The triumph of Augustan poetics offers an important and original re-evaluation of the transition from Baroque to Augustan in English literature. Starting with Butler's *Hudibras*, Blanford Parker describes Augustan satire as a movement away from the "controversial disputation" of the seventeenth century to a general satire which ridicules Protestant, Anglican, and Catholic in equal measure, as well as the poetic traditions that supported them. Once the dominant forms of late-medieval and Baroque thought – analogical and fideist, a fully symbolic world and an empty wilderness – were erased, a novel space for the imagination was created. Here a "literalism" new to European thought can be seen to have replaced the general satire, and at this moment Pope and Thomson create a new art of natural and quotidian description, in parallel with the rise of the novel. Parker's account concludes with the ambiguous or hostile reaction to this new mode seen in the works of Samuel Johnson and others.

CAMBRIDGE STUDIES IN EIGHTEENTH-CENTURY
ENGLISH LITERATURE AND THOUGHT 36

The triumph of Augustan poetics

A complete list of books in this series is given at the end of the volume.

The triumph of Augustan poetics

English literary culture from Butler to Johnson

BLANFORD PARKER

Visiting Professor at Claremont Graduate University

CAMBRIDGE
UNIVERSITY PRESS

PUBLISHED BY THE PRESS SYNDICATE OF THE UNIVERSITY OF CAMBRIDGE
The Pitt Building, Trumpington Street, Cambridge CB2 1RP, United Kingdom

CAMBRIDGE UNIVERSITY PRESS
The Edinburgh Building, Cambridge CB2 2RU, United Kingdom
40 West 20th Street, New York, NY 10011–4211, USA
10 Stamford Road, Oakleigh, Melbourne 3166, Australia

© Blanford Parker 1998

First published 1998

Printed in the United Kingdom at the University Press, Cambridge

Typeset in Baskerville $10\frac{1}{2}/12\frac{1}{2}$ pt   [CE]

A catalogue record for this book is available from the British Library

Library of Congress cataloguing in publication data

Parker, Blanford.
The triumph of Augustan poetics: English literary culture from
Butler to Johnson / Blanford Parker.
p.   cm. – (Cambridge studies in eighteenth-century English
literature and thought: 36)
Includes bibliographical references and index.
ISBN 0 521 59088 4 (hardback)
1. English poetry – 18th century – History and criticism.
2. English poetry – Early modern, 1500–1700 – History and criticism.
3. Verse satire, English – History and criticism.   4. Baroque
literature – History and criticism.   5. Johnson, Samuel, 1709–1784 –
Aesthetics.   6. Butler, Samuel, 1612–1680. Hudibras.   7. English
literature – Roman influences.   8. Aesthetics, British – 18th century.
9. Poetics.   I. Title.   II. Series.
PR561.P37 1997
821'.509 – dc21   96–51679 CIP

ISBN 0 521 59088 4 hardback

Contents

Contents

Acknowledgments

My earliest debt of gratitude in the preparation of this book goes to Professor W. J. Bate. I was fortunate to be his last thesis candidate. His advice was invaluable, and his willingness to accept my work with little revision was inspiring. Professor James Engell did a close and incisive reading of the manuscript. His comments always led to improvements. Professor Leopold Damrosch was kind enough to read the whole book in an early and mangled form. His support helped push the book into its more polished phase. Professor Anthony Low gave two meticulous readings of the manuscript, and was kind enough to make numerous adroit corrections of fact and style. He has been a friend to this project for many years. Professor David Venturo gave many helpful suggestions as well as kind support in the first days of working on the project. Professor James Cutsinger gave helpful guidance on theological matters relating to chapter 5. Professor Robert Faggen has been helpful in every stage of the production of this book. Professor Anthony Kemp was patient in listening to several phases of my argument. His perceptions have helped to guide my thinking. Mr. Daniel Dorogusker supported this project by his example of ardent commitment to eighteenth-century studies, and by numerous and detailed suggestions on several chapters. Professor Raphael Falco offered helpful advice and commiseration during my first years at New York University. Professor Steven Shankman was supportive and helpful. Mr. Alan Long has suffered through every version of this text, and has made his usual clairvoyant suggestions throughout the process of creating it. To Professor John Farrell I owe the greatest debt for tireless attention and innumerable conversations on the crux issues of the book. Whatever virtues the book may have must be largely attributed to his help. Professor John Crossett, my mentor and friend, influenced from afar every page of this work.

I also must thank Michael Raiger and Charles Henebry for their help in creating the final text. Elizabeth Duquette pointed out to me a helpful passage in Kant. My heartfelt thanks to my former students, John Tintera, Ronald Garrander, and Tammy Roth, for their help with typing. I should also mention the aid of the librarians of Harvard University, New York University, and Franklin and Marshall College.

Introduction

The European Baroque culture, along with the Humanistic tradition which preceded it, were Christian in all important aspects, with Christianity marking the limits of both aesthetics. Any application of the term "classical" to Renaissance writing must be qualified, because though it passed through the phases of Ovidian, Ciceronian, Platonic, and Virgilian fashion, those fashions were themselves shaped in a manner always syncretic and ambiguous. Petrarch's Cicero was an Augustinian Cicero, Ficino's Plato was both Scholastic and biblical, Pico's Virgil was a figure of esoteric Christian *preparatio*, and Chapman's Homer was an allegorical theologian. Even the most modern sensibilities reflected this dependency on Christian doctrine. As the Pyrrhonic elements of Erasmus and Montaigne came in the end to a kind of anti-Scholastic fideism thinly masking a Pauline topos, so Galileo's science leaned on the theology of the thirteenth century.

The Baroque, the last phase of the Renaissance in Europe, received four great traditions of Christian theology, and each had its own form of art. The *mystical* rhetoric of spiritual consummation, with the obliteration of the natural and the evaporation of self, produced the peculiar lyric of the Spanish mystics, an erotic allegory. The *logist* art produced spiritual acrostic, morphological verse, and paradox across Europe and in Britain, in which the biblical text forms an autonomous and all-explaining language with Christ, the Logos, as the underlying principle of grammar. The *fideist* rhetoric of the "good race," in which the salvific *telos* marks the limit of allegorical romance, had been common in Europe since Augustine but flourished especially in the Reformation under the authority of Luther. And finally the *analogical* art, in which the spiritual finds its analogy in the physical creation, was the last and most powerful of the aesthetic experiments of the Renaissance. In its first rumblings, it was measured and sublime, as in the erotic cosmologies of Dante and Petrarch, and by the seventeenth century it encompassed in its explosive extravagance all the central language cultures of Europe under the banners of Marino, Molina, Gongora, Ronsard, and Donne. Here the implications of the Scholastic *analogia entis* were dramatized, and the iconic repertoire of the late Middle Ages embellished and expanded.

All of these modes of poetry were present in the seventeenth century,
with the analogical mode dominating European and English lyric and
drama until mid-century. But in only one generation, sometimes only a few
years, these four modes of Christian poesis began to wither and fade. This
decay happened both on the Continent and in Britain, but it happened
most dramatically and absolutely in Britain. Vaughan, Crashaw, Cowley,
and Traherne, to name only a few, were writing in the old metaphysical
way in the decade preceding the Restoration, but how few poems of the
Baroque canon were written after? And what caused a reversal of taste so
complete?

In contrasting the poetic of Ignatius Loyola to that of later "classical
critics," Roland Barthes argued:

Classical ideology practices in the cultural order the same ecology as Bourgeois
democracy does in the political order: a separation and a balance of powers, a
broad but closely watched territory is conceded to literature, on condition that the
territory be isolated, hierarchically, from other domains; thus it is that literature,
whose function is a worldly one, is not compatible with spirituality; one is detour,
ornament, veil, the other is immediation, nudity: this is why one cannot be both a
saint and a writer.[1]

If we may replace "classical" with neoclassical, and this is what Barthes
always seems to mean by the "horizon of the classical," we may from these
words begin our search for solutions. The French neoclassical and the
British Augustan take as their starting point the excess, the abuse, of
figuration in the Baroque. The new poetry would depart from all four of
the previous models and would self-consciously set itself against them. The
English Civil War would circumscribe both the crest and the nadir of the
metaphysical writing era. The *Raison* of Boileau, or judgment of Dryden,
were created expressly to curb the excesses of the poetry of the earlier
seventeenth century. The Augustan culture could not abide the hubris of
an analogical age – its claim to mediated knowledge of the transcendent by
means of metaphor. Boileau, Butler, Rochester, Dryden, Swift, and their
contemporaries would mock the "acrostic land" of the logist; the maddened, inward "aeolist" imagination of the fideist; the self-lacerating
obsessions of the mystic; and most of all the empty conceits of the
analogists.

[1] Roland Barthes, *Sade/Fourier/Loyola* (New York: Hill and Wang, 1976), 39–40. It is interesting to
note that just such a bicameralism of the imagination was inscribed in the very language of *An
Essay on Man*. The House of Commons would be the motive force of the soul and the House of
Lords a body for advice and consent. "Most strength the moving principle requires: / Active its
task, it prompts, impels, inspires. / Sedate and quiet the comparing lies, / Form'd but to check,
delib'rate and advise" (Pope, *An Essay on Man*, II, 67–70). These correspond to the wit and
judgment of the *Essay on Criticism*. There must always, in enlightened theory, be a limiting
instrument to control and domesticate the "figure-making power."

Likewise, the Augustan would become classical in a new way. Its classicism would eschew syncresis and allegory and invent a novel literalism, a sober simplicity of representation. The cult of Horace was to become the first "Classicism" of Europe to oppose itself to the Baroque and to the Christian synthesis that had created all earlier "Classicisms."

In short, the empirical poetics invented in England in the seventeenth century brought on an irruption of consciousness which has until now never been completely described. It was construed at first by its Whiggish apologists, Locke, Shaftesbury, Hutcheson, and Addison, and more recently by their Victorian descendants, Macaulay, Lecky, and Stephen, as a reasonable and inevitable evolution. "The inevitable cooling of the imagination after the Restoration and the rational politics which is its twin"[2] was the saving instrument of the peace of the Augustans. The earlier age of superstitious energy, of, in Locke's words, "chimeras of conceit," had to be diffused by a program of moderation. "Quieting the cannon's mouth" was, for Bishop Sancroft in 1669, attended by "a like calming of those conceitful bigotries and ferocious fancies of the last age";[3] and Burnet, the greatest latitudinarian prelate of the time, found his country caught between "superstition and enthusiasm,"[4] attempting to construct a middle upon which to survive.

The balancing of Scholastic and Protestant elements which marked the Hookerian formula of the 1590s became instead a demolishing of traditions, an emptying of content, whether Protestant, Catholic, or Laudian. The *via media* of this latter culture was not a mean but a double expunging – an attempt at erasure. This Augustan project had great significance in the realm of politics – the building of a contractarian society, a modern constitutional monarchy, and its more democratic successor. The political evolution is by now proverbial, but the result for poetry, the precipitous transformation of imagination after 1660, is, perhaps, not so well understood. In fact the imaginative transformation is in part the ground for the political changes, and these two colossi of politics and art were built upon a change of theology of equally momentous proportions. The spirit of the age of Locke and Shaftesbury, and the succeeding one of Pope and Walpole, was not the inevitable result of the *Zeitgeist* of that century – an unconscious growth of empiricism and latitude – but in part a neatly crafted program founded upon the useful art of forgetting for the maintenance of public order. Among the feared residue of the Civil War culture was the very practice of Baroque art: conceitful, passionate, sacramental, iconic, communal, and traditional. This art, the product of centuries, had been so

[2] C. H. Firth, *Commentary on Macaulay's History* (London: Oxford University Press, 1938), 119.
[3] William Sancroft, Familiar Letters of (London: Cooper, 1757), 42.
[4] Gilbert Burnet, *History of His Own Time* (London: Reeves and Turner, 1883), 526.

nearly expunged that its recent apologists – Donne, Cowley, and Benlowes
(to name a few) – were themselves either openly censured as in Roscommon, Pope, and Swift, or rewritten, as in Pope's *Satires of Dr. Donne*, or,
more importantly, lampooned with ferocious energy. If we look at Spingarn's classic collection of seventeenth-century critical essays we find
Davenant, Rimer, Roscommon, Hobbes, Cowley, Dryden, and Pepys – the
whole line of forward-looking empirico-classicists – and aside from Dennis
(the whipping-boy of Pope and Swift), none of the numerous apologists for
the still flourishing religious school. The genius of the age was in obscuring
or lashing all opposition, not in the spirit of drawing-room complacency,
but in the active construction of the "myth of judgment."[5] In the words of
a pre-eminent Edwardian critic:

The scholastic philosophy had of course been challenged generations before.
Bacon, Descartes, and Hobbes, however, in the preceding century, had still treated
it as the incubus upon intellectual progress, and it was not yet exorcised from the
universities. It had, however, passed from the sphere of living thought . . . In the
time of Laud, the bishops in alliance with the Crown endeavored to enforce the
jurisdiction of the ecclesiastical courts upon the nation at large and to suppress all
non-conformity by law. Every subject of the King was also amenable to church
discipline. By the Revolution, any attempt to enforce such discipline had become
hopeless. The existence of non-conformist churches has to be recognised as a fact,
though perhaps an unpleasant fact. The Dissenters can be worried by disqualifica-
tions of various kinds, but the claim of toleration, of Protestant sects at least, is
admitted.[6]

These words of Leslie Stephen are not entirely true. The reform of Laud
was violent, rash, and unsuccessful. He had underestimated the Calvinist
and Independent elements within his own church and the willingness of the
gentry to come to the aid of dissenting groups. He misunderstood the deep
habit of iconoclasm that had grown up in England since the time of Jewell
(and perhaps even so far back as Wycliffe). Neither the Hookerian
compromise, with its residual Scholasticism, nor Laud's liturgical discipline
were in the spirit of the age. Laud was always associated in the popular
mind with creeping Catholicism, and such an imputation carried with it
the full weight of public censure. In fact, the propaganda of Sheldon's
church in the 1660s was far more subtle and effective than Laud's or
perhaps any earlier church hierarchy's had been. It manipulated anti-
Catholic feelings with great finesse. It brought the country clergy and
dissenting bishops into line by the most thorough and thoughtful coercion
– the distribution of older church lands and fees, the threatening of

---

[5] I elaborate the significance of the new concept of "judgment" superadded to the pre-existing
faculties of wit, invention, and fancy, in chapter 2.
[6] Leslie Stephen, *Selected Writings in British Intellectual History*, ed. John Clive (Chicago: University of
Chicago Press, 1979), 126.

benefices, and the meticulous control of parliamentary votes among sitting clergy.[7] From the time that the Bishops and the King's ministers tricked and deceived Baxter and his associates at the Savoy Conference of 1662,[8] the Presbyterian and dissenting interests were systematically excluded from the new national compromise. By the time such a party regained its feet, as in the era of Wesley or Whitefield, it had been hopelessly marginalized. Bishop Gibson treated Wesley like a child; Bishop Butler treated him like a madman. During the earlier phase the Anglican Church played a game of cat and mouse with Charles II and his successors and succeeded in preventing the Stuarts from granting any broad or enforceable Act of Toleration.[9] This was not done primarily because of fear of the king's Catholicism, though that fear was sometimes real, but as the means of diffusing Protestant dissent. The Church's control of publications after the Restoration was more successful even than Cromwell's had been, though there remained an enormous appetite for works of the most extreme dissent. We know that no works of the broad and middle Anglican culture came close to the popularity of Bunyan, and we should recall that nearly all the best-sellers of that age were of a similar cast.[10] Johnson was correct to say that the great popularity of Tillotson was basically a show of conformity and good taste, and if very few had read through those volumes of the bishop's tedious and commonplace moralism, few also had read the elegant and exacting tomes of Jeremy Taylor. The modern High-Churchman who reads Donne, Andrewes, Hooker, and Taylor is participating in nineteenth-century nostalgia.

The theater, late Cavalier poetry, lampoon, and, at a later phase, periodicals were the real taste of the broad church public, and this taste, though often denounced by the Anglican hierarchy, was of great value in the cause of diffusing the appetite for works of religious dissent. Not until the 1740s did the broader Protestant reading culture reemerge, and it is important to remember that Young's *Night Thoughts* and Richardson's *Clarissa* helped to rejuvenate the severe moralism and fideist allegory which had been so popular in the early years of the Restored government. If Scholasticism had passed "from the sphere of living thought," it was in part because the publication of Catholic (and some Protestant-Scholastic) books was often illegal. In fact both Francis de Sales and Thomas à Kempis remained popular after 1660, though sometimes in altered or even

[7] Cf. Gordon Rupp, *Religion in England 1688–1791* (Oxford: Clarendon Press, 1986).
[8] Norman Sykes, *Aspects of Religion in the Restoration Church* (Cambridge: Cambridge University Press, 1947), 4–5, 69.
[9] Ronald Hutton, *Charles the Second, King of England, Scotland and Ireland* (Oxford: Clarendon Press, 1987), 296–298.
[10] Cf. John Sommerville, *Popular Religion in Restoration England* (Gainesville: University of Florida Press, 1977), chs. 2 and 3.

emasculated editions. Scholasticism and its Neoplatonic cousin were, in fact, living elements in the writings of Norris and the Cambridge Platonists, of the unchurched nonjurors like Leslie and Sharpe, and even Edward Young, of whom it is reported that in his youth he had read Aquinas with great interest. It suited Leslie Stephen's own purpose (his own anti-metaphysical and agnostic bent) to imagine that the peace of the Augustans was smooth and natural – that it lacked the violence of earlier periods and that it had found an easy solution to the deep divisions in national opinion. It was the thesis of Arnold, and certainly championed by Lecky and Pattison, that the Hebraic element, that element of serious Calvinist theology and self-abnegating Protestantism, had remained an ineradicably bad element in the English national character to the end of the nineteenth century. The superstitious roots of this residual Protestant "bigotry" are a large part of the middle-class myth of George Eliot's fictional world, and are the subtext of Arnold's *Culture and Anarchy* and Lecky's *Rise of the Spirit of Rationalism in Europe*. Any apology for the literature of the eighteenth century since that time has tended to see the rise of empirical, rational thought as the keynote of the period, and the existence of Bunyan, Law, Wesley, Hervey, and Young as anomalous. Where Dissenters or protesting Anglicans have been treated seriously (leaving aside for the moment the important work of Donald Davie), they have been seen as connected to a laboring party or class. The thesis of the rising working class and the "poor man's ethic" of the Methodists has been of great importance, but it has also tended to obscure the deeper epistemological and theological issues of the Restoration culture.

Most studies of the Restoration and Hanoverian culture and literature have for a long time been rooted in apology. The admiration of common sense and empirical virtues has drawn many scholars to the period. Until recently those who have turned their attention away from Romanticism to explore the supposedly orderly confines of Augustan rhetoric have shown a remarkable degree of sympathy with the period's uncritical view of its own enlightened methods. It may have seemed inevitable that most critics of the period of spreading positivism, beginning in the age of Darwin and lasting till after World War II, would find their origins in the early eighteenth century. Those modern critics who have taken their cue from Locke, Burke, Johnson, and Adam Smith have preserved in their own work the myth of *judgment*, the narrative of the free and rational gentleman who is not the dupe of enthusiastic fancies or Romantic delusions. Locke, Burke, and Adam Smith are intimately connected to Romantic thinking itself. The capitalist individual of Smith is the forerunner and partner of the isolated Romantic of a later period. Hume's skepticism has a severe turn of solipsism and detachment from tradition which connects him to Rousseau and Byron. Burke's own nationalism, his sense of innate, primitive local tradition, his opposition to rationalism, and his cult for the sublime are part of the preparation for mature Romanticism. Similarly, Pope may be said to be one of the first truly modern sensibilities. He wrote the first important explicitly autobiographical poem in English, he helped to invent the cult of "private passion," and, as I shall show, he did a great deal by his poetic practice to take the edge off of the Humanism he is so often said to represent.

The Augustan period of literature in England remains today our most unread and, perhaps, unknowable body of texts. Strachey and Woolf were quite wrong to think we moderns could go back to the orderly souls of Pope and Hogarth, Walpole, and Sterne for contrast and relief. Augustan literature was the first great victory over the culture of analogy, memorial authority, and traditional theology, and their classicism is no more backward-looking or authentic than that of Shelley or even Joyce. The modern heterocosm and improvisational ethic began with the Augustan and have not moved far beyond it.

One of the great unsolved problems of Augustan studies is the true place of classicism in the major authors of the period. I hope to show that the Neoclassical dogmas of the late seventeenth century are qualified by an empirical poetic foreign to the Aristotelian–Platonic theories which dominated late-Medieval and Baroque culture, and that the classical was a kind of screen which the Augustans could place between themselves and the conceitful writing culture of the Civil War era. It should be obvious to us that the Roman gentleman could have known nothing of the incipient empiricism of the eighteenth century, but it may be less obvious that Virgil and Horace are themselves involved in the metaphysical and spiritual ambiguities which are seen in late ancient writing. The eighteenth century imagined a great divide of consciousness between those imperial Roman authors and the thought of St. Paul and Plotinus, but in reality the *honnête homme* and the English gentleman are much farther from the milieu of the patronized poets of the first century. Serious readers should recognize, I think, that the great age of syncretic Classicism in Europe was over by the time of *Gulliver's Travels*, and that, whatever advances were made thereafter in textual or historical scholarship, there was a great and singular decline in the imaginative use of classical materials.

Speaking of the differences between seventeenth- and eighteenth-century preachers, Leslie Stephen speaks the language of Augustan apology:

the persecution is political rather than ecclesiastical. The intellectual change is parallel. The great divines of the seventeenth century speak as members of a learned corporation, condescending to instruct the laity. The hearers are supposed to listen to the voice (as Donne puts it) as from "angels in the clouds." They are experts, steeped in a special science, above the comprehension of the vulgar. They have been trained in the schools of theology, and have been thoroughly drilled in the art of "syllogising." They are walking libraries with the ancient fathers at their finger-ends; they have studied Aquinas and Duns Scotus, and have shown their technical knowledge in controversies with the great Jesuits, Suarez and Bellarmine. They speak frankly, if not ostentatiously, as men of learning, and their sermons are overweighted with quotations, showing familiarity with the classics, and with the whole range of theological literature. Obviously the hearers are to be passive recipients, not judges of the doctrine. But by the end of the century, Tillotson has become the typical divine, whose authority was to be as marked in theology as that of Locke in philosophy. He addresses his hearers on a level with their capabilities, and assures that they are not "passive buckets to be pumped in to," but reasonable men who have the right to be critics as well as disciples.[11]

Tillotson's plain style, coming down to us in the contemporary flood of anti-dogmatic and anti-Baroque reactions which includes Sprat's *History of the Royal Society*, Glanvil's *Vanity of Dogmatizing*, and Locke's *Essay*, was not merely an evangelical and democratic gesture to his congregation. He did not only condescend to his audience's level, but he helped to create the audience for a style which, in Pepys' *Diary* and Baxter's *Reliquiae*, would be described as uninspired and mechanical. The unconscious and conscious clearing away of the residue of the metaphysical style in every genre was a mode of public control – of narrowing the public taste for a dangerous past. This clearing away is central to Sprat's argument that science is the best gift of providence to a peaceful nation. Such a gift must embrace the literal and unexceptional, and in Sprat's words "save us from the empty lure of words." Nor is Stephen correct in thinking that Donne was removed from his parishioners by a barrier of learned grandiloquence. Walton claimed that Donne was one of the best shows in town; his reputation as a preacher far exceeded that of Tillotson among his own contemporaries, and we know from Shakespeare's tragedies that the Jacobean audience of all classes had a genius for getting what it wanted and needed out of the most entangled materials. Donne's sermons are Scholastic and casuistical, but they also tap into that nerve of Protestant personal meditation and drama which sets them apart from Andrewes or Laud. The sermons of Donne's period are varied marvelously from the orotund and impenetrable to the straightforward. Though there was a lively debate over the "theory" of the sermon in the seventeenth century, no literature remains indicating any rigorous public program for the measuring and teaching of proper Anglican pulpit style in the period. Such a program is quite obvious in the later period. That there was still communication between the Roman Catholic and English clergy, and that it was carried on with the highest seriousness, shows the earlier age's advantage. A distrust of reasoned doctrine was not the glory but the folly of the eighteenth-century church. Swift and Sterne were great wits, but poor preachers. That the church-goers of the Restoration were independent spirits who thought for them-selves, and not "buckets to be pumped in to," is a typical piece of modern cant, and the fear of rational instruction and dialectical argument as an imposition upon freedom was an idea invented by the Augustans. Stephen fears figurative and theological language as Tillotson and Hoadly did before him. Such a fear of the figurative is deeply rooted in modern thought.

On the other hand, it was a peculiar accident of modern criticism that T. S. Eliot and a few of his contemporaries reclaimed for the larger English canon the poems of the metaphysical school. It was natural for Coleridge and Eliot (and Grierson) to take a personal interest in resuscitating the long-buried body of Baroque English lyric. Their own spiritual notions and their extreme reactions to positivist thinking may have driven them back to the seventeenth century for solace. The crucial moment of distortion in eighteenth-century studies came when Leavis in his *Revaluation* and Brooks in *The Well-Wrought Urn* (to name two obvious examples) began to see the same virtues of figural compression and even conceit in Pope and Gray that Eliot had discovered in Donne. At the time when Empsonian ambiguities had become the greatest differentia of good poetry, they suddenly appeared as a central element in Augustan writing. This was, perhaps, no more than the folly of professionalism which corrupts each generation of scholars in one way or another, but it had resounding significance. Since that time a continual attempt to conflate and blur the lines between metaphysical and Popeian wit has helped us to forget the serious breach in tradition that is implied by the theory and practice of the Augustans. One of the subjects of this study is the centrality for the Augustans of the newly discovered "literal," and how a poetics of contiguity and accretion is qualitatively different from a poetics of analogy and conceit.

A book of the kind I have conceived must go beyond a review of the problems of the Augustan canon. It must memorialize the remnants of the embattled Baroque culture, and must attempt to describe the survival of analogical thinking and writing throughout the Restoration and eighteenth century. For this reason I have included when possible a summary treatment of authors like Benlowes and Blackmore, and have tried to show the significance of Augustan hostility to their works without falling back on the uncritical acceptance of Augustan valuations. Pat Rogers claims that when he returned to read "the dunces" he found their works even more trivial and hackneyed than had been suggested by Pope.[12] This has not been my experience. Blackmore's *Creation* is an interesting if unwieldy

---

[12] Pat Rogers, *Grub Street: Studies in a Subculture* (London: Methuen, 1972), 101.

continuation of the European tradition of cosmological poems, and its
unlikeness to Pope's theodicy is of great importance. Likewise, I have
dedicated chapters 6 and 7 to the Protestant reaction to Augustanism. The
tensions created by the invention of a new literalism were enormous, and
Protestant writers from Watts to Johnson began to turn away from an
empirical poetic in order to escape the amorphous naturalism of poems
like *The Seasons*. This fideist reaction cannot be understood as an anomaly
within Augustanism, but as an inevitable return to one of the ancient
possibilities of Christian mimesis. Once nature had been stripped of its
analogical and specular qualities it could no longer be used for Christian
meditation, but it is instructive that the first important reaction against the
new limitations of Augustan writing came from within. Prior and Young in
their long meditative poems, the *Solomon* and the *Night Thoughts*, in part
repudiated their own earlier Augustan rhetoric and turned to the world-
weary and privative theology that we associate with Luther and Pascal. It
was essential, therefore, in this study to trace the origins and growth of the
Augustan and some important reactions to it.

Since I have claimed that Augustanism was an erasure – a new
beginning, neither Medieval, nor classical – it seemed incumbent upon me
to describe at least briefly the kinds of mimeses that it replaced and its
relation to those kinds. For this reason, in chapter 5 I have presented a
schematic of four traditional paradigms of medieval and Baroque writing,
each theological. In my early researches for this book I had contemplated a
study of English religious writing from 1660 to the middle of the eighteenth
century. But I came to realize that such a specialized study would be
misleading. Religious poetry was not a compartment of literature before
the Restoration. Religious analogies and images were the *sine qua non* of all
verse written from the Carolingian period to the earlier seventeenth
century in the European literatures. The Petrarchan and even Gongorist
modes were built from the same basic repertoire of images and had the
same conscious or unconscious theory of language that we find in hymns
and religious meditation. There was no really secular poetry in the late-
medieval culture, though there was a good deal of blasphemy, naturalism,
and eroticism. Villon's poetry, for example, is derived from the same
analogical conception of nature and autobiography that we see in the
Franciscan hymns. I have gone so far as to place even Rabelais, in whose
easy chair so much of Augustan literature is thought to sit, rather in the
context of the analogical habits of the sixteenth century than the ferocious
satirical literalism of Swift or Sterne.

With the late seventeenth century a new mimetic possibility enters the
scene. This novel art is no longer circumscribed by the old binarisms of
spiritual analogy against iconoclasm, or fideist against visionary poetics,
but issues from a thorough critique of all pre-existing modes of Baroque

art. In this sense Augustanism can be viewed as a challenge to the possibility of Christian and even classical "essentialist" theories of poetry. That this challenge was often unconscious, and often the work of poets ostensibly pious, makes the case even more complex.

I have chosen Samuel Butler to represent this new possibility in English. I begin with Butler (in chapter 1) because he helped to invent the satiric and popular path of the Augustan, which Dryden, Swift, Pope, Gay, and Sterne found irresistible. By a detailed treatment of *Hudibras* I hope to show the importance of the "low" element in all Augustan poetry, and dislodge the notion of unshakable canons of classical taste. The surface of Augustan literature was often hideously deformed, and I wish to argue that such realism is a necessary part of the reformulation of letters after the Restoration. In chapter 3 I analyze Pope's poetry to show that the high and low, the neoclassical and the Hudibrastic, are never far apart in this period, both serving an underlying "literalism" which was the particular discovery of Butler's era.

I have spoken briefly about the roots of our own apologies for the eighteenth century, and I hope to be forgiven for going back as far as Stephen for my examples. The defense of Augustan values and virtues has always been a tricky business in academic writing. I have heard one enthusiastic professor claim that eighteenth-century literature is for adults, Romantic for children. The trickiness is derived from the always relatively small and insular readership of both primary and secondary texts in the academic canon between Dryden and Johnson. The orderliness and abstraction which has so often been ascribed to the period, its solid common sense and its tough realism, are not likely to bring more readers to it. Yet it was in the intellectual interest of so many British and American critics since World War II to enhance and repeat those claims for the period. I have mentioned the attempt to draw Augustan poetry into the charmed sphere of witty ambiguity at the time of Leavis and Richards. But there is another kind of retrospective prestige that critics have attempted to recoup for the Augustans. We may call this the image of social and cosmic order. The monumental and invaluable works of critics like Mack, Price, and Battestin have attempted to shore up the edifice of Augustan literature on terms derived from it.[13] Battestin's *Providence of Wit* will always be a central study of Augustan writing, and perhaps no one can go farther in

---

[13] I have set out to show that a great appearance of order may be a disorder, and to address a number of studies on those grounds in my opening chapters. Among the many distinguished books on the order of Augustan rhetoric and cosmos I would mention particularly: Martin Battestin, *The Providence of Wit* (Charlottesville: University of Virginia Press, 1981); Maynard Mack, *The Garden and the City* (New Haven: Yale University Press, 1964); Martin Price, *To the Palace of Wisdom* (Garden City, New York: Doubleday, 1964); and Paul Fussell, *The Rhetorical World of Augustan Humanism* (Oxford: Clarendon Press, 1962).

defending the ideas of Providential and social order which the period wished for itself. But such an order was after the time of Dryden only wishful thinking. The heterocosmic vision of Pope's *Essay on Man*, like that of Hobbes' *Leviathan* and Butler's *Hudibras* before it, derived its astonishing originality from being perilously suspended, "self-balanced" like Pope's earth, between two great figure-making ages, the Baroque and the Romantic. This is not to say that the period is the prelude to Romanticism and the strong poetry of Blake and Wordsworth, but it is certainly to deny that Pope and Swift are the repositories of older humanistic culture. The very essence of poems like *The Rape of the Lock* and *The Seasons* is their capacity to collapse a world of fruitful analogies into the space of the trivial and quotidian. Their allusions to Virgilian and Miltonic sources are a mask which hides the thoroughness of their originality. I hope to show that the replacing of metonymic – that is, spatial associative structures – for metaphoric and analogical ones is a symptom of the rupture between Renaissance and Augustan thought.

Nor is it easy to return to the historical narrative at its moment of irruption, now so long obscured. After the Civil War, the remnants of the poetic culture of the Catholic, the Laudian, the Nonconformist, the Scholastic Presbyterian, the Quaker, and the nonjuror, were systematically pilloried – first in that master Augustan text *Hudibras*, and then with tireless satire down to the 1740s. What at first was merely burlesque about outworn customs of thought became the very definition of pathology, and the Augustans in their manipulation of the rhetoric of madness seem to add credence to the Foucauldian formula of cultural exclusion by a kind of socio-clinical propaganda.

The success of this age of satire was so complete as to have largely blotted out the reputation of authors of other poetic genres. The major Augustans produced by negation a space for their own peculiar concept of the reasonable man. The observant reader of *A Tale of a Tub* or *The Dunciad* has the same contempt for the enthusiastic and miraculous that his later counterpart felt in reading Hume's essay "On Miracles." There has always been a too rigorous distinction between the prose and poetic genres of the period. Mandeville and Hume seem to me to be among the most able Augustan satirists. The first was capable of subtle imitations of Hudibrastic verse, the second memorializes Butler on the last page of his great history. Their philosophies, like those of Butler and Rochester, were systems of pointed exclusion, and like the great verse satirists their chief enemies were conceited and conceitful traditionalists and self-vaunting spiritualists. The Augustan philosophers' indebtedness to Butler, Dryden, and Pope could be easily traced. Bacon and Hobbes are only one corner of their intellectual inheritance. Authors like Butler, Locke, Swift, and Hume engineered a tremendous narrowing of the uses of reason and wit. The "Age of Reason" had a contempt for the rational greater than any age before it. But by now the Augustan exclusion, the satiric apology for the forgetfulness of the age, is our own forgetfulness.

Beyond the degree to which subsequent generations have internalized the Augustan program, two other facts must be mentioned at the start. With few exceptions, most important studies of the Restoration and eighteenth century have been one of two types of prospective analyses: in the English tradition, the empiricism and skepticism of Hobbes' and Locke's epistemology is the forebear of several modern schools – the Scottish Associationists, the Benthamites, including Mill and Lecky, the psychological linguists like Richards and Empson, the Bloomsbury ironists, the social historians, and even (though paradoxically) Marxist critics like Williams, Hill, and Eagleton. All of these divergent schools look to the Augustan period as the origin and building blocks of their own potent critiques. All of them (even the ones who ostensibly despise the Whig and *laissez-faire* tendencies of the age) depend for their arguments on the epistemology invented in Augustan culture. The very notion of ideology has its roots in Shaftesbury and Hume, and modern positivism has its origins in the works of Locke, Hume, and their successors.[14] Marxism itself is a natural extension of Augustan psychology, and the great sources of Marx include Swift, Voltaire, and Hume. The notion of a general satire, beyond the limits of traditional religious controversy and calling into question the validity of debate itself, began in the age of Swift, and has been the instrument of the most potent of the moderns – Marx, Nietzsche, Freud. The cult of suspicion began with the eighteenth century and has since merely lost its polite surface. Who but a reader of Pope and Shaftesbury could fully appreciate the advice given in 1954 by the American humanist Sidney Lamprecht?

There is danger in a too-intense religious zeal. Religion ought to be the ornament of a rich life, not the driving passion of a fixed commitment. History is full of stories of cases of immature religious commitments. Religious commitments ought never to be drilled into men; they ought never be made too early in life . . . The odds are against any fine achievement by such means . . . The middle way is, in religion as generally in life, the best way. The middle way is to take religion with a sense of humor, a light touch, and a sensitive appreciation for what has, at least for the time being, no apparent religious import . . . In that way a religious way of life might coexist, as it has too seldom coexisted, with the emancipated mind.[15]

This is not the *via media* of "classical Anglicanism," which borrowed from

---

[14] We need only recall the remarkable tribute to Locke, Berkeley, and Hume in the first paragraph of A. J. Ayer's *Language, Truth, and Logic* (New York: Dover Books, 1952). The roots of modern positivism and Anglo-American language philosophy were in the Augustan project with its desire to stem the tide of the figurative "abuse of language."

[15] Sidney Lamprecht, *Observations* (New York: Harpers, 1954), 21.

two religious traditions, but the Augustan middle between the religious and
the secular life, between the excesses of enthusiasm and complete atheism –
a road to intellectual emancipation which could have been described in
almost the same words by Pope, or in Lord Chesterfield's "Letters" to his
son.

But it would be a great mistake to imagine that the heart of my argument
is simply a repetition, perhaps with more examples, of the thesis found in
various forms as far back as Arnold, and greatly expanded by Mario Praz,
H. J. C. Grierson, and T. S. Eliot, or in later academic critics like
Wasserman, Bate, and Abrams, that in the Augustan period there is a
metamorphosis of style from metaphysical conceit to Augustan wit, and
that this shows the inevitable transformation of consciousness from medieval to modern. The transformation of religious individualism and
personal rhetoric in Praz and Grierson, the "disassociation of sensibility"
in Eliot, or the movement towards a psychology of associationism in
Wasserman and Bate, are all important sources for my study, but none of
them lays out what I consider the central narrative of Augustanism. Nor
have these critics, brilliant as each of their analyses has been, come to grips
with the actual etiology of the Augustan – the genesis of the "literal." All of
them quite rightly mark the differences in thought and style between
Donne and Dryden, or between Crashaw and Watts, but none has
recognized the connection between satire, the leveling of all previous
modes of theology and psychology, and the subsequent literalism and
"descriptionism" of the eighteenth century. None of them has traced the
history of the public criticism of all the modes of meditation of the Civil
War culture and the attendant changes of style and thought during the
period after the Restoration.

One might have imagined that Eliot, a devout Anglican, would see the
transformation in specifically theological and social terms. But, instead, the
reader of "Thoughts after Lambeth" discovers that Eliot himself maintains
the same perennial conception of a wholesome Anglicanism balanced
between Roman and Evangelical excesses, as if that collection of attitudes
was part of the mystical and unchangeable character of the British race. He
speaks there of the great differences between the openness of the English
church as against the Roman church's doctrinaire qualities, while on the
other hand he claims that the bishops "have conceded nothing" to the
evangelicals. Although Eliot is often strident in his comments on Hoadly's
church, he has absorbed its own sense of neutral moderation. The theology
of Hooker and Andrewes was an amalgam, potent and traditional, of
Augustinian (one might say Protestant) and Scholastic elements, while
Eliot's supposedly "catholic" Anglicanism was very nearly that of the
church of Sheldon's era. Eliot, paraphrasing F. H. Bradley, said that
theology is "the finding of good reasons for what we believe upon instinct."

Such a position does not conjure up the "true Dantesque" or the drama of sin which Eliot discovered in Middleton or Baudelaire, but a truly Augustan complacency and anti-intellectualism. His own later "traditionalism" was always posed in opposition to full-blown agnostic modernism like that of Russell, Middleton Murry, or Shaw. Like Newman before him, he could never fully rid himself of the crippling narrowness of his conception of the ideal British gentleman – the superior and neutral observer invented by the Augustan culture.

It is remarkable how small a role metaphysical or theological considerations play in Eliot's analysis of English poetry from the Restoration to the nineteenth century. Like Grierson, Eliot never linked the precipitous changes of poetic taste to concrete historical events, but to a kind of gradual drift of consciousness effected in part by the growing prestige of science and a vague spiritual movement toward skepticism in modernity. Eliot linked the change even more directly to the literary examples of Milton and Dryden:

In the seventeenth century a disassociation of sensibility set in from which we have never recovered; and this disassociation, as is natural, was aggravated by the two most powerful poets of the century, Milton and Dryden . . . But while the language became more refined, the feeling became more crude . . .

The second effect of the influence of Milton and Dryden followed from the first, and was therefore slow in manifestation. The sentimental age began early in the eighteenth century, and continued. The poets revolted against the ratiocinative, the descriptive; they thought and felt by fits, unbalanced; they reflected.[16]

I myself have never understood exactly what Eliot meant by crudeness of feeling. That Tennyson's feelings were cruder than those of Middleton or Donne is at best an arguable point, but that Milton and Dryden were the twin fountains of sentimentality seems indefensible. That a poet would revolt against ratiocination on account of the influence of Milton, the most intellectually rigorous of all English poets, or Dryden, whom Johnson rightly described as a "master of argument in verse," is difficult to conceive. Eliot himself began to realize his youthful folly in the famous recantation in his second Milton essay. In one sense we may concede that Donne had a peculiar combination of rational and visceral elements in his poetry, and that later authors, even Milton, were relatively abstract and remote. That Donne had instruments to "seize and clutch and penetrate" beyond other authors is undeniable, but that he was more penetrating than Milton is doubtful. We may even concede that Milton's meter was received at great cost to subsequent generations who were crushed under the burden of its sonority while lacking the means to recreate the mythical and intellectual

---

[16] T. S. Eliot, "The Metaphysical Poets," in *Selected Essays* (New York: Harcourt, Brace and World, Inc., 1964), 247–248.

richness of *Paradise Lost*. But did Milton's meter and diction cause such a falling off, or was it the result of other cultural influences in the post-Restoration culture?

The influences which Eliot describes as "slow in manifestation" are not, it seems to me, the ones of the greatest interest in understanding the linguistic and literary changes after 1660. My own argument places Butler, Rochester, and the early Swift, what I have called the low road of the Augustan, at the center of this transformation from rich analogy and surprising conceit to the plainer and more prosaic rhetoric of the later period. These qualities were not "slow" but precipitous and sudden in manifestation, and they left an indelible mark on all subsequent Augustan writing, even on the polished couplets of Pope. Nor is the refinement of language that Eliot describes such an unmistakable mark of Augustan writing. As Margaret Doody and others have shown, the exuberant crudeness of much Augustan writing, its vulgarity, raciness, obscenity, and explosive directness goes far beyond the paradoxical titillations of Donne. If we see Butler and his raucous contemporaries as the true root and primitive exemplars of later Augustan authors, it will not be difficult to understand mature Augustan texts like *MacFlecknoe*, *The Dunciad*, and *Tristram Shandy*. That Romantic and Victorian critics did not have the stomach for the Hudibrastic[17] is no reason to write it out of the narrative of Augustan culture.

But at an even deeper level Eliot misread the situation of Augustan literary culture. He did not see its deep and self-conscious fear of, and pointed opposition to, all traces of the conceitful mentality of Donne and Herbert. He did not recognize that public satire of the kind Butler wrote was a perfect cultural parallel of the sober denunciations of rhetorical excess found in the numerous contemporary discussions on sermon, history writing, and other prose genres. Glanvil, Sprat, and Collier did the same cultural work of uprooting habits of analogical thinking in prose that Butler and Rochester had done in verse. Literary works of far different styles and with far different audiences were effectively flattening the exuberance of seventeenth-century rhetoric, and the documents of Sheldon's Church and Clarendon's Parliament point to the aggressive erasure of remnants of earlier writing cultures, while they manipulate the same vein of sometimes violent satire against the enemies of "the peace of the Augustans."[18] It was

[17] Hazlitt was an exception to this. He placed Butler very near the top of English humorists and praised his poetry in unequivocal terms.
[18] Anyone who has read through Restoration political or ecclesiastical documents will recall the emphasis placed on superstition, conceit, zeal, enthusiasm, and fancy. See, for example, the documents responding to Charles' "Declaration of Breda" and subsequent declarations of indulgence for Catholics and Dissenters in J. P. Kenyon, *The Stuart Constitution: Documents and Commentary* (London: Cambridge University Press, 1966), 357–413.

the language of the Quakers and Catholics that was the chief symptom of their hysterical attitudes. We see witness of this in state papers as well as in *Hudibras* and *A Tale of a Tub*. Here I must narrow my focus to well-known works of literature and can only throw out hints and pointers at the broader cultural nexus.

In fact, Eliot was wrong to imagine Milton as the precursor to Augustan style, and he was wrong in a different way to see Dryden as the clear and central example of Augustan poetry. Dryden was the master of the heroic couplet and the model of Pope, and he was the defender of the Augustan settlement in poems of brilliant apology – poems which reflect among other things his deep debt to the satiric formulae of Butler. But Dryden was a divided poet. He was a poet of two worlds, or as he memorably described it, "between two ages cast." The history of literary traditions is more than a history of style. It is a history of thought and a history of figuration. The dissonance between the earlier and later Dryden, and more importantly between the prosodic and the religious Dryden, is profound. Eliot, who had such melancholy feelings for Charles as the "broken Coriolanus" and the "king come at midnight," failed to see the sublime archaism of Dryden's own backward-looking poems, and he also failed to see the degree to which Dryden fought to return to and practice the canons of metaphysical verse after 1685.

But most importantly, Eliot, like Praz before him and many after, had only a partial understanding of the Augustan situation. The period is not simply the time when analogical structures of thought began to break down, but it was also a time when Protestant thought of a very opposite cast came under an attack equally severe. Eliot failed to realize that the eclipse of analogy was only half of the story of the Augustan revolution of taste. The other half was the attack upon the dissenting imagination – its spiritual typologies and its fideism. The seventeenth-century imagination was divided between analogists and poets of faith. By "poets of faith" I mean those writers who, like Luther, emphasized the emptiness and sterility of the natural world, and the warfare of the Christian knight against the prince of this world. This component of English culture was the rhetorical opposite of the metaphysical. Eliot did not notice that figures like Bunyan were fighting a rearguard action at least as difficult as that waged by the last remnant of the metaphysical writing culture.

The true peculiarity of the dominant strain of Augustan satire was the degree to which it excoriated both sides of Reformation culture. By associating the culture of analogy with Catholic superstition and the culture of faith with personal madness, Butler laid out the path for later Augustan ideology. *Hudibras*, like the tale of the brothers in Swift, equally condemned the two dominant theologies of the Baroque. Such a gesture was bound to bring on an explosion of novelty. Empiricism was one of

those novelties created in the wake of the general satire of the Restoration.
Locke's psychology and modern science were not the earliest foundations
of British Enlightenment, but were bolstered by an already highly developed tradition of satire. They were necessitated by the removal of analogy
on one side and world-negating faith on the other. The dichotomy of
superstition and enthusiasm as the twin enemies of good sense moved on
from verse satire to works of serious speculation like Glanvil's *Vanity of
Dogmatising* and Locke's *Essay*. The creation and manipulation of this
formula from Butler to Pope (and beyond) will be the subject of my first
three chapters.

This leads me to my final objection to Eliot. In the famous passage I
quote above, Eliot talks of a revolt against the "descriptive" element in
literature in the final phase of Augustan writing, that is, in the period after
1700. Nothing could be farther from the truth. The whole notion of
descriptive poetry is the invention of that period. Donne and Crashaw were
poets of physical analogy but not description. I shall discuss this at greater
length in my treatment of Thomson in chapter 4. Let it suffice to say that
the empty space brought on by the erasure of both analogy and fideist
theology was, in the last phase of Augustan writing, filled up with a plethora
of novel descriptions. The natural world and the world of incidental
appearances, stripped for the first time of their iconic burden, burst forth
and flooded the scene of eighteenth-century writing. Descriptive poetry
and the novel were the two great modes of the last phase of British
Augustan writing. They alone filled the vacuum of the imagination brought
on by corrosive satire. Eliot failed to realize that this movement from
"controversy," a mode in which various religious communities and their
theologies competed, to a *general satire* in which theology itself was laid
under siege, was bound to create a new art – one of sentiment and
description. Eliot's own theology, though learned and even archaic, was
concerned primarily with a certain kind of religious emotion – the
emotional richness of conversion. His own religion was traditional, but,
unlike like that of Newman, it was not involved with issues of orthodox
doctrine. He therefore was susceptible to making the mistake of thinking of
Dryden and Milton as the causes of a literary change which in fact was a
result of a deeper change of culture. In all these ways and more, I think it is
clear that I am not continuing Eliot's critique, and that, starting with the
well-known fact that there was a shrinkage of analogical wit in the late
seventeenth century, I have added a new etiology, a new narrative, and a
new vocabulary in order to understand Augustan writing.

There is one passage in Earl Wasserman's *Subtler Language* to which I
must pay special tribute. It was especially clarifying at the beginning of the
journey towards my final conclusions on the central issues of this book:

The other major Medieval and Renaissance patterns of thought tend to rest upon the assumption that the universe, physical, moral, and spiritual, is organized in analogical planes, and a brief glance at the fate of this concept will provide for all of them. The doctrine of the Great Chain, Shaftesburianism, and the physico-theological efforts to answer Deism by arguing the analogy of physical and spiritual truths kept the idea alive briefly, but in greatly attenuated form. And the doctrine of analogical correspondences was more talked about than employed as a poetic syntax.[19]

It was this passage in Wasserman's short but brilliant chapter, "Metaphors for Poetry," that first made me realize the long-standing confusion over two senses of analogy. Wasserman noticed that even the defenders of analogy like Joseph Butler and Warburton had a new and restricted conception of it. He further realized that the same Christian apologists that defended analogy as a tool in religious debate were themselves worried about "luxuriancy of fancy" and "enthusiastic conceits."[20] From this I came to realize more clearly the difference between analogy used for illustration, the kind of convenient analogies that Augustan theologians found between spiritual and physical existence, and the deeper *analogia entis* of Baroque culture. The later sense of analogy was mere formality, what Wasserman called a "thin atmosphere of logic." It claimed only an intellectual, not a metaphysical link between God and creature. Bishop Butler's *Analogy of Religion* is the very opposite of Donne's figural reality. For Butler, analogy helps to clarify the relations of remote orders of existence; for Donne, existence itself is analogical. The world and everything in it is part of the divine figuration. Butler has already conceived of a fully literal and autonomous creation that must be linked by analogy (by formal parallelisms) to the immaterial and original source of being. The order of things shows the existence of an orderer – God's mind, but not His person, is recognized as the necessary condition of creation. Butler's kind of analogy was the transition from a limited to a pure empiricism, a halfway house of the spiritual imagination. Wasserman was right to see all Augustan uses of analogy as merely vestigial. The late medieval or Baroque world did not have to conceive of a proof of God from physical creation, since creation was habitually thought of as the language, even the mirror of God. Wasserman (like Paul Ricoeur more recently)[21] recognized these as vastly different conceptions of analogy. His phrase, "poetic syntax" wonderfully captures the older sense of the world itself as God's text – Dante's "pages bound in a single volume" with Christ as the principle of grammar.

But Wasserman himself, like Eliot, did not see the connection of satire to the de-analogizing of nature, nor did he recognize the aggressive litera-

---

[19] Earl R. Wasserman, *The Subtler Language* (Baltimore: Johns Hopkins Press, 1959), 180.
[20] Ibid., 181–183.
[21] Paul Ricoeur, *The Rule of Metaphor* (Toronto: Toronto University Press, 1975), 273–280.

lizing program of the Restoration culture. Like so many other critics he
imagined the process as one of mere exhaustion – the gradual and
inevitable progress of modern consciousness. He could have seen in the
rewriting of *Cooper's Hill*, his own model Augustan poem, Denham's
participation in this sea change after the Civil War, but he did not do so.
The New Critical conventions within which he was operating would not
admit of an extra-textual or historical analysis. The absence of history, or
the imposition of a progressive dialectical theory of history, has helped to
obscure the grounds of Augustanism.

Of all the discoveries of the Augustans the idea of the *literal* is the most
important. It may be hard for us to imagine that the literal could have been
invented. To us it seems like the given within every system. But it was not
always so. For the Baroque culture figurative reality was made possible by
an underlying analogy of being. For Donne and Browne (as for Aquinas),
God or his preeminent creation, being, was the ground of, or solution to,
every metaphor. Though metaphor could be used as mere decoration (as in
classical grammars), it could also point to the relations and proportions
between things, or between God and his creatures. The emptying of the
space of analogy, and the shaking of confidence in language that such a
space betokens, was the most important gesture of the Augustans. I have
attempted to trace this emptying. For us, no doubt, the fiction of the literal
(and its twin the empirical) is by now unshakeable, and, since Hume, the
prejudice against analogical thinking has continually grown.

In addressing the subject of the *démon de l'analogie*, Roland Barthes
remarks:

Saussure's *bête noire* was the arbitrary [nature of the sign]. Mine is analogy . . .
Because analogy implies an effect of Nature: it constitutes the "natural" as a
source of truth; and what adds to the curse of analogy is that it is irrepressible: no
sooner is a form seen than it must resemble something, humanity seems doomed
to analogy . . . in the Edenic state of language, *analogy* used to mean *proportion*.
When I resist analogy, it is actually the imaginary that I am resisting: which is to
say: the coalescence of the sign, the similitude of signifier and signified, the
Homeomorphism of images, the Mirror, the captivating bait. All scientific
explanations which resort to analogy – and they are legion – participate in the
lure, they form the image repertory of Science.[22]

In Butler, Swift, and Locke we see the original of this emotion. But for
them the "proportion" at the root of analogy was still the medieval
proportionalitas, the relations of God to creature in Scholastic and Presbyterian theology. The "mirror" for them was not nature but God, and the
imagination which lures the subject to false and proud reasoning was the
still active conceit and syllogism of the culture of Donne and Browne. But a

---

[22] Roland Barthes, *Barthes by Barthes* (New York: Hill and Wang, 1977), 44.

resistance to analogy, what Locke was to call "the fanciful discovery of metaphysic relations,"[23] was one of the first moves in the chess game of the modern, and the fear of metaphor was its first great symptom. Its relation to the Catholic (as in its relation in Barthes to the methods of Loyola) is also part of that history, and in the age from Butler to Hume any imputation of a connection to the Papist was fatal.

But the history of our own modern obscuring of the breach between the world of analogy and that of the empirical, which figures in Barthes as a fearful corruption of science, is difficult to reconstruct from the moment of its Enlightenment origins. If British and American critics have obscured the interruption of the Baroque by their sometimes uncritical positivism, Continental critics, while more circumspect and less suspicious of metaphysics and theology, look to the Augustans, their invention of modern historicity and their critique of dogma, as the early terms of the master philosophical project which culminates in Kant or Hegel. So Cassirer cannot help but see the Cambridge Platonists, Locke, and Pope as the *preparatio* for the epistemological dualism of Kant. In this way, Becker, Lovejoy, and others give a narrative of uniform momentum – the enlightenment as the awakening to the possibilities of German critical ideology. This teleological structure envisions the interruption as part of a necessary dialectic. What began in many cases as the convenient actions of governments and interests after the English Civil War or at the end of the Thirty Years War in Europe appears at a later stage as the grand *Aufhebung* of history. Both the British and the German tendencies have obscured any thorough retrospective examination of the original crisis.

Michel Foucault in his epoch-making historiographical work, *The Order of Things*, has attempted to create one more version of the basic intellectual formulations of the Renaissance, the Enlightenment, and the nineteenth century.[24] It may be useful to make a few remarks about my chief differences from his conclusions. This would not be the place for a lengthy review of his theory, but two or three important points might help to clarify my own position. Foucault, from the opening of his marvelous chapter "The Prose of the World," finds himself as the confused modern swirling in a phantasmagoria of relations of resemblance which he rightly points to as the chief symptoms of the sixteenth-century episteme. With that electric and agitated style, which is both his greatness and his limitation, he imagines all the central ideas of the Baroque in terms of contortions of image. He does not wish to understand the world-view of the Baroque, but to get within its visual habits. In this he betrays the limitations of the

---

[23] John Locke, *Philosophical Works*, vol. 9 (London: Tegg, Sharpe and Son, 1823), 227. Reprinted in Berlin in 1963.

[24] Michael Foucault, *The Order of Things: An Archaeology of the Human Sciences* (New York: Vintage, 1973).

modern empirical personality attempting to disentangle the threads of Renaissance thought. His own intellectual stance is anti-metaphysical, illogical, and Romantic, and he can not help but see the *convenientia*, for example, as "adjacency of place," a panoply of visual contiguities; the *aemulatio* as the connections of far-flung bodies and beings, mysteriously brought into the same space; *analogy* he describes as the superimposition of the first two – a visual conflation of the contiguous and the remote. In fact his whole analysis of the Baroque is hampered by a visual/spatial prejudice which goes far beyond the habits of the episteme he is describing. He does not recognize the abstract, metaphysical sense of the terms he defines but invokes a chaotic imagery. The *convenientia*, as it was understood by Gerson or Cajetan, is a term from the Scholastic vocabulary meaning "fitness, harmony, wholeness," and in none of the six senses defined in the contemporary lexicon at Paris does it mean adjacency or contiguity.[25] In the passage which Foucault quotes from Porta, one of those fringe authors by which he delights to exemplify ideas, Porta in fact uses it in just this sense of harmonious connection. "The reciprocal and continuous connection" which Porta describes in this passage is essentially a logical, and only secondarily a physical relation. The *convenientia similitudinis* is the most atypical use of the term, but the one emphasized by Foucault. Foucault fails to understand the vocabulary of late-medieval theology because he wants to see the episteme of the sixteenth century as a moment of hysterical conceit and mad over-reading of resemblance among the physical objects of creation. Foucault's painterly mind cannot conceive of the relation of *convenientia*, *analogia*, and *proportio* as logical. He cannot conceive of the idea of cause at a distance, or logical cause, as anything short of magical reasoning. But there is nothing magical about it. *Convenientia* in its common acceptation describes the connection of cause and effect (*convenientia potentiae ad actum*) or of the numbers in a ratio (*convenientia proportionis*) and these are very far from the notions ascribed to the term by Foucault. I could make a similar analysis of "analogy," which is a far more complicated term, but let it suffice to say that all the flamboyant uses of these central sixteenth-century words have more tempered and rational counterparts (in fact Foucault's examples are mostly from the middle seventeenth century).

Just as in the poetry of Donne or Marino there are extreme experiments of casuistry and bizarre metaphorical connections with an underlying metaphysic of rational proportion, so in the work of most Renaissance writers there is both an extravagant and a moderate version of reality. By choosing the Paracelsan medicine and alchemy as his central examples, Foucault has exaggerated his case. He has in effect replayed the common

---

[25] See the *Verba Scholasticae philosophiae* (Paris: Sorbonne, 1884) reprinted from edition of 1577. Also, for further clarification see *A Latin–English Dictionary of St. Thomas Aquinas*, ed. R. J. Defferrari (Boston: St. Paul Books, 1960), 231.

technique of Augustan or enlightened satire by choosing the most extreme quality of earlier discourse as if it were typical. In that way critics like Dryden and Butler exemplify the whole epoch of Baroque writing by the examples of anagram and acrostic. Likewise, writers from Tillotson to Hume emphasize reliquary and prognostication as the typical modes of Catholic theology, or thrust the mystery of the real presence into the center of metaphysical thought. Like Foucault they are attempting to address logical or theological relations in purely physical terms. It was this visual and physical monism which produced the finest effects of Hobbesian irony and Hudibrastic sarcasm. Pope's satirical anatomy of figurative writing, the *Peri Bathous*, depends on the same kind of visual decentering. Foucault throughout those opening sections of his work, including the fanciful interpretation of the *Las Meninas* of Velázquez, plays upon the empirical prejudice of his audience, a prejudice which was handed down from the Augustan culture.

In describing the mad world of Baroque resemblances as a Borgesan fantasy he creates a feeling of absurdity in his reader – a sense of the absolute divide of consciousness between the Renaissance and the modern. For Foucault each episteme is so unique that it is opaque to those which follow it. The epistemes of Foucault can have, as he rigorously explains, no source, no history, no continuance into the future. They are the special speech of an autonomous community, and any attempt to reconstruct a history of ideas, a narrative of continuity, is doomed from the start. Foucault's structuralism forbids him access to the space outside the closed circle of signification which marks each epochal syntax. This, too, is the common gesture of Enlightenment thought. The past is inaccessible. Its language is foreign, opaque, mad. Such is the legacy of Butler, Voltaire, and Swift. Returning to the culture of the English Civil War was for Butler and Rochester like visiting an uninterpretable realm of fancy. This is the meaning of the coat which allegorizes primitive Christianity in *A Tale of a Tub*, the doctrinal debates of the third book of *Hudibras*, the foreign shores described in *The Persian Letters*. They are all indecipherable territories – realms of conceit. Foucault unconsciously replays the gambit of Augustan satire under the guise of structuralist neutrality.

Foucault was much closer to a great discovery in his treatment of the three great projects of what he calls the classical era. In the landscape of the history painter, the table of the physiocrat, the taxonomic diagram of the eighteenth-century naturalist, he brilliantly described the central and representative projects of empirical culture. The descriptions of the movement from resemblance to space, from image to type, are achieved with great incisiveness. But again Foucault oversimplifies the degree to which all eighteenth-century culture had a belief in the simple binarisms of the empirical. The taxonomies of Wilkens, Boyle, Buffon, and Condillac were not transparent. It was the impossibility of explanatory and constructive empiricism that led to Hume and La Mettrie; and they were, after all, within, not outside, the culture of Enlightenment. The simplicity and faith of the enlightened culture, like the swirling phantasmagoria of the Renaissance, are learned simplifications. Nonetheless, the sections on representing, speaking, and classifying are among the best analyses we have of the workings of Augustan intellectual culture, though British sources, which tend to be earlier, more formative, and often more profound, might have deepened the study. It was telling that Foucault was wedded to that magical term "classical" in describing the epoch of Enlightenment, even though what he describes does not in any way conjure up the mentality of antiquity. The screen of the classical used by Voltaire and Gibbon to escape traditional metaphysical thought, and to hide the ugly visage of the medieval, is rejuvenated by Foucault. Even this apostle of disjunctions, who imagines an absolute opacity between the periods of human history, could not deny the eighteenth century a real and living classicism.

Foucault, like Eliot and Wasserman, did not attempt an historical explanation of the classical age. He did not dirty himself by explaining how his world pictures came into being, or what political programs or human sacrifices attended the genesis of each episteme. Like many other theorists he exaggerates the univocity of the age he is describing. As in traditional English and American histories of ideas, there is one spirit, one form of thought in an era. This sharpens the modern sense of progress and inevitable supersession. But Augustan culture in England, like the classical French culture of the eighteenth century, is the culture of a narrow class of progressive individuals. They are the authors of their own history. But what of the other elements of a living culture? What of the Protestant, the Catholic, the women's, the laborers', the immigrants' culture in the period we are describing? Foucault, like so many others, obscures the fissures of interest and divisions of thought which mark every culture, and which it is the job of *Zeitgeist* historians to forget.

The process whereby English culture moved from the acrobatic credulity of Browne to the cool and abject skepticism of Hume in less than eighty years was neither automatic nor inevitable. The etiology of the change and the formation of a new and distinct conception of language and nature which accompanied it are not as obscure as Foucault imagined. The suddenness and severity of this moment of Augustan interruption is still of the greatest significance in our endless struggle to explain modernity. I have attempted to add something to our understanding of that moment in the following study.

Samuel Butler and the end of analogy

The curious man

It seems fair to speculate that Samuel Butler, like Swift and Johnson after him, spent a large part of his early adult life in far-ranging and sometimes esoteric study. From the time that his father bequeathed him all of his "Latine and Greek books" and a collection of works of rhetoric and logic to the time he served as secretary to the Countess of Kent, Butler was in the presence of antique learning.[1] Like Burton's and Browne's, all of his works are imbued with the spirit of fanciful Baroque erudition. Butler, the most subtle expositor of the scholarly minutiae of his age, was also its most peculiar renegade.[2] It is remarkable to recall that he spent perhaps two years as an amanuensis to John Selden, whom Milton called the most learned man of the age.

If Thomas Browne could exhaust himself on the learned paradoxes of the day, no such energy can be found in Butler.[3] It was Butler's fate to feel a growing revulsion for so much that he had absorbed, and he left to Swift especially among his younger contemporaries a sense of the general fatuousness of humane letters. His connection to Swift would be enough to make him a central figure in the writing culture of the Augustans, for he invented the prosodic and rhetorical conventions of Swift's verse and suggested the savage irony and moral formulae of Swift's mature prose. But Butler's position is even more central. He, even more than Hobbes, gave momentum to the rhetoric of exclusion – social, intellectual, and literary –

---

[1] John Aubrey, *Brief Lives* (London: Oxford University Press, 1898), vol. II, 115; also, Anthony à Wood, *Athenae Oxonienses* (London, 1820), vol. III, 87–89, in the article on William Prynne; and, *DNB*, II, 526–529. For some details on the breadth of his education and arcane learning see E. S. de Beer, "The Later Life of Samuel Butler," *Review of English Studies* 4 (1928), 159–166, and Michael Wilding, "Samuel Butler at Barboune," *Notes and Queries* 13 (1966), 15–19.

[2] See Edmund Gosse, *A History of English Literature (1660–1780)* (London: Russell and Russell, 1911), 107–109.

[3] Lytton Strachey's remarks on Browne are particularly apt. "For Browne was scientific just up to the point where the examination of detail ends, and its coordination begins. He knew little or nothing of general laws; but his interest in isolated phenomena was intense. The more singular the phenomena, the more he was attracted" *Literary Essays* (New York: Harvest Press, 1981), 43.

which is the *sine qua non* of Augustan writing. Revulsion for learning, which I have just mentioned, is only one symptom of the growing split between Baroque and Augustan conceptions of wit, and *Hudibras* helped to make this breach permanent and irreparable.

The "curious man" was for Browne "an ardent seeker after holy secrets,"[4] but for Butler every pearl had been cast before swine (his own pet metaphor for the virtuosi and extravagant scholars of the day). The curious soul, he says, "admires subtleties above all things, because the more subtle they are the nearer they are to nothing; and values no art but that which is spun so thin that it is no use at all."[5] We cannot help but think of the hobby-horses of Browne when we read, "He [the curious man] had rather have an iron chain hung about the neck of a flea, than an Alderman's Gold, and Homer's Iliad in a Nutshell than Alexander's Cabinet."[6] Hidden in these words is the cool and practical calculation of Butler's moral ethos. Power, civil and imperial – here the Alderman's chain and "Alexander's cabinet," as elsewhere the metonymies of "Cromwell's sleeves" and "the King's grave wand" – points to the mechanics of Butler's skeptical vision, and to characteristic literalizing and pragmatic gesturing, which he shares with Rochester, Garth, Swift, Pope, and Sterne. The spheres of curiosity – dogma, rhetoric, and "purple philosophy" – are the bugbears of the self-deluded, or the instruments of deception and control. Curious discourses are the paraphernalia of the outworn culture of the period leading up to and including the English Civil War, and they are in part to blame for the war "in which every dirtman had his own Theology, and a perpetual contrivance."[7]

The great discoveries Butler was to make would not have been suggested by their sources. Butler shared a skepticism with Hobbes which was neither Baconian nor Horatian. Theirs were slow-cooking and resentful intellects, late bloomers whose flowers could not have been harvested before the Restoration, and they invented that exquisite tone of Augustan moral superiority – the contorted smile of the sober gentleman thrust among the mad. Hobbes had mentioned his own timidity and agitation in his Latin autobiographical verses, and Aubrey and Wood agree that for all his wit and revelry Butler was fundamentally of a "gruching" humor. Butler's *Characters*, in its scope and thoroughness, even more than that of *Hudibras*, gives a dramatic caricature of the Hobbesian social world, tenuously kept in order by restraint of custom and force. It is little wonder that Mandeville chose Hudibrastics for his "Grumbling Hive," for Butler had created the grounds for the grim social carnival of the Augustans. In one sense, all those special elements of modernity in English Restoration and eighteenth-

[4] Samuel Butler, *Characters*, ed. Charles W. Davies (Cleveland: Case Western Reserve, 1970). From here on all references to *Characters* are marked (*Characters*, page) or if in sequence (page).
[5] Ibid., 105.   [6] Ibid., xx.   [7] Ibid., 98.

century writing – disaffection from ritual, alienated individualism, positivism, mistrust of language, and the cult of taste – may be seen in their infancy in Butler. Hobbes was all method and Butler pure insouciance, but they should always be connected in our minds with the origins of that dissolution of cosmos and incipient solipsism which is the most important element in European intellectual culture after 1660. Far from pointing to an Age of Reason, the acid critique of metaphysics and morals in *Hudibras*, like the *Leviathan* before it, shows the way to the broad and general contempt for human rationality and imagination shared by Locke, Voltaire, Pope, and Hume.

The frame of seventeenth-century humanism, whether Protestant or Catholic, held together by proverbial authorities, *imagines mundi*, analogical schema, and the residue of Scholasticism, was not fractured by Newton or Locke, who simply smoothed the rugged edges of Restoration cynicism, but by Hobbes and Butler, the *res* and *verba* of the modern English cultural critique. Butler's portraits of dissenters, Catholics, and even Anglicans as the moral freaks of the age went even further than Hobbes in creating the cult of Augustan "judgment." Butler helped to create the rhetoric of exclusion upon which the supposedly peaceful culture of latitude could be built. Much of that scaffolding is still obscure to us, but the myth of the gentleman and judge constructed in Book III of *Leviathan*, deepened in *A Tale of a Tub*, and polished in Shaftesbury's *Characteristics*, has its model in Butler's narrator. It should be no surprise that Butler illustrates for Addison (to name one example) a quirky but apt critique of the extravagant world of the mid-century.[8] Likewise, hudibrastic imagery and ethic is the backbone of Garth's *Dispensary*, Swift's "Mad Mullinix and Timothy" and *Baucis and Philemon*, Prior's *Alma*, and Gay's *Trivia*. More surprisingly, Butler ranks next only to Dryden and Milton as a verbal source for Pope, and *Hudibras* is, perhaps, a hidden parent text of *The Temple of Fame* and *The Dunciad*. Butler's method – both rhetorically and logically – proved infinitely elastic.

---

[8] Butler is mentioned or quoted (except in criticism of doggerel, always positively) in fifteen numbers of *The Spectator* and twelve of *The Tatler*. In *Spectator* 59 Addison remarks on false wit and metaphor (as it is exhibited in Erasmus and acrostic authors) and supports his theory by quoting forty lines of *Hudibras*. In *Spectator* 17, in describing the creation of the "ugly club," he suggests furnishing the busts of Duns Scotus, Scarron, Hudibras, and "the old man" in Oldham; along with pointing to the proverbial ugliness of the characters, this is a beautiful schematic for the repudiation of Scholastic, Jesuit, Recusant, and Puritan in Augustan culture. In *Spectator* 331 Addison employs a typical Augustan use of metonymy in his essay on beards. Popish beards and Moorish beards having been dispensed with humorously, Hudibras' Puritan beard ("too great a figure of the Civil War to be passed over") even in an age where such beards were extinct, is quoted at length. The technique of parody through anatomizing the dress of professions and parties, though used brilliantly by Cervantes and Rabelais, was domesticated for the English in *Hudibras*, and is one of the common modes of the "DeCoverley Papers." I shall discuss the central place of these methods of humor for Augustan writing.

It left a mark upon the whole later Augustan line – Dryden, Oldham, Rochester, Swift, Prior, Pope, Gay, Shaftesbury, and Churchill.

Butler and the formula of exclusion

It is commonly asserted that Butler's satire is morally and intellectually open, that it does not serve any particular program or interest. Satire, which Kernan and others have defined as a kind of bastion of public opinion, and the satirist as arbiter in manners and morals, do not seem to apply to Butler and his work.[9] For David Rothman, Butler is the type of the open-ended Varronian.

> *Hudibras* is not a satire with a clear "moral" or even a unified subject. Rather it draws on everything that comes to hand to assault the world, not to improve it. It resonates with the criticism of metaphysics in the *Novum Organum* and the *Leviathan*, but does not engage any new methods of understanding, as each of those works does. Rather the opposite: in employing a variety of knotty Menippean devices, the poem invites critical confusion and paralysis, upbraiding our attempts to make systematic sense.[10]

Likewise, for Michael Seidel the satiric intention of Butler moves in a circle.[11] The satirist becomes identified with the "lunatic single-mindedness" of his satiric subjects. For Margaret Doody "there is not, in *Hudibras*, any order appealed to that can counterbalance the energy and fascination of the misrule so celebrated here [the Skimmington ride in II, ii] and throughout the poem."[12] Others associate Butler's method with the explosive possibilities of the Bakhtinian carnival or with a pathology of melancholy, but it is almost never seen as moralism. The purifying possibilities of order associated in Augustan scholarship with the satire of Dryden and Pope, and the desperate moral indignation of Swift, are both, according to this view, missing in *Hudibras*. For Earl Miner, Butler's "terrible great poem takes from life any pretense to meaning, fullness, decency, or beauty."[13]

Those who have tried to defend Butler's humanity have said that the times in which he lived demanded such an image. Montague Bacon, writing of *Hudibras* in 1752, remarked, "Now if the testimony of these two authors which no party will refuse upon this occasion be true, the times we

[9] Ronald Paulson (ed.), *Modern Essays in Criticism: Satire* (Baltimore: Johns Hopkins University Press, 1972), 262–274.

[10] David Rothman, "*Hudibras* and Menippean Satire," *The Eighteenth Century* (1991), V, pp. 34, 40.

[11] Michael Seidel, *Satiric Inheritance: Rabelais to Sterne* (Princeton: Princeton University Press, 1979), 130.

[12] Margaret Doody, *The Daring Muse: Augustan Poetry Reconsidered* (Cambridge: Cambridge University Press: 1986), 122.

[13] Earl Miner, *The Restoration Mode from Milton to Dryden* (Princeton: Princeton University Press, 1974), 159.

are speaking of were so petty, so beneath all history, so full of madness, were they not fit subject for travestie? . . . Was it not a proper *burial* for a scene of pettiness, putridness, madness, and inconsistency?"[14]

There is no doubt that the age received a proper burial – in its own dirt, so to speak – in *Hudibras*. But in what sense was the age "buried" in the poem? A satirist, says Horace, "must bear the little indignities of men with a gracious smile" (*Satires.* VI. 89). Butler's satire shows no such forbearance. His satire is murderous in its breadth and sharpness. One senses that, at the end of the second part of *Hudibras*, no party in England is left standing. Butler's satiric persona is not a participant in the social drama like those of Horace or Donne, and not a teacher like the narrator in Juvenal. Butler's satiric narration is a kind of acid in which all materials dissolve. Such a dissolution of spirit, morality, and even poetry itself, into a kind of *prima materia* of wit, is the surface attraction of the text. Everything falls toward the bodily, everything is debased – the pig, the ass, the maggot, the worm, the dog, the spew, the dung, and the filth remain.

Our culture has been "matter-minded" for so long that we may forget the humiliation involved in such a treatment. The pre-Lenten carnival of the Middle Ages and the Renaissance *Walpurgisnacht* exist within the moral and theological tensions of a thoroughly Christian polity. The antic and the satyr are figures of traditional moral dualism, but they appear nowhere in *Hudibras*. The Skimmington ride[15] in *Hudibras* (II, ii, 81) is a picture of chaos within chaos. Such disorder in *Hudibras* cannot be allayed by ritual, because ritual itself is under condemnation. Butler, unlike Rabelais or Cervantes, is a non-participating bystander. If Swift was, in Coleridge's words, "Rabelais *in sicco* [in a dry place]," then *Hudibras* is Rabelais scorched with fire.

To understand the "burial" in Montague Bacon's metaphor we must understand what was buried in *Hudibras*. In that burial lies the moral or immoral possibility and purpose of the poem. It seems to me that every critic has left out the question of Hudibras' justice. Is something hidden or obscured in the text? Are the objects rendered rightly? What method of selection is being used in the poem's construction? Does Butler give a reasonable assessment of his age? Now the fact that the questions have never been asked, and because they seemed at the time of Dryden, and later Warton, to be perfectly obvious, may appear troubling to us.

I should begin my answer by saying that nothing less than a whole culture, its intellectual and moral *modus vivendi* and its great and puzzling divisions, are being buried in the text. The great "joy at court" which the king and his ministers felt, the convulsions of laughter that the text

---

[14] Quoted in Michael Wilding, *Dragon's Teeth: Literature in the English Revolution* (Oxford: Clarendon Press, 1987), 127.
[15] Cf. Doody, *The Daring Muse*, 123.

precipitated in Clarendon and Rochester alike, the public reading and constant quotation of the first part of Canto I in the House of Lords, and in the country houses of the gentry, are a part of the burial. These reactions imply at least a partial misreading. The courtiers of the Restoration, no doubt, saw the poem as a compendium of their own resentments towards the Roundheads and factious parties of the Civil War. The Royalist partisan was unlikely to recognize how much his own social and moral claims were uprooted in *Hudibras* (and in the later poems, *Notebooks*, and *Characters*, which he could not have read).

The misprision at court, however, is not, I think, as drastic as the miscalculation of the modern reader. To imagine that the politics, the theology, the science, the logic, and even the violence of an era can be pilloried without moral significance, is indeed improbable. The earlier reader could not have known Butler's words, unpublished before 1759, "Whatsoever makes an impression on the imagination works itself in like a screw, and the more he turns and winds it, the deeper it sticks, till it never can be got out again" (*Characters*, 263). The method of mockery by literalizing and parody, the marshaling of ludicrous authorities, the *reductio ad absurdum* of the argument, and quotidian and scatological images were the screws that turned and wound themselves into the minds of every important Augustan poet down to Churchill. *MacFlecknoe*, "The Alma," *The Spleen, The Dispensary, The Rape of the Lock, The Dunciad, Trivia, A Tale of a Tub*, and "The Grumbling Hive" take their central note and measure from *Hudibras*, and not from any classical or Renaissance text. The constant fluctuation in Augustan writing between Gallic decorum (Boileau's *Raison*) and native English chaos was in part made possible by the existence of the hudibrastic at the first stage of the post-Civil War satiric formulation. From the time of *Hudibras*, the possibility of dissolution and solipsism was always at hand. The obvious heterodoxy and epicureanism of the Hobbist kept him at least nominally from the mainstream of culture, but the Butlerian cynic, whose critique of religion and social ordering was even more damning, entered into the Hanoverian consciousness almost without resistance.[16] The notion of a laughing wisdom has numerous sources. In Burton's *Anatomy* the smile of Democritus mocks the false solemnity of the melancholic and the zealot. But from Butler on, satire is one of the chief measures of superior wisdom, and by his example, long before Shaftesbury had conceived of humor as the chief attribute of the reasonable man, it preserved its prestige.

The subject of the opening couplet of *Hudibras* is ignorance: "When Civil fury first grew high, / And men fell out they know not why." Ignorance of

---

[16] See Edward Ames Richards, *Hudibras in the Burlesque Tradition* (New York, unknown: 1937), 39–87.

one sort or another could be said to be Butler's main subject. His idea of "ignorance" is not the starting point of a process of enlightenment, but an explosive and dangerous force in society. For Butler, "When he [the ignorant man] is possest with an Opinion, the less he understands of it, the more confident and obstinate he is in asserting it; the more false the better satisfy'd with the Truth of it."[17] Though quarrelsome and confident, the ignorant soul, paradoxically, is also "most readily and easily impos'd upon" (*Observations*, 64). "Impregnable against reason," ignorant men "can be governed by those with even less understanding than their own" (63). The portrait of ignorance in the *Notebooks* looks forward to the images of debasement and animality found in Rochester and Swift: "prop'd (like a Cripple)," "led by . . . a dog," "a mutant and belly ignorance," and "bruit Beast" (63). These are the flourishes of animality which all the Augustans associated with those who breach public moral or aesthetic conventions. Excepting the imperfect attempt of Dryden's *The Hind and the Panther*, the animal cannot be reclaimed for this later canon as *vestigia* of God or a figure in religious allegory. If in Rochester the animal has become man's moral superior, in Butler the beast illustrates perfectly the appetite of religious zeal and party ignorance. "He [the devoted Anabaptist] may bawl like a great wolf of the countryside, and fill the woods with terror" (*Characters*, 139). The dissenter is "stuffed with straw, like an alligator, and has nothing of humanity." Fools, dunces, melancholics, and clowns (members of factions and mental defectives) are like "crabs engrafted on apples," "worms in dunghills," "a dog in a slip that will not follow but is dragged till he is about hanged" (167). Quakers, Catholics, fanatics, lawyers, clowns, and all the others are dogs, pigs, bears, parrots, and horses – either Cartesian automatons driven by blind appetite, or an epitome of lust and simplicity.[18]

Where the noise of ignorance is not bestial it is merely vacuous. In his *Characters* (264), "The ignorant man makes more noise with his emptiness, like a tub, than others do that are full." This is the same resounding tub that Swift floats beside "Leviathan" in the opening of his *Tale*, and it is the "Tympany of sense" that echoes in *MacFlecknoe*. Oldham's "ringing tub of the enthusiast" is the cousin of Butler's, and it fills the air with the "passionate ignorance" which betokens the disruption of orderly life.

We meet with this noisy ignorance everywhere in *Hudibras*, whether in the great backward black trumpet of rumor, the wrangling horns of the

[17] Samuel Butler, *Prose Observations*, ed. Hugh De Quehen (Oxford: Clarendon Press, 1979), 62.
[18] For this see *Characters*, 251 and 275. Butler was fascinated by the notion of a person with a single motivation, like an animal or a machine. He transformed the humoral into a mechanist psychology. Each hobby-horse of religion or profession produced such a simplicity in a person. This kind of moral analysis is closely connected to Bacon's and Hobbes' interest in finding simple explanatory causes. Butler's morality is analogous to a kind of early modern physics.

Skimmington ride, or the coarse fiddlings of Crowdero. This same ignorance puts the world out of pitch and as a figure of discord survives down to the bawling asses of *The Dunciad.* The origin of this universal noise for the Augustan is the English Civil War. If the low road of Augustan rhetoric is derived in part, as Margaret Doody remarks, from the raucous broadsides and scurrilous ballads of the mid century, it is also built upon a complete revulsion for the character of the parties involved. We must remember that Butler was not really a public advocate of the king's cause after the manner of John Taylor or Robert Vance. He was not the radical Royalist that Christopher Hill has described. His scathing portrait of the "Duke of Bucks," of court wits, and the sitting bishops, demonstrate his distrust for all traditional institutions. Though it may be unprovable, it would certainly not be surprising if Butler had at an earlier phase (as some have argued) been a dissenter himself, since any allegorical reading of the second canto of Part 1 of *Hudibras* would have to be thoroughly anti-Royalist.[19] In his later years Butler attacked the claims of the Royal party explicitly in prose and verse. Intellectualist Royalism of the Filmerian sort was repugnant to Butler, and he could not have gone so far even as Dryden in accepting the mythology of a golden age come round again, or a king who was a spiritual instrument of Providence. The falling out of all the parties in Butler's version of the Civil War was equally derived from ignorance. Most of the well-known victims of his lampooning (aside from his two great heroes, Hudibras and Ralpho), were in fact Anglicans, and some even Royalists. It was not one party which Butler was aiming at, nor was it every party. The ignorant devotion to outworn and empty modes of thought – religious and philosophical – is the real subject of *Hudibras.* Butler is the enemy of ignorant faith and haughty speculation, a descendant of Hobbes without the habit of rationalism. Therefore, the subject of his poem is the transition from, and the annihilation of, the Baroque and the enthusiastic Protestant culture still alive in his great contemporaries, Milton and Bunyan. It may be true that Butler sees the end of martial heroism and the classical epic, but that end was foreseen by the previous century and marked in the peculiar failures of Daniel and Cowley. Milton (as Michael Wilding has shown)[20] was on Butler's side on this one issue – the moribund state of classical heroism – and Dryden and Pope found themselves thrown back upon translation in their rearguard attempts to save the traditional martial narrative. The question of martial poetry was

---

[19] This is the view of several critics who have read the opening part of *Hudibras* as an elaborate political allegory. Most important among them is Hardin Craig, "*Hudibras,* Part 1, and the Politics of 1647," in *The Manly Anniversary Studies in Language and Literature* (Chicago: University of Chicago Press, 1923), 145–155; and Ward S. Miller, "The Allegory in Part 1 of *Hudibras,*" *Huntington Library Quarterly* 21 (1958): 323–343.

[20] Michael Wilding, *The Last of the Epics* (New York: Oxford University Press, 1987).

only an aside for Butler. His subject, which discovered its central idea in "ignorance," was the moribund condition of the Baroque and late-medieval intellect.

That the parties in the English Civil War did not know why they fell out is of course impossible. They knew all too well. The self-consciousness of doctrine, the struggle over every point of conscience between the factions from the time of the Bishops' War (1639), is the peculiar mark of pre-Restoration culture. We may say that the richness and profundity of the debate among Milton, Filmer, and Hobbes (to name only one corner of seventeenth-century controversy) could not be equaled in any other period of English writing. We can say the same for the history of style. The peculiar power and extreme unlikeness of the plain style of Hobbes, the middle style of Jeremy Taylor, and the plenary style of Browne is one of the fruits of the tension of the period. Such an intellectual pitch would not return; the fireworks of the earlier period would have to be diffused by any successful Augustan culture of peace. Butler's attempt to imagine an ignorance which can include all of these parties and styles was, I think, the great fiction of Augustan culture, a chief source of Stuart panegyric as well as mock-heroic.

The most important gesture in Butler's rhetoric is the collapsing of difference into sameness. Butler accomplishes this effect on two levels. First, and most obviously, he collapses the multiplicity of theological culture. "Ignorance," he says, "is easily possest with any opinion, that is but strange and monstrous" (*Characters*, 121). For Butler every zealous religionist – Puritan, Independent, Catholic, Lutheran, Quaker – is monstrous. It was Butler's genius to discover the underlying likeness between all the varieties of religious imagination. He was in a sense an early anthropologist. As with his modern counterpart, the discovery of any physical or formal likeness was to him the discovery of an identity. For the positivist all analogical structure is factitious, and for Butler, one of the parents of modern positivism, all the claims of ritual and magic could be reduced through metonymy to the merely physical. Like our modern structuralists Butler imagined a basic code or syntax of ignorance which bound together the faithful of every party. From the start he built his heroes not, like those in Milton or Spenser, out of the elements of motive, character, and belief, but out of their surfaces – their beards, clothing, horses, and most importantly, their food. The Catholic "takes a liking to his religion as some do to old cheese, only for the blue rottenness of it" (*Characters*, 103).

Butler's appetitive man is the Augustan counterpart to the spiritual man of Donne or Bunyan; and if that spiritual man is for Donne a metaphor, "a little world made cunningly," or in Shakespeare's phrase, "of imagination all compact," the Butlerian man is a metonym for a world made only for cunning devices – one compact of flesh. The metonym, the figure of association and contiguity, is the natural figure for a poetics of mundane and spatial description. When the literal invaded the domain of metaphor, all analogical structures were weakened and a material monism began to take its place. It was with this acidic literalism that Augustan culture produced its greatest victories of wit. As Butler demolishes the claims of the heroic and supernatural in *Hudibras*, so the mocking parallelisms in Pope, drawn from the Miltonic or Virgilian text, leave *The Rape of the Lock* and *The Dunciad* in a world of brilliant and mundane monism. The spiritual analogs of Rosicrucian cosmology become extensions of personal habits (cosmetic, clothing) and temperament. In Butler the clothing, language, and manners of his heroes, so fraught with theological and metaphysical meaning for the culture of the Civil War, became the expression of appetite and interest:

> To poise this equally he bore
> A *Paunch* of the same bulk before:
> Which still he had a special care
> To keep well cramm'd with thrifty fare;
> As Whit-pot, Butter-milk, and Curds,
> Such as a Countrey house affords.
>
> (*Hudibras* I, i, 293–298)[21]

This, coming in the middle of the extended physical topology of Sir Hudibras, which includes his beard, bum, doublet, breeches, sword, dagger, and pistol, is a subtle weaving and refraction of epic and historical sources. The country house had never been seen in a more practical light, and the realism of the field mess looks forward to Sterne. Unlike the portraits in Chaucer's "Prologue" (to which Butler may be indebted), where a single salient physical trait (the Pardoner's hair, the Wife of Bath's gap-tooth, or the French pronunciation of the Prioress) often serves to concentrate an issue of character and to give nuance to the wider social scene, the method of Butler is one of an exhaustive and minute physical description. It is accumulation rather than symbolic point that creates the force of the characterization. Such a cataloging makes Hudibras a man of accidents without purpose – a kind of cartoon version of the ethereal knights of the *Faerie Queene*. Spenser is, of course, the source for the character of Hudibras, and the underlying humor involved in the contrast between the fairy realm and the hudibrastic does a good deal of the satirical work in the first canto. We may say that the whole poem is an inversion of the Spenserian – metrical elaboration and suavity into doggerel, and spiritual allegory into brute literalism. In larger historical terms, Butler is moving from romance and allegorical topoi toward the novelistic. In giving

[21] All passages from Samuel Butler, *Hudibras*, ed. John Wilders (Oxford: Clarendon Press, 1967). Passages are marked in text (*Hudibras*, Part, canto, lines).

the history of the dagger, for example (which has cut no flesh, only bacon, beef, and cheese), he draws his hero into the sphere of selfish appetite, and cleverly manipulates a technique of epic symbolism, derived from Homer and used by both Chaucer and Spenser. Again this was to become an Augustan staple, as in the clothing metaphors in *A Tale of a Tub* or the history of Sir Plume's "seal rings" in *The Rape of the Lock*.

The history of the dagger is in fact structured as an inversion of *Faerie Queene* (III, iii, 29–48), which is Spenser's mirror of English history stretching from Arthur/Artegall to the Tudors. If Spenser wished to establish a spiritual pedigree for Elizabeth, Butler wishes to show the animal parentage of English royalty from Arthur to Henry VIII, and the likeness between Hudibras (along with his Roundhead counterparts in the Interregnum) and all previous English kings. In light of this passage, it is not strange that the *Notebooks* equate the claims of Cromwell with those of earlier kings. Butler's politics are as pragmatic and untraditional as Hobbes', which is a further stumbling block to the reading of *Hudibras* as a specifically Royalist poem. The mythic claims of royalty, like those of religion, are lampooned throughout the poem. Hudibras' breeches are old and worn, perhaps as ancient as Henry VIII, whose "siege of Bullen" is a pun on his sexual pursuit of Ann Boleyn. We might imagine that the "magazine" which Hudibras stocks with bread and black pudding enhances his connection to "fat King Harry." In point of fact Arthur's Round Table was the perfect progenitor of Hudibras' marvelous shirt:

> For *Arthur* wore in Hall
> Round-Table like a Farthingal,
> On which with shirt pull'd out behind,
> And eke before, his good Knights din'd.
> Though 'twas no Table, some suppose,
> But a huge pair of round Trunk-hose. (*Hudibras* I, i, 335–340)

In another extraordinary moment, Butler equates Henry to the Pope. "He [the Popish priest] believes the Pope's Chain is fastened to the Gates of Heaven like Prince Harry's in the Privy Gallery" (*Characters*, 101). For Butler power always corrupts.

Returning to the world of appetite, Hudibras crams his hose and shirt with all manner of victuals and is attacked by an army of rats. This recalls the pseudo-Homeric epic of the mice and the cranes, which was always a favorite of Augustan culture, and more importantly draws Hudibras into conflict with his animal brethren. These vermin are the unenchanted counterparts of Spenser's dragons. Butler takes up the debate over whether knights errant need to take food and drink. Don Quixote had attempted in several places to convince Sancho Panza that knights were above the petty requirements of food or rest when "through desarts vast / And regions desolate they passed," but the narrator of *Hudibras* answers this conundrum with a simple, "'Tis false." So in a remarkable sweep of thirty lines, the Spenserian mirror of history becomes a gustatory burlesque. The motives of Roundhead knights, like those of their animal opponents, are reduced to a single appetite derived from the mythical Arthurian origin. Piety and courage are now and have always been self-interest. Hudibras carries no Anchises on his back, but his own dead weight:

> For as Aeneas bore his Sire
> Upon his Shoulders through the Fire:
> Our knight did bear no less a Pack
> Of his own Buttocks on his Back   (*Hudibras* I, ii, 284–287).

Butler brilliantly developed these two modes of reduction. The leveling of factions and ideas, and the leveling of the spiritual, or dual, into the physical. For the first technique he borrowed the casuistry of the age he was condemning. For the second he discovered an empirical poetics, an original literalism. The three chief instruments of his literary imagination are borrowed (and inverted) casuistry, literalism, and the vulgarity of his poetic technique. Each is a rebuke to the metaphysical writing culture he is attacking, and each proved corrosive to the survival of the conceitful and Scholastic culture of the seventeenth century. If Hudibras "speaks Greek as naturally as pigs squeak," it is because his learning is mere sound, and any such esoterica mask a pig-like simplicity and appetite. "The ignorant man is a true natural," with the undertone of the true idiot, and the noise of the squeaking pig and the reciting scholar are equally empty of import. The great mystery of language and intellect, which Henry More saw "framed and illumined in the sweetness of Greek,"[22] is here once more reduced to the metonymy of noise.

The same technique is brilliantly illustrated at *Hudibras* I, i, 519–525:

> Thus Ralph became infallible,
> As three or four legg'd Oracle,
> The ancient Cup, or modern Chair;
> Spoke truth point-blank, though unaware:
> For Magick, *Talisman*, and *Cabal*,
> Whose primitive tradition reaches
> As far as *Adam*'s first green breeches.

I mention this passage because of its marvelous economy in producing the central Butlerian (and Augustan) effect. The breeches, the cup, the chair, draw us down into the sphere of the literal, while calling to mind the deeper likeness of all that these metonymies represent. The papal throne, the three-legged stool of the prophesying New Model soldier, and the

---

[22] Henry More, *Prose Works* (London: Hatcher, 1815), 186.

ancient seat of the Egyptian priest are all drawn together as a single image. Each claims a lineage august and primitive. The Catholic infallibility and fail-proof Protestant prophecy are fundamental delusions, having the same empty confidence of the ancient *auriscuper*. Like most of Butler's image repertoire, this genealogy of the chair was endlessly reworkable in Augustan poetry. It became the false throne of the Quaker prophet for Swift, and, a century after the publication of *Hudibras*, in Charles Churchill's *Ghost* we find the evangelist, Whitefield, occupying it.

> At Delphos to Apollo dear
> All men the voice of Fate might hear;
> Each subtle Priest on three-legg'd stool,
> To take in wise men played the fool;
> A mystery so made for gain,
> E'en now in fashion must remain.
> Enthusiasts never will let drop
> What brings such business to their shop;
> And that great saint, we Whitefield call
> Keeps up the humbug spiritual.[23]   (*The Ghost*, 1, 63–72)

As we shall see, two opposite (and equally bad) kinds of fraud, the enthusiastic and the superstitious, have occupied the seat of humbug. At the bottom of Butler's humor and conceit is the real humble chair, derived perhaps from nothing greater than Adam's own fallen ignorance – a place for the sons of Adam to rest their heavy bums.

But the most important single element in this equation is the Catholic. From the taint of a likeness to Papist pretense, and from the undeniable analogy between all religious claims, the Protestant is besmirched. For the social mind of the English seventeenth century the Catholic is the horrid enemy, the spanner in the works of any defense of the Baroque. It was central to the success of *Hudibras* that Butler continually and with great ingenuity drew the Protestant into guilty association with the Catholic. In Michael McKeon's words, "the critique of Calvinist sufficiency drew strength from the perception that it only perpetuated, in stealthy form, the theology of works of Roman Catholicism."[24] Butler learned how to conflate and intermingle the qualities of the Catholic religion with that of Calvinists, Independents, Presbyterians, and Quakers.

It is hard for us to imagine the depth of anti-Catholic feeling after 1660, but Butler, like Oldham and Swift after him, always played the Catholic card with the most powerful results. It may be obvious to us that the Lutheran and Calvinistic doctrines are in one sense only a strain of the

---

[23] Charles Churchill, *The Poetical Works*, edited by Douglas Grant (Oxford: Clarendon Press, 1956).

[24] Michael McKeon, *The Origins of the English Novel 1600–1740* (Baltimore: Johns Hopkins University Press, 1987), 195.

larger Christianity – Augustinian and Pauline – which resist the possibilities
of the Scholastic. But in the heated arena of Reformed theology and
politics no such concession could be made. Donne, for example, was both
the most obviously Catholicized consciousness and one of the most
vehemently anti-Catholic of Anglican writers. As Louis Martz and others
have shown, the conceitful method itself resonated with the central
tendency of Catholic continental lyric of the period.[25] But these connections were not obvious to the Protestant writing culture in England until
after the Restoration. Butler forced this unpleasant revelation upon the
intelligent reader of his age, and by doing so helped to de-center and
weaken the fabric of Anglican and Protestant religion.

The whole range of Butler's satirical characters are drawn into the
dreaded circle of Catholic thought and practice. A prostitute is the "devil's
Nuncia resident with the rosey flesh, a superintendent of the *family of love*, a
seminary sister with a mission to reconcile those who differ, and confirm
the weak" (*Characters*, 213). "*An Host*" is like a "Roman Cardinal that
resigns up the whole command of himself and his family to all that visit
him" (280). *An Envious Man* "like a Catholic penitent, whips himself for
another's enjoyment" (271). *A Cruel Man* "like a zealous Catholic worships
the relic more than the saint" (265). *A Pert* (or pickpocket) like a simple
Catholic "feels free with other men's superabundant merits, which he
believes he has right (as being one of the same society) to share in" (251).

The Catholic is an epitome of the possible vices of English society. He
puts no value in property or law, but is a kind of gypsy spirit. He wraps
himself in the disguises of empty words and dissimulating costume. *A Pimp*
is a Jesuit maintaining constant "Correspondence and Intelligence, not
only domestic . . . but also foreign, that is with all willing lay-sisters" (235).
The *Proud Lady at Court* is a "secular whore of Babylon" (302). A
"*Complementer*. . . has certain set Formes and Routines of Speech, which he
says over, while he thinks on anything else, as a Catholic does his Prayers;
and therefore never means what he says" (167). *The Court Beggar* "how rich
soever he proves is resolved never to be satisfied, as being like a *Friar Minor*,
bound by his order to be always a beggar and a liar" (72–73). *The Cheat, The
Gamester,* and *The Modern Politician* all are like that *Magus* of superstition, the
Catholic Priest. *The lawyer* is a Gothic monster patched in medievalisms:
"He has as little kindness for the Statute Law as Catholics have for the
Scripture, but adores the Common Law as they do Tradition, and both for
the very same reason: for the Statute Law being certain, written and
designed to prevent Corruptions and Abuses in the affairs of the world (as
the Scriptures are in matters of Religion) he finds it many Times a great
Obstruction to the Advantage and Profit of his practice" (111). The

---

[25] Louis L. Martz, *The Poetry of Meditation* (New Haven: Yale University Press, 1954), ch. 2.

Catholic himself is a veritable inventory of ignorances – idolatry, submission, credulity, illiteracy, lying, fancy and cowardice (103–104).

It could be urged that the Protestant culture in England as far back even as the Wycliffites had been well stocked with anti-Catholic rhetoric. This is no doubt true, and Butler's originality was not in discovering the manifold evil of the Catholic faith. Luther had written scathing and often scatological criticism of the papacy and the holy orders. The Humanists like Von Hutten and Erasmus had cataloged in satirical terms the vices and corruptions of the Catholic clergy. The virulence of rhetoric in Butler would have been a mere recapitulation of Reformation sarcasm, but he went further and took the Catholic critique in unexpected directions. First, he was much more thorough in his *Characters* than anyone before him had been in presenting both lay and priestly Catholic vices, and secondly, he had diverged from the main current of English character writing by putting religious obsession and zeal at the heart of every human error. Religious bigotry became the type of all human ignorance. For Butler, religious errors are the origin of secular errors, and the whole range of religious conviction is inherently irrational and dangerous.

The earlier English characterologies had followed a distinctly different route. Bishop Hall in his *Characters of Vices and Virtues* (1608) took a narrowly homiletic tone, even borrowing illustrations from his own sermons. The Theophrastian elements are muted with the classical professional characters being replaced by ethical types. The moralism is Anglican of the earnestly Protestant sort, and about half the studies are idealized portraits of Christian virtue. Douglas Bush[26] points out that classical realism is rarely found in Hall, and that the witty side of English character writing was taken up in the Overbury group, which included Dekker and Webster. The victims of the Overburian character are scholars, lawyers, and gentlemen. The Puritans are commonly ridiculed for the irrational pride and arrogance which we also see lampooned in Ben Jonson's *Every Man in His Humour* and *Volpone*. The authors of earlier character books are witty and moderate Anglicans who consciously or unconsciously uphold Christian Humanist values in theology and ethics. They do not "scrutinize the fundamentals of orthodox doctrine" as Butler was to do.[27] Nor do they imagine a world held together by mutual hostility and deception. A note of Baconianism sometimes enters in these earlier books, but never the more violent pragmatism of Hobbes. The best of the Character books in the period was John Earle's *Microcosmographie* (1628). The *Microcosmographie* is a book of great stylistic and dramatic accomplishment. It may be said to be the precise moral opposite of Butler's *Characters*. Earle is a moderate and

---

[26] Douglas Bush, *English Literature in the Earlier Seventeenth Century* (Oxford: Clarendon Press, 1945), 204–207.

[27] Ibid., 206.

serious Anglican who spent his years of exile (1642–8) translating Hooker and the *Eikon Basilike* into Latin and devising plans for the reconciliation of religious factions. There is a touch of anti-Catholic feeling in him, but it is not cloying or doctrinaire.[28] Earle's ameliorative theology is learned and traditional, and his *Grave Divine* "is a Protestant out of judgment, not faction."[29] The second and third portraits, "A Young Raw Preacher" and "A Grave Divine," lay out the limits of piety in an age of theological conflict. The raw preacher is a failure as a student of Bible and theology. Barely catechized, he can impress only tradesmen and laborers with his rhetoric. The grave divine is a model of balance – neither hostile to the perennial truths of the Catholic Fathers, nor wanton in his applications of novel doctrines. He wishes to assuage all Christian parties, and sees some truth in every tradition.

In matters of ceremony, he is not ceremonious, but thinks he owes that reverence to the church to bow his judgment to it, and make more conscience of schism than a surplice. He esteems the church hierarchy as the Church's glory, and however we jar with Rome would not have our confusion distinguish us.[30]

Butler's *Characters*, like the portraits in his *Hudibras*, are entirely out of the main road of pre-Restoration character writing. Although Butler has been praised for his athletic wit by critics from H. J. C. Grierson to George Wasserman,[31] his mind was not in any way typical of the culture of Browne, Vaughan, Taylor, or Benlowes, and he was not a devotee but a sworn enemy of the conceitful meditation. He has been praised as the last of the metaphysical poets on account of his esoteric syntheses and casuistical logic, but his casuistry is self-conscious mockery, his esoteric knowledge the parodic simulacrum of the serious analogies of Donne's school. Calling Butler a metaphysical poet is like calling Joyce a neo-Thomist. Such a claim is itself a kind of veiled attack on the possibility of the serious use of metaphysical lore. The playful casuistry of the seventeenth century is nothing less than the last fruits of generations of Scholastic meditation, and its poetry the extreme European example of a method

---

[28] Charles W. Davies in his Preface to Butler's *Characters* (Cleveland: Case Western Reserve, 1970), 16, makes the following remarks: "Earle's example of the antiquarian's preoccupation include his interest in his own agedness (of course to him a virtue) and even in death itself since it will '[gather] him to his Fathers.' Butler's Catholic also dotes on his religion because of its vintage quality, the point being intensified by a comparison, perhaps borrowed from Earle, with the love of old cheese for its rottenness. Butler's interest soon shifts, however, away from the man to the institution of the Church, to the fallibility of the infallible Pope and other deceptions that demolish the efficacy of the Church and underline the misplaced devotion of its believers."

[29] John Earle, *Microcosmographie or A Piece of the World Discovered* (London: Dent, n.d.), 8.

[30] Ibid., 9.

[31] See the preface to H. J. C. Grierson's famous anthology, *Metaphysical Lyrics of the English Renaissance* (Oxford: Oxford University Press, 1921), 21; and George Wasserman, *Samuel "Hudibras" Butler* (Boston: Twayne, 1980).

whose roots are in the thirteenth century. None of the practitioners of metaphysical wit would have sympathized with Butler. The question asked by Locke in respect to *Gil Blas* and *Don Quixote* could have been asked by the scholars of mid-century England:

Would it not be an insufferable thing for a learned scholar, and that which his scarlet would blush at, to have his authority of forty years standing wrought out of Hard Rocks, Latin and Greek, with no small expense of time and candle, and confirmed by immemorial tradition and a reverend beard in an instant overturned by an upstart.[32]

Butler was such an upstart, but as I have said, his overturning of traditions, his reversal of the theory of character writing, his acidic Pyrrhonism and physical monism, his mockery of the conventions of theological dispute and the rhetoric of the schools, would have remained only representative of earlier satire except for one fact. In writing *Hudibras* he discovered, almost for the first time, and without the veils and subtlety of Montaigne or Bacon, the extraordinary likeness of all religious parties of the seventeenth century. His anthropology of the faithful man blurred and conflated Catholic, Calvinist, Anabaptist, Lutheran, Quaker, Anglican, Jew, and even "Mohammedan."

I have shown that for Butler every vice in society called to mind the Catholic, but that was only of secondary importance. Central to Butler's project was showing that the hated Catholic was the spiritual twin of his moral enemy, the zealous Reformer. The *Hypocritical Non-conformist*, "though they abominate that [the Church of Rome], yet they endeavour to come as near it as they can, and serve in an unknown sense" (*Characters*, 49). Likewise the *Popish Priest* "gathers his church as *Fanatics* do, yet despises them for it, and keeps his flock always in hurdles, to be removed at his pleasure" (100). A *Silenced Presbyterian* "is a seminary minister, a Reformado reformer, and a Carthusian Calvinist, that holds only two things by his order, seditious opinions and his tongue" (312). *The Republicans* (or Levelers) are a marvelous amphibian in Butler's taxonomy: "they are State-Recusants, politic Non-conformists, that out of tenderness of Humour cannot comply with the present Government, nor be obedient to the Laws of the Land with a safe Fancy.[33] They were all Freeborn in Fairy-Land" (59).[34] But the most perfect expression of the conflation and moral identity of Reformer and Catholic appears in the third canto of the first part of *Hudibras*, where the magical apostolic authority has been transferred from

---

[32] John Locke, *Essay Concerning Human Understanding* (New York: Dover, 1959), Book 4, chapter xx, 11, 2.

[33] This connection of the civil disobedience of the Independents to Catholicism is taken up again in *Hudibras* III, i, 1463–1606.

[34] We shall see the importance of the connection of "Fairyland" to both the Catholic and the enthusiastic Protestant when we turn to *The Rape of the Lock* in chapter 3.

Rome to every shire in England. Like Dryden and Swift after him (and
Milton before), Butler imagines old Presbyter as new Pope, and the
Commonwealth as the idol of Moloch:

> For then to sacrifice a Bullock,
> Or now and then a child to *Moloch*,
> They count a vile Abomination,
> But not to slaughter a whole *Nation*.
> *Presbyterie* does but translate
> The Papacy to *Free State*,
> A *Common-wealth* of *Poperie*,
> Where every Village is a *See*
> As well as Rome, and must maintain
> A *Tithe-pig-Metropolitan*:
> Where ev'ry *Presbyter* and *Deacon*
> Commands the *Keyes* for Cheese and Bacon;
> And ev'ry Hamlet's governed
> By's *Holiness*, the *Churche's head*,
> More haughty and severe in's place
> Than *Gregorie* and *Boniface*.   (*Hudibras* I, iii, 1197–1212)

The chief note of Hudibras' own education is its Scholasticism, and from
the opening section the Puritan knight is subtly drawn into the dreaded
circle of Catholic thought. Butler rightly recognized the fundamental
likenesses at the root of religious denominations, and more importantly the
violent exaggeration of differences that arose between all the Christian
parties in the polemics of the age. He recognized that the theology of
analogy, the language of Scholasticism, and the specular theory of nature
were the shared material of Catholic and Presbyterian culture, and he
returns to this sore spot again and again:

> Beside he was a shrewd *Philosopher*,
> And had read every Text and gloss over:
> What e'er the crabbed'st Author hath
> He understood by implicit Faith,
> What every *Sceptic* could inquere for;
> For every *why* he had a *wherefore*:
> Knew more than forty of them do,
> As far as words and termes could goe.   (*Hudibras* I, i, 127–134)

> Where Entity and Quiddity,
> The Ghosts of defunct Bodies, flie.   (*Hudibras* I, i, 145–146)

Here Butler looks back to Hobbes and forward to Locke in satirically
attributing two errors to the methods of Hudibras. First, Hudibras can not
distinguish a verbal formula from a substantial one; secondly, he believes in
the ghostly existence of the fictitious "quiddity" or essence. Bacon had
pronounced against the confusion of words with things – the fetish for

delicate and empty terms – which was the main error of the Scholastic philosophers. He distinguishes

two marks and badges of suspected and falsified science: the one, the novelty and strangeness of terms; the other, the strictness of positions, which of necessity doth induce oppositions, and so questions and altercations. Surely, like as many substances in nature which are solid do putrify and corrupt into worms; so it is the property of good and sound knowledge to putrify and dissolve into a number of subtle, idle, unwholesome, and, as I may term them, vermiculate questions, which have indeed a kind of quickness and life of the spirit, but no soundness of matter or goodness of quality.[35]

Hudibras is just such a mere verbalist, though he lacks even the quickness of spirit which is for Bacon the deceptive bait of Scholastic rhetoric. The tick of Aristotelian logic in *Hudibras* is a kind of ritual babbling. One gets the feeling that Butler recognizes the seventeenth century as the moment of the final decay of old habits of argument. Throughout the poem Butler grants at least a marginal advantage to the logic of the more radical Protestant discourse of Ralpho, in part to show the false will-to-power in the Presbyterian interest, and in part to place metaphysical analogy at the very heart of human error. Butler was correct to note the deep connection between medieval and Puritan discourse, which has also been described by Perry Miller:

Though Puritan literature abounds with condemnations of scholasticism, almost no limits can be set to its actual influence. At every turn we encounter ideas and themes which descend, by whatever stages, from Medieval philosophy, while the forms of the thinking, the terminology, the method of logic – though this was believed to have been drastically revolutionized in the sixteenth century – were still duplications of Medieval habits, modified but not transformed. Indeed, in seventeenth-century Puritanism the scholastic elements were more pronounced than in the sixteenth century.[36]

The mixture of an implicit faith with the nonsense of Scholastic logic is one side of Hudibras' delusion, the other is his misreading of nature. Hudibras believes in the ghostly and fanciful notions of quiddity and quality, the invisible and immaterial principle within the individual substance which makes it intelligible. This had been one of the chief objects of Hobbes' derision. In one of the final and most passionate passages of *Leviathan* he had connected Scholasticism rather oddly to the calamities of the Civil War, and to the superstitious doctrines of Catholicism:

It is to this purpose, that this doctrine of *Separated Essences*, built on the Vain Philosophy of Aristotle, would fright them from Obeying the Laws of their

[35] Francis Bacon, *The Advancement of Learning*, ed. G. W. Kitchin (London: J. M. Dent, 1973), 25–6.
[36] Perry Miller, *The New England Mind: The Seventeenth Century* (Cambridge, Mass.: Harvard University Press, 1954), 104.

Countrey, with empty names; as men fright Birds from the Corn with an empty doublet, a hat, and a crooked stick. For it is upon this ground, that when a man is dead and buried, they say his Soule (that is his Life) can walk separated from his Body, and is seen by night among the graves. Upon the same ground they say that the Figure, the Colour and the Tast of a peece of Bread has a being, there, where they say there is no Bread: And upon the same ground they say that Faith, and Wisdome, and other Vertues are sometimes *pow'red* into a Man, sometimes *blown* into him from Heaven, as if the Vertuous and their Vertues could be asunder; and a great number of other things that serve to lessen the dependence of Subjects on the Sovereign Power of their Countrey.[37]

This may be the source of the famous "scarecrow deity" in Cowley's "Verses on the Royal Society," as well as some of the spiritual military imagery of *Hudibras* ("infallible Artillery," etc.), and it neatly lays out the usual network of associations in Augustan religious satire. There is a typical progression from the Aristotelian metaphysical discourse of "separated essences" (to which Aristotle himself, of course, did not subscribe) to the ghostly apparitions of the graveyard, and on to the folly of transubstantiation, itself a separated and mystical essence, moving at last to the notion of personal inspiration and prophecy, which was at first the Catholic theory of Pentecost as the divine inspiration of the Apostolic interpreters and in its more modern guise the prophetic vocation common among the dissenting preachers of the Civil War.

I should note in passing that the "bloody communion" and Catholic ghost stories are the origins of the Gothic in England, which had a long history before *The Castle of Otranto*. What began as mockery of superstition ended as fascination. Such a fiction flourished best in Britain, where the recusant population was at once small and obsequious. Literary Gothicism, the enticing twin of Protestant bigotry, was bound to grow up there. An important study could be made of the role of Bacon, Hobbes, Glanville, and the early Hume in the formation of Gothic conventions in literature. Gothicism was at first a strategy of intellectual and social containment. It was used with great skill in the program of Bishop Sheldon at the time of the creation of the Clarendon Code (1661–3), which effectively thwarted the religious culture of both Roman Catholics and Dissenters. "The Papist," he said, "may corrupt our childe-like congregations, and fill their hearts and eyes with the Ghostly Shows and sanguineous Sacrifices of his luride banquetinges."[38] Readers of Monk Lewis will recognize the bishop's

---

[37] Thomas Hobbes, *Leviathan*, ed. Richard Tuck (Cambridge: Cambridge University Press, 1991), 465. I have used this text (for reasons of the new collation of MS texts and the use of the Egerton 109 MS) instead of Molesworth.

[38] Archbishop Sheldon, *Lectures and Sermons* (London: Foster Company, 1811), 214. For a good recent treatment of Restoration censorship and containment see the essay "The Theory of Religious Intolerance in Restoration England" by Mark Goldie, in *From Persecution to Toleration*, eds. O. P. Grell, J. I. Israel, and N. Tyacke (Oxford: Clarendon Press, 1991), 331–368.

imagery. Such dangerous excesses of imagination are the chief subject of *Hudibras*.

Hobbes connects Scholastic metaphysical and logical discourse with the narrative of the fantastic, and connects Catholic superstition with Protestant enthusiasm. I mentioned a moment ago the detailed linking of these two forms of ignorance (Hobbes calls them "absurdities") in the *Characters* and *Hudibras*, and it is no exaggeration to say that Hudibras himself has all the symptoms of Papist overreaching – transcendent verbalism, theological anomalies, confusion of spiritual and physical existence, veiled pragmatism and chicanery, and timid credulity. It is interesting to note how explicitly Hobbes links these "absurdities" to threats to the state. The formula of exclusion in Butler, Swift, and others was always linked to the maintenance of order in the state, and it is not sufficient to call the Augustan attitude tepid or Erastian – it was often bigoted and violent. Long after the period of religious uneasiness had passed (and the Catholic dangers had always been exaggerated) the bitter satire remained. It is as strong in Churchill and Crabbe as it was in Swift.

The structure of *Hudibras* is not dramatic, not even narrative, but didactic. This may seem odd for a poem which seems so amorphous and open-ended. Nonetheless, the only principle of organization it has, its animating logic, is one of instruction. The instruction is completely negative, but it is complete and coherent – more single-minded than the dialectics of Bacon and Hobbes, because more unyielding. Hobbes sometimes enters into traditional debate, as in the argument over papacy and monarchy, in which he addresses in great detail the opinions of Cardinal Bellarmine, or in his detailed objections to Descartes' *Meditations*. Hobbes sometimes concedes something to his antagonist, as Bacon did before him, for example, in his strange sympathy with the Jesuits. But in Butler, Augustan satire has matured. It no longer admits the possibility of a rational interlocutor, and in this refusal it looks forward to Locke and Hume It will no longer grant any validity to traditional discourse.

In *Hudibras* Butler calls into question all the major contemporary modes of religious and metaphysical thought. The first step in his expanding field of satire is moving from Hudibras to Ralpho. Ralpho is the logical and moral opposite of his master. If Hudibras overvalues speech, the social medium and the customs of rhetoric and logic, Ralpho overestimates the internal sphere of silent judgment, the place of conscience and "the inner light."

> His *Knowledge* was not far behind
> The Knight's, but of another kind,
> And he another way came by't:
> Some call it *Gifts*, and some *New light*;
> A Liberal Art, that costs no pains

Of Study, Industry, or Brains.
His wits were sent him for a Token,
But in the Carriage crackt and broken.
Like Commendation Nine-pence, crookt
With to and from my Love, it lookt.   (*Hudibras* I, i, 473–482)

For as of Vagabonds we say,
That they are ne're beside their way:
Whate're men speak by this *new Light*,
Still they are sure to be i'th'right.
Tis a *dark-Lanthorn* of the Spirit,
Which none see by but those that bear it:
A Light which falls down from on high,
For Spiritual trades to cousen by:
An *Ignis Fatuus*, that bewitches,
And leads men into Pools and Ditches.

(*Hudibras* I, i, 495–504)

  Hudibras' error is one of false logic and empty rhetoric. It was mere verbal formality that made him swell in confidence in the face of the mysteries of Eden. He believed that words bore a sure if flexible relation to the real, and that the "real" included every subject of wayward speculation. There was, therefore, very little that he could not "unriddle in a moment / In proper terms, such as men smatter / When they throw out and miss the matter"(I, i, 184–186). While Hudibras, like the Scholastics on which he was modeled, found a too perfect relation between word and object, Ralpho has the same misguided confidence in the relation of inner light to outer reality. His inner-light has warrant from heaven without need of "Study, Industry, or Brains." His gifts, though slightly "behind the Knight's," were truly awe inspiring. Unbounded by language, and richest in the absence of education, they are the epistemological opposite of those of his master. Though his wits may have been injured in the delivery, they had no difficulty attaining to prophetic and mystical perfection. Not language but silence was the mark of Ralpho's skills:

The Light . . .
Speaks through hollow empty soul,
As through a Trunk or whisp'ring hole,
Such language as no mortall ear
But spiritual Eaves-droppers can hear.   (I, i, 511–515)

Although Ralpho knew well the "intelligible world" and the mysteries of anthroposophy and the Rosicrucians, he knew them by an immediate, not a studied method. He did not need the help of natural signs:

All this without th'eclipse of Sun,
Or dreadful Comet, he hath done,

By inward light, a way as good,
And easy to be understood.

(I, i, 574–577)

And he has been more "lucky" (happy, that is) in his spiritual guesswork than the guild of astrologers and white magicians which are described in contrast to him at the end of his portrait. In fact, Ralpho, doubting the powers of astrology (which the Independents and Quakers roundly condemned), "therefore took / The other course," of inward meditation and prophecy. It would not be until the second part, canto iii that Butler's satirical cosmos would be completed with the addition of the astrologer, Sidrophel.

It seems to me that Butler had imagined at the beginning of his project, probably in the early stages of the Civil War, and perhaps at the behest of a Royalist patron, an extended allegory of the various actions of the Long Parliament. There are hints of this especially in the second canto of the first part. It may be that Butler envisioned a parody of Spenserian allegory, which would serve to belittle the enemies of the Crown rather than enlarging the royal person, and there are a number of veiled parallels with Spenser in the opening cantos, including the one which I have already described. Doggerel might have served in this project to create a humorous contrast between the artless decorum of the dissenting culture and the ceremonious habits of the Elizabethan court. This project was never completed; it apparently trailed off at about the time the king was being pursued to Carisbrooke in the period before his arrest. A poem so brutal and so offhanded may have seemed inappropriate as a memorial of the martyred king. Cowley's narrative of the Civil War, though far more serious, met a similar fate. Insofar as the poem has historical interest, it seems to be concerned with the national situation from the time of the Bishops' War until about 1646. It may have been a kind of prognostic work, showing the dangers of Protestant populism in that era. Obviously whatever allegorical reading is possible now must be intermittent and unconvincing, because from the time that Cromwell enters the scene, the poem seems to have taken on a different cast.

It would, nevertheless, be a mistake to think that the poem was entirely playful and improvisational. Having lost its original purpose, a purpose for which Butler was in any event ill-suited, it developed by degrees a far different structure which would prove endlessly imitable in the writing culture after 1660. Like all the central figures of Augustan poetry except Swift, Butler's talent did not lie in the direction of narrative. He does not tell a story well, nor can he interweave the action in such a way as to produce interest. He did not share with Defoe a serious concern for the moral culture of everyday life, and his own callous attitude toward teleological and metaphysical discourse made a traditional romance un-

palatable to him. Like *The Dispensary*, *The Trivia*, *The Dunciad*, and many
other important Augustan poems after it, the genius of his work does not lie
in the story – the narrative appears on the whole as an impediment – but in
its spatial-logical arrangement. Very few modern readers have read past
the first part of *Hudibras*, and even in the nineteenth century (when patience
was not at a premium) critics like Southey and Hazlitt rarely quote from its
later cantos. But such a closer reading yields certain fruits. By pursuing the
complete text we see the range of satire and the degree of intellectual
dislocation which Swift and Pope inherited.

Having forsaken the narrative of Part I, Butler lays out the last two parts
to show the full range of analogical error. Canto I of Part II deals primarily
with the subject of poetry, and secondarily with matters of ideal love. That
canto opens with an allusion to Renaissance romance and has four
subsequent references to *Don Quixote*. While Quixote's Dulcinea represented the picaresque sphere, the ultimate rebuke to the figural excess of
his delusion, the Lady whom Hudibras pursues recognizes the emptiness of
the conceits with which he attempts to woo her. She connects the
Petrarchan hyperbole of his speech – here, and in the first canto of the third
part – with both love-delusion and hypocritical fortune-hunting. She lays
out for Hudibras the problems of his rhetoric:

> Hold, hold, Quoth she, no more of this,
> Sir *knight*, you take your aim amiss;
> For you will find it a hard *Chapter*,
> To catch me with *Poetic Rapture*,
> In which your *Mastery* of *Art*
> Doth shew it self, and not your *Heart:*
> Nor will you raise in mine *combustion*,
> By dint of high *Heroique* fustian:
> Shee that with *Poetry* is won,
> Is but a *Desk* to write upon;[39]
> And what men say of her, they mean,
> No more, than that on which they *lean*.
>
> (*Hudibras* II, i, 583–594)

The place of the Lady in *Hudibras* has been widely debated. She is one of
the earliest figures of English feminism. But her feminism may be a screen
behind which the Butlerian cynic can hide. By making the Lady a neutral
and superior observer, Butler is able to enact the distance between the folly
of the age and the narrator. The Lady stands in for Butler. She plays the
part of the Augustan outsider. Like the Turk in Hogarth's *Credulity, Superstition, and Fanaticism*, she is on the outside of male, conventional European

---

[39] The reader may notice this image (perhaps by way of allusion) was used in a remarkable scene
in Laclos' *Les Liaisons dangereuses* where Valmont describes his desk as a figure of his true love
while writing his letter on the back of one of his mistresses.

discourse. As the victim of both conceitful poetry and empty rhetoric, she is also a metonymy for Mother England at the hands of the villainous revolutionaries of the Civil War. Like the author, she is a true rational patriot.

Canto II of Part II deals entirely with rhetoric. Every kind of arcane casuistry is employed in the debate between Ralpho and Hudibras. The same role played by poetry in matters of love is played by rhetoric in matters of religion. For Butler, poetry and rhetoric are both untrustworthy instruments of argumentation. In the third canto of the second part, Butler addresses the errors of science. By introducing the alchemist, Sidrophel, he broadens his critique of human knowledge. Hudibras represents the purely verbal side of Baroque culture. Sidrophel embodies its fantastic misinterpretations of nature. Sidrophel has mastered all the false magical arts of the seventeenth century – astrology, alchemy, fortune-telling, and phrenology.

In Part III of *Hudibras,* Butler returns to the formula which he had devised for the second part. In the first canto, he pursues once again the question of ideal love and the collateral issue of the poetic imagination. In the second canto, he returns to false wit, but this time he historicizes the debate of the knight and his squire. This canto is the most tedious one for a modern reader. Butler turns to historical analysis, which we have not seen since Part I. Unfortunately, this detailed revision, probably written in the Interregnum, smothers the reader in irretrievable historical subtleties.

The last canto of the poem parallels the concluding canto of Part II, but not as closely as the parallels I have just noted. The subject of the last canto is legal discourse rather than science. As in *Tristram Shandy,* which is modeled upon it, the love plot devolves into an issue of legal contract. Here again, the effect of the Lady's superior sanity forces us to see the inequities of Renaissance love. The "Epistle" written by the Lady, and appended to the canto, explains to Hudibras the absurdity of his suit in terms both literary and legal.

The arrangement of Parts II and III in three closely parallel cantos (with slightly altered subject matter) helps us to understand Butler's project. The genre of *Hudibras* is neither romance nor mock-heroic, but anatomy. *Hudibras* is the satirical anatomy of the Baroque. Having dispensed in Part I with the absurdity of the martial epic, Butler moves on to address the popular, non-narrative elements of Humanistic culture – the love lyric, rhetoric, science and law. Following Bacon, he regarded both physical science and law as branches of true history, while poetry and rhetoric are outworn instruments of a dying culture. Science and law, the whole of discourse, must be rationalized. As in Bacon, the history of facts unencumbered by distracting metaphor is the true object of human intelligence. Butler's anatomy dramatizes the need for a new Baconian beginning.

The failure of narrative and the corresponding success of satire in Butler is natural enough. It is difficult to construct a myth out of the denigration of other myths, and the *satira*, in the Roman sense of a bowl for throwing in the oddments and diverse elements of the imagination, was an ideal vehicle for the kind of negation of form that is at the heart of *Hudibras*. *Hudibras* is an exhaustive collection of false wit and moral self-delusions. The arrangement of satirical arguments and parodic images of characters is not accidental. The structure is logical and even economical in the specific sense that Butler discovered a set of oppositions which could accelerate the demise of his *bête noire* – medieval and Baroque thinking.

To understand Butler's anatomy of delusion we must consider a wider history. There appear to be three stages in the history of the idea of superstition since antiquity. The first is derived from long-standing Catholic and Orthodox notions, which were still alive in the seventeenth century. In this stage superstition is no more than the various false or imperfect forms of religion. Augustine had set out in his "Letter xvii" to the pagan Maximus of Madaura a list of the things Christians could not believe and these he termed *superstitiosus*, things full of superstition, borrowing the language of the late-ancient pagans. He says simply that no dead person or created thing can be worshiped.[40] Elsewhere he lays out a number of superstitious practices which Christians should avoid including astrology, numerology (*mathematici*), and fortune-telling. Aquinas also uses the term *superstitio* to describe practices opposed to *vera religio*. He lists chiefly, *superstitio divinationis*, which includes fortune-telling and other divination; *superstitio idololatriae*, idolatry; *superstitio indebiti cultus veri Dei*, illegal or sacrilegious worship of the true God; and *superstitio observantiarum*, superstitious observances and performances, which may have included participating in local pagan celebrations.[41] One last category is of special interest: *superstitio nugatoria* included all minor and relatively harmless forms of folly; he sometimes called this form *noxia* indicating a limited moral danger.

This kind of Scholastic taxonomy was preserved down to the time of the Council of Trent and well into the modern period. The word *superstitio* appears only twice in the documents of Trent. In the decretal on the proper observance of the Mass it is defined as *verae pietatis falsa imitatrix*, the false

---

[40] Augustine's words are instructive. "Scias Christianis catholicis (quorum in vestro oppido etiam ecclesia constituta est) nullum coeli mortuorum, nihil denique ut numen adorari quod sit factum et conditum a Deo, sed unum ipsum deum qui fecit et condidit omnia." ["You should know that for Catholic Christians (who even now have built a church in your town) not one of the dead in heaven, and indeed no divine image which is made or built from a god is to be adored, but only the one God who made and built all things."] St. Augustine, *Prolegomena, Confessions, Letters* (in vol. 1, *Nicene and Post-Nicene Fathers*, First Series) (Buffalo: Christian Literature Press, 1886), 235. Also, see Letter CCXLVI, 588–589.

[41] *A Latin-English Dictionary of St. Thomas Aquinas* (Boston: St. Paul Editions, 1986), 1016–1017. See also, Thomas Aquinas, *Commentary on Thessalonians*, Leonine Edition (Toronto: 1957), 67–69 and *passim*.

imitation of true piety.[42] It is obvious that it applied mainly to idolatry and other forms of false worship, and was less frequently applied (as in the *Brevior synopsis theologiae moralis*) to false opinions on matters of faith or doctrine.[43]

The concept was greatly expanded by Humanists of the sixteenth century, including the reformers who extended it to include the false practices of the Roman church as described by Luther and others, especially indulgences, belief in purgatory, the use of images, the rosary, and relics. One branch of this tradition comes to maturity in Casaubon's important treatise in which the pagan sources, Pliny, Cicero, and Plato are evaluated, and fear and ignorance are seen as the common sources of credulity and superstition. The fourth part of Burton's *Anatomy of Melancholy* is a massive collection of the moral and psychological dangers of superstition – one of the chief causes of religious melancholy. Like Erasmus and Rabelais before him, Burton attributes a good deal of the problem to celibate orders and monastic life, and this fits with the contemporary English attack upon Catholicism in the early seventeenth century:

In our days we have seen a new scene of superstitious impostors and heretics. A new company of actors, of Antichrists, that great Antichrist himself; a rope of Popes, and by their greatness and authority bear down all before them; who from that time they proclaimed themselves universal bishops, to establish their own kingdom, sovereignty, greatness, and to enrich themselves, brought in such a company of human traditions, purgatory, Limbus Patrum, Infantum, and all that subterranean geography, mass, adoration of saints, alms, fasting, bulls, indulgences, orders, friars, images, shrines, musty relics, excommunications, confessions, satisfactions blind obedience, . . . that the light of the Gospel was quite eclipsed, darkness over all, the scriptures concealed, legion brought in, and religion banished, hypocritical superstition exhalted and the church itself obscured and persecuted.[44]

Burton lays out the Protestant side of Anglican apologetics in the early seventeenth century. Hooker of course plots a middle path. In the first book of *The Laws of Ecclesiastical Polity*, he lays out the good and the bad of Roman Catholicism, and on the whole he is more conciliatory to Catholic practices than to dissenting Protestant ones. Following the medieval opinion, "superstition" for Hooker was simply false doctrine and idolatrous ritual.

It is easy to see that the Counter Reformation Catholics from Gerson to Cajetan and Bellarmine would oppose any doctrine of inner-light, and all but the most restrained theories of conscience. They had to defend perennial doctrines and the authority of the Catholic *magisterium*. It was enthusiasm, the inward conviction of prophetic or spiritual light, that

[42] H. J. Schroeder, ed., *Canons and Decrees of the Council of Trent* (London: B. Herder, 1941), 423.

[43] J. Tanquery, ed., *Brevior synopsis theologiae moralis* (Paris: Declée and Company, 1924).

[44] Robert Burton, *The Anatomy of Melancholy* (Boston: Dana Estes, n.d.), 375.

moved their ire. Both Anglicans and Catholics accepted a tempered concept of zeal, though even as early as Jeremy Taylor's *Holy Living* it was seen as particularly dangerous to mature faith.[45] Donne and Taylor were close to Continental models in their understanding of the dangers of a too enthusiastic conscience.

After 1660 much more was written against enthusiasm, which sometimes simply meant dissent. By then Fox and his followers were taken as the exemplars of extraordinary and civilly disruptive enthusiasm – they followed the light of the spirit wherever it led, and it led in many cases to imprisonment and severe fines. The subtle distinctions between true and false zeal in the earlier Anglican divines were discarded by the preachers of the age. Authors as various as Glanvil, Tillotson, Sharpe, and South began to associate enthusiasm with mental and civil disturbance. At the same time the whole field of theological thought began to shrink. The great systems of analogical metaphysics, preserved briefly in some of the works of the Cambridge Platonists, were now disappearing. Bacon and Hobbes had come of age, and all traditional theology could be tarred with the imputation of Catholic superstition.

It was at this historical juncture that Butler fell upon a remarkable discovery: that the dissenting interests were fundamentally divided, that some, particularly the Presbyterians like Hudibras, were Scholastic in their rhetoric and metaphysics, and that others like Ralpho were their spiritual opposites. Most Anglicans fell out on one side or the other. All the greatest victims of Butler's lampoons were in fact Anglican – Ross, Partridge, Thomas Vaughan, Benlowes. Butler was piecing together a general satire of Christian thought, one that would attack with equal power the enthusiastic and the superstitious. His most important gesture was to move away from controversy toward total satire. From the time of Butler, Augustanism began to adopt a stance of neutral and general satire. No longer involving itself in the minutiae of doctrine, nor siding with either of the great parties of Civil War controversy, Butler and his successors attacked the very notion of doctrine.

Although Cowley had published the "Puritan and the Papist" before him, Butler more subtly negotiated the binary oppositions of the enthusiastic and superstitious parties. He collected the literary jibes and nasty legends of the pamphlet literature of the Civil War era. He could borrow equally from the broadsides of dissenting or High Church authors. The rather narrow conception of superstition that we saw in Aquinas or Hooker was hugely expanded. The *superstitio nugatoria* was no longer harmless. Every folk cult of fairies, goblins, angels, devils, and every branch of false learning – alchemy, Rosicrucianism, astrology, prophecy, magic – was packed into

---

[45] Jeremy Taylor, *Works*, ed. C. P. Eden (London: Oxford University Press, 1847–53), vol. II, 126.

the new sphere of superstition. Hobbes had already seen the rich possibilities of conflating a wide array of absurdities under a small number of headings, but Butler went one better. He mastered the peculiar arcana of every party. His work is a kind of heteroglossic manual of burlesque. Science itself, especially the improvisational experiments of the masters of Gresham College, was to be lumped with the delusory arts. With the introduction of Sidrophel into *Hudibras* the pseudo-scientific and merely verbal forms of superstition come into contact. So in later Augustan poetry, as we shall see in our treatment of Pope, the old wives' tale and the theological doctrines of the Jesuit were to become one.

This formula of exclusion, as I have called it, was to become a staple of Augustan poetry. Sometimes, as in the case of Denham, the conflation was historical. The parties of Reformation culture could be thrown together under the Butlerian ignorance.

> When Lucifer no longer could advance
> His works on the false ground of ignorance,
> New arts he tries and new designs he lays:
> Then his well-studied masterpiece he plays –
> Loyola, Luther, Calvin he inspires
> And kindles with infernal flames their fires.[46]

Such conflations were not unpopular in pulpit oratory. Robert South connects the Dissenters and Papists – the enthusiastic and superstitious enemies of the Church – in a torrent of abuse:

[T]hat sort of men place *their whole Acceptance with God,* and indeed, their whole *Religion,* upon a *Mighty Zeal* (or rather out-cry) against *Popery, and Supersitition;* verbally, indeed, uttered *against the Church of Rome,* but really meant against the *Church of England.* To which Sort of Persons I shall say no more but this, (and that in the Spirit of Truth and Meekness) *namely;* That Zeal and Noise *against Popery,* and real Services *for it,* are no such inconsistent Things, as some may imagine; indeed no more than *Invectives against Papists, and solemn Addresses of thanks to them,* for that very Thing, by which they would have brought in Popery upon us. And if those of the *Separation* [Dissenters] do not yet know so much, (thanks to them for it) we of the Church of *England* do; and so may themselves too, in due time. I speak not this by way of *Sarcasm,* to reproach them, (I leave that to their own Consciences, which will do it more effectually) but by way of *Charity* to warn them: For let them be assured, that this whole Scene and Practice of theirs, is as really *Superstition,* and as false at Bottom to rest their Souls upon, as either *the Jews alledging Abraham for their Father,* while the *Devil* claimed them for his *Children;* or the Papists relying upon *their Indulgences, their Saints Merits,* and *Supererogations,* and such other Fopperies.[47]

---

[46] John Denham, "The Progress of Learning" in *Poems* (New York: AMS, 1974), 64.
[47] H. White, R. Wallerstein, and R. Quintana, eds., *Seventeenth Century Verse and Prose* (New York: Macmillan, 1952), 189–190.

One could point out the same formula in Cleveland, Cotton, and others of the 1670s. Oldham's *Satires on the Jesuits* return again and again to the relation of enthusiastic dissenters to secret Jesuitical cabals. A long paper might be written on Oldham's use of Butler's material.

The greatest work to handle the superstition and enthusiasm dichotomy after *Hudibras* is *A Tale of a Tub*. The opposition of the brothers is divided along the same lines as the Ralpho/Hudibras duality. In one respect Swift simplified the model by bringing in the Catholic, Peter. While Butler had used the Scholastic Hudibras to represent the Catholic vices, Swift went back to the source. In the myth of the coats Swift employs the clothing metonymies of Butler (and Rabelais) with a subtlety and depth beyond the scope of Butler. Although the primitive Christianity of the father's will is uninterpretable, it at least gives the impression of an original truth. Butler did not even try to fool the reader into imagining a decline from an original. But in the latter sections of the *Tale* the brothers begin to sympathize with each other, and Swift enacts the association of Calvinist and Catholic thought which Butler had discovered. In laying out the logic of oppositions between the outward analogical man, Peter, and the inward enthusiastic man, Jack, Swift goes far beyond Butler in exhausting the possibilities for humorous analysis. Swift more explicitly connects enthusiasm with mania, and superstition with fetishism. Like Butler, Swift leans heavily on sacramental theology for his satire. It is here that Swift's *Tale* must have been offensive to Anglicans. In fact Martin, who represents the Anglican faith in the allegory, is not shown in a better light than his brothers. Even in the later editions when Swift apparently tried to give Martin some distinctly pious characteristics, the attempt fails. Martin has the insubstantial quality of much post-Restoration Anglican apology. Rather than borrowing elements from the Roman and Protestant traditions as Hooker had done, these later apologists emptied the church of all known doctrine. The tendency of complete monism in Swift is shown in his bitter mockery of the doctrine of the Eucharist. Both Swift and Butler make fun of the intelligible world and the various versions of microcosm. Both have a style digressive and circling, but Swift's argument is much more condensed and pointed. Swift derived more from Butler than from any other English author. To him he owes a good deal of his humor and the semi-doggerel style of his poems.

Pope too occasionally leans on the Butlerian formula of exclusion. The structure of the second book of *The Dunciad*, which brings together the preachers in the field (under the title "enthusiasts") with the writers of conceitful nonsense like Benlowes and Wither, is a subtle reworking of the paradigm. Although Churchill, Lloyd, and others were to carry those now perennial figures of the superstitious Catholic and enthusiastic Protestant into the satire of the later eighteenth century, they find their last mature and subtle realization in the text and notes of the Variorum text of *The*

Dunciad. While Butler and Swift had associated their satirical heroes with the modes of false wit and religion of the seventeenth century, Pope places the greatest significance on the transformation of poetry itself. Superstition and enthusiasm are absorbed into the dialectic of Augustan poetic. Luther, Loyola, the Scholastics, and Calvin are replaced by Dennis, Blackmore, Defoe, and Cibber; the theological debate becomes a debate of style. Pope moves even closer to the neutral aesthetic stance of the modern critic.

The effect of the enthusiasm/superstition formula runs very deep in European culture. Hume, following the tradition of Swift, describes enthusiasm and superstition in terms of psychology. Enthusiasm, for Hume, is the product of pride, warmth of spirit, delusion, and ignorance; superstition caused by fear, infantile credulity, and childish cravings for ceremony. The former is the possession of Dissenters, the latter of Catholics, and both lead to civil unrest and intellectual folly. The former is the work of passionate souls deluded by zeal, the latter by pusillanimous souls deceived by priests. Hume's "Essay on Enthusiasm and Superstition,"[48] is the most perfect statement of the tradition which began with Butler, and he does not fail to pay tribute to his master on the last page of his *History of England*:

Though Hudibras was published, and probably composed during the reign of Charles II, Butler may justly, as well as Milton, be thought to belong to the forgoing period. No composition abounds so much as Hudibras in strokes of just and inimitable wit; yet are there many performances, which give us as great or greater entertainment on the whole perusal. The allusions in Butler are often dark and far-fetched; and though scarcely any author was ever able to express his thoughts in so few words, he often employs too many thoughts on one subject, and thereby becomes prolix after an unusual manner. It is surprising how much erudition Butler has introduced with so good a grace into a work of pleasantry and humour: Hudibras is perhaps one of the most learned compositions, that is to be found in any language. The advantage which the royal cause received from this poem, in exposing the fanaticism and false pretences of the former parliamentary party, was prodigious. The king himself had so good a taste as to be highly pleased with the merit of the work, and had even got a great part of it by heart.[49]

The celebrity of Butler and his effect on the great men of letters of the eighteenth century is remarkable. The whole European Enlightenment struggled with the problem of superstition and enthusiasm, and the trace of Butler in the discussion was inirradicable. Voltaire mentions him in the article on *Enthusiasme* in his *Philosophical Dictionary*. Kant, too, was familiar with Butler's great poem, which he read in the French translation made by Tawnley in 1757. Caught up in the spirit of Hudibrastic scatology he remarked,

---

[48] David Hume, *Essays Moral, Political, and Literary* (Indianapolis: Liberty Classics, 1985), 73–79.
[49] David Hume, *The History of England* (Indianapolis: Liberty Classics, 1983), 544–545.

If I were to adopt this point of view I would also have to adopt a different treatment for the disciples of the occult kingdom, different from the one meted out to them before. If in the past it was found necessary now and again to burn some of them at the stake, it would be more appropriate now-a-days to administer purgatives to these people. In such a situation, it would not have been necessary for me to go so deeply into the whole subject [of the occult] in order to unravel by the aid of metaphysics the secrets contained in the fever-stricken brains of some deluded dreamers. Perhaps the clever Hudibras alone could have solved the riddle for us; according to his opinion, when a hypochondriac wind rattles through the intestines, it all depends on the direction it takes: if down, it becomes a f__, if up, it turns into an apparition or a holy inspiration.[50]

The low road of the Augustan

Hudibras, more effectively even than *Leviathan*, promotes the emptying-out of the two dominant forms of Christian humanistic discourse – the symbolical and the faithful. We have seen how thoroughly Butler connected the two forms of conceit, the metaphorical and the private meditation. The false images which the King James translators had placed "in man's own conceit," now with the help of the new Hobbesian psychology, could expand to include nearly every metaphor and nearly all inward contemplation. Iconophobia spread throughout the eighteenth century. Berkeley spoke often of the crippling obscurities of the simile, Steele defined the best style as one "the least figurative and subtle."[51] Metaphor was under attack on all sides.

> The trivial turns, the borrowed wit,
> The similes that nothing fit;
> The cant which every fool repeats,
> Town jests, and coffee-house conceits;[52]

The program of literalizing which was advertised by Glanvil and Sprat, and perfected in Locke's *Essay*, had at first been dramatized in *Hudibras*. Butler was the first to expose poetry as a mundane (and political) rather than a divine madness:

> Great *Wits* and *Valours*, like great *States*,
> Do sometime sink with their own weights:
> Th'extreams of *Glory*, and of *Shame*,
> Like *East* and *West*,[53] become the same.   (II, i, 269–272)

---

[50] Imanuel Kant, *Dreams of a Spirit-Seer, and Other Related Writings*, trans. John Manolesco (New York: Vantage Press, 1969), 66.

[51] Richard Steele, *Correspondence*, ed. R. Blanchard (Oxford: Clarendon Press, 1921), 127.

[52] Jonathan Swift, *The Complete Poems*, ed. Pat Rogers (London: Penguin, 1983), 526.

[53] The sardonic inversion, a favorite figure of Donne, here is a fine example of Butler's use of conceitful materials. In Donne's great elegy "Hymn to God my God, in My Sickness" we see:

In this sense it was necessary for *Hudibras* to be a joke on poetry writing, and the Hudibrastic bravado serves to impress upon the reader the folly of the figure-making excesses of the superstitious without being itself an implicit defense of verse-writing. The prosodic wreck of *Hudibras* suggests in its own body the distortions in all poetry. Butler handed down to his descendants a willingness to denigrate the office of the poet – a willingness almost as strong in Pope and Gay as it was in Rochester and Swift. Swift describes the fate of poets in a beautiful Butlerian pastiche in which the "littering under hedges" is a direct borrowing:

> No beggar's brat, on bulk begot;
> Not bastard of a pedlar Scot,
> Not boy brought up to cleaning shoes,
> The spawn of Bridewell or the stews;
> Nor infants dropped, the spurious pledges
> Of gypsies littering under hedges,
> Are so disqualified by fate
> To rise in church or law or state,
> As he whom Phoebus in his ire
> Hath blasted with poetic fire.[54]

Pope denigrates the office of poet as few Renaissance and fewer Romantic poets would have countenanced:

> What tho' my Name stood rubric on the walls?
> Or plaister'd posts, with Claps in capitals?
> Or smoaking forth, a hundred Hawkers load,
> On Wings of Winds came flying all abroad?
> I sought no homage from the race that write;
> I kept, like *Asian* Monarchs, from their sight:
> Poems I heeded (now be-rym'd so long)
> No more than Thou, Great GEORGE! a Birth-day Song...
> Nor like a Puppy daggled thro' the Town,
> To fetch and carry Sing-song up and down;[55]

Butler's work also looks forward to the heteroglossic and vulgar elements of the novel. The novel was made possible by the dissolving of the moral teleology and metaphoric encrustation of romance, and by the expansion of the art of contiguity and association as opposed to that of conceit. A narrative in which all iconic and teleological elements appear in "a mad discomposure" is a manifestation of what Roland Barthes called "the

"As East and West / In All flat Maps (and I am one) are one, / So death doth touch the Resurrection."

[54] Swift, "On Poetry: A Rhapsody," lines 33–42 in *Complete Poems*, 522.

[55] Alexander Pope, "Epistle to Doctor Arbuthnot" (215–222: 225–226), in *The Poems*, Twickenham edition (New Haven: Yale University Press, 1960), vol. IV, 197.

horizon of the empirical."[56] The hysterical fullness of things in *Hudibras* is an important parallel to the mature condition of the novel. In this limited sense, *Hudibras* is the modern Verronian, the parent of the prosaic novel, and the direct and most important precursor to *Tristram Shandy*. It is no accident that the crux of the plot of *Hudibras* – the impossible pursuit of the hero's lady – is repeated in Uncle Toby's courtship of the Widow Wadman, and in terms that mix a parody of the Petrarchan with mock-legal discourse. The obsession with the relationship of legal discourse to courtship and the denigration of traditional attitudes toward idealized love are played out, not in the dramatic terms of Clarissa's struggle, but in terms that call into question the linguistic norms of seventeenth-century Europe. Both *Hudibras* and *Tristram Shandy* are parodies of romance at those very elements of analogy and hyperbole which Augustanism seeks to purge.

Likewise these two narratives, together with *A Tale of a Tub*, are the most thorough attacks on the tradition of medieval and Baroque rhetoric. When Walter Shandy buries his emotional response to his own son's death in a swirl of classical and Baroque allusions; when he attempts to replace real thought with an avalanche of famous mottoes, he is replaying the casuistical technique of *Hudibras*. Likewise, when the "white bear" appears in chapter 43 of *Tristram Shandy*, it is carried out of the frame of the empirical and back into the extravagant verbal frame of scholastic grammar:

A WHITE BEAR! Very well. Have I ever seen one? Might I have ever seen one ? Am I ever to see one? Ought I ever to have seen one? Or can I ever see one?

Would I had seen a white bear! (for how can I imagine it?) If I should see a white bear, what should I say? If I should never see a white bear, what then?[57]

This is parodic casuistry after the manner of Butler's grammatical bear in canto II of *Hudibras*. In the final crescendo of Sterne's anatomy of the bear he asks how his relatives and he "would have behaved had they seen a white bear," and "how would the bear have behaved?" The human subject and the bear begin to blur. The same conflation occurs in Butler's passage.

> Quoth *Hudibras*, Thou offer'st much,
> But art not able to keep touch.
> *Mira de lente*, as 'tis i'th' Adage,
> *Id est*, to make a Leek a Cabbage.
> Thou canst at best but overstrain
> A Paradox, and th' own hot brain.
> For what can *Synods* have at all
> With *Bears* that's analogicall?
> Or what relation has debating

[56] Roland Barthes, *Writing Degree Zero* (New York: Hill and Wang, 1972), 40.
[57] Laurence Sterne, *Tristram Shandy* (Indianapolis: Odyssey Press, 1940), 406–407.

Of church affairs with *Bear-baiting*?
A just comparison still is,
Of things *ejusdem generis*.
And then what *Genus* rightly doth
Include, and comprehend them both?
If *Animal*, both of us may
As justly pass for bears as they.   (*Hudibras*, I, i, 839–854)

The end that Hudibras reaches almost by accident in his argument is that men and animals are moral and natural equals. This collapsing of difference – the humbling of man – and downward metaphors, are important notions of the Augustan culture. Swift gives it tremendous weight in the self-discovery of his narrator in the fourth book of *Gulliver's Travels*. In Rochester man sinks even below the animal existence "I'd be a dog, a monkey, or a bear, / Or anything but that vain animal / That is so proud of being rational."[58] This was an inevitable part of the shrinking boundaries of analogy. In the Baroque poetic the creature bore a shifting and often exalted position. On one extreme the animal existence was purely iconic – the deer recalls the suffering of Christ, and the dove the charity of God; on the other side, the animal's existence bore the marks of purpose – the turtle is a fortress built by the all-protecting divinity. But most importantly, the Baroque creature is always known by its relation to divinity. It is a sign, a vehicle, and window of God's perpetual act of creation. All of these kinds of analogy dwindle from the Restoration on. In a poetics of appearance even differences of kind begin to disappear. Locke's *Essay* did not invent the idea of an empirical epistemology. He merely extended and generalized the implications of Augustan satire.

Hudibras is at once self-conscious wit and an approach to the limits of the prosaic. Its novelism is in fact more thorough than that of Richardson or even Dickens. It looks forward to the complete erasure of romance in the modern novel. In this, *Hudibras* is the great example of the low road of Augustan rhetoric – the path which includes the quotidian satire in Garth's *Dispensary*, the literalist debunking of metaphysics in *A Tale of a Tub*, and the cultural opportunism of Mandeville. Similarly, the empirical world expressed by metonymy in canto I of *The Rape of the Lock* serves as the true subject of Pope's poem, while the Virgilian and Miltonic material simply serve to make the quotidian more palpable and vulgar. In Butler we find:

Be under Vows to *hang* and *dy*
Loves Sacrifice, and all a *lie*?
With *China-orenges* and *Tarts*,
And winning *Plays*, lay baits for Hearts?

[58] John Wilmot, Earl of Rochester, "Satire against Reason and Mankind," 3–5, in *Poems* (New Haven: Yale University Press, 1978).

Bribe *Chamber-maids* with *love* and *money*,
To break no Roguish *jeasts* upon yee?
For Lillyes limn'd on *Cheeks*, and Roses,
With painted perfumes, hazard noses?
Or vent'ring to be brisk and wanton
Do penance in a *Paper-lanthorn*?   (*Hudibras* II, i, 871–880)

Pope removes the doggerel, but retains the world of *Hudibras*:

Whether the nymph shall break *Diana's* law,
Or some frail *China* Jar receive a Flaw,
Or stay her Honour, or her new Brocade,
Forget her Pray'rs, or miss a Masquerade,
Or lose her Heart, or Necklace at a Ball;   (*Poems*, II, 164–168)

Butler's technique of conflating the high and low is carried to a higher level in the work of his successors, but the tensions remain the same.

The attack upon the claims of the inward man and the outer world leads to a new space – an emptiness. The original mode of Restoration imagination (as represented by Butler and Rochester) is just such a privative topos – the space left after the evacuation of the two reigning discourses of the transcendent. It is no exaggeration to say that the emptiness implied by the decay of analogy and the simultaneous challenge to the poetics of Protestant faith precipitated an aesthetic rupture. *A Tale of a Tub* and *Tristram Shandy* negotiate and mine this space with supreme adroitness. Pope in *The Rape of the Lock* (105–109) masks this emptiness with a ritual classicism – a classicism which deflects our thoughts from the vacuity of the analogical cosmos of his sylphs. In *An Essay on Man* and in the last book of *The Dunciad* he attempts to rebuild the analogical edifice of an earlier period while maintaining the rhetoric of Butler. The projects are doomed to failure, but the failure is of the greatest importance to understanding the Augustan. The peculiar search for the "literal," for a language which evades the necessity of the metaphor, is the project and problem of every great work of Augustan literature. The first movement of Augustan poetry was satire, general and destructive – a search for a world loosed from the authority of perennial European casuistry. This search (a Baconian experiment of the imagination) was first attempted in the pages of *Hudibras*.

2

Transitional Augustan poetry

The eclipse of analogy

The chief subjects of Renaissance meditative poetry in Europe are God and man in relation to God. The art of that period differs from Romantic and Modernist art in denying to the self in its particular and accidental sense a place of absolute centrality. The human self that is important in the common metaphysical schemata of the Renaissance (and earlier seventeenth century) is either the utterly spiritual type of microcosm, "a little world made cunningly" and a map of creation, or one of utter sinfulness and privation. The Catholic culture of Humanism, as represented by Pico, Ficino, and Ronsard, and the Counter Reformation versions of Bellarmine, Molinas, and Crashaw, at bottom both embrace the microcosmic man – a being only "a little lower than the angels." The ancient sources of this paradigm are neoplatonic and Johannine, and the system of equivalencies and proportions between this ideal man and God were worked out systematically in the theology of the high Middle Ages, particularly in the works of Bonaventure and Aquinas. The Scholastic theory of *analogia entis*, that man and the other creatures bear the vestiges and signature of their creator, or that they are a refracted mirroring or emanation of the divine being, is the conscious or unconscious underpinning of nearly all Humanist and Baroque theologies. The laughing versions of this tradition – Erasmus, Rabelais, Von Hutten, and More – depend as much on this system of analogies as do the more serious and academic modes.

The second and opposite version of man in the period before the middle of the seventeenth century is the Pauline and Augustinian one. Borne down by sin and living in absolute dependence on a God unknown, this man's darkness is penetrated only by the candle of faith. The most important expositor of this view is Luther, but it has many advocates before and after the Reformation. In one sense these two versions of human nature are permanent archetypes of Christian imagination. I discuss them at some length in the fifth chapter.

The period from the Restoration to the mid-eighteenth century was a time of sudden and even precipitous transition from the figural mentality of

earlier periods. I have already pointed out in the example of Butler the
strong tendency of this later culture to attack both archetypal figures: the
analogical and the privative/faithful man. Butler embellished and deepened the implications of Bacon, Burton, and Hobbes and their radical
reinterpretation of human nature. His extraordinary *reductio ad absurdum*
looked forward to Swift and Mandeville. With the clever conflation of the
Catholic with the English Calvinist as types of the superstitious man, and
with the association of the dissenting man of faith with madmen and
criminals, Butler accelerated the satiric frenzy of the period after the Civil
War. The analogical man was henceforth associated (as he still is) with
magical reasoning, extravagant over-confidence in the power of language,
and empty doctrinal subtlety. The faithful man (whom Butler always
equates with the doctrine of the inner light) was from then on associated
with self-vaunting mysticism, ignorant and formulaic fundamentalism, and
madness.

The Butler and his contemporaries had begun to empty out the old repertoire
of theological and poetic figures which were the products of habitual
analogy, and had begun the process of de- or disfiguring the conventional
consciousness of British and European culture. Such an operation – the
satirical evacuation of traditional discourse – is the first and determining
mark of Augustan writing. It was through this emptying of conceitful
traditions together with the closely connected discovery of the art of the
literal, that Augustanism made its mark on European thought. The other
superficial elements of Augustan writing – its classicism, its vaunted
correctness, its residual humanism – are of secondary importance. They
are not definitive.

The great age of classicizing was the long period of Humanistic syncresis
beginning with Petrarch and including Ficino, Erasmus, Castiglione, Vives,
and surviving down to the time of Milton. In its idea of style, like many
earlier periods and schools, the eighteenth century wished to associate itself
with the prestige of the classical inheritance, and in its later phase in
England particularly with the figures of Virgil and Horace. In this connection it attempted to connect its own project to that of the Humanists. We
may recall Swift laughing in the "easy chair" of Rabelais, or Pope as the
"Montaigne of Twickenham." The "praisers of folly" were natural sources
for Augustan satire, though it was a transformation of both folly and satire.
In some important respects the cult of Virgil and Horace survives the other
disruptions of intellectual culture after 1660, but in other ways the movement from syncretic to "modern" classicism, one purged of Neoplatonism,
medievalisms, typology, and allegory, is itself a breach with Humanism. By
the time of Dryden, Pope, and Thomson, Classicism was very old indeed,
nor were these authors the most distinguished manipulators in English of
that inheritance. The classical is an endlessly amorphous configuration,

and it was used by Pope and Hume and Gibbon as a kind of screen between themselves and the perennial Christian tradition which they were uprooting with varying degrees of enthusiasm. As for the cult of judgment in the eighteenth century, it seems to me to have been formed in the various vulgar literatures of Europe – particularly in England and France – as a particular reaction to the Baroque. The Ciceronian, Senecan, and Horatian fashions were highly developed by the beginning of the seventeenth century, and the peculiar narrowing of the classical inheritance afterward may be seen in the weight placed on Virgil and the *sermone*-style of Horace in England after 1700.

As for the term "Augustan", which has been hotly debated in recent years by Howard Erskine-Hill, Howard Weinbrot, and others, I use it only out of convenience. There was no doubt a cult for Augustan Rome in Britain in the period, and that cult was no doubt (as Weinbrot has shown) not uncritical or monolithic. The manipulation of a body of allusions and symbols from Roman poetry which continued at least to the sixteenth century, and which are mined with growing dexterity by Ben Jonson and his contemporaries, is, no doubt, one of the chief sources of Augustan poetry. The subtle analogies between the *pax Romana* and the Stuart Restoration are an important subject for any student of the period, but any connections between the late-ancient culture and the enlightened culture of Butler and Dryden are deeply problematic. We must not imagine that the *imago vitae* of Horace and Virgil has any more than a fanciful connection to the actual living, mentality of Augustan England. The true horizon of the classical in epistemology, in religion, in language, is not merely adapted by the Augustans, it is transfomed. I have used the term "empirico-classical" to describe this transformation. None of the ancient sources of Dryden, Pope, and Gibbon could have recognized themselves in the portrait of the ideal Augustan observer – an observer superior to the temptations of metaphysics and magic. In preserving Battestin's or Mack's conception of the eighteenth century, brilliant as their work may be, we are preserving (as the Victorians and Edwardians did before us) one of the period's ideas of itself. I have chosen instead to use "Augustan" to refer to what I believe is the larger and more fundamental invention of the period, an invention which shows its peculiar originality in its relation to earlier indigenous modes, not in its own self-presentation. Augustan, for me, refers to that particular band of cultural associations, the interest not of eighteenth-century culture as a whole, but of a small class of enlightened and forward-looking intellectuals who discovered through satire, empiricism, and a reconstituted idea of the "classical" really new possibilities of thought.

In the English Renaissance, non-dramatic verse generally fell into one of two distinct modes. The first, and until the time of Donne perhaps the dominant one, was amorous and courtly verse, representing one of the affluent branches of the once unified stream of the medieval imagination. The other was devotional poetry. The first of these branches of the Renaissance imagination was not really, in our sense, secular, though it partakes of something of the profane. The most important fact in the formation of Renaissance love poetry was its likeness to religious writing. The love object was a displaced divinity, who could call up all the ardor and attention that in orthodox Christian thought was reserved for God.

In that way Sidney's Stella, for example, acquired a number of God's attributes: she is the center and principle of a cosmos, she is written upon the heart and conscience, she is the unchanging principle in a chaotic world, and she is the purveyor of a special and enlivening grace.[1] No doubt she was a version of the Piconian microcosmic man, and in realizing the ideal of moral and metaphysical epitome she outstripped any male figure in sixteenth-century British literature. Yet, in another and opposing sense, the absence of the beloved, the absolute inaccessibility of the love object, reminds us of the literature of Christian faith. Stella, like Laura before her, synthesized the dominant modes of theological discourse – the analogical and the fideist. The figural path from Stella to Pope's Belinda, with the intermediary steps of Milton's Eve and Dryden's Eleanora, might be a convenient way to diagram the transition from Baroque to Augustan. Belinda is as surely a type of Augustan literalizing as Stella is a type of the earlier mode of hyperbole and microcosm. Unlike Eve's and Eleanora's, Belinda's context, her defining milieu and figural center, are secular, ironic, and naturalistic.

Though the close relations between supposedly secular and religious verse are most evident in Christian culture, it has been argued that classical love poetry bears the same original relationship to classical hymnology.[2] It is almost a principle in the history of genre that religious forms are the archetypes of secular ones; the temporalizing reality of modern fiction, for example, was made possible by the cessation of older forms of spiritual narration.[3] In the same way Richardson and Defoe are the repository of a good deal of deflected or displaced material from the Protestant tradition of allegory and Reformation hagiography.[4] Mature Augustan literature, on

---

[1] See *Astrophil and Stella*, sonnets 10, 41, 68.

[2] For this argument cf. Mircea Eliade, *Patterns in Comparative Religion* (Chicago: University of Chicago Press, 1971), 111–125; also, cf. F. J. E. Raby, *Secular Poetry in the Middle Ages* (Oxford, Clarendon, 1930).

[3] Michael McKeon, *The Rise of the English Novel* (Baltimore: Johns Hopkins University Press, 1987), Introduction and chapter 1. This is a summary of a theory which is familiar in Lévi-Strauss and in the myth criticism of Frye and the Jungians.

[4] Although it is beyond the scope of argument possible here, I should point out that Protestant fideism in the form of teleological romance (which is mocked in Butler's narrative), intermittently returns in the British novel. Dickens is a high moment in the revitalization of the model –

the other hand, presents us with an original and surprising moral land-scape. The relation of secular to religious genre and of spiritual to physical description began to change in the middle seventeenth century, and the possibilities of the modern were accelerated by this change. It is clear, as we have seen in *Hudibras*, that the collapsing by satire of analogical structures into a physical monism is a gesture as radical and novel as the geometric and physical monism of Hobbes. For a long time scholars have maintained that the imaginative procedures of Rochester, Butler, Swift, and Pope were in some peculiar sense conservative and traditional – that their satire had the role of preserving a threatened order. From this tradition has come the notion of the public poet as cultural guardian and umpire, and the old saws about gloomy, backward-looking Tories, and recasters of the medieval great chain and graduated plenitude. Critics have pointed out that Swift and Pope were not Hobbesians, and there is no doubt that the word "Hobbist" was a very bad word well into the eighteenth century. But we must here as elsewhere be careful not to take Augustan self-presentation as truth. The method of Hudibrastic and Swiftian satire is analogous in its form and in its results to the Hobbesian critique of older thinking. In one sense it is more novel and compelling, because, unlike Hobbes, the later Tories (and Hobbes was the pre-eminent Tory intellectual) did not deign to address their intellectual opponents directly as Hobbes did in his responses to Bellarmine, Descartes, and others; rather they posit a dullness and irrelevance in their opponents which are quite unwarranted. Because the Augustan culture is formed upon the denunciation of real controversy, and a prejudice against dialectical discourse, it possesses a tremendous rheto-rical advantage. Rhetoric free from the strictures of philosophical dialectic roves freely among the duncical arguments of its opponents. Therefore, the argument that Swift is making in the *Tale* against his past and contem-porary opponents – the Scholastics, rationalists, metaphysical stylists, Catholic and Protestant apologists, Dryden, Wotton, Blackmore, Boyle – is all the more powerful for being itself undefined and indefinable. The notion of sense and judgment, like its forebear, Boileau's *Raison*, has only a negative force, and is associated with no intellectual method. That the motives of Protestant enthusiasts could be reduced to the Hobbesian metaphors of the "Mechanical Operation of the Spirit,"[5] is evidence of a kinship on a deeper level. The form of satirical rhetoric and the figural bias

A Christmas Carol and *Hard Times* replaying those archetypal spiritual conflicts which were the staple of the earlier period. It is no great stretch to see Cratchit and Stephen Blackpool as combining qualities of the wise fool and the substitutionary victim. In the same way their antagonists Scrooge and Bounderby fulfill the role of the demonic opponent. Any accusation of unreality or caricature in Dickens (and we can recall the criticism of Thackeray or James) is a continuation of the canons of Augustan realism and morality.
[5] On this particularly see Irvin Ehrenpreis, *Swift, The Man, His Works and the Age* (Cambridge, Mass.: Harvard University Press, 1962), vol. I, 240–241.

of Swift and Pope are never far from a conscious repudiation of perennialist European thought. Moreover, the repudiation of Bacon's experimentalism, and Descartes' dualism in the major Augustans (especially Rochester, Swift, and Pope) pushes their project to an even headier extreme of skepticism. Aside from the school of minor physico-theologists like Ray and Jago, science was not much more generally credited than metaphysics until later in the century. It is probably an anachronism to attribute the turn to literalism and empiricism in the great Augustans to an interest in science. Cowley at the beginning of the movement and Thomson near the end embraced science, and their work found a solid center in contemporary physical theory, but this was by no means the general rule among major writers of the period.

There is an extraordinary gulf, then, between the "humanism" of Swift and Pope and that of the Renaissance. This gulf has been largely invisible to literary critics. It was the habit of critics and historians of the period as far back as Lecky and Stephen to confirm the position of Swift and Pope (and even Butler) in terms which these authors crafted for themselves: thus the vaunted sanity and manliness of spirit which critics attributed to this tough "age of prose" while at the same time accepting the Romantic conception of these works as mechanical and uninspired. At a later phase even this degree of hostility disappeared and New Critics and period academic critics like Brooks, Leavis, Wimsatt, and Mack started to describe the witty complexity and ambiguity of Dryden and Pope in terms originally devised for the metaphysical poets. For Maynard Mack, the *Essay on Man* was the last great document of Renaissance system-building; for Reuben Brower, "*The Rape of the Lock* stands as Pope's *Midsummer Night's Dream,* the last successful work in the Renaissance mythological tradition that includes the tales of Marlowe, Lodge, and Drayton, and the plays of Lyly."[6] Similarly, Grierson included Butler in his famous anthology of Metaphysical lyrics, and Ian Jack, recalling the words of R. W. Church, says Butler was "a mind keenly sensitive to all analogies and affinities . . . spreading as it were tentacles on all sides in quest of chance prey."[7] According to Jack, the satirical element was always important to metaphysical writers like Donne and Cleveland; Butler had just pushed their methods further. Butler was for many critics a neutral and playful humorist bitten by the demon of analogy, and in some sense even a throwback. Surely, though, the serious playfulness of *A Midsummer Night's Dream*, whose poet looks "from Earth to Heaven / From Heaven to Earth" and who gives us one of the finest examples of the linked realms of the natural, the magical, and the theological in all of literature, is remote from the quotidian irony and

---

[6] Reuben A. Brower, *Alexander Pope, The Poetry of Allusion* (Oxford: Oxford University Press, 1968), 150.

[7] Ian Jack, *Augustan Satire* (Oxford: Oxford University Press, 1970), 31.

mundane moralism of *The Rape of the Lock*. And even more surely, the ransacking of learned allusions and metaphysical arcana have a different and opposite purpose in Butler from that which they have in the poems of Donne, Herbert, Vaughan, or Marvell. Butler's "Small Poet" is the type of the deluded metaphysical casuist, and I think that Donne's "Ecstasie" or Herbert's "Church Monuments" would have made Butler smile derisively. The passages I have excerpted from Butler are indeed in no sense metaphysical poetry, but hostile vulgarisms which place the fruits of analogy in a completely unsympathetic light. Here is Butler's genre theory:

> He would an *Elegie* compose
> On Maggots squeezed out of his Nose;
> In *Lyrick* numbers, write an *Ode* on
> His Mistress, eating a Black-pudden:
> And when imprisoned Air escap'd her,
> It puft him with *Poetic Rapture*.   (*Hudibras* ii, iii, 377–382)

There have always been those who find Swift's manner and mind unpalatable and uncharitable – Johnson and Leavis come to mind – but the far greater number of his critics have advocated his humanity. Numerous critics have attributed the qualities of the traditional humanist to this most inhumane of wits. He was a typical Augustan humanist to Paul Fussell and a champion of tradition to Martin Price.[8] Nigel Dennis' words are representative:

The High Churchman who ridicules the dissenters does so with an "enthusiasm" that would shock any Presbyterian; the upholder of the "golden mean" supports, really, nothing but one of his more amiable moods. If we refuse to accept Swift as an idealist of dignity and a man of rigid, passionate principles, we cannot hope to understand why he is driven so easily by any betrayal of these into the most scabrous rages and revengeful emotions. His wiser friends understand this very well, and refuse flatly to credit the misanthropy and disdain of the human race that we, today, believe to have been true of Swift . . . We are far less understanding in this matter today. We allow no distinction to be made between the person of Swift and the art of Swift. When Swift shows Gulliver's revulsion at last to the whole human race we reject not only the fictitious conclusion but the man who wrote it. We react to *A Tale of the Tub* in exactly the spirit of Queen Anne, denying the possibility that so much coarseness and vehemence can be expressed by a priest who is truly religious. In this way we not only deny the writer of fiction his need to push satire as far as it will go, but deny the priest his right to uphold a High Church orthodoxy in the teeth of his enemies. When certain of the saints assure us that we are a good for nothing pack of scoundrels and mere belly-bags of excrement, disgusting in the Lord's sight, we not only regard them as indubitably pious but point to their disgust as evidence of their piety; similarly, when Dante shows us over Hell and points out our human flesh being boiled or frozen stiff we

---

[8] Martin Price, *Swift's Rhetorical Art* (London: Archon, 1963), 114.

respond with a high respect for the poet and a mournful acceptance of his message. That we should refuse to do as much for Swift is very unimaginative on our part and very unjust to him: we carry on down through the centuries precisely the disapproval that ruined him when he was alive.[9]

I give this quotation at length because it is a representative defense of Swift and, by analogy, of Augustan culture. Notice how it replays with great exactitude Swift's conception of himself as a beleaguered and mistreated truth-teller. According to Dennis, Swift is best understood as "his wiser friends" understood him. We must enter the Scriblerian sense of alienated companionship and moral aloofness. At a deeper level Dennis replays the archetypal gesture of the Augustans, reducing the differences between the Presbyterian and the "golden meaners" of the High Church to one of private humor. Lastly, the two unacceptable modes of Catholic superstition (as represented in the passage by Dante's cosmos) and Protestant fideism (as represented by the doctrine of total depravity) are subtly positioned to clarify the place of the Augustan. These older orthodoxies are unmasked as petty and irrational fantasies which justify the humane skepticism of Swift. This passage typifies the way many critics of Augustan culture and poetry have made its moral parameters their own. It is a natural transition. We are to a large extent the products of a satiric critique which helped to usher in, and has since supported, the rational bigotries and de-mythologizing elements of the modern. We, like our Augustan precursors, have moved beyond controversy into that wilderness of general and indefinable satire. We, like the first of the moderns, feel the supreme generosity of a skepticism freed from proud dogmatism, and the superiority of the prosaic and practical over the overreaching conceits of our forefathers.

The intellectual milieu of the early modern Europeans which Swift and Voltaire spent a lifetime exposing was quite different. The representative intellectual problem of Petrarchism and metaphysical poetry as it survives till the time of Cowley's *Mistress*, was one of accommodation between the claims of courtly hyperbole and the counter-claims of Protestant devotion. It was a balancing of figures and doctrines – a set of paradoxes connected to the root paradoxes of theology and metaphysics. The blending of metaphysical strata, the coalescing of moral profundity with profane wit, and the confusion of sexual and mystical passion together marked the vague borders between religious and amorous art. The literal had not yet been invented, and the secular and religious strands could not yet be unraveled. The conflation of the two modes is well known in the poetry and prose of the Spanish mystics. In the case of the more rigorously Lutheran and Puritan consciousness, this blending was sometimes considered blas-

---

[9] Nigel Dennis, *Jonathan Swift* (New York: Collier, 1967), 44–45.

phemous. Greville's *Caelica*,[10] to name one of many, can be read as a battleground where these two imaginative modes contend for the upper hand, so that the first eight numbers of that sequence are a mirror of Sidney's Petrarchism, while the latter twenty pass into unequivocal Calvinist devotion to Christ. Greville is an interesting case of the total abandonment of the resources of analogy on behalf of rigorous fideism and iconoclasm. His "Treatise poems" are an extreme excoriation of figural reasoning. Nonetheless, Greville's gesture is not Augustan (or satirical), but one of controversial Protestantism. The Augustan mode was never that of controversy – of the pitting of one doctrine against another – but rather it was one which opposed from the start the very idea of rational doctrine and of fixed methods and conclusions in theology. The Augustans were above the traditional restraint of argument. In a sense the ironic spirit of the Deists and Latitudinarians and the general and withering satire of Butler and Swift both have the same motivation and the same anti-intellectualist prejudices.[11] All traditional method for them was abominable casuistry. The attempts of Descartes and the rationalists to restore a path, a method, which would be definitive and explanatory was met with the coldest mockery by Butler and Swift: Descartes was a Pythagorean, his mind never came in contact with his body, he believed animals were tops spinning perpetually for no reason, he believed he was surrounded by devils. These were the jests of the Augustans toward the last great Scholastic personality of Europe.

By keeping its distance from metaphysical controversy and analogy, the

---

[10] The *Caelica* is a perfect case for our argument. In the famous opening numbers Greville imitates his friend Sydney in ascribing to Caelica certain extramundane powers of influence, but as the sequence proceeds both the objects of martial conflict and those of courtly love are seen as instruments of corruption. The absent and unapproachable beauty of Caelica is easily transformed, in the final apocalyptic numbers (sonnets 95–108), into the qualities of the Father as a *Deus absconditus*.

[11] I use the term "anti-intellectualist" in the sense of turning away from the long-standing elaborations of metaphysical system and the perennial esoteric philosophies (Neoplatonism, Scholasticism, Neostoicism, and Cabbalism) on the grounds of honest simplicity either verbal or methodological. The new "common sense" of Hobbes and Locke was considered by its proponents as a mere extension of normal thought unprejudiced by subtle doctrines. In the first phase of this critique it was natural to answer the old questions (the problem of the one and the many, the nature of the intelligible, and others) directly and thoroughly. This was the rationalist phase. But any such answering renders the moderns at a distinct disadvantage, for the modern could not compete with traditional discourse within the nomenclature and moral atmosphere of the Renaissance. Any participation in this older milieu gives credence to the program of the ancient and medieval thinkers, and it involves itself in the paradoxes which are inescapable in dialectical debates. There was also the problem of the authority and inertia of intellectual institutions – academic and ecclesiastical – which both the rationalist and Augustan thinkers always discredited until in the last phase the very activities of those institutions were called into question. We should recall the attitude that Descartes, Hobbes, and Locke took towards their own teachers. The next phase (which was foreshadowed by Bacon) considered the very questions themselves impertinent and fanciful. This latter phase began with the satiric gestures of Butler and Swift, and was completed by Voltaire, Hume, and their followers.

Augustan culture placed itself in stark opposition to the dominant modes of Baroque and Reformation imagination. In every genre the plenary conceitfulness of the earlier period was evolving, often with remarkable rapidity, into an artful plainness. The archetypal structure of Augustan thought can be divided for the purpose of analysis into two separate and coordinated gestures. The first is negation by satire and the second the construction of a novel mode of description – a kind of literalism which includes on one side quotidian verse and on the other the novel. Satire went about the business of clearing a space for a new way of thinking and the empiricists attempted to fill it up.

The forms of satire in the late seventeenth century are diverse and flexible. Not only the verse satire of Butler, Rochester, and Garth, and the Menippean prose of Swift, but also the discursive prose of Burnet, Hobbes, Locke, and Sprat, were at bottom instruments devised to negate the claims of an earlier age. This was in every case (at least in part) a negation of the claims of metaphor, and most often a negation of the metaphysical systems in which metaphorical procedures thrived. So Rochester mocks on the one hand the analogical hyperbole of courtly love in "Fair Chloris in a pigsty lay," and on the other Baroque metaphysics in "Upon Nothing." Swift ridicules the whole system of conventional theology in *A Tale of a Tub*, while Burnet's *History* and Tillotson's *Sermons* navigate the new space between superstitious overreaching and dissenting enthusiasm with a smug and sneering moderation.

All of these versions of the Augustan are attempts to find a space for a new naturalistic and "rational" discourse unencumbered by figural excesses. The common enemy of all Augustan authors from the Restoration down to the time of Pope was the fancy or "imagination." Imagination, as we have seen, was the source of world-wearying ignorance for Butler and the source of uncritical rationalization according to Hobbes. For Bacon there are three chief branches of human learning – History, Reason, and Poetry. History was the source of all real knowledge, human and natural, and was the storehouse of the observing and experiencing powers; Reason was an ordering faculty concerned with the arrangement of things garnered from experience and memory; and Poetry was the product of "imagination," a kind of "feigned or dissimulating history." History then became a shorthand term for the whole discourse of real experience. In actual history writing this meant going back to uncover the superstitions and prejudices of the immediate and more distant past, as in Clarendon, Bolingbroke, and Hume; in theology it meant going back to judge the veracity and "honesty" of the documents and witnesses of the Apostolic miracles, as in Locke's *Reasonableness of Christianity*, or, with more devastating skepticism, in Gibbon's *Decline and Fall*; in natural history it meant collecting large heterogeneous bodies of data and applying honest and original methods of observation to them; and in the writing of fiction it meant creating narratives of "real experience" unencumbered by the fancies of romance. Hence, the origin of the "histories" of Moll Flanders, Tom Jones, or Peregrine Pickle. The term "history" then, comprised all that Bacon had defined as untainted by extravagances of the imagination. Taken as a faculty, imagination is for Bacon a kind of messenger of sense, reason, and action, but it is only trustworthy when it is in bondage to sense and reason.[12] In two realms, religion and poetry, imagination runs dangerously free. For Bacon the chief symptom of the misuse of mind is the appearance of analogy in all of its forms:

In matters of Faith and Religion, we raise our imagination above our Reason; which is the cause why Religion sought ever access to the mind by similitudes, figures, types, parables, visions, dreams; and likewise in all persuasions that are wrought by eloquence, and other impressions of like nature, which do paint and disguise the true nature of things, the chief recommendation unto Reason is from the Imagination.[13]

For Bacon the chief instruments of religion appear to be those over-reaching modes of analogy ranging from similitude to dream vision. Like the dream world or the world of enthusiastic rhetoric, the world of analogy, we might easily say poetry, is always in danger of losing its mooring in experience and going out of rational control. In Butler's words, "Fancy is (like Caligula) an excellent Servant to reason and judgment but the most unfit thing in the world to governe."[14]

Making sure that imagination, which Pope and Swift generally term "wit," was under the control of judgment was the special concern of neo-classical writers in France and Britain. The cult of judgment in the poetic theory of the Restoration, as I have mentioned, was an analogue to several tempering faculties in other discourses; just as the civil order after 1660 wished to quell the excesses of revolution, so the writing culture set out to govern the monstrous extravagances of conceit. The abuse of language, as Locke was to call it, like the abuse of religion, was based on the autonomous fancy and "chimeras of wit," which had naturally accompanied the fanciful Catholic superstitions of late-medieval culture, but which along with ungoverned inwardness (Protestant faction) were the greatest enemies of rational order.

---

[12] "It is true that the Imagination is an agent or *nuncius*, in both provinces, both the judicial and the ministerial. For Sense sendeth over to Imagination before Reason hath judged: and Reason sendeth over to Imagination before the decree can be acted: for Imagination ever proceedeth Voluntary Motion. Saving that this Janus of Imagination has differing faces . . . Neither is the Imagination simply and only a messenger; but is invested with, or at leastwise usurpeth no small authority in itself" (Francis Bacon, *Advancement of Learning* [London: Dent, 1973], 120–121).

[13] Francis Bacon, *Works*, ed. J. Spedding, F. Ellis, and L. Heath (London: Russel, 1858), vol. iii, 112.

[14] Samuel Butler, *Prose Observations*, ed. Hugh De Quehen (Oxford: Clarendon Press, 1979), 130.

The cases of Cowley and Dryden

I mentioned Cowley in my first chapter as one of the earliest manipulators of the twofold formula of enthusiasm and superstition, and his work
is a good place to begin to investigate the general problem of poetry after
1660. Cowley, who was ten years younger than Milton, and thirteen years
older than Dryden, bears an interesting relation to those two unlike
poets. He was a favorite of Milton's, next only to Spenser and Shakespeare. He was the last poet trained in that thorough and curious
Classical-Biblism, which is the special mark of Milton himself. Like
Milton, Cowley's learning was at once multifarious and profound, and
like him, Cowley devised a biblical epic from Old Testament materials, a
drama after the manner of the Greeks, and a body of intellectualist
poems about love and leisure. It would not be too much to say that
Cowley's "In Memory of Hervey" is second, though a distant second, to
"Lycidas" among the elegies of the period. They both wrote works of
prose apology, though for opposing parties; Cowley, a wavering but
probably dedicated Royalist, survived long enough to offend both Roundheads and Cavaliers.[15]

Having said this much, it must be immediately added that there is a
great unlikeness of imagination between Milton and Cowley. Milton's
great project is *sui generis*, and if he "wrote no language,"[16] what he did
write has in some sense survived as a large part of our received heritage.
"Miltonism," as it marked the last really vital and serious moment in
English Christian Humanism, became the particular possession of
subsequent English poets. Cowley has had no Thomson, no Wordsworth, no Keats to follow his example. Cowley has by now almost no
reputation, and this is a fact of literary history that bears some
explanation.

In Cowley the two confluent streams of Renaissance imagination, the
amorous and the religious, were, for the first time since the fifteenth
century, parted. The *Mistress* attempts to duplicate the paradoxical sleights
of rhetoric that abound in Donne. It attempts, also, to capture the drama
and psychology of *Astrophil and Stella*. In both it fails, though it fails under an
enormous weight of ingenuity and learning:

> Will cry, Absurd! and ask me, how I live;
> And syllogisms against it give;
> A curse on all your vain Philosophies
> Which on weak Nature's Law depend,

---

[15] "Abraham Cowley," *The Dictionary of National Biography* (London: Macmillan, 1937), vol. III, 165.
[16] Samuel Johnson, *The Lives of the English Poets* ed. Birkbeck Hill (London: Oxford University
Press, 1964), vol. I, 132.

And know not how to comprehend
Love and Religion, those great Mysteries.

("The Soul," 7–12)[17]

This unassuming stanza is quite revealing. First, its separation of Nature on
the one side, and Love and Religion on the other, was not yet a commonplace in 1647. Nature is seen here as an independent ground of reality.[18] It
apparently has a law of its own, distinct from the transcendent.[19] It is
connected to syllogistic logic, while Love and Religion are connected to
"Mystery." There is a stiffness, an atmosphere of abstraction, throughout
the early work of Cowley which betrays this separation of materials. *The
Mistress* lacks the unifying analogies of body and soul which we see in
Donne's "Ecstasie" or King's *Elegies*. It lacks the abundance and movement
of even the slightest of Milton's poems.

Those vain philosophies of nature, which Cowley castigates in *The
Mistress*, were shortly to become his own chief interest. By 1660 he had
imbibed the program of Hobbes with whom he was for many years a
friend. He had given up on his unfinished biblical epyllion, *The Davideis*,
and turned to verse and prose, in which he championed Horatian leisure
and the new science. If his first biographer and encomiast is correct,
Cowley knew more, perhaps, than any of our important English poets
about science. Bishop Sprat was in a good position to judge, being himself
among that new brand of clerics whose interests wandered rather far from
theology.[20] Sprat was the first historian of the Royal Society, a friend of
Newton, and an adept at mathematics. He was also involved in the
contemporary process of rhetorical simplification in the writing of sermons
and "histories," which I discuss at the end of this chapter.

---

[17] Abraham Cowley, *Poems of Abraham Cowley* ed. A. Waller (Cambridge: Cambridge University Press, 1905), 107.

[18] The development of the idea of "nature" is of the utmost importance to this study. In his *Studies in Words* (Cambridge: Cambridge University Press, 1960), 24–74, C. S. Lewis has traced a good deal of its development from the sense of the characteristic of any species – the "nature of a thing" – to our more modern sense of "scenery" and the place of purity. What Lewis fails to notice is the development in the later seventeenth century, during the first wave of "scientism," of a completely independent entity – "nature." The "state of nature" in Hobbes is a rude state, a state without the covenant of civilization. In this sense Hobbes is not departing from Hooker's sense (cf. Book III, *The Laws of Ecclesiastical Polity* [1642]) and is well within the bounds of Calvinist orthodoxy. But nature as a system with independent laws was introduced after 1660. It is, perhaps, impossible to see where it was first used, but it abounds in the poetry of Blackmore, Ray, and Jago, and is one of the common senses of "nature" in Thomson (cf. *Liberty*, II, 543; *In Memory of Sir Isaac Newton* [1727], 33–37). Some of the impulse for this sense of "nature" can be seen in the fashion for the *De rerum natura*, and its allegorical Venus. Pope's *Essay on Criticism*, 67–75, provides the most famous example.

[19] See the beginning of the fourth section of this chapter for a larger discussion of the tradition of transcendental "naturalism" both in its Metaphysical and its Augustan phases.

[20] R. F. Jones, et al, *Studies in the Seventeenth Century* (Stanford: Stanford University Press, 1951), 96–108; also, Johnson, *Lives*, 371–375.

The distinct phases of Cowley's career mark the decay of Christian poetry from the time of Herbert's *The Temple* and Vaughan's *Silex Scintillans* to the early years of the Restoration. The *Mistress* shows the complete separation of secular from spiritual material, the strong division between love themes and religious ones. It further shows that the conceit, once the ground for elaborate spiritual analogy, had hardened into mere decoration. Cowley's metaphors by the time of the "Pindarique Odes" (1655) do not serve to advance a central argument, but merely embellish the literal core of the poem's meaning. The accusation of logicism and disparateness made by Johnson, Coleridge, and others against both Donne and Cowley is more especially true of Cowley. The reasons for Johnson's preference for Cowley as a poet are still difficult to understand. It may be that Cowley served for Pope and Johnson as the point of dissolution of the old Baroque method. His mature work looked forward to Augustan descriptive writing. He was a master of the epithetic style which was perfected by his contemporaries Waller and Denham, and his meter labors toward that fullness and regularity which we associate with Dryden, but which is found nowhere in the couplet poems of Donne or Carew. More importantly, he helped to make a space for a specifically secular image repertoire foreign to the "school of Donne" and requisite to the construction of Augustan literalism.

The separation in Cowley of amorous and religious materials, and secondly, of religious and "natural arguments," marks the stages of decay of the older Baroque synthesis. The earlier Renaissance was, as Roland Bainton and others have argued,[21] the last phase of Medieval European culture. The older analogies between theology and science, between God and nature, were becoming inoperative. In Cowley's later work this process is almost complete. We might examine a passage from his extraordinary late poem, "To the Royal Society."

> Three or four thousand years one might have thought
> To ripeness and perfection might have brought
> A Science so well bred and nurst,
> And of such hopeful parts too at the first.
> But, oh, the Guardians and the Tutors then,
> (Some negligent, and some ambitious men)
> Would ne'er consent to set him Free,
> Or his own natural powers to let him see,
> Lest that should put an end to their Autoritie.
>
> ("To the Royal Society," 10–18)[22]

"Stifling" authority takes three forms in the poem: first, the Roman church, then Aristotle, with his "glozing words," and last the human mind

[21] Roland Bainton, *The Reformation of the Sixteenth Century* (New York: Beacon Press, 1970), 3–11.
[22] Cowley, *Poems*, 448.

without the guide of the senses. I have observed how thoroughly Butler had lashed out against these elements of Baroque culture, and it is no exaggeration to say that nobody could convincingly defend them in Britain again till the later nineteenth century. When Dryden tried to do so in *The Hind and the Panther*, he was mercilessly lampooned in the *The Hind and the Panther Transversed*, a rebuttal by Charles Montague and Prior that unleashed all the forces of Augustan bigotry. Much of the method of this response can be seen also in the argument of the anti-Jesuit diatribes by Oldham, and in a number of "state poems" of the 1670s and 1680s. All true philosophy for Cowley and his successors is natural philosophy, which has been kept away from starving man by a conspiracy of words. Poetry, which, in earlier Cowley poems had been a divine agency,[23] now comes under attack. Returning to the subject of science Cowley says,

> That his own business he might quite forget,
> They amused him with the sports of wanton Wit,
> With the Deserts of poetry they fed him,
> Instead of solid meats t'increase his force;
> Instead of vigorous exercize they led him
> Into the pleasant labyrinths of ever-fresh discourse.
>
> ("To the Royal Society," 21–26)

Here the most "wanton wit" of the period inveighs against the unhealthy sweets of verse and the dangers of Socratic dialectic. This poem looks forward to the famous attack on poetry by Newton himself,[24] and to the comments on the deceptiveness of "figurative speech and poetry" in Locke's *Essay concerning Human Understanding*.[25] The hero of this poem is, of course, Bacon, who, appearing three times (once as Moses), rises to slay the poets, mythologizers, and "autorities." In a passage which calls to mind the mildly blasphemous epitaph on Newton by Pope,[26] we see the Bible story mocked:

The orchard's open now and free;
Bacon has broke the scarecrow Deity;
Come enter all that will,
Behold the ripened Fruit, come gather now your Fill. (Cowley, *Poems*, 449)

How far the tone and substance of this diverges from that of Baroque religious poetry is by now obvious. Donne was terrified at the prospect of the crack made in the old world picture by the new science.[27] He could rather

---

[23] For example, Cowley, *Poems*, 18, 87.
[24] Norman Hampson, *The Enlightenment* (London: Penguin, 1972), 23.
[25] John Locke, *An Essay concerning Human Understanding*, III, x, 34 (New York: Dover Books, 1959), 146–147.
[26] Epitaph. Intended for Sir Isaac Newton, in Westminster Abbey: Nature, and Nature's Law lay hid in Night. God said, *Let Newton be!* and All was *Light*.
[27] John Donne, *The Complete Poems*, ed. A. J. M. Smith (London: Oxford University Press, 1974), cf. "The Anatomy of the World," ll. 205–217.

casually deny the significance of sea exploration and astronomy on behalf of
love: "Let sea discoverers to new worlds have gone, / Let maps to other
worlds on worlds have shown."[28] He preferred the microcosmic images of
man, biblical typologies, and the fabulous creatures of mythology to the
materials of science. But such an archaic stance became increasingly rare
after 1660, and those who, like Benlowes and the later Dryden, showed any
sign of it walked into the teeth of the highly developed Butlerian burlesque.

   Cowley's unlikeness to Donne (and Milton) is most obvious in his great
quatrain poem, "Hymn. To Light." This is one of the first physico-
naturalist poems in the language and looks forward to Ray, Blackmore, and
Jago, the encomiasts of Newtonian cosmology. Admired by Johnson for its
perspicuity, it marks an epoch of English poetry. In its twenty-six quatrains
there is but one oblique mention of God. The relation of light to God as
origin or sustainer is not stressed, and the common biblical analogies are
not invoked. The divinities of the poem are pagan – thinly veiled figures for
natural phenomena. Unlike the first-born creation of Milton, or the
"divine child" of Herbert, this light is purely mundane. Its relation to
natural things is drawn out at great length. We discover its speed and
subtlety, and its relation to heat.

> Hail active Nature's watchful Life and Health!
> Her joy, her ornament, her wealth!
> Hail to the Husband, Heat, and Thee!
> Thou thy world's beauteous Bride, the lusty Bridegroom He.
>
> ("Hymn. To Light," 9–12)

   The marriage of heat and light, the newly established relationship of two
forms of energy, is here clothed in the language of Christ's marriage to the
church. The syncretism of the poem, conflating images of Apollo and other
deities with natural forces, is commonplace, but the emphasis on the sheer
phenomenon of light is remarkable. It may be contrasted to the "Light"
which opens Book III of *Paradise Lost*, the heavenly, distant beams of
Dryden's *Religio Laici*, or the "light of worlds" in Taylor's *Holy Living*. It is
easy to forget the long intellectual process which revolutionized and de-
analogized a large part of the older language. By now we are accustomed
to this process of scientific literalism, and it is nothing for us to talk about
the "software" required for human thought and the "hard wiring" of the
human brain! But in the mid-seventeenth century this possibility was just
coming into the culture. Within a very few years, scores of poems of this
sort would appear, and their fashion would last until the time of Thomson's
Seasons, which marked both the end and the perfection of the Augustan
phase of poetic naturalism.[29]

---

[28] Donne, *Complete Poems*, 14. ("The Good Morrow").
[29] This is one of the problems addressed in chapter 4, the failure of this mode to survive, and the
    relation of Thomson's *Seasons* to Young's *Night Thoughts* and other mid-century poems.

Milton himself eschewed the dominant Neoplatonism and "analogism" of Baroque literary culture for an original mixture of biblical mythos and "mortalism." He had enough of the incipient materialism of Hobbes to be unable to imagine a fully disembodied angel, and even his God seems to possess a kind of rarefied body. Nor could he abide either Trinitarianism or the *ex nihilist* orthodoxy of the period, and a list of his "physicalist and paganizing heresies" would take some space.[30] It is sufficient to remark that there was an element in him of the literalizing tendency of the religious culture of the day.[31] On the other hand, Milton's great poem includes within it most scholastic and Baroque techniques of analogy: the gradations of being ending in the "bright consummate flower," the vestigial and specular illumination of "His face / Express, and of his steps divine," and others.

Cowley took the mortalist (and rationalist) tendency a good deal further. He should be read beside his near contemporaries, Vaughan, King, and Herrick, in order to see how far out of the common way his "scientific" outlook took his mature poetry.[32] But if it took him away from the common practices and literary prejudices of the Caroline poets, it also made him the first figure in the rising Augustan line.[33]

Cowley's poetry marks the decay of metaphysical wit. More importantly it marks the growth of specific techniques of Augustan rhetoric. Dryden borrowed a great deal of the content and manner of the *Davideis* for his *Absalom and Achitophel* and Cowley's unfinished couplet narrative of the Civil War is one of the first good examples of polished Tory-Augustan verse. It calls to mind the style of Dryden's *Astraea Redux*.

[30] See George Williamson, "Milton and the Mortalist Heresy," *Studies in Philology* 32 (1935), 553–579.

[31] The complicated but still important problem of Milton's relation to orthodox Christianity and to seventeenth-century trends in theology and epistemology is central to my argument.

It is important to recall Dorothy Sayers' argument about the relation of Dante to Milton. She argues that without "a Beatrice" Milton had no window to God, no imaginative ground for analogy, and, therefore, was forced towards a kind of literalism in his reworking of the Biblical motifs. Cf. Dorothy Sayers, *Dante and Milton* (New York: Harpers, 1957), 148–182. Joseph Frank, in his article "John Milton's Movement toward Deism" (*Journal of British Studies* 1 (1961), 39–51), goes so far as to say that Milton's mortalism was a form of proto-Deism. Milton's Arianism seems to aggravate the possibilities, and recently in the work of Professor Robert Faggen a strong link has been shown between his metaphors of the tree of life and Darwin's evolutionism. Whatever may be the case, Milton was more useful to the teleo-physical and Deist poets of the eighteenth century, and to the Augustan latitudinarians, than any other poet. See Robert Faggen, *Robert Frost and the Challenge of Darwin* (Ann Arbor: University of Michigan, 1997), chapter 2.

[32] This, of course, was partly because of the rage for ruminative blank verse, but also, as we shall see, it was a turning away from the analogism of medieval and Metaphysical poetry. It is important to note here that Young and Johnson, who themselves were critical of the new naturalism, were also, perhaps, most remote in their own verse from Miltonism. In the case of Young, Milton's influence upon his blank verse is very small.

[33] See Alexander Ward Allison, *Toward an Augustan Poetic* (Knoxville, Tenn.: University of Kentucky Press, 1961), 47–68.

How could a war so sad and barbarous please,
But first by slandering those blest days of Peace?
Through all the excrements of States they pry,
Like Emp'ricks to find out a Malady;
And Cowardice did Valours place supply,
Like those that kill themselves for fear to die.[34]

This verse does not have the density or refinement of Dryden's, but it does have a distinctly Augustan turn of syntax and diction. "Through all the excrements of States they pry" recalls the tenor of *Absalom and Achitophel*. There is a tempered quality throughout, and a roundedness that cannot be found in *The Mistress* or the *Pindarique Odes*. For our purposes the history of style is of great importance, since every narrative of changes in style is a history of the use of figures, and a chief sign of intellectual change.

The reason we began with Cowley is twofold. In him, more even than in Dryden, we can see the loss of a sense of the old hierarchical and analogical world view. In Alexander Allison's words,

techniques entering into the conceit were a survival from the gothic past – a period in which analogical reasoning unchecked by the Baconian spirit of criticism had contributed much to human error. For these reasons, both general and specific, poets during the second and third quarters of the century reposed increasingly less confidence in the power of the wit to apprehend an objective truth, and of a conceit to express such a truth. The later disciples of Donne, of whom Abraham Cowley was the type, give the impression of remembering that poets should be witty but of having forgotten why.[35]

Now this forgetfulness is a remarkable problem. Had metaphysical poetry merely become jaded by continued practice, or tortured (like some Victorian poetry) into a melancholy and empty act of emulation, then it would be a problem of forgetting. But in the case of Cowley it was a new recognition that prompted his conversion. Cowley was one of the first to feel the failure of analogy as an extension of the skepticism of Hobbes and Bacon. He was one of the first to reckon with the problem of a necessary revision of consciousness.

Cowley has been lost to us for this reason. He is a belated and unfaithful Renaissance lyricist, and an unpolished and experimental Augustan. It was his fate that he could change in an age of change. Herrick and Waller, much lesser talents, have given us a few great poems. Cowley has given us the history of his failure. Unfaithful in the mode of faithful analogy, and unpolished where correctness was to become the measure of judgment,

---

[34] Cowley, *On the late Civil War* in *Essays and Plays*, ed. A. R. Walker (Cambridge: Cambridge University Press, 1906), 470.
[35] Allison, *Toward an Augustan Poetic*, 55.

Cowley has left behind an indecipherable legacy. More truly than Dryden he was "between two ages cast."[36]

Dryden's own world-view retains more of the authentic life of Renaissance culture. His comic biblical typologies are real to him. His faithful adherence to the implications of divine right, and his subtle reworking of all but moribund analogies in the musical odes have a remarkable resonance. The earlier "Ode for Saint Cecilia's Day" is one of the last poems in English where Humanist syncresis is fruitful. In that poem the Jewish, Greek, and Christian musical mythologies are linked. The hagiographical tableau of St. Cecilia in which she rises above the natural wonders of Orpheus to entertain the angelic existences ushers in a remarkable apocalypse. Although the famous lines on the new science in "To my Noble Friend, Mr. Charleton," show a certain "modern" flexibility of imagination, the general cast of his mind is archaic.[37] It is unfortunate that many of his important critics beginning with Van Doren have overemphasized Dryden's scientific and Lucretian elements.[38]

Dryden made Augustan rhetoric his own, giving it a rapidity, a "treading upon the brink of meaning,"[39] which it never again recovered. This serendipitous and associative quality is the remnant of an earlier era, and the best passages in Dryden have the quickness almost of Donne. When he says that Donne "had more wit than any of us,"[40] one hears a tone of admiration and nostalgia. In fact, Dryden mentioned in the same preface that he had admired the genius of Donne, and that twenty years had passed since he could escape the limitations of his laureateship to write a true pindaric – a spiritual apotheosis. He reaches in that poem a heady pitch of conceit.

> O happy Soul! if thou canst view from high
> Where thou art all Intelligence, all Eye.   (*Eleanora*, 340–341)[41]

[36] John Dryden, ed. James Kinsley, *Poems* (Oxford: Oxford University Press, 1966), 104. See "Prologue" to *Aureng-Zebe*, 21.

[37] Dryden, *Poems*, 97. The important passage reads as follows: "Had we still paid that homage to a name/ Which only God and Nature justly claim, / The western seas had been our utmost bound, / Where poets still might dream the sun was drowned / And all the stars that shine in Southern skies, / Had been admired by none but savage eyes./ Among the asserters of free reason's claim, / The English are not least in worth or fame, / The world to Bacon does not only owe / Its present knowledge, but its future, too."

[38] Mark Van Daren, *John Dryden, A Study of his Poetry* (Bloomington: University of Indiana, 1960). Here I seem to be opposed to the conclusions of Earl Miner (*Dryden's Poetry* [Bloomington: University of Indiana, 1967]), and Dryden's recent biographer, James Winn (*John Dryden and his World* [New Haven: Yale University Press, 1987]), but it is merely a matter of the balance. The place of Hobbes and Bacon is significant, but does not counterbalance the backward-looking quality of his major religious and political poetry.

[39] Johnson, *Lives*, vol. I, 325.

[40] John Dryden, "Preface" to *Eleanora* in *Works*, ed. E. N. Hooker, H. T. Swedenberg and A. Roper (Berkeley and Los Angeles: University of California Press, 1972), 16 vols., vol. III, 137.

[41] Ibid., 140.

What he failed to make more explicit in prose was that all of his later poems reclaim the possibilities of conceit, microcosm, and analogy. *Eleanora*, *Killigrew*, *Threnodia Augustalis*, and many of his later verse prologues swerve back towards the archaic mode of his youthful poem on Hastings. A longer study than I can offer in this summary should be given to the Baroque Dryden, for his late conversion to Catholicism was attended by a really doctrinaire reversal of taste, and that reversal took place within the confines of a mature Augustan couplet. Dryden also experimented with the possibilities of Anglican compromise, but pushed himself into an untenable corner in the logic of *Religio Laici*, and so made concessions about authority and scripture that would have made Milton swoon.

> Such an *Omniscient* Church we wished indeed;
> 'Twere worth *Both Testaments*, and cast in the *Creed*.
> (*Religio Laici*, 282–3)[42]

What Philip Harth and others have described as rational Anglicanism was in fact a revelation of the nearness of Anglicanism to the dreaded Deism which Dryden attacks. I believe that Dryden recognized this in the mid-1680s. The formula of exclusion in Butler leaves an emptiness between Protestant conscience and Catholic authority. Dryden could not accept the vacuum of doctrine and authority implied by such an amorphous orthodoxy, and the same elements of iconic traditionalism and need of certainty that inform his Royalism explain his Romanism. Even in *Eleanora*, an express imitation of Donne's *Anatomy of the World*, his housewife, by a strange reversal, becomes not only a microcosm of the spiritual and physical worlds, as in the example of Elizabeth Drury, but also a monarch with distinctly paternal characteristics. Dryden's monarchism has a kind of depth that no subsequent Tory writer could equal. He was not a pragmatic Royalist like Swift, Pope, and Bolingbroke, but one who had always longed for a quasi-sacramental link between the king's person and the promise of law.

> So willing to forgive th' Offending Age,
> So much the Father did the King asswage . . .
> (*Absalom and Achitophel*, 941–2)

> Kings are the publick Pillars of the State,
> Born to sustain and prop the Nations weight:
> (*Absalom and Achitophel*, 954–955)[43]

The later Augustans themselves, particularly Prior and Dryden's unsympathetic cousin, Swift, did not approve of this later poetry. Swift took every chance to mock Dryden, calling his *Hind and the Panther* the greatest

---

[42] Dryden, *Works*, vol. II, 117.   [43] Ibid., 33–34.

collection of wit since Duns Scotus, and dressing him up like a poetic Don Quixote in his hopeless jousting contest with his master Virgil. Indeed, Dryden's nostalgia for the Baroque was not shared by those who borrowed the most from his remarkable prosody and language – Pope, Swift, Thomson, and Johnson. The settlement of 1689 was unsettling to Dryden, as was the whole memory of the Civil War and the Restoration. A few months before he died, in the waning moments of the seventeenth century, he could produce an emotion almost Elizabethan in its wistful gravity.

> All, all, of a Piece throughout,
> Our Chase had a Beast in view,
> Our Wars brought Nothing about,
> Our Lovers were all untrue.
> Tis good an old Age is out,
> And Time to begin anew.
>
> (Chorus in the *Secular Masque*)[44]

Dryden was the last author before Smart and Blake to come to his poems with an established ground of analogy – a fully realized imaginative world with religious seriousness. He had a narrow round of emotions, a some-times frigid spiritualism, but his imagination, especially in his later poems, retained the flexible figurative cast of earlier seventeenth-century verse.

This kind of traditionalism is not found in Cowley, Denham, or even Waller.[45] The establishment of the Augustan line, which in Johnson's opinion refined and codified the proper use of diction and meter, was also the establishment of a new intellectual world. The attentiveness to physical science in Cowley, to mundane politics and simplified eroticism in Waller, and to landscape in Denham, pointed the direction and marked the limits of imagination from 1670 to the 1740s. Cowley and Dryden, the two most important British poets after Milton in the last half of the seventeenth century, passed each other on their imaginative journeys going in opposite directions, both attempting to escape the limitations of a way of writing which they had helped to create.

The transformation of prose style

Many forces combined to advance the anti-analogical and literalist tendency in the later Cowley and in his distinguished contemporaries. First, any form of the Gothic smacked of an evil and encroaching Romanism, which, combining with the Tudor legacy of the Spanish dread, was finally to bring about the downfall of James II. The conceit itself and

[44] Dryden, *Poems*, ed. J. Kinsley (Oxford: Clarendon, 1979), vol. IV, 203.
[45] The opposite view of Denham is suggested in an extraordinary essay by Earl Wasserman, who sees *Cooper's Hill* as an involved Royalist (and religious) allegory. See Earl Wasserman, *The Subtler Language* (Baltimore: Johns Hopkins University Press, 1959) 45–88.

other Baroque rhetorical figures were expressly connected to Catholicism.[46] This produced the double offense of imitating "the Papist mind" and of colliding with Puritan iconoclasm. After the English Civil War and the Thirty Years War in Europe there was a growing sense that the cost of faction in religion was intolerable. It is not surprising to find that, during the week of the King's return in 1660, Richard Baxter (the most brilliant of the Restoration dissenting ministers) and Bishop Bramhall gave very similar admonitions against "bloody wars of religious opinion."[47]

God knows how soon sickness may cast us upon our restless beds, and change our sweet repose into wearisome tossings. God knows how soon we may be choaked with the fumes of a restless stomach or drowned with hydropical humors, or burnt up with cholerical tempers, or buried alive in the grave of melancholic imaginations. Now we sit in the beauty of peace, every man under his own vine and his own fig-tree. We know how soon our ringing of bells may be changed into roaring of cannons. It is the mercy of the Lord that these mischiefs do not overwhelm us.[48]

These words of Bramhall, already in his own final illness, are hauntingly archaic. Trained as he was in the parish of Bishop Andrewes, and carrying the full baggage of Andrewes' (or perhaps Jewell's) own remarkable prose, Bramhall is transformed into a kind of Janus. His own style, a tempered but fanciful manipulation of phrases from the Gospel in the strong irregular iambic cadence of the Book of Common Prayer, would in the very early years of the Restoration become impossibly antique. It looks back to the generation which transformed pulpit oratory into an art of the highest distinction – incomparable in its moral electricity, its rhetorical variety, and its casuistical acuteness.[49] This oratory was one of the great products of Baroque culture.[50] So far from the fashion that Tillotson was about to usher in, these sentences of Bramhall's, with their strong parallelisms and fertile associations, will not be found again in England after the beginning of the eighteenth century, aside from a few Jacobite extremists.

But we are straying away from the main point. All of these causes – the obsession with ecclesiastical and civil peace, the growth of a new reading public, the stigma of Catholic literary and religious culture, and the growth of the new science – work to dull the preexisting potentials of Christian imagination. Three distinct moments mark the trajectory of the old

---

[46] The use of "Gothic" to describe the metaphysical style is found in Addison and Swift. Helen White's *Bibliography to Seventeenth-Century Protestant Pamphlets* has several titles specifically about this problem. In Helen C. White, *Bibliography of English Devotional Literature* (1600–1670)

[47] John Chandos, ed., *In God's Name: Preaching in England 1634–1662*, (New York: Bobbs-Merril, 1971), 542–546.

[48] *In God's Name*, 553–554.

[49] Cf. Douglas Bush, *English Literature in the Early Seventeenth Century* (Oxford: Clarendon Press, 1957), chapter 10.

[50] John Toller, *The Imagery of Donne's Sermons* (Cambridge, Mass.: Harvard University Press, 1983) Preface.

analogical Christian tradition. In history writing, for example, the late sixteenth and early seventeenth centuries saw the printing of several incomparably conceitful narratives. The most important was Ralegh's *History of the World* (1614), which combines an almost euphuistic density with luxurious fancy:

> For seeing God who is the Author of all our tragedies, has written out for us and showed us all the parts we have to play: and hath not in their distribution been partiall to the most mighty Princes of the world; that gave unto Darius the part of the greatest Emperor, and the part of the most miserable begger, a begger begging water of an enemie, to quench the great drought of Death; who appointed Bajazet to play the Gran Signior of the Turkes in the morning, and in the same day the footstoole of Tamerlane . . . why should other men, who are of but the least wormes, complain of wrongs?[51]

This form of historical narrative corresponds in time and figurative energy to the maturing of metaphysical poetry and Baroque homily. Euphuism itself, the most self-consciously elaborate of all Renaissance prose, is the descendant of the late medieval Latin sermon with its use of transverse alliteration, internal rhyme, syntactical doubling, and oblique illustration.[52]

Ralegh's prose and the tenor of his thought depend upon the heaping-up of analogies between the biblical and classical, the mundane and the eternal. Every creature, and every man's biography, is a "window" to God. There is in Ralegh a completely fluid relation between the mythic and the historical, as there is between the human and the divine:

> And whereas God created three sorts of living natures, to wit, angelical, rational, and brutal; giving to angels an intellectual, and to beasts a sensual nature, he vouchsafed unto man both the intellectual of angels, the sensitive of beasts, and the proper rational belonging unto man, and therefore, saith Gregory Nazienzen, *homo est utriusque naturae vinculum:* "Man is the bond and chain which tieth together both natures." And because in the little frame of man's body there is a representation of the universal, and (by allusion) a kind of participation of all the parts thereof, therefore was man called *microcosmos*, or the little world. *Deus igitur hominem factum, velut alterum quendam mundum, in brevi magnum, atque exiguo totum, in terris statuit:* "God therefore placed in the earth the man whom he had made, as it were another world, the great and large world in the small and little world." For out of earth and dust was formed the flesh of man, and therefore heavy and lumpish; the bones of his body we may compare to the hard rocks and stones, and therefore strong and durable, of which Ovid:

> > *Inde genus durum sumus, experiensque laborum,*
> > *Et documenta damus qua simus origine nati.*[53]

---

[51] Reprinted in Walter Ralegh, *Selections from His Writings*, ed. S. Greenblatt (Oxford: Clarendon Press, 1917), 56.

[52] See Morris Croll, *Lyly and English Rhetoric* (New York: Harpers, 1931), 33–47.

[53] Ralegh, *Selections*, 42.

Ralegh displays the kind of syncretic classicism that could find spiritual parallels between classical and late-Medieval texts. His allegorical interpretation of Ovid supports his claims about microcosm. He recalls the story of Deucalion throwing the stones over his shoulder to create a new race of men – "thus we derive our hardness, and our endurance shows from what we were born." There is a kind of unbroken continuum of the miraculous from which this man of wide experience can draw. Such microcosm became for Butler one of the most despised figures of Renaissance writing. Butler thought microcosm, like other forms of exaggerated analogy, to be the supreme form of superstitious delusion. He offered some choice burlesque on the subject in *Hudibras*:

> Th'Intelligible world he knew,
> And all men dream on't, to be true:
> That in this *World*, there's not a *Wart*,
> That has not there a Counterpart;
> Nor can there on the *face* of Ground,
> An individual *Beard* be found,
> That has not in that Forrain *Nation*,
> A fellow of the self-same fashion.   (*Hudibras* I, iii, 225–232)

"Nature," which appears seven times in Ralegh's Preface, always means "this lower world of dust," "this place of dissimulation,"[54] and has the general sense of the condition of changing things. Having no existence apart from God's will, it is said to be the "toy of man's wit." Not only Ralegh's unconscious Platonism, but his highly personal use of Calvinist historiography, mark him as a typical figure of English "metaphysical" culture.

Clarendon's history, which I shall touch on briefly, is a work of transition. Its prose does not rise to the level of Burton's or Ralegh's in complexity, having a regular and even flow with long but unadorned periods. Recalling Hooker, but simpler and more idiomatic, it is the middle term in an equation of change. Clarendon's royalism, his almost superstitious concentration on Charles' martyrology, links him imaginatively with Baroque culture. As in Dryden, metaphors of kingship are the chief traditional residue of analogy in his thought, and, like Dryden, his vocabulary is touched at several points by a Hobbesian sobriety. In describing King Charles' character, he says:

He was very fearless in his person, but not very enterprising. He had an excellent understanding, but was not confident enough of it; which made him oftentimes change his own opinion for a worse, and follow the advice of men that did not judge so well as himself. This made him more irresolute than the conjecture of his

---

[54] Ibid., 38 and *passim*.

affairs would admit: if he had been of a rougher and more imperious nature he would have found more respect and duty.[55]

This is close to the kind of plainness advocated by Sprat and Glanvil. It is a style that can be uninterrupted by metaphor for several sentences. The syntax is not rhythmically contrived and the diction is that of a man of the world. Clarendon was not a skeptic, but beside Ralegh he seems to be playing rather close to the rhetorical vest. Like Tillotson, his near contemporary, Clarendon has developed a kind of "realism" and transparency which is part of the atmosphere of his time. There are a few passages in Clarendon which hark back to the style popular in his youth. In these passages, sometimes brought on by wrath, he appears as a transitional stylist, simpler than Burton but less prosaic than later Augustan writers:

But, in that learned and unbiased (I mean unprovoked) men, in that science, who knew the frame and constitution of the kingdom, and that the bishops were no less the representative body of the clergy, than the house of commons was of the people; and, consequently, that the depriving them of voice in parliament, was a violence, and removing landmarks, and not a shaking (which might settle again) but dissolving foundations; which must leave the building unsafe for habitation: (that such men) who knew the ecclesiastical and civil state was so wrought and interwoven together, and in truth, so incorporated in each other, that like Hippocrates' twins, they cannot but laugh and cry together; and that the professors of the law were never at so great a height, as even in this time that they so unjustly envied the greatness of the church.[56]

There is more excitement in this passage. The energy of the verbs "shaking," "dissolving," " wrought and interwoven," push the conceit of the building (a favorite Baroque figure) along. The mixture of mythological allusion and the humorous reference to lawyers gives the effect of spontaneous comparison. The syntax has marked parallelism, and in the closing clauses something close to metrical repetition.

The final phase, the one in which history is, to use a fashionable expression, "temporalized" (that is, freed completely from the mythic) is the period of Hume and Gibbon. Their histories honor the Lockeian and quasi-scientific notion of evidence. Biblical typologies and other spiritual analogies do not appear. The prose itself has a rationalist balance, though in Gibbon's case it maintains an almost tiresome latinity. This completes the three phases. The last and most prosaic can very fairly be termed Augustan. It is no accident that the prosaic rhetoric invented by Sprat and Glanvil would be the instrument of Hume, though with a native energy. With perfect sureness he manipulates the satirical formulae of exclusion I

[55] Edward Hyde, Earl of Clarendon, *The History of the Rebellion and Civil Warres* (London: Oxford University Press, 1956), 155.
[56] Edward Hyde, Earl of Clarendon, *History of the Rebellion*, volume II (Oxford: Oxford University Press, 1974), 107.

have described in chapter 1. He uses the Butlerian "superstition and enthusiasm" to frame the causal nexus of his *History*. He gently mocks the superstitious consciousness which survives in the late seventeenth century. In describing the Prayer Book, which he no doubt considered a tribute to human credulity, he says:

The book of Common Prayer suffered in England a new revisal, and some rites and ceremonies, which had given offence, were omitted. The speculative doctrines, or the metaphysics of the religion, were also reduced to forty-two articles. These were intended to obviate farther divisions and variations; and the compiling of them had been postponed till the establishment of the liturgy, which was justly regarded as a more material object to the people. The eternity of hell torments is asserted in this confession of faith; and care is also taken to inculcate, not only that no heathen, how virtuous soever, can escape an endless state of the most exquisite misery, but also that every one who presumes to maintain, that any pagan can possibly be saved, is himself exposed to the penalty of eternal perdition.

The theological zeal of the council, though seemingly fervent, went not so far as to make them neglect their own temporal concerns, which seem to have ever been uppermost in their thoughts: They even found leisure to attend to the public interest; nay, to the commerce of the nation, which was, at that time, very little the object of general study or attention.[57]

Hume's style is unadorned but sure-handed. Though he uses little metaphor there is a supple movement of thought and image and an irony far subtler than that of Gibbon or Boswell. "Suffered a revisal" is brilliant, and the uncovering of venal motives in the clergy arrives at the end without fanfare and with the typical eighteenth-century deference of "seemingly . . . seem." The sarcasm of "they even found leisure to attend the public interest" and that the liturgy was "more material" for the general run of the congregation than theological speculations are part of the Humean sense of the remote rational observer at a festival of nonsense. Like Adam Smith he extends no sympathy to the instruments or victims of superstition. More explicitly, and with an unusually broad humor, he illuminates the absurdities of Catholic faith and the self-interest of the English church. In the last sentence he enters into that anthropological detachment which I mention in chapter 1 when discussing Butler's idea of religion. Another passage shows Hume at his best:

The better to reconcile the people to this great innovation, stories were propagated of the detestable lives of the friars in many of the convents; and great care was taken to defame those whom the court had determined to ruin. The reliques also and other superstitions, which had so long been the object of the people's veneration, were exposed to their ridicule; and the religious spirit, now less bent on exterior observances and sensible objects, was encouraged in this new direction. It is needless to be prolix in an enumeration of particulars: Protestant historians

[57] David Hume, *The History of England* (Indianapolis: Liberty Classics, 1983), 385–386.

mention on this occasion with great triumph the sacred repositories of convents; the parings of St. Edmond's toes; some the coals that roasted St. Laurence; the girdle of the Virgin shown in eleven several places; two or three heads of St. Ursula; the felt of St. Thomas of Lancaster, an infallible cure for the head-ache; part of St. Thomas of Canterbury's shirt, much reverenced by big-bellied women; some reliques, an excellent preventive against rain; others, a remedy to weeds in corn. But such fooleries, as they are to be found in all ages and nations, and even took place during the most refined periods of antiquity, form no particular or violent reproach to the Catholic religion.[58]

Hume here exhibits the satirical idea of Butler brought to higher level of subtlety and elegance. Without the impediments of hyperbole and doggerel he traces the history of delusion which is the shared narrative of all religious interests. Even the "most refined periods of antiquity," so superior to the absurd ages of Christian Europe, could not entirely escape the "fooleries" of superstition. As in the three-legged stool of the Roman oracle and Protestant enthusiast, the reliquary tradition is a perennial folly of mankind. Like Butler, Hume doubts equally the motives of the local Protestant culture "who defame those [Catholic friars] whom the court had determined to ruin," and the Catholics themselves who built up a "system of fantasies." Priestly deception is replaced by Anglican manipulation. As in Restoration lampoon, the satire is general – all parties are tarred with the same brush. The style in the litany of superstitions is as balanced and "objective" as the subject is fantastic. Hume ingeniously moves from the toes to the girdle to the head in his burlesque of the saintly body; like Butler and Swift he discovers in clothing the best symbols of false representation. His casualness is felt in his hardly having to mention the standard symbolic repertoire of conventional Christianity. It is needless for him "to be prolix" when confronted with absurdity so rich, and the simplicity and ease of his style sets in sharper contrast the excess of his subject matter. One could scarcely realize the possibilities of the Augustan formula of exclusion more adroitly.

History was not the only genre that passed through these stages. After our brief excursus we may safely return to Cowley. His work divides clearly and, perhaps, uniquely, into these three species – metaphysical, transitional, and Augustan – which we have just been illustrating with the example of history writing. But for Cowley, of all the forces that contribute to his later Augustanism, the growth of a scientific way of thinking is the most important. In this respect Cowley is an anomaly. For Butler, Rochester, Swift, and sometimes Pope the scientists of the Royal Society and the experimenters in astronomy were described as madmen akin to religious overreachers and foolish projectors. Butler's "Elephant in the Moon" and the third book of *Gulliver's Travels* are the best examples of this tendency, but there are many more examples down to the 1720s. For Butler and Swift, astrology and alchemy (the enemies of Bacon) were the fundamental paradigms of the physical sciences. They both doubted the ethical relevance of science, and they thought of it as an extension of the Pandoran curiosity of the Civil War era.

In this regard the "Preface" that Cowley wrote to his collected poems two years before his death is an important document. In it, Cowley, making puns upon his early titles in phrases like, I "have dispensed with my long loved Mistress" and "my infant Muse, who I came to wed too early," turns against his own earlier work. He mocks the metaphorical style of Donne, his old master, and claims that the new religion must not stand upon old fancies, but upon the solidity of new learning. In this he foreshadows the great project of Sprat (who edited Cowley's poems) as well as the latitude of Tyndall and Toland, and while his tone is not completely deistical, it is completely detached from his own earlier thinking. One passage should be quoted at length:

> But as the Marriages of Infants do but rarely prosper, so no man ought to wonder at the diminution or decay of my affection to Poesie; to which I had contracted myself so much under Age, and so much to my own prejudice in regard of those more profitable matches which I might have made among the richer Sciences.[59]

There is something almost melancholy in Cowley's self-denunciation throughout this "Preface," something which cannot be attributed simply to an aging author's conventional indifference to his earlier work. This "new scientism" marks a change in cultural history. The unconscious or habitual rejection (from the Restoration onward) of the old, staple Christian analogies and "mysteries" is in Cowley a conscious choosing. Cowley saw that the language of science would replace the language of analogy, and no major author before Thomson paid greater tribute to the positivist momentum of modern British intellectual culture.

Pope, to take one of many later examples, did not even recognize the problems for his own Catholicism of Newtonian science. He had no solid conception of orthodox theology or the methodological implications of contemporary astronomy. Cowley in this sense leaped ahead of the later Augustans. For although Pope shows in his response to Crousaz and in his letter to Louis Racine that the traditional issues of grace, typology, biblical authority, and original sin had lost their meaning for him, he did not turn to science or any particular mode of rational skepticism.[60] The *Essay on Man* was the final tribute to his confusion. Pope was to become the perfect

---

[59] Cowley, Preface (to the first collected edition, 1665), *Poems*, 6.
[60] Alexander Pope, *The Correspondence of A. P.*, edited by George Sherbun (Oxford: Clarendon Press, 1956), 415–416.

Augustan, imbibing as he did Denham's landscape art, the metonymic
plainness of Waller, and Dryden's satiric method without the real seriousness
and complexity of Dryden's world-picture. Pope, as I will show in the next
chapter, was a new kind of secular poet. Pope's apocalypse, unlike Dryden's
"crumbling pageant," is an apocalypse of "taste," and looks forward to the
endless crises of culture recorded since the eighteenth century. No writer
before Pope could have written an epitaph for Isaac Newton which, perhaps
without malice, parodies the Old Testament: "Nature and Nature's Laws
lay hid in Night, / God said, *Let Newton be*, and All was *Light*." Here Newton,
a metonymy for the new enclosed and intelligible system of Nature, is the
principle of a cosmos, usurping the revealing wisdom traditionally granted
to the Logos himself. Before this is dismissed as mere witticism, we should
remember that it was seriously considered for Newton's tomb in Westminster. In the Latin lines which preceded the epitaph, Newton is said to have
received testimonials from *Natura* and *Tempus*, those new twin deities which
in the minds of Vaughan and Bishop King (only 40 years before) had
represented nothing more than the "rags of time." The old idea of "nature"
as corruption which was held by Ralegh, Donne, Herbert, Clarendon, and
even Dryden, had by now been replaced by a new and independent entity.
Dryden could have seen the epigram as blasphemy; Cowley might have
hailed it as an inevitable revelation.

The reinvention of nature

When we find in Herbert's "The Pulley,"

> For if I should (said He),
> Bestow this Jewell also on my Creature
> He would adore my gifts instead of me
> And rest in Nature, not the God of Nature
> So both should losers be,[61]

we know that for Herbert "Nature" is a body of signs given by God for the
edification of the militant spiritual man. Nature is not only beneath God
(and man) in dignity but more importantly for our argument, it is a jewel
(in Ralegh's words a "toy") for contemplation. It is a window for the
contemplation of God.[62] The nature which "underneath a heap of jarring
Atomes lay"[63] in Dryden is in contrast to this an inert material substratum.
Its harmony and intelligibility comes directly from God. God is not made

---

[61] George Herbert, *Poems*, ed. F. E. Hutchinson (London: Oxford University Press, 1941), 117.
[62] This is of the utmost importance for my fifth chapter which attempts to describe a complete
phenomenology of Christian poetry, especially as it stood before the Enlightenment. This sort of
analogical or "transparent" symbolism, as we shall see, dominated the late medieval and
Renaissance imagination. The notion of nature as an end or a system is, of course, inimical to it.
[63] Dryden, "Song for St. Cecilia's Day," *Poems*, 196.

known by nature; rather, nature is made knowable, and arises from its "more than dead" condition, by the *fiat* of God. This may seem like a tissue of commonplaces, but we must keep these two distinctly Renaissance conceptions of nature in mind if we wish to understand the profound changes wrought upon the idea in the eighteenth century. We must also recall that Dryden's conception, still roughly orthodox, has a touch of that classical atomist heresy and opposition to the doctrine of ex-nihilistic creation which we have already discussed in the case of Milton.

In at least three kinds of poetry, the Augustans created a new conception of nature. In landscape poetry like *Cooper's Hill, Windsor-Forest, Grongar Hill,* and *The Fleece* they produced our modern conception of scenic nature. In this "new-Edenism," as it was called by the elder Warton,[64] they revolutionized the pastoral mode. They not only returned to a distinctly classical form, forsaking the older Christian allegorical machinery which had dominated the "pastorelle" and which could still be seen in Marot in France, Spenser's *Shephard's Calendar* in England,[65] and elsewhere in the sixteenth and seventeenth centuries, but they also enhanced the realistic elements of the Virgilian model. This movement toward naturalism precipitated the famous debate between the school of Fontenelle,[66] which supported the Golden Age thesis, and the incipient realism of many of his French and English contemporaries. Pope's short prefatory essay on the pastoral, prefixed to his own *Pastorals,* shows him wavering on the issue of the proper pastoral mode, and siding at last with the Golden Agers. But a very few years later he forsook this mode for the historico-political form of the pastoral in *Windsor Forest.*[67] It was within the Augustan tradition of Denham, Pope, and Thomson that the pastoral material was fully temporalized, and brought into history. From that time the mythical Arcadia, which had served as the spiritual haven of the practical man (as in Sidney's *Arcadia,* Book VI of the *Faerie Queen,* or the "country house" poems of Jonson and Carew), ceded to the local and the historical.

No longer a utopian other-world, the pastoral became emblematic of national or local pride of place. Divested by the 1720s of its monarchical and genteel conventions, it became a form of Whiggish description. In the final step of this transformation, not only scenery, but work itself, was brought into the displaced pastoral situation. Again the transition was not smooth. Classicism was the middle term between the earlier Christian

[64] Thomas Warton, *Correspondence* (Cambridge: Cambridge University Press, 1856), 79.
[65] See Patrick Cullen, *Spenser, Marvell, and Renaissance Pastoral* (Cambridge, Mass.: Harvard University Press, 1970).
[66] Cf. Alexander Pope, *Poems of Alexander Pope,* vol. 1, ed. E. Audra and Aubrey Williams (New Haven: Yale University Press, 1968), Preface.
[67] See the argument of David Morris in his *Alexander Pope: The Genius of Sense* (Cambridge, Mass.: Harvard University Press, 1984), ch. 4.

allegorical mode, in which Arcadia was a figure for the "second Eden" and
the Shepherd a figure for Christ, and the final movement toward scenic
description and historical accident. The transition can also be seen in the
evolution of the pastoral elegy. In Milton's *Lycidas* the syncretism is
complex, but the older Christian analogies of the priestly pasture and the
shepherd's duty remain. *Lycidas* is the last fully Christian pastoral of this
kind, and the last poem, perhaps, which returns to the tradition of
Mantuan.[68] Cowley's nearly contemporary "Elegy for Hervey" shows an
already advanced realism in which the actual Cambridge locations of
youthful friendship are invoked. We look forward to the criticism of *Lycidas*
in Johnson, and in his starkly naturalistic theory of the pastoral in numbers
36 and 37 of *The Rambler*.

Although the displacement of original generic material is never
complete, this final transformation of pastoral as in *Grongar Hill* and *The
Seasons* is an important moment. In Thomson, the tradition described by
Curtius, in which every shrub and animal was part of an emblematical
taxonomy,[69] had become moribund. Thomson's nature is a place of natural
beings and natural forces. His classicism is decorative and his Christianity
is cold. I shall give more space to this issue in my treatment of *Summer* in
chapter 4.

The cult of Lucretius was another force behind the naturalism which
transformed the pastoral *locus amoenus* into our modern conception of
landscape. Ovid and Virgil (as in the *Metamorphoses* and the Fourth *Eclogue*)
had been allegorized in the Renaissance by the Florentine Platonists, and
in England by Golding, Sandys, and even the young Pope. They had
seemed a part of the prophetic or imaginative *preparatio* for Christ and
Christian culture. Lucretius was a very different case. He was brought into
favor in England largely by the authority granted to him by Hobbes and
especially Bacon, who said of the atomists that they "went further into
Nature than the rest. We also should be more concerned with matter than
forms."[70] Similar encomia are common in the works of the early members
of the Royal Society and the *De rerum natura* was deeply admired by Dryden,
Roscommon, and others. The partial translation of Dryden, and the
important complete translation by Creech (1682), enhanced the fashion for
Lucretius. As I mentioned above, the *alma Venus* figure began to usurp
other poetic conceptions of Nature, and for the first time brought the
notion of a general procreative energy throughout nature into the post-
Medieval mind. This was not merely the attraction of kind as in Chaucer's
Prologue, but a comprehensive, independent and unitary force.

---

[68] See W. W. Gregg, *The Pastoral and Pastoral Drama* (London: Macmillan, 1933), 102–112.
[69] Ernst Robert Curtius, *European Literature and the Latin Middle Ages* (Princeton: Princeton
University Press, 1973), 193–201.
[70] Francis Bacon, *Novum organum* (New York: Bobbs-Merril, 1972), 51.

William Ellery Leonard is right that Lucretius brought the notion of "a universal Law of Nature, an absolute system of cause and effect," along with a conception of "inconceivably vast stretches of time and space, and multiple worlds,"[71] more strongly into the western mind. These notions became popular for the first time only after 1660, and a sober thinker like Addison can imagine "an untold expanse of the sky" and "many worlds like our own."[72] These notions were easily combined with Hobbesian nominalism and Newtonian physics to produce a new place for the imagination. Lucretius bears the same relation to Augustan cosmology as Horace does to Augustan ethics. We do not have time here to trace the influence of Horace and his place in the secularization of consciousness. Although Horace is used illustratively in the sermons of Lancelot Andrewes, for example, and often in Burton's *Melancholy*, he did not attain to the rank of cultural arbiter until after 1670. His mix of bland Epicureanism and ironic nationalism were attractive. He was a more rational and leisurely figure than most other classical or Renaissance authors. His form of the ode did not eclipse the Pindaric fashion, but grew up beside it, and his epistolary style, loose, worldly, and circumspectly satiric, was a natural mode for Rochester, Pope, Swift, and others. This Roman curriculum served to further secularize poetic consciousness.

The last and most extreme form of post-Restoration naturalist poetry was the "teleo-physical" or cosmological poem, which Ray made famous and Blackmore enlarged. In this the claims primarily of Newtonian physics and Gilbert's astronomy are poeticized. This is the first distinctly secular form of cosmological verse. The concept of Nature, ambiguous until then, became fully modernized, and we may say, de-analogized. This new-found form of imagination marked the way toward a more complete severance of cosmological thinking from biblical and Medieval models.

The growth of these three genres is merely representative of the larger change in British conceptions of nature and, more importantly for our study, conceptions of metaphor and theology. The traditional reaction to these developments, which began with Prior's *Solomon* and continued in the important poems of Young, Johnson, the hymn writers, and the prose works of Wesley and Hervey shows the inevitable if intermittent return of Protestant poetics in England. Far from reflective of sentimental decay, these works show the resilience of the ancient paradigms of Christian poetry, as I shall show in chapter 6.

---

[71] Lucretius, *De rerum natura*, ed. W. E. Leonard and S. B. Smith (Madison: University of Wisconsin, 1942), 58–59.

[72] Quoted from Basil Willey, *The Eighteenth Century Background* (Boston: Beacon Press, 1954), 12.

Benlowes: the survival of conceit

Comforting as it may be to see each era as intellectually univocal, it is also important to recall that the old devotional and amorous poetry of the earlier seventeenth century marked by microcosmic analogy and conceit did not completely die out. Philip Ayres, Katherine Philips, Anne Killigrew, and others pursued the older modes even after 1660. The case of Edward Benlowes is interesting. His *Theophila* is one of the most anomalous creations of the period. At turns brilliant and monstrous, it re-creates the whole poetic ethos of the Baroque period. Like Burnet's *Sacred History*, it attempts to swallow up and mimic the new scientific material. In fact, that material is lost or transmogrified into something entirely alien. Benlowes, the butt of Dryden, Butler, Swift, and Pope, and the Augustan symbol of deranged fancy, stands at the impossible crossroads of Christian poetics. Saintsbury's comment is telling:

We know that Crashaw and his contemporaries were not fools; and though there is no reason for adopting the opinion of parasites and pensioners about Benlowes, there is nearly as little for agreeing with Butler that our poet was one. We come in him to one of the most remarkable examples provided by English literature of the extreme autumn of the Elizabethan *annus mirabilis*. The belief in conceits is as strong as ever: though the power of producing them poetically is dying down, and except for flickers has almost died. A fresh deliberate, critical belief in *furor poeticus* has come to blow the embers . . . one sees why contemporary men not particularly moved by a like enthusiasm, turned to the other method – the method of the scientific, the familiar, or the ordinary.[73]

"Enthusiasm" is an important word here. It recalls the condemnatory arguments of Butler, Swift, and Locke. Enthusiasm, when it came to represent and to condemn both the qualities of the Protestant dissenting imagination with its emphasis on allegory and typology, and Catholic imagination with its use of analogy, *compositio loci*, and conceit, had foreclosed Christian poetry on two sides. And enthusiasm was precisely the temper of Butler's enemy Benlowes.

> Who art by light-surrounding powers obeyed
> (Heaven's host thy minist'ring spirits made)
> Clothed with UBIQUITY, to whom all light is shade!
>
> Whose thunder-clasping hand does grasp the scroll
> Of total Nature, and unroll
> The spangled canopy of Heav'n from pole to pole![74]

---

[73] George Saintsbury (ed.), *The Major Poets of the Caroline Period*, vol. 1 (Oxford: Clarendon Press, 1919), 311.
[74] Ibid., 378–379.

This was heady stuff, backward-looking and fantastic. What was left to
the truly original religious poets of the day, as Ray makes clear in the
preface to his *Wisdom of God Manifested in Works of Creation* (1691),[75] was
science and experience, the only viable ground of religious apology. This
was the view of Newton and Voltaire, the first a pious Christian, the second
an outspoken iconoclast. But if the doctrine of "gravity" as explained by
Newton proved the existence of God,[76] because He alone could hold such
a force in place, it also left a ground of hope for the Tolandite Deists of a
naturalized God, and by an easy declivity, led within about fifty years to the
almost complete extinction of specifically Christian poetry. The core of
Augustan literature, as we read it, does not include Blackmore and Ray.
Augustan norms could not permit either the novel subject matter of the
physico-theological poets, or the preservation of traditional cosmology. As I
have mentioned, Butler, Swift, and Rochester condemned experimental
science with all the maniacal energy they could muster. Nonetheless, the
central Augustans reserved their most withering attacks for the residual
archaists of the declining Christian poetics.

From Butler onward the major Augustans knew their enemy. Benlowes
and the emblem-book authors Wither and Quarles embodied everything
bad. These three appear in Butler, Dryden, Swift, and Oldham. They are
discovered amidst the preachers in the fields, the raving populist Defoe,
and the lunatics of Bedlam in *The Dunciad*. In the three-pronged attack of
Hudibras, Butler had distinguished the madness of three great figures –
Hudibras, Ralpho, and Sidrophel. He had thereby found a connection
between the over-interpreting of natural (the literal) by theological analogy,
by inward meditation, and by astrology. In his *Characters* he employs a
similar taxonomy, but replaces the astrologer, Sidrophel, with "A Small
Poet." Although there is a good deal about the horrors of poetry and
especially the dangers of conceit and fancy throughout *Hudibras*, especially
in the first canto of the second part, this portrait is his greatest achievement
in denigrating the imaginative conventions of the metaphysical writing
culture. It may be his greatest satirical achievement. The poet chosen to be
placed on Butler's rack was Benlowes himself, and the qualities of
ignorance and absurdity which invest his two other singular contributions
to the character – the Hypocritical Non-conformist and the Hermetic
Philosopher – burst forth in the portrait of the poet in a torrent of abuse.

For *Metaphors*, he uses to chuse the hardest, and most far-fet that he can light upon
– These are the Jewels of Eloquence, and therefore the harder they are, the more
precious they must be.

---

[75] Basil Willey, *The Eighteenth Century Background* (New York: Beacon Press, 1957), 37.
[76] Newton argued that gravity, though present in the universe, was not a necessary force. For him
    this proved it obtained at the behest of a necessary and unlimited God.

He'll take a scant Piece of coarse Sense, and stretch it on the Tenter-hooks of half a score Rhimes, until it crack that you may see through it, and it rattle like a Drum-Head . . .

He'll make one Word of as many Joints, as the Tin-Pudding, that a Juggler pulls out of his Throat, and chops in again – What think you of *glud-fum-flam-hasta-minantes*? Some of the old *Latin* Poets bragged that their Verses were tougher than Brass, and harder than Marble; what would they have done, if they had seen these? . . .

There was one, that lined a Hat-Case with a Paper of *Benlowse's* Poetry – *Prynne* bought it by Chance, and put a new Demi-Castor into it. The first Time he wore it he felt only a singing in his Head, which within two Days turned into a Vertigo – He was let Blood in the Ear by one of the State-Physicians, and recovered; but before he went abroad he writ a Poem of Rocks and Seas, in a Style so proper and natural, that it was hard to determine which was ruggeder.

There is no Feat of Activity, nor Gambol of Wit, that ever was performed by Man, from him that vaults on *Pegasus*, to him that tumbles through the Hoop of an Anagram, but *Benlows* has got the mastery of it, whether it be high-rope Wit, or low-rope Wit. He has all sorts of *Echoes, Rebus's, Chronograms*, &c. besides *Carwithchets, Clenches*, and *Quibbles* – As for Altars and Pyramids in Poetry, he has outdone all Men in that Way; for he has made a *Gridiron*, and a *Frying-Pan* in Verse, that besides the likeness in Shape, the very Tone and Sense of the Words did perfectly represent the Noise, that is made by those Utensils, such as the old Poet called *sartago loquendi*.[77]

The whole gamut of Augustan criticism, though in a mad form, is in this passage. The English Augustans had learned from French and Italian critics of the 1630s to accuse those they disliked of writing the most airy and contrived forms of verse – morphological poem, acrostic, anagram, paradox. Here Benlowes' conceits are so extreme as to be dangerous to a reader's mental health. This was to become a standard motif in Swift and Pope. The thin partition between bad taste and madness recalls the Foucauldian thesis of the cultural asylum of the Enlightenment. Prynne, the old Parliamentary nemesis of Royalists and an important figure in *Hudibras*, is connected to the Baroque poet. Popular government is analogous to the riddling nonsense of Benlowesian rhetoric. The "far-fet" metaphors, "quibbles and clenches" are the flimsy building blocks of the Baroque. The world of the low-life laborers and artisans – pudding-eating jugglers in the circus and hatmakers – are the crass figures of Augustan carnival.

What is clear is that a figure like Benlowes, whose passion for creaturely emblem and analogy would not appear again in English poetry until the time of Smart and Blake, marks the end of a tradition.

[77] Samuel Butler, *Characters*, ed. C. W. Davies (Cleveland: Case Western Reserve, 1970), 87–90.

3

Pope and mature Augustanism

Belinda alone in the world of things

Pope will always be the great problem for students of eighteenth-century poetry. Without the intellectual edge of Dryden, or the savage moralism of Swift, he has been presented as the mature representative of the Augustan middle. Lovejoy, Cassirer, and Becker chose to place the *Essay on Man* as a centerpiece of rational humanizing in the period, and Mack (Pope's most important academic champion), through his splendid commentary on the *Essay on Man*, has made Pope appear as a late Renaissance syncretist.

Speaking of the sweep and power of the *Essay*, Mack situates Pope as the last great figure of Renaissance Humanism. Therefore, he must be understood in

the light of Renaissance thought and literature. Here the ideas we have dealt with so far on the philosophical plane can be studied in formulations elaborated and particularized by the literary imagination of centuries, and arranged in a pattern or formed *Weltanschauung* that seeks to take hold of the relations of God and man not through theorem but through symbol . . .

In Renaissance thinking, as a number of recent studies have emphasized, one of the most striking features is the powerful conception of the universe as order with its twofold aspect of hierarchy (the principle of plenitude circumstantially filled out) and union.[1]

Pope by Mack's estimation was creating a massive and synthetic symbol of Renaissance plenitude and late-Medieval theology. According to this view Pope combined the virtues of humanistic inclusiveness so admired by the older "history of ideas school" and the imagistic complexity – the richness of the symbol – which was the requirement of New Critical fashion. Leavis in his *Revaluation* would show that Pope had the same virtues of ambiguity and density that had been claimed for Donne and Marvell. Mack could discover in Pope's amorphous system the Hookerian and Thomist distinctions of Divine and natural law, the microcosmic man of

---

[1] Maynard Mack in his Preface to *The Essay on Man* in *Poems of Alexander Pope* ed. J. Butt (New Haven: Yale University Press, 1950), vol. III, xlvii–xlviii.

Pico, the macrocosmic speculum (mirror of creation) of Neoplatonism, and the cosmology of Milton. No doubt, some of these matters appear in Pope, but surely they are seen through the refractions of doubt and novelty which I have been tracing from Butler to Swift, and also in Pope's contemporaries. I hope it is not too disparaging of several important critics to say that this imagined continuity with the Renaissance, which neatly dovetailed with the project of New Criticism, was rather fanciful in placing Pope in the intellectual confines of the earlier period. An author who felt the anxieties of cultural and imaginative change as sharply as the author of *The Dunciad*, whose chief use of Milton was in constructing effects of burlesque, and who was all his life a stern critic of the "Baroque confusion" of Donne and his contemporaries – who, indeed, offered in the *Peri Bathous* the most complete criticism of the conceitful style in the whole epoch – cannot, without reservations, be called the last bastion of the English Renaissance. His "rewriting" of Donne's Satires is, in one sense, a writing them into the Augustan canon by polishing their formal and intellectual indelicacies. Even as a student of Dryden, and there can be no greater, Pope failed to put to use all those elements which most intimately connect the older poet to his own century. Pope was uninterested in or incapable of following the example of those poems of Dryden where the Baroque elements constitute the heart of the project – the *Eleanora, Killigrew*, the allegorical narrative of *The Hind and the Panther*, and the first of the "St. Cecilia's Day Odes." Reuben Brower went even farther than Mack and placed Pope in the line of Shakespeare. Speaking about *The Rape of the Lock*, he explained:

Significantly enough, Ariel comes from *The Tempest*, the Shakespearean play that is most thoroughly permeated by Ovidian metamorphosis. In its union of the comedy of young love with classical myth and fairy lore, *The Rape of the Lock* stands as Pope's *Midsummer Night's Dream*, the last successful work in the Renaissance mythological tradition that includes the tales of Marlowe, Lodge, and Drayton, and the plays of Lyly. Pope's success in this mode, like the Elizabethans', depends less on learning than on a happy gift of mythological invention.[2]

My own revaluation of Pope must begin with *The Rape of the Lock*. If Mack's notion of Pope's intellectual solidarity with the Renaissance worldview appears dubious, Brower's claim for *The Rape of the Lock* is more subtle. There is no doubt some of the atmosphere of gaudiness and translucence in the *Rape* which abounds in Drayton's *Nimphidia* or Shakespeare's *A Midsummer Night's Dream*, and Pope wished to produce a fanciful web of imagery. His shimmering surface effects call to mind the pyrotechnics of Marlowe's *Hero and Leander*.

[2] Reuben A. Brower, *Alexander Pope: The Poetry of Allusion* (Oxford: Oxford University Press, 1968), 150.

> So fair a church as this had Venus none;
> The walls were of discolored jasper stone,
> Wherein was Proteus carved, and o'erhead
> A lively vine of green sea agate spread,
> Where, by one hand, light-headed Bacchus hung,
> And with the other wine from grapes outwrung.
> Of crystal shining fair the pavement was;
> The town of Sestos called it Venus' glass.
>
> (*Hero and Leander*, 135–142)

The Rape of the Lock is a fully realized poem, well enameled and finely polished, but the mirror of Belinda does not quite attain to the lavishness of the mirror of Venus:

> And now, unveil'd, the *Toilet* stands display'd,
> Each Silver Vase in mystic Order laid.
> First, rob'd in White, the Nymph intent adores
> With head uncover'd, the *Cosmetic Pow'rs*.
> A heav'nly Image in the Glass appears,
> To that she bends, to that her eyes she rears;
> Th' inferior Priestess, at her Altar's side,
> Trembling, begins the sacred Rites of Pride.
>
> (*The Rape of the Lock*, I, 121–128)

Marlowe's mirror is, in the broadest sense, allegorical. It is the mirror of love in Ovidian terms, but the larger poem embraces several other specular relations, most importantly, the Neoplatonic reflection of the particular in the ideal. The Marlovian world, while a cartoon, is a cartoon of a metaphysical reality. As Shakespeare's fine, frenzied poet (in *A Midsummer Night's Dream*) looks "from heaven to earth, from earth to heaven," he "bodies forth forms," not only reenacting the Christian-Platonic Creation from nothing, but viewing life in the mirror of ideal existence. Pope's world is not a world of allegory in the true sense, and certainly not a dualistic world. Shortly before the lines quoted above, Belinda's spiritual guardian, Ariel, observes the world in another mirror.

> Late, as I ranged the Crystal Wilds of Air,
> In the clear mirror of thy ruling *Star*
> I saw, alas! some dread Event impend.
>
> (*The Rape of the Lock*, I, 108–110)

That is to say that Ariel has astrological and spiritual powers, and comes to inform his charge of the future. Pope's own note to the line reads simply, "in the clear Mirror] *The Language of the Platonists, the writers of the intelligible world of the Spirits, etc.*"[3] This note is an attempt to sharpen and clarify Pope's own satirical attitude toward the spiritual extravagances of an

---

[3] Pope, *Poems*, vol. II, 117.

earlier age. The language of the "intelligible world" is taken from the
lengthy excoriation of Platonists and astrologers in the second book of
Hudibras. In a poem of mockery like *The Rape of the Lock*, we do not expect
metaphysical seriousness, but we do expect a certain playing of the game.
We expect the poet to pursue the tenor of his own language, and to make
good on the logic of his myth. Shakespeare and Marlowe are true to the
implications of the metaphysical binarism we have been describing and
illustrate it by the double world (real/ideal, practical/meditative,
mundane/transcendent, and human/fairy). These binarisms are the
central mark in the dominant tradition of Renaissance analogy. The tragic
love plot (in the case of *Hero and Leander*) and the magical marriage plot (in
the case of *Midsummer Night's Dream*) are realized over all impediments. The
machinery of the woodland transformation, supernatural contrivance and
the like, however fanciful, are part of the economy of the moral denoue-
ment. By contrast the Sylphs have no effect on *The Rape of the Lock*. Pope,
apparently, did not place them in the poem to put the action forward, and
they neither impede nor hasten it. Although they do participate in the
purely quotidian activities of Belinda's day – "These set the Head, and
those divide the hair" (I, 146) – and sometimes fire the sleeping imagination
to attend more minutely to sartorial affairs, "in Dreams, Invention we
bestow, / To change a *Flounce* or add a *Furbelo*" (II, 99–100) – their role in
the action of the poem is infinitesimal. The admonitions of Ariel are
obliterated by the first casual event upon Belinda's awaking, and Crispissa's
evanescent body is irrelevantly divided by the fatal scissors at the moment
of truth. The blowing "back of her hair" and the twitching of "Diamond in
her ear" (III, 13 and 137) are ineffectual warnings – the amassed army of
sylphs cannot even be perceived by Belinda. This one point Johnson
concedes to John Dennis, who savagely attacked Pope's poem.

It is remarked by Dennis likewise, that the machinery is superfluous; that by all the
bustle of preternatural operation, the main event is neither hastened nor retarded.
To this charge an efficacious answer is not easily made. The sylphs cannot be said
to help or to oppose, and it must be allowed to imply some want of art, that their
power has not been sufficiently intermingled with the action.[4]

The irrelevance of the sylphs is maintained to the very end. The power
of the gnomes is placed in the subjunctive throughout – "*If* e'er thy Gnome
could spoil a grace, / Or raise a Pimple on a beauteous Face" (IV, 67–68).
Again they have nothing to do with the Lock's apotheosis. They merely
"behold it kindling as it flies / And pleas'd pursue its progress through the
skies" (V, 131–132). In a sense they are a double for the pointed voyeurism
of the narrator and his characters. They "watch," "o'erlook," "survey,"

[4] Samuel Johnson, *The Lives of the English Poets*, ed. G. Birkbeck Hill (Oxford: Clarendon Press,
1905), vol. II, 155.

and their chief, Ariel, when the Lock is threatened, is "Amazed, confused."
Incapable of action and frozen in the fanciful tableau, Ariel "found his
Pow'r expired / Resigned to Fate, and with a sigh retired" (III, 145–146).

The element of the sylphs is tea (which is also the element of the queen's
court), and their substance air. They display the trivial social energy which
is introduced in the opening lines, but they do not even really arrange the
incidental props of the bedroom. "The light militia" is a provincial army
that (unlike the regular redcoats) is rarely called into battle. They have the
same power that honor has to stave off male advances in "midnight
masquerades," which from the example of the poem appears to be an
unexercised power. In their most extraordinary moment in the poem they
fly luxuriantly amid the breezes that waft Belinda's boat down the Thames
to Hampton Court.

> He summons strait his Denizens of Air
> The lucid Squadrons round the Sails repair . . .
> Some to the Sun their Insect-Wings unfold,
> Waft on the Breeze, or sink in Clouds of Gold.
> Transparent Forms too fine for mortal Sight,
> Their fluid Bodies half dissolv'd in Light.
> Loose to the Wind their airy Garments flew,
> Thin glittering Textures of the filmy Dew;
>
> (*The Rape of the Lock*, II, 55–64)

Here Pope uses "denizens" in its eighteenth-century legal sense as "naturalized aliens"[5] and they seem beings at once alien and fanciful, vaguely
atmospheric like the aureate cupids of rococo paintings. We are surprised
in the succeeding speech of Ariel that such minimal substances are
sometimes charged not only with guiding "all the actions" of mortals, but
rolling the planets, painting the rainbow, and straightening the paths of
comets. These offices have been dexterously chosen by Pope, for they are
exactly the activities which Newton had so recently proved to be the
passive results of the general laws of gravity and optics. "God said *Let
Newton be!* and All was *Light*" are the words of Pope, and there is a good deal
of pathos in the arcane machinery of medieval *topos* dissolving into the
Newtonian landscape.

We know that Pope expended great labor on the sylphs, expanding his
original two-canto poem of 330 lines (in which they do not appear) to the
five-canto version we read today. I think we must concede that the sylphs
(along with Belinda and the single moment of Sir Plume) are the most
successful elements of the poem. This sense of their looming over the poem
– almost constituting the poem's *raison d'être* – demands some better
explanation of their work in the fable. One school of critics has sexualized

[5] Pope, *Poems*, vol. II, 224.

their role. David Morris, who has written one of the best studies of Pope's poems, says:

It is the sylphs, however, added to the original poem in 1714, who perfectly represent the abstracted sexuality of the beau monde. These airy creatures have achieved a state of virtual disembodiment. Although less "refined" (ii 81) than pure angelic spirits, they have shed the flesh and blood of their previous existence as coquettes (i 65) and function now as the reigning deities of fashion. They characterize a world of folly which Pope depicts as a refraction of its prototype in Restoration comedy . . . In the sylph-governed realm of the beau monde, by contrast, sexual desire is not satisfied in concealment but endlessly and openly deferred through perpetual displacements onto objects, images and words. Thus the marbled cane and namesake feather of Sir Plume – the phallic emblems of his overrefinement – display something like a self-induced impotence, comically duplicated in his blustering speech.[6]

Aside from the standard Freudian inversions of logic there are several problems here. First of all, the world of the poem is in no sense "sylph-governed"; it is governed by human whim and appetite. The sylphs are observers and ineffectual agents. Secondly, they are exactly as refined as Miltonic angels, upon which they are partly modeled. Milton's angels are rarefied bodies with digestive and sexual natures – they are not orthodox, immaterial angels in any respect except their powers. Lastly, Sir Plume's impotence and the symbols of it are irrelevant to an analysis of the sylphs, and if the humans and the sylphs have the same kind of deferrals and inhibitions, what could be the point of adding preternatural agents to the poem? On his point about the sylphs returning as specular doubles of earthly women, more in a moment. I do not think the ethos of the beau monde is very far at all in its sexual reality from that of Restoration drama. In fact, Arabella Fermor, the original of Belinda, was disturbed by the realism of the poem. In this regard, Leopold Damrosch remarks:

In the *Rape* the sexual truth is finally admitted when Belinda wishes the Baron had been "content to seize / Hairs less in sight, or any hairs but these" (IV. 175–76). This sort of innuendo was remarkably popular.[7]

Damrosch goes on to illustrate a parallel sexual innuendo in Elijah Fenton's "The Fair Nun," a poem which combines anti-Catholic, Hudibrastic, and overt sexual humor.

In the perennially quoted and re-quoted essay of Cleanth Brooks the sylphs are treated differently. I will pass by his remark, at once facile and embarrassing, that they "represent Pope's attempt to do justice to the

---

[6] David Morris, *Alexander Pope: The Genius of Sense* (Cambridge, Mass.: Harvard University Press, 1984), 92.

[7] Leopold Damrosch Jr., *The Imaginative World of Alexander Pope* (Berkeley and Los Angeles: University of California Press, 1987), 46.

female mind," and move on to more fertile ground. Laying out the place of
the sylphs in the poem Brooks explains:

The sylphs do represent the supernatural, though the supernatural reduced, of
course, to its flimsiest proportions. The poet has been very careful here. Even
Belinda is not made to take their existence too seriously . . .
    It is precisely the poet's handling of the supernatural – the level at which he is
willing to entertain it – the amused qualifications which he demands of it – that
makes it possible for him to state his attitude with full complexity.[8]

For Brooks this deeper complexity is social. The sylphs are the symbols or
signs of honor, and honor is part of the slippery grammar of personal
relations. In what sense this social strategizing involves or ought to involve
the supernatural, however diminished, is not made clear. But Brooks has
begun to give us some insight. What does it mean to ask the question about
the degree, or to use Brooks' word, "level," at which Pope is "willing to
entertain" the possibility of the supernatural and what "qualifications he
demands of" the supernatural? This is a peculiar problem, indeed. If it were
asked of Shakespeare, Donne, Milton, or even Dryden, what would it mean?
It hints glimmeringly at the real problem of the sylphs. To pursue this track
further we must look at what very well might be called the central passage of
the whole poem. It is the passage most likely to help us answer the question
of the qualifications and levels of the supernatural, and Pope's willingness to
entertain them. At line 29 of the opening canto, Ariel addresses Belinda:

> If e'er one Vision touch'd thy infant Thought,
> Of all the Nurse and all the Priest have taught,
> Of airy Elves by Moonlight Shadows seen,
> The silver Token, and the circled Green,
> Or Virgins visited by Angel-Pow'rs,
> With Golden Crowns and Wreaths of heav'nly Flow'rs,
> Hear and Believe! thy own Importance know,
> Nor bound thy narrow Views to Things below.
> Some secret Truths from Learned Pride conceal'd,
> To Maids alone and Children are reveal'd:
> What tho' no credit doubting Wits may give?
> The Fair and Innocent shall still believe.
>
> (*The Rape of the Lock*, 1, 29–40)

In chapter 1 I tried to lay out the satirical formula of Samuel Butler in a
way that might help explain the remarkable shrinkage of spiritual imagination, particularly in the sphere of poetry, during the later seventeenth
century. In a way infinitely subtler than *Hudibras*, and in a tone infinitely
sweeter than *A Tale of a Tub*, Pope has introduced the same satirical
formula, and by analyzing it we may see the real value of the sylphs in

[8] Cleanth Brooks, *The Well Wrought Urn* (New York: Harvest, 1947), 88–89.

Pope's imaginative cosmos. Here we see the two forms of ignorance – the superstitious and the enthusiastic – introduced as the formative (infant) modes of Belinda's moral education. The superstitious here is the learned ignorance of priestly instruction, the kind Belinda (and Pope) as a wealthy Catholic recusant would have received from a Jesuit or parish tutor; on the other hand, the nurse represents unlearned and popular error, what Butler calls "zeal." We remember from Butler's *Characters* that religious culture depends on the ignorance of women, who listen to the preposterous tales of the Jesuit or the Quaker. This theory was endlessly reworked in the eighteenth century – the numerous tracts on the credulity of women in the face of the Methodist temptation replaced earlier fears of the "womanish conventicles" and holy meeting houses of the Civil War. The nurse takes her place among the deceiving and deceived folk – what Hobbes called "base-born lunacy." Swift's Lilliputians made this a central issue of feminine *paideia*.

> In the Female Nurseries, the young Girls of Quality are educated much like the Males, only they are dressed by orderly Servants of their own Sex, but always in the Presence of a Professor or Deputy, until they come to dress themselves, which is at five Years old. And if it be found that these Nurses ever presume to entertain the Girls with frightful or foolish Stories, or the common Follies practised by Chamber-Maids among us; they are publicly whipped thrice about the City, imprisoned for a Year, and banished for Life to the most desolate Parts of the Country.[9]

The specific lore that Pope had chosen for his parent superstition was the Rosicrucian system. He imagines it from the start as a special temptation (like ombre and ghost stories) for young women. This may have been taken directly from Butler, who lays out, in canto iii of the second part of *Hudibras*, the mysteries of the "Rosey-Cross" in a way oddly applicable to the *Rape*.

> The *Rosy-crucian* way's more sure,
> To bring the Lady to the Lure,
> Each of 'em has a sev'ral Gin,
> To catch *Intelligences* in.
> Some by the Nose with fumes trap'an em,
> As *Dunstan* did the *Devil's Grannum*,
> Others with *Characters* and *Words*,
> Catch 'em as men in nets do birds.
> And some with *Symbols, Songs,* and *Tricks*
> Engrav'd in *Planetary* nicks.   (*Hudibras*, ii, iii, 613–622)

From this and other passages of the Sidrophel narrative Pope derives his language of the "intelligible world," "mystic mazes" and the like. The Rosy-crucian himself is simply an extravagant mountebank who preys

---

[9] Jonathan Swift, *Gulliver's Travels* (New York: Norton, 1961), 43.

upon the innocent faithful. This charlatan spiritualism is expressly connected to the popular reading culture of women and the rising popularity
of the novel in Pope's prefatory letter to Arabella Fermor.

> The Rosicrucians are a people I must bring you acquainted with. The best
> account I know of them is in a French book call'd *Le Comte de Gabalis*, which both
> in its title and size is so like a *Novel*, that many of the fair Sex have read it for one
> by mistake.   ("To Miss Arabella Fermor," 217)

The episode described in *The Rape* is the material of the novel. As the
opening gambit in a story of sexual temptation and humiliation at court, it
looks forward to Fanny Burney. The novelistic landscape of the domestic
scene is unmistakable and the metonymies of billet doux, two letters and a
page, the toilet, and the game of ombre help to indicate the impossibility of
any real transcendence. All the poems of the volume of 1717, except the
Essay on Criticism, are dominated by synecdochal and metonymic figures,
and the principal mode of organization in the non-narrative *Temple of Fame*
and *Windsor Forest* is spatial association. In lieu of iconic schema, Pope
arranges things in an artful chaos. In so doing he contributes to the ethos of
the novel.

   If we look closer at the passage of the Nurse and Priest we find that the
vision has two sources. There is the tutelary angel of Baroque Catholic
theology, which guards the maiden's virginity, and there is the fairy world
of "Moonlight shadows." The sylphs combine the qualities of both the
tutelary angel and the fairy. By combining the two, Pope can make light of
particular providence, a doctrine which he several times argues against in
his letters,[10] as a part of the world of purely literary fancy. In his letter to
Edward Blount he describes the prayers of the Catholics besieged at
Barcelona in August 1714 in terms of the martial and divine forces he has
been recently considering in his translation of the *Iliad*:

> To disarm me indeed may be but prudential, considering what armies I have at
> present on foot, and in my service: a hundred thousand *Grecians* are no contemptible
> body; for all that I can tell, they may be as formidable as four thousand *Priests*; and
> they seem proper forces to send against those in *Barcelona*. That siege deserves as
> great a poem as the *Iliad*, and the machining part of poetry would be the juster in it,
> as they say the inhabitants expect Angels from Heaven to come to their assistance.
> May I venture to say, who am a Papist, and to say to you who are a Papist, that
> nothing is more astonishing to me, than that the people so greatly warmed with a
> sense of Liberty, should be capable of harbouring such weak Superstition, and that
> so much bravery and so much folly, can inhabit the same breast.

Here the "machinery" is part of popular superstition. By so equating moral
theology with imagination in *The Rape*, as he was to do at greater length

---

[10] *The Correspondence of Alexander Pope*, ed. G. Sherburn (Oxford: Clarendon Press, 1956), vol. I,
    246–247.

one year later in *Eloisa to Abelard*, Pope places himself as a Catholic in an ambiguous position. Pope's Catholicism was neither orthodox nor zealous, and appears to have been preserved primarily as a means of honoring his parents. Of course, a formulation which conflates Catholicism and the realm of fancy did not start with Pope. Hobbes in the penultimate section of *Leviathan* had drawn an elaborate analogy between the Catholic church and the land of Fairy:

For from the time that the Bishop of Rome had gotten to be acknowledged for Bishop Universall, by pretense of Succession to St. Peter, their whole Hierarchy, or Kingdome of Darknesse, may be compared not unfitly to the *Kingdome of Fairies*; that is to the old Wives *Fables* in England, concerning *ghosts* and *spirits* and the feats they play in the night . . . The *Ecclesiatiques* are *Spirituall* men, and *Ghostly* Fathers, the Fairies are *Spirits* and *Ghosts*. *Fairies* and *Ghosts* inhabit Darknesse, Solitude, and Graves. The *Ecclesiatiques* walk in obscurity of Doctrine, in Monasteries, Churches, and Churchyards . . . The *Ecclesiastiques* have their Cathedral Churches, . . . Holy Water, and certain Charmes called Excorcismes . . . The Fairies also have their enchanted Castles, and certain Gigantique Ghosts, that domineer over the regions round about them . . . In what Shop, or Operatory the *Fairies* make their Enchantment, the old Wives have not determined. But the Operatories of the Clergy are known well enough to be the Universities.[11]

This passage comes near the end of a long discourse on the impossibility of angelic and spiritual existences, and the springs of "phantasme" and superstition. The old wives stand in for the Nurse of *The Rape*, the force of popular opinion in preserving ignorance[12] as the Priest in Pope represents more sophisticated superstition. English culture was by no means monolithic on this point. Twenty years after *Leviathan* we see John Aubrey speak of the controversy over the fairy world in terms of the spread of educated culture.

Before Printing, Old-wives Tales were ingeniose: and since Printing came in fashion, till a little before the Civil-warre, the ordinary sort of people were not taught to read: now-a-days Bookes are common, and most of the poor people understand letters: and the many good Bookes, and Variety of Turnes of Affaires, have put all the old Fables out of dores: and the divine art of Printing and Gunpowder have frighted away Robin-good-fellow and the Fayries.[13]

[11] Thomas Hobbes, *Leviathan*, ed. Richard Tuck (Cambridge: Cambridge University Press, 1991), 481.

[12] There is a typical passage of this kind in Swift's mentor, William Temple. Speaking of the dubious (and "Gothic") side of poetic imagination he remarks: "From the same perhaps may be derived all the visionary Tribe of *Faries*, *Elves*, and *Goblins*, of *Sprites* and of *Bul-beggars*, that serve not only to fright Children into whatever their nurses please, but sometimes, by lasting Impressions, to disquiet the sleeps and the very Lives of Men and Women, till they grow to years of Discretion; and that, God knows, is the Period of time which some People Arrive to but very late, and perhaps others never" quoted from "Of Poetry," in *Critical Essays of the Seventeenth Century*, vol. III, 1685–1700, ed. J. E. Spingarn (London: Oxford University Press, 1909), 97.

[13] From John Aubrey, *Remaines of Gentilisme and Judaisme*; quoted in *The Oxford Book of the Supernatural*, ed. D. J. Enright (New York: Oxford, 1994), 262.

The association of Catholic and fairy, like the association of Catholic with gypsy, throughout the period from the Restoration to the nineteenth century helped to color the Papist religion with childishness, ignorance, secrecy, and stealth; it begins to usher in the mature phase of Gothicism in England which was formed upon the anxiety that superstitious forces were indestructible and omnipresent. The shadowy monks that crowd the pages of Augustan poetry from the dark brother at the start of Parnell's "Night Piece on Death" to the nun hidden in William Collins' apostrophe to "Evening" betoken the magnitude of this resilience, and chart a sure course to the better known Gothic fiction of Walpole, Radcliffe, and Lewis. In one sense Pope's work is such a work of refracted Gothicism.

This helps us finally to understand the sylphs. The sylphs in Pope are not symbols of oppressed sexual emotions, nor are they the noble residue of the Christian religion. The sylphs do not exist. Their non-existence, the complete evaporation of the spiritual apparatus of the Baroque, is the very reason why they are placed in the poem. They can move nothing in "the Toyshop" of Belinda's heart, because they are not present. They are not possible either in their fairy or angelic form, nor do they intervene in the manner of Homeric gods. If they support the claims of honor, it is only because honor is also merely a word – an inactive fiction in the period after the decline of the romance. Falstaff says that "Honour is a name for the man who died o' Wednesday," and the sylphs like honor are incompatible with the moral world of Pope. The imagination alone can add them. They are beautiful traces of cultural memory. Their elaboration only enforces the strict realization of their metaphysical impossibility.

In the absence of spiritual machinery the reader is forced to recognize the autonomy of Belinda – and through Belinda the autonomy of the man or woman of sentiment. By collapsing the heavenly and the demonic spheres, the binarism of Renaissance spirituality becomes purely psychological. What replaces them are the higher sphere of charm and lower sphere of spleen. As the spleen was originally associated in Burton with an overactive religious imagination, it is now associated with any religious habit. The poet has endowed Belinda's desire with all the qualities of the Renaissance macrocosm, and in so doing he has shown like Butler and Rochester before him that those cosmic forces were a fiction – as fanciful and flimsy as honor, virginity, and manners. At the same time Pope marks, perhaps unconsciously, the eclipse of the literature of *gentillesse* and ideal Eros. Like the "Nothing" of Rochester,

> Great Negative, how vainly would the wise
> Inquire, define, distinguish, teach, devise,
> Didst thou not stand to point their blind philosophies.
>
> (Rochester, "Upon Nothing", 28–30)

Pope's sylphs underline the emptiness of moral vision. The sylphs represent what has no force, the horizon of the impossible.

The sylphs, the sphere of the angelic and the fatal, lack the real force and weight of the personified "Discord" of Boileau, the "Ignorance" of Butler, the "Absurdity" of Hobbes, or Dryden's "Dullness." All these are substantial elements in the moral landscape of the Augustan world. Their role is to anatomize the vices of the vain and ignorant and to clear a space for the Lockeian *sensus communis*. Such a withering critique retains the normative power of traditional satire. In this difference lies the peculiar power and charm of Pope's poem. For the modern reader, Butler and Swift may appear to bludgeon mankind. Their satire is often violent, sometimes repellent. *The Rape of the Lock*, while performing the cultural work of Augustan satire – that is, clearing away the rubble of the past, and making a space for the imperturbable observer – does it with such grace and *élan* that it goes unnoticed. The sylphs, which "bask and whiten in the blaze of day" are innocent and joyous. They may cast only a mild shadow of regret over the reader, but they leave behind the appearance of play. *Saeva indignatio* is replaced with unflappable charm. For this reason the vulgar and strident elements which Pope borrows from *Hudibras* are invisible. The misty Rosicrucian spirits, the cane of Sir Plume, like the trumpet of fame in *The Temple*, seem far removed from the bloody burlesque of Butler. But they are all borrowed from it.[14] With *The Rape of the Lock* Augustan satire is domesticated and elevated, and from then on it can disarm its audience.

For this task Pope was uniquely suited. He, like Keats after him, was enamored of the surfaces of things. Rochester and Dryden were sinewy and argumentative rhetoricians; neither excelled in scene painting. Butler was incapable of imagining ideal beauty. Swift was a deeply prosaic and agitated soul. He had no interest in ideal beauty, either in its primitive or in its civilized mode. But Pope was born to create an ideal décor, and the set

---

[14] I should mention one important scene in *Hudibras*. In the third part, canto i, 1423–1434, Hudibras is terrified by the voice of a ghost in the dark which is in fact the voice of his squire, Ralpho, who is hiding behind a sofa. Ralpho, in league with Hudibras' beloved Lady, is repaying his master for a series of deceptions and injustices. This guardian power explains himself with sylph-like irony:

> *Sir (Quoth the Voice) Y' are no such Sophy,*
> *As You would have the World judge of Ye,*
> *If You design to weigh Talents,*
> *I'th' Standard of Your own false Ballance:*
> *Or think it possible to know,*
> *Us Ghosts, as well as we so you.*
> *We, who have been the everlasting*
> *Companions of Your Drubs and Basting:*
> *And never left you in Contest*
> *With Male or Female, Man or Beast,*
> *But prov'd as true t' ye, and intire*
> *In all adventures as your Squire.*

pieces of *The Rape of the Lock* and *The Temple of Fame* are the most perfect realizations of the Rococo element in the Augustan project. Before he "stoop'd to Truth and moralized his Song," Pope created four great works of fantasy. By fantasy I mean perception elevated and brightened as in the Greek φαντασία.[15] Pope and Keats were geniuses of description. Not penetrating thought, but penetrating sight, enabled them to recast the work of the eye as the work of imagination. This was because they shared a rare gift – the gift of enjoying the things before them. This enjoyment, though, was heightened by the fact that these things in the world could be so perfectly realized for them as things of art. For both poets the only residue of the medieval was an aesthetic aura, and there is a strange, unrecognized kinship between "Eloisa to Abelard" and "The Eve of St. Agnes." Likewise, Shelley received from Pope those sylph-like projections of the poet's imagination which he placed in the tomb of Keats. He presented them in a diction and meter only slightly altered from their original.

> *One from a lucid urn of starry dew*
> *Washed his light limbs* as if embalming them;
> *Another clipt her profuse locks, and threw*
> *The wreath* upon him like an anadem.[16]

> (*Adonais*, 91–94, italics added)

I must quote at length from a letter Pope wrote to his friend Edward Blount on June 2, 1725.

Let the young ladies be assured I make nothing new in my Gardens without wishing to see the print of their Fairy Steps in every part of 'em. I have put the last hand to my works of this kind, in happily finishing the subterraneous Way and Grotto; I there found a Spring of the clearest Water, which falls in a perpetual Rill, which echoes through the Cavern day and night. From the River Thames, you see thro' my Arch up a Walk of the Wilderness to a kind of open Temple, wholly composed of Shells in the Rustic Manner; and from the distance under the Temple you look down through a sloping Arcade of Trees, and see the Sails on the River passing suddenly and vanishing, as through a Perspective Glass. When you shoot the Doors of this Grotto, it becomes on the instant, from a luminous Room, a *Camera Obscura*; on the Walls of which all the objects of the River, Hills, Woods and Boats, are forming a moving Picture in their visible Radiations: And when you have a mind to light it up, it affords you a very different Scene: it is finished with Shells interspersed with Pieces of Looking-glass in angular forms; and in the Ceiling is a Star of the same Material, at which when a Lamp (of an orbicular figure of thin Alabaster) is hung in the Middle, a thousand pointed Rays glitter and are reflected over the Place. There are connected to this Grotto by a narrower

---

[15] Among the numerous meanings of this word, an ideal image formed of the thing percieved (or natural object) is important. It was used in this sense by Plutarch and other late ancient academic Platonists. Of course, it is also St. Paul's term for tempting and carnal imagination.

[16] *Shelley's Poetry and Prose*, ed. D. H. Reiman and S. B. Powers (New York: Norton, 1977), 394.

Passage two Porches, with niches and Seats; One towards the River, of smooth Stones, full of light and open; the other towards the Arch of Trees, rough with Shells, Flints and Iron Ore. The Bottom is paved with simple Pebble, as the adjoining walk up the Wilderness to the Temple is to be Cockle-shells in the natural Taste, agreeing not ill with the little dripping Murmur, and the Aquatic Idea of the whole Place. It wants nothing to complete it but a good Statue with an Inscription, like that beautiful antique one which you know I am so fond of,

> Huius Nympha loci, sacri, custodia fontis,
> Dormio, dum blandae sentio murmur aquae.
> Parce meum, quisquis tangis cava marmora somnum
> Rumpere, seu bibas, sive lavere, tace.

> Nymph of the grot these sacred Springs I keep,
> And to the Murmur of the Waters sleep;
> Whoe'er thou art, ah gently tread the Cave,
> To bathe in Silence, or in Silence lave.

You'll think I have been very Poetical in this Description, but it is pretty near the Truth. I wish you were here to bear Testimony how little it owes to Art, either the place itself, or the Image I give of it.[17]

In a world of artificial divinities and broken statuary Pope creates a startling image of beauty. The image has an artful naturalness, but it is a fantasy. In Pope's mind neither the letter nor the scene owe much to art. Pope's excitement over the spatial, the colorful, and the mundane enables him, more than any of his contemporaries, to fill the void of description left by the annihilating wave of satire. He does not require a moral or metaphysical schema upon which to build, but, like Keats, can construct an edifice upon appearances, and imbue them with an atmosphere of transcendence.

Pope's grotto is an example of the domination of spatial over moral landscape, for unlike Milton's Eden or Dryden's *Golden Age*, in the Popeian scene the visual supersedes all other considerations. Pope was like the sparrow in Keats' garden, a master of negative capability – "always in uncertainties, mysteries, doubts without any irritable reaching after fact or reason," his "sense of beauty overcame every difficulty."[18] Like Keats, and unlike any other English poet, he wrote a number of massive works of imagination, certainly equal to his best, before his twenty-eighth year. I agree with the many critics, beginning with Johnson, who see the *Essay on Man* as a great (even glorious) failure. It was an attempt to slow down the sense, growing throughout the eighteenth century, that the empirical man bore no resemblance or proportion to God, and that man lived in an accidentalist rather than providential realm. The *Essay on Man* points more vividly to the problem than the solution in its attempt to combine the

---

[17] *Correspondence of Alexander Pope*; vol. II, 297–298.
[18] John Keats, *Letters*, ed. H. E. Rollins (Cambridge, Mass.: Harvard University Press, 1971), 132.

unlike materials of humoral psychology, Mandevillean competition, and rationalist metaphysics in a network of loosely connected apothegms. Leaving aside *The Dunciad*, *Arbuthnot*, and the *Horatian Poems*, where Pope successfully entered the main stream of Augustan public satire, he should always be remembered for his singular capacity to raise edifices of great beauty under the enormous burden of an empirical poetic. He created in those early years four great works of fantasy – four works which seize upon the instruments of associative and metonymic art with marvelous results. In *Windsor Forest*, the fantasy of commerce; in *The Temple of Fame*, the fantasy of art; in "Eloisa to Abelard", the fantasy of love; and in *The Rape of the Lock*, his greatest poem, the fantasy of the quotidian.

It makes sense that the great poem following upon the irruption of Restoration satire should be a poem of the literal – of everyday life. The merely negative part of the Augustan project had succeeded in casting doubts upon perennial habits of the European mind. The broader field of spiritual figures had been leveled, and a new level of objectification was unavoidable. For this reason the sylphs must be portrayed as identical in nature to the various characters they protect – the prude, the coquette, and the others. They are in fact merely another name for those temporal women. The sylphs are nominal existences which add nothing to the real. They take the place in narrative that Hobbes grants to spiritual existences in nature – ontological fictions, props of fancy, charming delusions. This may explain why Pope apparently removed the angelic powers from "Eloisa to Abelard", where they may have more naturally been accommodated.[19]

The real subject of Pope's poem is the autonomous physical realm in which Belinda finds herself. Like the madmen of Foucault's enlightened empiricism, she is trapped in the company of objects, which being seen as the whole of reality, must define her. "Those eyes that must eclipse the day" are no longer the eyes of Petrarch's Laura, "tipped with central fire of the sun," but eyes attached to the apparent heterocosm of objects: the billet-doux, the fan, the lapdog, and the rest. The game of ombre, far from allegorizing Belinda's situation, merely gives microscopic attention to its existence as a game. It is not Middleton's *A Game at Chess*, which circumscribes the action of the pieces in a moral and political analogy. In Pope it is the literal game that counts, the sylphs resting comfortably on the card equivalent to his or her own part in the play. Pope added his *Key to the Rape of the Lock* to further deepen the sense in which the game of ombre and the sylphs are literal. By mocking the notion of a key which unlocks the

---

[19] In a letter about the poem to Richard Steele (November 16, 1712), written while it was in an early draft, Pope refers to the presence of angels: "I have confined the attendance of Guardian spirits to Heaven's favourites only?" These spirits do not appear in the published text (*The Correspondence of Alexander Pope*, vol. I, 153–154).

mysteries of the spiritual signatures of the poem, he mocks the very notion of allegoresis, as he was to do a few years later in his witty poems on *Gulliver's Travels*.

Belinda is the finest dramatization of what Charles Taylor calls the "punctual" self. Taylor begins by describing the building-block theory of Lockeian epistemology as an attempt to disassemble the atomic elements of experience, or consciousness, and goes on to say:

The aim of the disassembly is to reassemble our picture of the world, this time on a solid foundation, by following reliable rules of concatenation . . . In effecting the double movement of suspension and examination, we wrest the control of our thinking and outlook away from passion or custom or authority and assume responsibility for ourselves.[20]

And again,

Here I want to look at it [Locke's epistemology] in its aspect as a new, unprecedentedly radical form of self-objectification. The disengagement both from the activities of thought and from our unreflecting desires and tastes allows us to see ourselves as objects of far-reaching reformation. Rational control can extend to the re-creations of our habits, and hence of ourselves. The notion of "habit" has undergone a shift: it no longer carries its Aristotelian force, where our *"hexeis"* are formed against the background of a nature with a certain bent. Habits now link elements between which there are no more relations of natural fit. The proper connections are determined purely instrumentally, by what will bring the best results, pleasure, or happiness.[21]

Now Belinda does not exactly do this disassembling and reassembling for herself like a conscious acolyte of Lockeian self-fashioning. But her world is a reassembled and particularized world bereft of obvious purpose, and stripped of obvious principles of moral fitness. Belinda cannot help but represent the anxiety of a world released from the ordering figures of traditional analogy. We watch her as Glumdalclitch watches Gulliver in Book II of *Gulliver's Travels*. It is not surprising then that when Pope wrote his odd prefatory verses for the Scriblerian edition of Gulliver he recast Glumdalclitch, the type of the neurotic Augustan observer, in terms derived from Belinda, almost two decades after *The Rape of the Lock*.

> Soon as *Glumdalclitch* mist her pleasing Care,
> She wept, she blubbered and she tore her Hair.
> No *British* Miss sincerer grief has known,
> Her squirrel missing, or her Sparrow flown.
> She furl'd her Sampler, and hawl'd in her Thread,
> And stuck her Needle into *Grildrig*'s Bed.
>
> (*Verses on Gulliver's Travels*, II, 1–6)

[20] Charles Taylor, *Sources of the Self: The Making of Modern Identity* (Cambridge, Mass.: Harvard University Press, 1989), 167.
[21] Ibid., 171.

Here are the accouterments and structures of the quotidian world, and the syntax of *The Rape of the Lock*. Glumdalclitch's world bears the same relation to Britain that Belinda's does to the Homeric. Here the "British Miss" that has known "no sincerer grief" connects the world of the Brobdingnagians to that of England as "Not youthful Kings in Battel seiz'd alive" (*Rape*, IV, 3) connected Belinda to the world of martial epic. The English scene is the tenor of these two sublime vehicles – the Homeric and the Brobdingnagian. Pope retrospectively hints that we might observe Belinda, objectified and isolated, as the heroine in Swift viewed her captive giant.

Unlike the Petrarchan woman, Belinda judges all by appearances – fearing the loss of her lock more than the capture of "hairs less in sight than these." She has no pride of nature, only of place. She is also judged as an appearance and, in our modern sense, objectified. Pope's creation was truly novel. Boileau's *Le Lutrin*, on which it is modeled, is by comparison archaic. The "Discord" which fosters the rebellion of the choir master from the abbot in that poem is real. Boileau feels the destructiveness of a petty and polluted church, and pokes fun to admonish. The burlesque is actually rather subtle because the ecclesiastical sphere is being recast in the language of classical epic – but the church retains some weight and authority. When the *chanter* dreams of the new altar rising up out of Hell, Boileau is not making fun of altars or hell, he is making fun of the misplaced vocations of a corrupt priesthood.[22] Boileau, troubled by the reaction to some passages of his travesty, added two long cantos, the last rising up to a level of high theological seriousness. The work in the end can be called controversial and as I have shown in chapter 1, mature Augustan satire – Rochester, Butler, Swift, Pope – cannot accept the concept of meaningful controversy. Augustan ridicule must question the claims of reason itself. In this particularly, Augustan satire foreshadows the Romantic fear of public rationality.

Pope, no doubt troubled by the moral vacuum he had created, made one last addition to *The Rape of the Lock* before the *Poems* of 1717 was published. This was the soliloquy of Clarissa, a straightforward and irrelevant moral speech in imitation of the famous admonitions of Sarpedon to Glaucon in

---

[22] The history of the uses of Boileau in English is convoluted, but of central importance. The first English translator of *Le Lutrin*, O. N., chose to frame his poem with canto "arguments" in the style of Butler and use the important vocabulary of *Hudibras*: "lunacy," "zeal," "fanatic," etc. In fact, the whole range of Boileau translators, who appeared on the scene between 1678 and 1684 at the time of the Popish Plot and Exclusion Crisis, politicized and localized their translations largely through "Butlerisms" in language, thought, and meter. This was true particularly of John Crowne, the best and most interesting of them, who appears to have had a more direct influence on Dryden, Oldham, and Pope. Thus, Crowne, like N. O., presents the poem as a kind of intermittent allegory of the British scene. Bulter himself (like Rochester) had translated one of Boileau's Satires (the second), which he entitled "A Satire to a Bad Poet."

the *Iliad*. Much ink has been wasted on this speech already, and I do not wish to treat the poem again as a simple and serious moralization of the "vanities of women." The vanity of Belinda is the vanity of the unmoored perceiver surrounded by shifting tokens of empirical existence. No moral can console the loss of her lock, because it has no moral significance. That, in a sense, creates the surface humor of the poem. But the deeper significance of the poem has nothing to do with Arabella Fermor or the accidental customs of the time. The pathos of the poem comes from our own sense of its novelty framed in the gorgeous nonsense of a once potent symbolism. We pursue, like the sylphs, the lock into the sky created by the poet as a memorial of his own genius and as an elegy to the tradition of classical and Renaissance transcendence. It is the muse, the embodiment of fancy, alone that sees the lock ascend. The eye of the poet is no longer the instrument which pierces the metaphysical veil, but rather the power that concocts the transcendent. The lock ascended into heaven like Romulus, seen only by one man. This man is Pope himself. Like the comet of Marvell's "Cromwell Ode," it shot through nature beyond the narrow limits of traditional morality. Only Butler's lunatic, the prognosticating wizard Partridge, can see it now, but the Fall of Rome, which is foreshadowed in it, unbeknownst to Pope, betokened the fall from grace of the whole Italianate culture, conquered by the cosmetic empire of Britain, of which Belinda is queen. The pains suffered by wayward sylphs in the first canto leave behind a "rivelled essence." Silken wings beaten in vain or spirits transfixed on pins are the symbols of the emasculated ghosts which populate the wasteland between an analogical and an empirical culture.

Geoffrey Tillotson was quite wrong to say that the sylphs, like the Virgilian gods or Miltonic angels before them, perfectly represented the religion of Europe.[23] They in fact represent the loss of a system of spirits which had dominated that culture for over fifteen hundred years. Pope does allow a fuller and literal reality to those larger extensions of social power – the court and the empire. Although the poem is truly the epic of the quotidian, the domestic sphere extends, as Laura Brown and others have shown,[24] into the space of empire. Just as the sylphs do not impinge upon the fate of Belinda, neither do such powers control the destiny of the larger world. If the Petrarchan woman is the epitome of the ideal of feudal and Scholastic cosmology, so Belinda is a little world made cunningly out of the elements of the incipient commercial culture. Queen Anne is simply another Belinda, and the famous zeugma "Here Thou, Great Anna! whom three Realms obey, / Dost sometimes Counsel take – and sometimes Tea"(III, 7–8) expressly refers to the British Isles and those "realms beyond

[23] Geoffrey Tillotson, *On the Poetry of Pope* (Oxford: Clarendon Press, 1950).
[24] See the section "Imperialism and Poetic Form," in Laura Brown, *Alexander Pope* (Oxford: Blackwell, 1985).

the seas" (India, America) that were added to her coronation oath. The
verb "take" does not only make light of her lack of a sense of royal
proportion, but also indicates the literal taking of tea from her distant
colonies. It is important that the opening of Canto III (1–30), where these
lines (and the more famous ones in which "Wretches hang that Jurymen
may dine") have no trace of the sylphs. The sylphs do not rule the political
or commercial world. For Pope such a world, as in the loco-descriptive
ideal of *Windsor Forest*, is invested with all the authority of the literal.
Perhaps in the end the invisible and powerless sylphs are being replaced
unconsciously by the looming and equally invisible "hand" of trade.

Martin Price has argued that "'the light militia of the lower sky" are a
travesty of both Homeric deities and Miltonic guardian angels. Like their
originals, they have ambiguous status: they exist within and without the
characters."[25] In fact Milton's angels are real, entirely separate beings, and
Homer's gods are the denizens of a remote and august sphere (though they
amuse themselves sometimes in the lives of men). The sylphs are never
outside of Belinda (or Pope), nor are they the arbiters of conscience. They
are gone for ever in the enlightened haze of the empirical to seek their fate
in the kingdom of absurdity.

Pope's spatial art

After describing the ideal classical description of *Windsor-Forest* in which
Pope "offers a systematically 'poetic' world, committed to allegorizing the
darker human passions in a painterly harmony, using a compound of
classical allusion and pictorial hints based on the landscape tradition of
Claude Lorrain and others,"[26] Leopold Damrosch goes on to discuss the
quotidian realism of *The Rape of the Lock*.

But *The Rape of the Lock*, dating from exactly the same period, is far more
circumstantial about everyday phenomena, and much of the pleasure is in seeing
the surprising periphrases with which Pope can describe what everybody knows.
The ombre game is significantly translated into the language of heroic combat, but
as scholars have shown it is technically accurate; Wharton says, "I question
whether Hoyle could have played it better than Belinda." Here we approach the
point where mock-epic topples over into mockery of epic, permitting (sometimes
inadvertently) familiar experience to cut the stilts out from under the epic
elevation.[27]

Damrosch is right to see the "descent" (as he terms it) of Pope to truth, but
I think it is important to add that *Windsor-Forest* itself participates in such a
descent. For while the poem is to a greater extent than the mature rhetoric

[25] Martin Price, *To the Palace of Wisdom* (Carbondale, Ill.: Southern Illinois, 1964), 151.
[26] Damrosch, *Imaginative World*, 202.   [27] Ibid.

of Pope a classical and idealized pastiche, specific observation and spatial
organization have already reached a level in the poem not found in earlier
loco-descriptive texts.

If we take the example of the piscatorial scene, we may discover the
originality of Pope. Since Denham leaves fishing out of "Cooper's Hill,"
Jonson's "To Penshurst," Drayton's *Poly-Olbion*, and Marvell's "Upon
Appleton House" are Pope's most obvious English sources. Drayton's
fishing passage in *Poly-Olbion* xxvi is the chief seventeenth-century source.
Drayton's descriptions are realistic and didactic. He discusses the fishing
trade through the whole extent of the river system of Britain, and explains
angling techniques for catching the salmon, chub, perch, trout, and other
species. Pope's catalogue is derived from Drayton, and Pope borrows a few
key words from him – most particularly, "Tyrant." Pope has depended less
on other important piscatorial sources – Virgil and Sannazzaro, for
example – than one might have guessed, and Drayton shows Pope the way
to serious local description unencumbered by allegory. It is not surprising
that Pope's main classical source is the late-ancient fishing poem of
Ausonius. In the *Mosella* Pope discovered a kind of acute realism and spatial
organization foreign to the landscape of Golden Roman poetry. The
methodological kinship can be seen in several passages of the Roman poem.

> [A]st hic, tranquillo qua labitur agmine flumen,
> ducit corticeis fluitantia retia signis;
> ille autem scopulis deiectas pronus in undas
> inclinat lentae convexa cacumina virgae . . .

[Here where the river rolls in its peaceful path, one lays out his net with floating
corks. Another leaning over the waters which roll over boulders, dips the end of his
rod . . .][28]

Like Drayton, Ausonius had gone a long way to de-mythologize the natural
scene. Both Ausonius and Pope are at their worst when they introduce
mythological epyllia and classical conceits into their otherwise descriptive
poems.[29] The *Mosella* is injured by its facile Ovidian props, and Johnson

---

[28] Ausonius, *Works*, ed. H. G. Evelyn White (London: Loeb Classical Library, 1919), vol. 1, 63.
[*Mosella*, 245–248. Translation my own.]

[29] Professor Robert Browning gives a portrait of Ausonius as a writer which bears striking
similarities to the character of Pope. He says: "A prodigious memory, a facile talent for
versification, a cheerful optimism, and an avoidance of all that was serious or profound . . . He
can express everyday thoughts and emotions clearly and with infinite variety. Completely at
home in the classical tradition he is never overwhelmed by it. Though his poetry is filled with
conscious and unconscious reminiscences of Virgil, Horace, Ovid, Lucan, Statius, it is his own
poetic voice that we hear. In a few poems, particularly those on Bissula and the *Mosella*, he
displays a talent for sympathetic observation and strikingly vivid description which suggest that
had he looked less at his books and more at the world about him he might have been a better
poet." See *The Cambridge History of Classical Literature*, vol. II, part v, 19 (Cambridge: Cambridge
University Press). In applying this passage to Pope we could not in good conscience use the
word "facile," but there is no doubt that the greatest power of Pope was observation – practical

was right to question the propriety of the Latona passage of *Windsor-Forest*. The poem would be better, even more original without it. In that one passage Pope lapses into the formulaic meter and language of his *Pastorals* and *Messiah*, which he himself mocks in the *Essay on Criticism*. Moving from the standard pastiche of the *gradus* epithet and auxiliary words (especially "do"), which fill out those earlier poems, to the easy variety of *The Rape of the Lock* was his first great artistic victory. Moving from pseudo-classical description to novelistic observation was his second victory. Such a complete maturity comes in several stages, from his translations through *The Dunciad* and culminating in the infinite flexibility of *An Epistle to Dr. Arbuthnot*.

The originality of Pope may be seen best against the backdrop of his most important seventeenth-century models in loco-descriptive poetry. Jonson gives us an important parallel to Pope in his famous passage.

> And if the high-swollen Medway fail thy dish,
> Thou hast thy ponds which pay thee tribute fish:
> Fat agèd carps that run into thy net,
> And pikes, now weary their own kind to eat,
> As loath the second draught or cast to stay,
> Officiously at first themselves betray;
> Bright eels that emulate them, and leap on land.
> Before the fisher, or into his hand.[30]

In this Edenic fantasy the fish leap joyously into the boat without the rigors of angling. They so desire to feed the Sidneys that they refuse to eat each other. "Fat" is the single descriptive gesture in an otherwise fully moralized and abstract passage. The fowls, the fish, and the fruit of Penshurst form a kind of linked series of idealized analogs to the largesse which emanates from Jonson's patrons.

In an even more luminous allegory Marvell makes his Maria the tutelary angel of the stream. After viewing her perfect beauty in the Neoplatonic speculum of the water she mesmerizes the fish.

> The viscous Air, wheres'ere She fly,
> Follows and sucks her Azure dy;
> The gellying Stream compacts below,
> If it might fix her shadow so;
> The stupid Fishes hang, as plain

and visual. He, like Ausonius, uses his great models, Horace and Virgil, without penetrating to their richer philosophical and moral implications. Pope too is not overwhelmed by his sources but fashions from them a novel descriptive art. Both authors were Christians in a time of intellectual upheaval, who for different reasons chose an almost entirely secular and quasi-classical tone in their poems.

30 Ben Jonson "To Penshurst," *Works*, ed. C. H. Herford and P. Simpson (Baltimore: Johns Hopkins University Press, 1952), vol. II, 123.

As *Flies* in *Chrystal* over'tane;
And Men the silent scene assist,
Charmed with the *Saphir-winged* mist.[31]

("Upon Appleton House," 673–680)

The contrast of Pope's extended fishing scene is interesting for its relative realism.

In genial Spring beneath the quiv'ring Shade
Where cooling Vapours breathe along the Meade,
The patient Fisher takes his silent Stand
Intent, his angle trembling in his Hand;
With Looks unmoved, he hopes the Scaly Breed,
And eyes the dancing Cork and bending Reed.
Our plenteous Streams a various Race supply;
The bright-ey'd Perch with Fins of *Tyrian* Dye,
The silver Eel, in shining Volumes roll'd,
The yellow Carp, in Scales bedrop'd with Gold,
Swift Trouts, diversify'd with Crimson Stains,
And Pikes the Tyrants of the watry Plains.

(*Windsor-Forest*, 135–146)

In this passage Pope is laboring towards his mature style. The first couplet has three conventional epithets obviously to fill out the lines metrically. "Genial" and "quivering" have appeared in the earlier *Pastorals*, and "cooling" is a favorite of the late seventeenth century. But in moving from Bucolic to Georgic imagery Pope finds a higher degree of observant description. The "trembling" angle is a real improvement on Drayton, and the enjambment with "Intent" effectively breaks up the syntactical monotony. "The Scaly Breed" is a favorite kind of generic abstraction (not personification) which goes back to Sylvester's translation of Du Bartas. These generalized images – "feath'ry troops," "hungry tribes" – are often more specific than a simple word would be. Rather than a sign of crippling evasion they point to the desire for taxonomic analogy and visual specificity. Such a language is supremely visual, and sometimes approaching to the scientific. In dropping this language Wordsworth was returning to a less not more exact mode of description. The Romantic sublime depends on a poetic of vagueness, and raising the "smoking tube" is neither vague nor sublime. Such abstract descriptive language is often found in the novelistic discourse of the period, especially in Behn and Defoe.

From "dancing Cork" onwards the passage becomes more lively and immediate. Pope's natural descriptions are painted, but they owe little to Salvator or Lorrain. Aside from "Tyrian" all his adjectives are sharper than

[31] Andrew Marvell, *Poems and Letters*, ed. H. M. Margoliouth (Oxford: Clarendon Press, 1952), vol. 1, 80.

Drayton's. The whole passage is actually about fishing, not in the Neoplatonic allegorical sense of Marvell or in the Protestant typological one of Walton's *Compleat Angler*, but in the spatial, visual sense which slowly overtakes Pope's poems, and which succeeds only intermittently in *Windsor-Forest*.

In the translations, we see the workings of the Augustan – the empirico-classical – reaching its stride. Pope's *Iliad* is a gathering place for all his earlier and many of his most original rhetorical effects. What began as classical pastiche and mockery is taken directly over into translation, so that the quotidian, spatial elements of *The Rape of the Lock* and *The Temple of Fame* are developed and manipulated within the Homeric text. The original gesture of satire, which emptied the classical and Humanist of its special claims as cultural interpreter, becomes the means of presenting the classical itself. This is part of the strangeness of Pope's Homer, and also why it is the greatest proving ground for Pope's poetic arsenal. Without the discipline of metaphrase Pope would not have so swiftly expanded the flexibility of meter and image which we see afterwards. By the time of his Horatian experiments the quotidian pictorial quality had moved from means to end, entirely blotting out in some cases the content of the original. Popeian imitation became a form of expunging, rather than the reciprocal illumination described by Thomas Greene. It might be useful to quote from the closing section of *The Light in Troy* at some length.

In the long run the achievements of *imitatio* would ensure its decay in the form analyzed by this study. After the age of Jonson, ancient culture acquired in England that straddling status it already possessed on the Continent: it was foreign but at the same time it *belonged*. It had undergone its process of reception, and now it was progressively a native possession. It lent itself to the play of parody and travesty without imposing the threat – or allowing the thrill – of sacrilege. It merged with post-classical Continental literature as a kind of penumbra or extension of the domestic tradition. After the Restoration, as Bate has shown, it was the Elizabethan-Jacobean past that represented the heaviest burden upon the English imagination.

Thus after the turn of the seventeenth century on the Continent, a generation later in England, a history of imitations would require different assumptions, perhaps different terms, than those employed in this book. The movement was past when, in Croll's terms, men wanted to Hellenize or Romanize themselves. If one were to address like Petrarch missives to the age of light, if one were to honor Plato with banquets like the Florentine Academy's, these would have lost their reverential seriousness. Partly through the activity of imitation in all its forms and usages, the classics were domesticated, *apprivoisés*. The superb formal imitations of Pope, Swift, and Doctor Johnson adjust the idiom of familiars who have lost their numinous ghostliness.[32]

---

[32] Thomas M. Greene, *The Light in Troy: Imitation and Discovery in Renaissance Poetry* (New Haven: Yale University Press, 1982), 293.

The transformation which Greene describes was not one of the familiarity
which breeds contentment and occasional parody. The changes were more
incisive, radical, and political than a model of gradualism could explain.
The kind of spiritual syncresis of the sixteenth century (Protestant and
Catholic alike) was never appealing to the later period. In some respects
the Florentine Plato and the Petrarchan Cicero, like the Saint Socrates that
More prayed to in his final imprisonment, were figures of great spiritual
complexity. The great Renaissance Humanists believed explicitly or im-
plicitly that Cicero, Plato, and even Ovid were part of an ancient *preparatio*
for the mysteries of Christianity. For Pico Hermes Trismegistus, and
Pythagoras are types of Christ, as Socrates was for More. The Platonic
dialogues were the core of perennial esoterica for Ficino. Ovid himself was
moralized and allegorized throughout the Renaissance down to Milton.

The stage of Neoclassicism represented by Boileau in France and
Dryden and Pope in England was not one of merely hardening and
regularizing the habits of *imitatio*. It was a period of vast shrinkage of the
possibilities of Classicism. What I have called empirico-classicism was, in
fact, an editing and rewriting of the classical. Rather than a synthesis of
intellectual traditions like the Platonic and Scholastic in Ficino, the
Augustans attempted to separate the classical from the Christian, imagining a sober naturalism and literalism where the humanists had often
imagined imbedded analogies. The "thrill" or "threat of sacrilege" which
Greene mentions was no longer as embarrassing as the fanciful claims of
orthodox religious writing, and just such orthodoxy (as in *Bachis and
Philemon*, *The Rape of the Lock*, and others) was the subject of parody by
means of the classical imitation. Montaigne's Pyrrhonism was the chief
survival of Humanism, and it had been a relatively small part of late-
Renaissance thought. Added to it was a novel empiricism. The work of
Hume and Gibbon was simply the last phase of reworking the classical
gentleman as the antagonist of the superstitious Christian, and as the
imaginary precursor to later empiricism. That was the direction of all
Neoclassical thinking.

Pope himself was antagonistic to the Platonic and transcendent end of
humanism. In chastising the absurd spiritual ambitions of man he remarks:

> Go, soar with Plato to th' empyreal sphere,
> To the first good, first perfect, and first fair;
> Or tread the mazy round his follow'rs trod,
> And quitting sense call imitating God;
> As Eastern priests in giddy circles run,
> And turn their heads to imitate the Sun.
> Go teach eternal Wisdom how to rule –
> Then drop into thyself and be a fool!
>
> (*An Essay on Man*, II, 23–30)

This represents one of the norms of English Neoclassicism, cut off from traditional metaphysical discourse, now tainted by its connection to the culture of the Civil War. Pope makes a cartoon out of the Platonic exemplarism, associating it as Butler and Rochester had with the giddy philosophy of Brahmin priests. For Pope any philosophy which "quits" sensation (and sensibility) has soared beyond human powers.

Thomas Greene misinterprets the new ordinariness of the classical imitation because he forgets that it has been refashioned to suit the humble and prosaic purposes of political allegory (as in early Dryden) or mere literalism (as in Pope and Swift). The Petrarchan and Neoplatonic classicism of the Renaissance had come to be seen as a grotesque and superstitious mask by the late seventeenth century. Because the classical culture itself had no notion of empiricism and the spatial poetics it ushered in, this new empirico-classicism was very limited in its sources. Horace was promoted as a great realist. His *nil admirari* was used by Pope anachronistically to indicate a doubt about the *mira* of Baroque theology, as Hume and Gibbon were to find in the classical man the true judge of Christian credulity and barbarism. The classical became a way to criticize both the folk and intellectualist elements of early modern Christianity. Removed as it was from the spiritual conflicts of the seventeenth century, the classical could often be more comfortably domesticated than recent European and British literature.

In domesticating the classical a good deal of its original content and atmosphere had to be removed. Homer was a good place for Pope to center his labors as a translator, because the Homeric, though it had often been allegorized, was less obviously connected to an ambitious spiritual program than the Renaissance Virgil or Plato. Nevertheless, Pope's transformation of Homer's sprawling energy into a kind of walking picture gallery of lacquered set pieces and his fine block compositions are where we may see this new classicism at its most obvious distance from its sources. He renders the Homeric image as:

> Strait to the Tree, his sanguine Spire he roll'd,
> And curl'd around in many a winding Fold.
> The topmost Branch a Mother-Bird possessed;
> Eight callow infants filled the mossy Nest,
> Herself the ninth: The Serpent as he hung
> Stretched his black Jaws, and crushed the crying Young.[33]

(*Iliad*, II, 374–379)

[33] Homer, *Iliad*, II, 311–315. The text is as follows: "ἔνθα δ' ἔσαν στρουθοῖο νεοσσοί, νήπια τέκνα, ὄζῳ ἐπ' ἀκροτάτῳ, πετάλοις ὑποπεπτηῶτες, ὀκτώ, ἀτὰρ μήτηρ ἐνάτη ἦν, τέκε τέκνα. ἔνθ' ὅ γε τοὺς ἐλεεινὰ κατήσθιε τετριγῶτας · μήτηρ δ' ἀμφιποτᾶτο ὀδυρομένη φίλα τέκνα."

Many readers will note the debt to Milton from two passages of *Paradise Lost*, and may recall the "mossy nest" from *Macbeth*, but fewer will recognize this as the typical kind of empirical abstraction of the period, looking forward to the naturalism of Thomson's *Spring*. The passage has a synthesis of English allusions, but an original and uniform rhetoric. What in Homer is unadorned simile, in Pope is the art of an observer. No one would confuse this with seventeenth-century emblem, and aside from the *Pharonnida* and some sections of the *Poly-Olbion*, nothing in the earlier period is so inclined to draw from the empirical. All poetry is abstraction, but Pope's abstraction is no longer iconic. The adjectives are far more determinate and visual than Homer's – "topmost," "curled," "mossy," and "black" deepen the sense of the spatial. Nor is this a specific tradition drawn from painting, but rather, like Thomson, is involved in the invention of an empirical art which by mid-century had profoundly influenced British painting.[34] The frozen image of the birds who "leave their little Lives in Air" and the "glossy varying Dyes" of the pheasant in *Windsor-Forest* were part of the preparation of these outcroppings of the modern picture, the dramatic contour of still life found throughout Pope's *Iliad*.

> As when the Fig's pressed Juice, infused in Cream,
> To Curds coagulates the liquid Stream.   (*Iliad*, v, 1111–1112)

> The tint is brightened with a rising Blaze:
> Then when the languid Flames at length subside,
> He strews a Bed of glowing Embers wide
> Above the Coals, the smoking Fragment turns,
> And sprinkles sacred Salt from lifted Urns;
> With bread the glittering Canisters they load.   (*Iliad*, xiv, 156–161)

Here, the "smoking Fragments" and "glittering Canisters" recall the poetry of mechanical description, which is the major subject of Gay's *Trivia*, and shows a touch throughout of bourgeois modernity. Achilles' moving, squaring, separating, and dividing the ritual sacrifice subtly draws the language of the passage into the sphere of the industrial; and the

---

[34] There has been some exaggeration of the influence of specific traditions of painting upon poetry since the time of Jean Hagstrum's important work. Poetry seems more commonly to be the model for a new spatial and descriptive attitude in painting in Britain throughout the period. Hogarth was influenced by Butler's realism and began his career by illustrating *Hudibras*. Thomson and Pope had an important, perhaps definitive, influence on Wilson, Gainsborough, and Constable. Poetry and painting alike resisted the movement from icon to empirical image. Though modern perspective was developed in the Renaissance, the subject matter of most paintings before the seventeenth century was still conventional and iconic. The notion of an autonomous observational art is part of the heritage of the eighteenth century, though it is preceded by the domestic and still-life painting of the Dutch and Flemish painters of the middle seventeeth century, which may be seen as part of an inevitable development.

"coagulated curds" and figs "infused in cream" recall the typical language of the experimental records of the Royal Society in the 1680s.

Hither also may we most congruously refer to the *coagulation* of milk, upon the injection of rennet, vinegre, juice of limons, and the like acid things. For, the hamous possessed of hooks, and inviscating atoms, whereof the acid is mostly composed, meeting with the ramous and grosser particles of the milk . . . this may be confirmed from hence; that whenever the cheese or butter made of the coagulation is held to the fire, they recover their former fluidity.[35]

The language of Hoole's *Science of Winemaking* or *Art of Dehydration*, or the Charleton papers mentioned above is echoed throughout the sacrificial scenes of Pope's *Iliad* and is a good example of his normal practice of observant expansion. Homer's detail is never an end in itself. His descriptive formulae are neither precious nor strictly visual. Pope has imposed the idea of the modern literal upon the Homeric text.

Just as the pheasant and dogs in *Windsor-Forest* helped to free the creature from the bondage to analogy, so long preserved by the drawings in the bestiary (still popular in the seventeenth century), or the symbolic animal substitution of beast-fable surviving down to the time of Dryden's *Hind and the Panther*, so the movement in most mature Augustan verse from conceit to metonymy helps to create a space for realism, that is, a physical contiguity and association. The spatial poetic is connected in recent Augustan criticism to Marvell's, Waller's, and Pope's special interest in the art of painting, and the domestication of principles of perspective, color, and shade in Fresnoy, Kneller, and others. Pope had some talent as a painter, but the real issue is the method of the empirical within poetry. Any analogy between two arts is always metaphorical and imperfect. The supposed synesthesia in Keats, like the "painterly" qualities in Pope, remain issues of language and verbal construction. Although the low Augustan, the Hudibrastic, has an obvious counterpart in the practice of Hogarth, and the higher in Gainsborough and Wilson, these connections point to an underlying departure from emblem and icon. Landscape and history painting invoke the classical as literal. A whole class of painters down to Constable worked to strip their canvases of the residue of Christian icon, not with complete success. In so doing, they hoped, along with Pope and Thomson, to create a new idea of classical realism, a detachment from conceitful enthusiasm in art, a cult of judgment. Classical history, classical ruin, Roman composition, become the signs of the occlusion of seventeenth-century symbolism; and the myth of Rome as the grandparent of England, its typological twin of Roman *imperium*, helped to obscure the indigenous

---

[35] Walter Charleton, *Notes for the Royal Society* (London: Wells and Wells, 1811), vol. IV, 117. Also see Richard Foster Jones, "The Rhetoric of Science in England of the mid-17th Century," *Philological Quarterly* 51 (1954), 77–79.

origins of English poetic culture. The cult for old Rome (as against Catholic Rome) which has been traced in recent studies may be seen in Pope and Dryden.[36] Pope centers his own historical critique on Catholic and Mediterranean culture (though he was a practicing Catholic). This points not so much to the centrality of an idea of classical authority, as to the enduring place of Catholic Rome (as also in Butler, Oldham, and Swift), as the demonic enemy of modernity.

> Thus long succeeding critics justly reign'd,
> License repressed and useful laws ordain'd.
> Learning and Rome alike an empire grew,
> And Art still followed where her eagles flew;
> From the same foes, at last, both felt their doom,
> And the same age saw learning fall, and Rome.
> With tyranny, then superstition join'd,
> As that the body, this enslav'd the mind;
> Much was believ'd, but little understood,
> And to be dull was constru'd to be good;
> A second deluge learning thus o'erun,
> And the monks finished what the Goths begun.
>
> (*Essay on Criticism*, 681–92)

I have already discussed the common Augustan analogy between Scholastic and Protestant thinking. And I have attempted to point to Pope's contribution to that attitude. I mention it here only to point out that "classical" was commonly conflated after the Restoration with practical, visual, and empirical. My term "empirico-classical" was carefully selected, because it shows the special combination of exclusions upon which Augustan art was constructed. Classical *mimesis* as it is derived from Aristotle or from Dionysius of Halicarnassus was not an empirical aesthetic. The *mimesis* of Aristotle depends on the notion of intelligible essence and *entelechy* and without those notions there can be no Aristotelian imitation. "Poetry is more general than history," because it deals with intelligibles and classes rather than accidents – what a thing is essentially rather than materially. "Numbering the streaks of the tulip" is in fact a marked tendency in Garth, Gay, Pope, Thomson, and Akenside, and their new descriptionist art is original to their own time. It has no classical counterpart. Although Aristotle was a great observer himself, he would have abhorred the qualities of spatial organization and accidental detail found in mature English Augustanism. His own great poem, *Arête*, is the antithesis of this latter-day classicism.[37] Dionysius' own formulation (the

---

[36] See Howard Weinbrot, *Augustus Caesar in "Augustan" England: The Decline of a Classical Norm* (Princeton: Princeton University Press, 1978); and Howard Erskine-Hill, *The Augustan Idea in English Literature* (London: Edward Arnold, 1983).

[37] Ἀρετὰ πολυμόχθε γενεῖ βροτείῳ, / θήραμα κάλλιστον βίῳ / σὰς περὶ παρθένε μόρφας / καὶ

only surviving definition of *mimesis* from antiquity), as "a paradigm made from nature for contemplation," clarifies the point. A παράδειγμα is a *figura essentiale* – a figure abstracted from the members of a class. Just such an essential composite is the goal for serious intellectual contemplation, for it purges the image or action of accidental or empirical excrescences. Such a doctrine was Christianized by Aquinas under the headings of *unitas* and *claritas*, the transparency of the idea in the object. Such "translucence" is shared by every illuminative poetics – Thomist, Scotist, or Baroque. This kind of aesthetic dominated European culture for most of its history, but it was not the poetic practiced by Pope and Thomson. This is not to say that the *Essay on Criticism* does not contain the common maxims of classical and French neo-classical theory. The idea of a general nature, what the painting theorist de Piles calls "visible nature as an object," was no doubt important to Pope. But de Piles, who is of an earlier intellectual culture, goes on to say, "He must have an image of her in his mind, not only as he happens to see her in particular subjects, but as she ought to be in herself and as she would be, were she not hindered by certain accidents."[38] This seems to be a great distance from Pope's own theory and practice. So the concepts of general nature, the imitation of the ancients as equivalent to nature, the tempering of wit by judgment, are commonplaces of the Renaissance, but are evolving in the hands of the Augustan critics into something new. All of these notions are in Rapin, Boileau, even Dryden and Davenant, and Pope follows the general line in his opposition to metaphysical poetry. First, there is the specific criticism of conceitful composition, Baroque poetic *sprezzatura*:

> Some to *Conceit* alone their Taste confine,
> And glittering Thoughts struck out at every Line;
> Pleas'd with a Work where nothing's just or fit
> One *glaring Chaos* and *wild Heap* of *Wit*.
>
> (*Essay on Criticism*, 289–292)

This recalls Dryden's critique of Donne, who "had more wit than any of us," but lacked judgment to control it, or Boileau's detailed rebuke to Jesuit meditation, "le grand débâcle d'imagination." To say, as Pope does, that the conceitful manner is a taste which confines, must give readers of Marino, Donne, and Vaughan pause. "Taste" implies a self-conscious rhetoric of surprise. Judgment, of course, preserves the Augustan poet from "glittering Thoughts struck out at every Line," but the real change is deeper. The world of Donne, Marino, and Gongora was a moral and iconic

ἀνεῖν ζηλώτος ἕν Ἑλλάδι πότμος / καί πονόυσ' τλῆναι μαλέρουσ' ἄκαμαντας [Virtue cause of much labor for men, the best prize to obtain in this life; even to perish for a look at your face, virgin goddess, and to suffer terrible and never-ending hardships, is an honorable fate in Greece.] My own translation.

[38] Alexander Pope, *Poems*, ed. G. Tillotson (New Haven: Yale University Press, 1959), vol. II, xliv.

extravaganza, likely to surprise; and its multiplicity and vividness were unified by God as the mirror in which all things are refracted. The appearance of wildness and chaos can only be derived from a prejudice for spatio-temporal contiguity and uniformity. Pope's imaginative field is associative, not assimilative, and the accumulations of continuous embellishment and surprise, of "glittering thoughts struck out," seem at least as proper when applied to "Eloisa," *The Temple of Fame*, or *The Dunciad*, as to almost any other English poems. The pacing of Vaughan's "The World" or Herbert's "Man," though conceitful and even crowded, is much more deliberate and easy than Augustan practice. The couplet as Pope practiced it depends more on the effect of the independent, even ostentatious, distich and the architectonic layering of verse paragraph than in any earlier English verse, even the Pindaric. Nothing is more surprising to a culture habituated to metaphysical design than an empirical field. The surprise is not one of the Marinist *mira*, the wonder discovered or selected from experience, but of the novelty of realistic observation.

Beneath the surface practice of classical and Gallic theory, even the *Essay on Criticism* betrays Pope's mature empiricism.

> True Wit is Nature to Advantage drest,
> What oft was *Thought*, but ne'er so well *Exprest*.
> *Something*, whose Truth convinced at Sight we find,
> That gives us back the Image of our Mind.
>
> (*Essay on Criticism*, 296–299)

We expect to find the doctrine of *res* and *verba*, of the decorous combination of rhetoric and tried truths in any Neoclassical system, but the truth convinced at sight and the giving back "the image of the mind" are not in Pope either Platonic or specular, but empirical. It is visual memory and the eye which arbitrates in matters of taste. Nature is not the repository of the essential figure, but a decorated space. It is no surprise that we find the theory exemplified throughout with the Popeian prospect.

> In *Prospects*, thus, some *Objects* please our Eyes,
> Which *out* of Nature's *common Order* rise,
> The shapeless *Rock*, or hanging *Precipice*.
>
> (*Essay on Criticism*, 158–160)

In classical *mimesis*, as in Baroque, the inventive power is selective and rational, but in Pope's it is passive and visual. "Out of Nature's common Order" betrays his conscious or unconscious Baconianism (Bacon's own phrase is "the common ordering of Nature's body"). "The shapeless Rock, or hanging Precipice," are very early examples of the new concept of sublimity, but the objects which "please the eye" look forward to Burke's theory of beauty, Addison's "variety," and especially Thomson's "hungry eye." Burke was to produce one of the first fully developed spatial and structural theories of beauty. He describes tactile and visual qualities which necessarily create an empirical sense of beauty. His idea of beauty is sometimes a sexual instinct, sometimes an empirical reflex. Baroque and medieval theories of beauty (like that of Aquinas and Bonaventure) are always aesthetics of analogy. Unity, radiance, and translucence are qualities at root theological. All art must show its source in God or ideal creation; it must produce an intuition of its origin. With ideals of art such as variety and novelty (Addison), or shape and color (Burke and Wolf), art has become one of the literal appearance of the natural – the possible in an accidental descriptive field. This is the aesthetic that Pope almost unconsciously advocates in the rhetoric of the *Essay on Criticism*. Johnson was correct to admire the *Essay on Criticism* less for its theory and more for its illustrative matter. "Hills peep o'er hills, and Alps on Alps arise," Pope's most famous figure for the struggling poet, is at once a marvelous example of Augustan perspectivism and a figure of the uncontrollable expanse of empirical objects. The peculiarity of Pope's success is that it is always better in the excrescenses than in the argument, and that like the *Essay on Man*, his theory is merely a frame for the accidental and descriptive vitality of his rhetoric. This is understandable if we realize that the central problem of empiricism is finding a governing principle of intelligibility in heterogeneous experience. The degree of Pope's success within such a poetic is in proportion to his inability to solve just such a problem.

Returning to Pope's Homer, we can illustrate this spatial method in its mature form. In the invocation of the muses (*Iliad* II, 485–487), before the catalog of the ships, Pope renders the following three lines of Homer

> ἔσπετε νῦν μοι, μοῦσαι Ὀλύμπια δώματ᾽ ἔχουσαι,
> ὑμεῖς γὰρ θεαί ἐστε πάρεστέ τε ἴστέ τε πάντα,
> ἡμεῖς δὲ κλέος, οἷον ἀκούομεν οὐδέ τι ἴδμεν,

as:

> Say, Virgins, seated 'round the Throne Divine,
> All-Knowing Goddesses! Immortal Nine!
> Since Earth's wide Regions, Heaven's unmeasur'd Height,
> And Hell's Abyss, hide nothing from your Sight.

> (*Iliad* II, 572–575)

In Homer's words, construed literally, "Muses who have homes on Olympus / You are present, and you know all things, / And we hear only rumor and know nothing." "Throne Divine," "Immortal Nine," "Earth's wide Regions," "Heaven's unmeasur'd Height," and "Hell's Abyss," do not appear in Homer, but serve the typical purpose of Pope to visualize, schematize, and particularize the Homeric language. We may remember the same alteration in the "earth, sea, and sky" passage at the opening of Pope's "Temple of Fame" – the expanding of Chaucer's simplicities into scenic vista. The wide, high, and low give Pope a chance to schematize the scene in terms of extensive view. The catalog of the ships, which Pope minutely anatomized in an essay printed at the end of his translation of the second book of the *Iliad*, gives him a chance to draw Homer into the sphere of his own empirical project. Pope remarks,

We may observe first what an *Air of Probability* is spread over the whole Poem by the *particularizing* of every Nation and People concerned in this War. Secondly, what an entertaining *Scene* he presents to us, of so many Countries drawn in the liveliest and most *natural Colors*, while we *wander* along with him amidst a beautiful *Variety*, Towers, Havens, Forests, Vineyards, Groves, Mountains, and Rivers, and are perpetually amused with his *Observations* on the different Soils, Products, Situations, or *Prospects*.[39] [emphasis added]

The entire Addisonian aesthetic of color, novelty, and variety is combined with the language of prospect and scene. Pope imagines with very little evidence that Homer is making a kind of visual map of the Greek culture, a kind of Poly-Hellenica which would embody the qualities he admired in Drayton and Denham. This is far from Homer's actual method. Pope is forced to find some kinship with his great author, but rather than a metaphysical and political typology, like that which Chapman had found in Homer or Dryden in Virgil, he embraces Homer as a genius of description – a travel guide through the realm of geographical and martial appearances.[40] Having questioned the metaphysical and theological insights of Homer in his brilliant "Preface," he has to move to firmer ground. This same movement away from religious and metaphysical borrowing toward the practical and descriptive can be seen throughout British Augustan poetry. It helps to explain why Milton's Edenscapes and Georgic materials in books 4 and 5 of *Paradise Lost* were so important to his eighteenth-century imitators like Philips, Thomson, and Cowper. These authors could no longer fully digest the controversial, intellectualist elements of the poem. There is a general retreat to landscape in the period. The same might be said about uses of the leisure country poems among Horace's *sermones* – the place, the atmosphere, the tone, but not the philosophical nuance, are exploited by popular poets like Pomfret and Somerville.

We can see in Pope's note to Book III (and elsewhere) that Pope also considered Homer a model in figurative writing. Although Homer had the

---

[39] Pope, *Poems*, VII, 173. This is the *Observations* on the catalog appended to Book II of his translation of the *Iliad*.

[40] Pope has a bit of anxiety concerning his descriptive expansions of the text, and makes some muted remarks in his *Observations*: "I have ventured to open the Prospect a little, by the addition of a few Epithets or short Hints of Description to some of the places mentioned; tho' seldom exceeding the Compass of half a Verse (the Space to which my Author himself generally confines these Pictures in Miniature)." See Pope, *Poems*, 177. Pope's expansions are much greater than he admits in this passage.

energy and novelty of perception which Pope felt was at the heart of all great writing, he did not belabor and twist his figures as the Baroque artists of the seventeenth century had done. He (like Horace) is a model of correctness, but unlike Horace he is capable of the Longinian sublime – a torrent of visual and rhetorical effects which Pope envied. It is now proverbial to say that Pope's *Iliad* is a tribute to the impossibility of the epic in the eighteenth century. This is no more than to say a vaguely Deist, satirically open, and literalizing art could not produce Homer, Virgil, or Milton. But the loss of the dense fabric of Christian and Humanist analogies, which Pope from the first imagines as grotesquerie, is a more considerable problem.

It is often said that Dryden and Jonson are the great seventeenth-century models for Augustan moral vision. These two authors seem to lack the Baroque extremism of Donne or the early Marvell. Ben Jonson in *The Alchemist* and *Volpone* is the obvious antecedent to the mature and electric style of *The Dunciad* and *Arbuthnot*, but with a difference. In Jonson these dense concatenations of mundane and social detail are part of a dramatic order, a moral order of an almost allegorical timbre. Jonson's dialog, in other ways so much like that of Pope's mature poetry, has a different purpose and a deeper level of suggestion. If Pope is our first fully and almost naively secular poet, it is because he is drawn in by his own worldly fabric. Jonson's world of dark realism and sordid detail is a world in which the moral center is lost to his characters, but never to him. It is the world at large which has forsaken that peculiar mix of Classical restraint and Christian humanism, which remained the heart of his own private literary emotion. Pope is a representative figure of his age, and Belinda, Sappho, and even Atticus have that touch of projection, of modern psychological empathy, which is nowhere in Jonson. This is why Pope's apocalypse is one of "taste," while the coldly just ending of *Volpone* still touches a darkly Christian moral. But the rhetoric of the two is not unlike, and both seem to combine with the effects of Restoration drama to make the Dickensian, that is, the modern novelistic world, possible.

As I have remarked in chapter 2, there are two distinct Drydens. The return of Dryden, however imperfectly, to the mode of British Baroque after his laureateship, is one of the important stories of literary history. Pope's career moved in the opposite direction – to a more and more associative and realistic art. Pope imitated and improved upon every part of Dryden's repertoire except two – the ode and the argument poem. The ode of the seventeenth century depends on a texture of elaborated figures; the argument poem depends on rational coherence and continuity. Greville, Davies, and Dryden have all far outdone Pope in this direction. Swift, in recognizing the satirical miasma of his own world view, was wise enough to give up even the appearance of rational explanation in his long poems.

I will not repeat the splendid language of Johnson on the failure of the *Essay on Man*. The world is still divided on the relative success of that project. Northrop Frye's remarks are ingenious and charitable.

> The *Essay on Man* does not expound a system of metaphysical optimism founded on the chain of being: it uses such a system as a model on which to construct a series of hypothetical statements which are more or less useless as propositions, but inexhaustibly rich and suggestive when read in their proper context as epigrams. As epigrams, as solid, resonant, and centripetal verbal structures, they may apply pointedly to millions of human situations which have nothing to do with metaphysical optimism.[41]

Frye begs the question as to what the proper context of the epigrams should be. To say that they are "centripetal," self-justifying literary creations which happen to apply to human life is a bit confusing. But not as confusing as the *Essay* itself. Nonetheless, the ground of Pope's confusion is still an interesting question. Hegel somewhere remarked that the philosophical mind must shed its habit of picturing things if it wishes to penetrate to the depths of metaphysical speculation. Pope's greatest power was visual, and he could construct a spatial field for every poetic situation. *The Rape of the Lock* and *Eloisa to Abelard* are perfectly realized dramatic spaces – experiments in ideal décor. The same can be said for the landscape of *Windsor-Forest*. These techniques were not so well suited for vindicating God. Milton had constructed a moral landscape of mammoth proportions – heaven, hell, "wide interrupt," "chaos old." Pope intended, no doubt, to construct a similar space, but he was impeded by a too literal sense of cosmic plenitude. The great chain of being was not for him, as it had been for Aquinas or Leibniz, the convenient illustration of metaphysical order. It did not simply point to the kinds of metaphysical participation which take place between God and the created essences or emanations. In Pope's mind the great chain was an actual structure of physical existence – the image of a quasi-Newtonian field of vast spaces.

> Thro' worlds unnumber'd tho' the God be known,
> Tis ours to trace him only in our own,
> He, who thro' vast immensity can pierce,
> See worlds on worlds compose one universe,
> Observe how system into system runs,
> What other planets circle other suns,
> What vary'd being peoples ev'ry star,
> May tell us why Heav'n made us as we are.
>
> (*An Essay on Man*, i, 221–128)

---

[41] Northrop Frye, *Anatomy of Criticism* (New York: Atheneum, 1970), 85.

For Pope "the connections and dependencies" of this system were to be visualized. He was the true avatar of Locke. As in *The Temple of Fame* the thing allegorized is swallowed up in the vehicle of the allegory.

The great passages of the poem, and there are many, show the degree to which obsessive visualization haunted his imagination.

> What modes of sight between each wide extreme,
> The mole's dim curtain and the lynx's beam: . . .
> What thin partitions sense and thought divide!
>
> (*An Essay on Man*, I, 211–212; 226)

It was natural for Pope to be enticed into an irrational optimism. Having first removed the Christian theodicy as provincial and unphilosophical, and having moved on to an incalculable physical cosmos, he was stuck with the ethical results. Having replaced *analogia entis*, the theory of proportion between creature and God, with a notion of remote and unknowable dependencies, he had to fall back on the favorite Augustan solution – Providence. This providence was no longer one of provision (a God holding up existence itself) but of *providens*, seeing from afar. Like the invisible hand of Adam Smith, the great circling ripples at the end of the *Essay* somehow move out from person to person and from appetite to appetite to hold together by a miraculous accident the whole social and cosmic order.

> Self-love but serves the virtuous mind to wake,
> As the small pebble stirs the peaceful lake;
> The centre mov'd, a circle strait succeeds,
> Another still, and still another spreads,
> Friend, parent, neighbour first it will embrace,
> His county next, and next all human race,
> Wide and more wide, th' o'erflowings of the mind
> Take every creature in of every kind;
> Earth smiles around, with boundless bounty blest,
> And Heav'n beholds its image in his breast.
>
> (*An Essay on Man*, IV, 363–372)

Again images of accidental proximity replace those of essential connection, and the personal passion deflected occasionally by reason, like human wit bound in by saving judgment, will fulfill the hopes of universal order. Reason is no longer the source of order or its image, but a tool used to control the primary motive force of the world – self-love. It is interesting to note that the whole passage is a reworking of Pope's description of Rumor in *The Temple of Fame* (431–447), and that it appears again as the image of "nutation" in the great diving scene of *The Dunciad* (397–410).

> Hither, as to their proper Place, arise
> All various Sounds from Earth, and Seas, and Skies,
> Or spoke aloud or whisper'd in the Ear;

Nor ever Silence, Rest or Peace is here.
As on the smooth Expanse or Chrystal lakes,
The sinking Stone at first a Circle makes;
The trembling Surface by the Motion stir'd,
Spreads in a second Circle, then a third;
Wide and more wide, the floating Rings advance,
Fill all the wat'ry Plain and to the Margin dance.
Thus ev'ry Voice and Sound, when first they break,
On neighb'ring Air a soft Impression make;
Another ambient Circle then they move,
That in its turn, impels the next above.

(*The Temple of Fame*, 432–445)

Then down are roll'd the books; stretch'd o'er 'em lies
Each gentle clerk, and mutt'ring seals his eyes.
As what a Dutchman plumps into the lakes,
One circle first, and then a second makes,
What Dulness dropt among her sons imprest
Like motion from one circle to the rest;
So from the midmost the nutation spreads,
Round and more round, o'er all the sea of heads.

(*The Dunciad*, 1728 edn, Book ii, 371–378)

The sinking stone of *The Temple of Fame* is replaced by human dung in *The Dunciad*. Rumor which fills the world with report of loss and gain, sickness and health, war and peace, prodigies, portents, fires, plagues, storms, projects, mismanagements, and taxes works by the same ineluctable motion as the Providential power. The circle on circle of dullness which echoes through London from Westminster to Hungerford operates with the same inexplicable force of association as the "Self-love" of the *Essay*. All spheres are bound together in a system of contiguities and associations which look forward to the casualist ethics of Hartley. The scatological mechanisms of the carnival are absorbed into theodicy. What was at first cynical becomes the saving grace of mankind. The Hudibrastic is once again parent to the sublime. As in so many other cases the image had taken over the mind of Pope and could be fashioned and refashioned at will. The image, the roving repertoire of description, was the end, not the instrument.

Such an effect is fatal in a philosophical poem, but Pope was not working from clear principles and could not have recouped his losses without a massive project of re-education, for he had spent most of his life reading and reworking a body of classical and early modern poems. The elements of his mind were not thoughts, but a collection of image-blocks from Homer, Horace, Statius, Milton, Dryden, and Butler.

That Pope to the end was no friend to the analogical style can be seen in

his prosaic "corrections" of Donne's verse in his *Imitations of Doctor Donne,*
and in the narrow range of figures he accepts in the *Peri Bathous*, which is
itself a document of the utmost importance in the period. We may find the
brilliant tone and circumspect satire still very amusing. But we must also
realize that our own modern taste for "Clevelandism" would have horrified
Pope. The figures which Pope culls from Blackmore and others are hardly
extravagant in light of our recent revitalization of Donne, Crashaw,
Traherne, and Vaughan, and we must recognize the genius of Pope's
polemic. Pope is arguing against a large tradition of verse, and against a
way of thinking. We must also recognize that *The Dunciad* seems to release
in Pope an underlying and repressed metaphorical and bombastic energy.
It is a place in which Pope can escape into the atmosphere of conceit which
he usually denigrates, and it is a place in which a complex of spiritual and
artistic ghosts are being laid to rest. Margaret Doody has emphasized,
more than I, the occasional bursts of wildness and fantasy throughout the
period, and those moments of mad association are very often at the point
where the superstitious, the enthusiastic are being invoked for ridicule. The
thin partition between decorum and madness, which is so often the subject
of Butler, Swift, and Pope, may easily be torn away by the Augustan writer.
At such moments, like the opening of *MacFlecknoe*, we may feel most at
home, and we may see what an imposition upon imagination the doctrines
of judgment and decorum were in the whole period. What in the
Renaissance could be invoked as an analogous field of existence – allegory,
romance, and vision – in the Enlightened culture must be viewed as
satirical fantasy and repudiation. In part because Benlowes and Shadwell
belong to an older order, they are the practitioners of a freer (if a weaker)
craft than Pope's, and in castigating them he seems to cross over into their
own imaginative territory. This causes a good deal of confusion in *The
Dunciad*. Of all the confusions the one presented at the end of the poem is
the most amazing. Pope's final apocalypse is an unconscious attack on his
own habitual optimism, literalism, and "Lockeianism".

> Before her, *Fancy's* gilded clouds decay,
> And all its varying Rain-bows die away.
> *Wit* shoots in vain its momentary fires,
> The meteor drops, and in a flash expires

(*The Dunciad*, 631–634)

> *Philosophy,* that leaned on Heav'n before,
> Shrinks to her second cause, and is no more.
> *Physic* of *Metaphysic* begs defence,
> And *Metaphysic* calls for aid on *Sense!*
> See *Mystery* to *Mathematics* fly![42]

(*The Dunciad*, 643–647)

[42] Pope, *Poems*, 799–800.

These lines demand a close examination. The "gilded clouds" and "Rain-bows" of Fancy here recall the imagery of Donne or Vaughan. The rainbow itself is an archetypal example of the great change wrought upon the poetic fancy by Newton's *Optics* and by the general trend towards "scientism."[43] The rainbow of Thomson's *Spring*, written in the decade preceding *The Dunciad*, and the rainbows of Akenside and Jago, which follow it, are denuded of their symbolical and religious force. They are the objects of mechanical sensation. We can only guess the unconscious suggestion in Pope's use of this image, but we can not help but notice that he is bemoaning, in this passage, the mathematization and "empiricizing" of the world. The argument in these lines about the retreat of metaphysic to physics, and the incapacity of Sense as a moral and philosophical faculty, seems to oppose the more typical attitude of Pope, and certainly the method of all his earlier poems. They suggest a Scholastic nostalgia which Pope never before or after entertained.

The undigested influence of Warburton is undoubtedly part of the explanation, but there is more.[44] This passage in Pope's final version of *The Dunciad* (composed originally in 1726–28) marks the late 1730s and the early 1740s as the period in which the intellectual prejudices and imaginative habits of Augustanism started to be scrutinized. Young's *Night Thoughts*, Hervey's *Meditations*, and Johnson's *Vanity of Human Wishes* make more absolute and explicit the claims which Pope here intimates. There was never before the age of "imagism" a less metaphysical, and a more empirical-minded poet than Pope. It was part of his peculiar self-deception to write the apocalypse of a kind of art which he had been attacking for twenty years. At the end of *The Dunciad* Pope has made a completely unconscious contribution to the criticism of those conventions which he, by supreme artifice, helped to popularize.

No discussion of Pope could be complete without some mention of Horace. Pope did not borrow a specific set of images or themes from Horace, but a notion of the poet's ideal existence. The cult of literary friendship and leisure was derived from his reading of Horace's *sermones*. The *carpe diem* aspects of Horace, which had so affected Herrick and Waller, exist as a secular counter to their own passionate religious poetry. The pagan theme has the appeal of a moral oasis, what is now usually called the "carnivalesque". But in Pope's poetry the influence goes much farther. Horace's world becomes the moral ballast and window of Pope's. This is not to say that Pope thinks of the Horatian milieu as a kind of golden age. Quite the contrary, he expects Horace to have seen the same evils and vanities as he and shields himself from painful exposure by a fiction of

[43] Cf. M. H. Abrams, *The Mirror and the Lamp* (New York: Norton, 1953), 303–311; and Marjorie Nicolson, *Newton Demands the Muse* (Princeton: Princeton University Press, 1960), ch. 2.

[44] Maynard Mack, *Alexander Pope: A Life* (New York: Norton, 1986), 744–745, 749.

poetic fraternity. The words of his self-composed epitaph show the moral superiority he felt with respect to his Latin masters, but it shows also the moral ethos he lived and died in.[45] Such a classicism, remote as it is from Christian gravity, was impossible for Donne or Jonson.

Horace also informs the arch and indulgent *otium* of the circle of Mason, Gray, and Walpole. In fact, the supposedly pre-Romantic effervescence of Gray, Mallet, and Mason, is the last, somewhat diluted form of Augustanism. They show the same sort of naturalism, rational observation, and "classicism" of the earlier Augustans. We may be distracted by a superficial change of meter and stanza into missing the essential likeness of Pope's *Rape*, and Gray's "Ode on a Cat Drowned in a Tub of Gold Fishes": mock-heroic parallelism, minute and painterly description, and moral irony. There is the same fetishism for the objects of the drawing-room, the same comically ambiguous view of women (deflected by the metonymies of sylph and cat), the same facile classicism. The real opposition within the world of letters is not between Augustans and later sentimentalists, or between social poets and naturalists, least of all between classical and Gothic poets, but between all of these and the Protestant poetry of reaction. This may seem exaggerated by the demands of my argument, but it cuts rather deeply. The new objects of Lockeian consciousness, which include the stuff of incipient industrialism as well as scenic naturalism, are the common materials of Pope, Gay, Thomson, and Gray. The moral and religious prejudices, and the resulting methods of description and reasoning found in Watts, Norris, Prior, Young, Berkeley, Lowth, Johnson, and Cowper are quite another matter. It is these two worlds which are held in perilous opposition during the whole eighteenth century. Christian reaction to Augustanism dates from the time of Benlowes and Bishop Ken in the 1670s to the time of Watts and Law (1712–23). But this reaction reached its peak at the moment when Augustanism had exhausted its genius in the "Horatian Poems" of Pope and Thomson's *Seasons*.

Many have seen Pope, if not as a great Renaissance synthesizer, at least as a great classical artist, a perfect Horatian, "an acrobat of wit," and a preternaturally gifted metrist. In one sense, the best qualities of the era seem to meet in Pope. He gleaned from the Roman poets, and especially Horace, the qualities of both courtly decorum and freewheeling satire, which meshed so opportunely with the sophisticated novelty of his realism. Pope's ability to transform the most diverse materials into Popisms is astonishing. But the crux of Pope's genius is in his odd ability to project

---

[45] Cf. Mack, *Alexander Pope: A Life*, 733. The words of his last epitaph (he wrote several), are: "Heroes and Kings! your distance keep. / In peace let one poor Poet sleep, / Who never flattered folks like you: / Let Horace blush, and Virgil too." Considering that Pope's life was a "long disease" his other epitaph ends with a grimly ambiguous line, "Trusts in God, that as well as he was, he shall be." This shows the general tenor of Pope's piety.

real, racy, and immediate experience into what Hazlitt called "filigree."[46]
The decorous atmosphere which is said to surround his work is really the
imprint of his special verbal finesse. His Homer is not Homeric, his Ovid is
not Ovidian, and most importantly, his Horace is not Horatian. His lack of
brutal forward energy (always excepting *The Dunciad*, the portraits in
Arbuthnot and a few sections of the *Horatian Poems*) and his fluid artfulness
doomed his translations, if we may accept modern canons of accuracy; but
Johnson was quite right to say that his *Iliad* has a high place among the
whole work of the century. In it Johnson saw the maturing of his own idea
of poetic language, and he saw it as a great gift to English readers from an
artist who could resist the impious and extravagant allegorizing of
Chapman and Golding. I have only attempted through the example of
Pope to indicate the degree of conscious and unconscious repudiation of
both classical and Christian *mimesis* in the building of a satire suited to the
shrunken field of Augustan figuration, and the correlative discovery of a
truly novel descriptive art.

[46] William Hazlitt, "On Dryden and Pope," *Lectures on the English Poets*, 1818, in *Complete Works*, ed.
P. P. Howe (London: Oxford University Press, 1934), vol. VII.

4

Thomson and the invention of the literal

The new objects of poetry

Of all the qualities which distinguish the poetry in England from 1690 to 1730, its breadth of subject matter is perhaps the most extraordinary. New objects were entering poetry every day, and the grave old business of verse was being transformed by these objects. The three genres which I mentioned as the particular creation of English Augustanism, or at least, the three which gained a new place in the national poetic consciousness after 1670, were scenic or landscape poetry, teleo-physical verse, and what I have called, for want of a better phrase, general satire. These are all aspects of a new literalizing tendency, and this tendency did not end with nature poetry. The objects of the home, the tavern, and the garden were soon to enter English poetry, and the city, already the possession of comedy, was in the time of Gay and Garth to become a familiar place in lyric and didactic verse.

Even this does not begin to describe the sweep of Augustan description. Not only was no object too common or too small for wit's new empire, but smallness seemed to be the measure of a good deal of the most popular (if not lasting) poetry of the age. Mock-heroism was at first merely a vehicle for ridicule or burlesque, but in the end it became the highly self-conscious repository of "a world of so many simple things."[1] The superficial brilliance of Belinda's toilet, or of Timon's mansion, with their plethora of new things, are all that remain for most readers of anthologies of this wider eighteenth-century habit of minute and mundane description. In fact such material, whether in absolute mockery or in the serious play of Garth, Tickell, or Somerville, flooded in upon the contemporary reader with the force of a new world. Margaret Doody has described this expansion of poetry in terms of growing appetite:

"Rise, kill, and eat" might be taken as the motto of English poets of the Restoration, from Butler on, and, to only a slightly lesser extent, of all the succeeding poets to the end of the century. Nothing is so common, so bizarre, so

[1] Oliver Elton, *A Survey of English Literature*, vol. III (London: Oxford University Press), 197.

136

unclean – or so grand – that it can't be apprehended and consumed by the poetic process. Everything that has being, physical or mental, is available to the poet.[2]

It was, of course, also the world of Defoe's novels and *The Spectator*, but the case of poetry is more singular. It might be fairly said that no period before 1660 and after 1740 was so fascinated with the poetry of the trivial, as none was ever so taken up with the objects near at hand. Even the "objectivism" of W. C. Williams or the "vorticism" of Pound were more selective of its materials, and *Spring and All* is a new bottle for old Romantic wine. Even this loose field of metonymic objects and modernist analogues could not outdo the Augustans in the game of objectivity.

This is important to my study for two reasons. First, it marks the final displacement of generic material, the beginning of which I marked in the writing of Cowley and Denham. By 1720 poetry was no longer a basically religious or even courtly matter. It was for the first time the art of everything. It was the vehicle of the fully literal, the realization of the physical and detached nature of things. In John Donne's church the stays, buttresses, windows, and doors were part of a pictorial analogy to the church spiritual or New Jerusalem.[3] The building of the church was symbolical and illustrative, and to say that Donne was interested in the "facts" of the church or the physical presence of the building would be misleading. In Swift's *Baucis and Philemon* the church is a complex of its material parts and their new moral significations.[4] Part of the humor of these newly contrived comic objects was their novelty. Nothing is more remote from our old poetry than the real chaos of objects. A good deal of the new poetry after 1690 must have appeared to learned readers like an old and dignified friend seen for the first time in his coarsest and most casual clothes. Never before had such a large body of non-dramatic verse served to explore the contours of middle-class life. The poems of Gay were among the most remarkable for this quality. The older Renaissance form of the town progress,[5] a staple of the Cavalier love poets, was replaced by the first thoroughly realistic urban landscape poetry in the *Trivia*:

> Where the fair columns of St Clement stand,
> Whose straightened bounds encroach upon the Strand;
> Where the low penthouse bows the walker's head,
> And the rough pavement yields the wounding tread;

[2] Margaret Anne Doody, *The Daring Muse: Augustan Poetry Reconsidered* (Cambridge: Cambridge University Press, 1985), 9.

[3] John Donne, *Devotions on Emergent Occasions* (Ann Arbor: University of Michigan Press, 1959); see "Death's Duelle."

[4] See *Baucis and Philemon*, lines 101–116. Jonathan Swift, *The Complete Poems*, ed. Pat Rogers (London: Penguin, 1983), 104–105.

[5] Herrick's "Corinna's Going A-Maying" is a good contrast. In that poem each of the town's corners or gardens recalls Christian and Classical conventions of *amor*. There are examples of the older method in Rowlands and Carew as well.

> Where not a post protects the narrow space,
> And strung in twines, combs dangle in thy face;
> Summon at once thy courage, rouse thy care,
> Stand firm, look back, be resolute, beware.
> Forth issuing from steep lanes the collier's steeds
> Drag the black load; another cart succeeds,
> Teams follow teams, crowds heaped on crowds appear,
> And wait impatient till the road grows clear,
> Now all the pavement sounds with trampling feet,
> And the mixed hurry barricades the street.   (*Trivia*, III, 117–30)

And:

> If cloath'd in black you tread the busy town,
> Or if distinguished by the reverend Gown,
> Three trades avoid; oft in the mingling Press,
> The Barber's apron soils the sable dress;
> Shun the perfumer's touch with cautious eye,
> Nor let the Baker's step advance too nigh . . .
> The little chimney-sweeper skulks along,
> And marks with sooty stains the headless throng;
> The dustman's coat offends the cloaths and eyes,
> When through the street a cloud of ashes flies.
>   (*Trivia*, III, 25–34)[6]

The first passage has the racy and realistic quality in its detail which we look for in the novel. The scene itself is the distant cousin of both the beginning of *Bleak House* and the London of *The Waste Land*, but its observations are less infected by metaphor, or by any intervening intellectualism. This is an unsentimental art. In the succeeding lines it playfully describes the evening violence of fisticuffs and robbery, and in several places shows that mild and ironically blasphemous allusions to Bible reference which was a common element of Augustanism.[7] Classical and biblical material is always out of place in this poetry; one could say that it is out of scale with the surrounding material. The most perfect use of the contrast between the mundane and the older literary order is in Pope's *Rape*, but it is a common element in the larger Augustan repertoire. This unlikeness to the past, to the classical, or even the Miltonic is a discrepancy felt by the age, and part of the atmosphere of anxiety which W. J. Bate has described.[8]

The second passage of Gay above is taken from the daytime scene of the *Trivia*. It looks forward to a fiction of social conscience, and to the dreadful realism and scatology of *The Dunciad*. The characters of Cloacina and

---

[6] John Gay, *Poetry and Prose* (Oxford: Clarendon Press, 1974), 160–161, and 144.
[7] See above in the discussion of Pope's epigram on Newton.
[8] W. J. Bate, *The Burden of the Past and the English Poet* (New York: Norton Publishers, 1970), 101–103, and *passim*.

several of the laborers in Pope first appeared in the *Trivia*. The mixed sense of whimsical attraction and moral aloofness of Gay distinguishes him from the imitators of Juvenal's urban satires, and the languid pacing of details distinguishes him from the Swift of "A Description of a City Shower." Gay, like Garth and Shenstone after him, is an unambitious poet, and suited by a strange mixture of realism and complacency to be the perfect precursor to the later phase of Augustanism. There is nothing in him of Professor Greene's "Augustinian"(least of all in the *Beggar's Opera*), as there is none in Garth or Pope.[9] Conceptions of sin, repentance, spiritual militarism, and world-weariness are not central to this poetry as they are to that of Young, Johnson, and many of the writers of the later period of Protestant reaction. It might be remarked that this mundane revelation found its voice for the first and last time in the Augustan period. Eliot's London streets are full of nauseated regret, as is the image of the city in Keats, Coleridge, and especially De Quincey. But though the Augustans held the life of the middle class and the court up to ridicule, there was also a sense of attraction, a relishing of new social energies and expectations. Pope, Addison, Steele, Gay, Garth, Tickell, Parnell, and many others, were both the disclosers and the defenders of this new world of things.

One of the surprising aspects of this revolution of taste is the new possibility of subject matter it discovers. In Garth's *Dispensary*, to take an early and popular example, the issue of charitable medical aid is taken up. The general method, like that of *The Rape of the Lock*, is mock-heroism borrowed from Boileau, but unlike *The Rape*, Garth's poem seems to lose track of the relations between the heroic and medical themes. The objects of the hospital in a sense overwhelm their epic counterparts, and dissolve the "plan" of the poem. In this Garth represents (with great charm) the new realism:

> And now the staggering braves, led by despair,
> Advance, and to return the charge prepare.
> Each seizes for his shield a spacious scale,
> And the brass weights fly thick as showers of hail.
> Whole heaps of warriors labor on the ground,
> With galley-pots and broken phials crowned,
> While empty jars the dire defeat resound.

[9] Professor Donald Greene argues that the gloomy and pensive qualities of Swift and Johnson (and many of their contemporaries) might best be seen as "Augustinian." Their consciousness of human fallibility, of the general level of human immorality and sin, could be construed as the residual effect of Calvinism in their religion. I have opted to remove Johnson (for different reasons) from the Augustan camp altogether, and instead, to associate that term with the particular strain of empiricism, irony, and scientific rationalism, often combined with a worldly and circumspect humor. The real models are Waller and Denham, Pope, Gay, Steele, Tickell, the earlier works of Dryden, and several less important figures like Garth, Granville, and Bolingbroke.

This poem, printed in 1699, has an obvious connection to the method of
The Dunciad, but more importantly it shows that, by the turn of the
eighteenth century, subject matter of all kinds, even the popular modes of
contemporary journalism, had entered into poetry. Nor should we think of
this as mere "vers société," when it was taken seriously by so many of
Garth's contemporaries. Pope and Swift, who were not sympathetic with
the Whiggish, Kit-cat Club connections of Garth, were nonetheless
appreciative of his victory over intractable materials; and the poem recalls
the words of Sprat, himself a "scientific moralist," that "poetry must
encompass new things, and in a new way gain a place among the serious
subjects of our time."[10] It is important to note that Garth also wrote a long
landscape poem, *Claremont*, in the tradition of Denham's *Cooper's Hill*, a
number of medical treatises, and Latin translations (including a partial
Lucretius). Like Gay in his *Rural Sports* and *Shepherd's Week*, Garth contributed to the new literalizing and spatializing of the traditional pastoral.
These projects of Garth – urban satire, scientific apology, de-idealized
landscape – as I indicate in chapter 3, are all part of a unified and empirical
imaginative movement, and the scientific and descriptive characteristics
combine to replace the remaining traces of Christian iconic lore.

Garth, Gay, and Pope were simply the most successful of numerous poets
of the quotidian. The number of poems on precious and hitherto unpoe-
tical topics was astounding. Even lyric poetry of the period, like that of
Ramsay, is larded with incidental description:

> While kettles dringe on ingles drour,
> Or clashes stay the lazy lass,
> The songs may ward ye frae the sour,
> And gaily vacant minutes pass.
>
> ("The Dedication prefixed to the Tea-table Miscellany," 18–21 from
> [*English Poetry of the Eighteenth Century*, edited by C. A. Moore (New York:
> Henry Holt and Company, 1935), 363.]

These "gaily vacant minutes" pass in a good deal of eighteenth-century
verse, as if time had slowed down to make the world of sight more readily
available for inspection.[11] In this sense the poetry of Pope dwells upon tiny
objects, and, as in the coming of "Fate" in the scissors scene in *The Rape of
the Lock* shrinks time to a narrow span. The whole tradition of Augustan
trivialization and mockery is ironically summarized in the first book of
Cowper's *Task*, which in its subsequent books looks back and imitates all
the phases of eighteenth-century poetry from Augustan mock-heroism to

[10] Thomas Sprat, *History of the Royal Society* (Cambridge: Cambridge University Press, 1865), 48.
[11] This is true of a good deal of colonial American poetry as well. For example, "The Hasty
Pudding" and "John Bell's Walk," employ the same prosaic but accurate observation. This
form of poetry remained popular in nineteenth-century poems of worldly wit like those of
Oliver Wendell Holmes.

proto-Romantic sublimity (in the "Winter's Evening Walk"). Shenstone is another important case, for though Thomson had put new wine into Spenserian bottles before him, Shenstone was the most successful at producing pathos and humor by juxtaposing a serious Renaissance form with humble and descriptive matter. *The Schoolmistress* is one of the most interesting lessons in the Augustan art of scale, and perhaps nothing can bring home the breach of poetic consciousness between the Renaissance and the Enlightenment more clearly than this humble poem.

> Algates from silk misfortune free.
> Stir'n but as nature doth abroad them call;
> Then squatten down with hand beneath each knee,
> Ne seeken out or secret nook or wall,
> But cack in open street – no shame doth them appal.[12]

More could be said about Shenstone's morality, his relation to the problems of the village and city, of capitalism, of changing ideas of metaphor, and of the uses of allegory, but we must move on to larger matters.

These changes also affected the general poetic idea of man. Man in seventeenth-century poems held a distinguished position. The human was a microcosm of the whole creation, a perfect anatomy of the world, and it was not until the Augustan period that he was made fully and distinctly physical. This process is seen in Defoe and Sterne and in the grotesque and uninhibited descriptions of prostitutes, young lovers, and others in the poetry of Swift. It was a commonplace in medieval moralities that a corpse resided just a little below the living human skin – that there was a native rottenness about the flesh. But Swift brought a new zeal for the literal to this observation:

> The black, which would not be confined,
> A more inferior station seeks,
> Leaving the fiery red behind,
> And mingles in her muddy cheeks.
>
> The paint by perspiration cracks,
> And falls in rivulets of sweat;
> On either side you see the tracks,
> While at her chin the confluents met.
>
> A skillful housewife thus her thumb
> With spittle while she spins anoints;
> And thus the brown meanders come
> In trickling streams betwixt her joints . . .

---

[12] William Shenstone, The School-Mistress. A Poem in Imitation of Spencer's style, 73–77 in *The New Oxford Book of Eighteenth Century Verse*, ed. Roger Lonsdale (London: Oxford University Press, 1984), 307.

> Two balls of glass may serve for eyes,
> White lead can plaster up a cleft:
> But these, alas, are poor supplies
> If neither cheeks or lips be left.
>
> Ye powers who over love preside,
> Since mortal beauties drop so soon,
> If you would have us well supplied,
> Send us new Nymphs with each new moon.[13]

When we read these lines, we recall the hyperbolic and brutal technique of
A Modest Proposal, and that such vulgarity was one of the peculiar territories
of Swift's imagination. This is not the lusty and poignant pornographic
style of Rochester, nor the complicated sensuality of Donne or Middleton.
It affects the cool and mechanical mode of observation then associated
with the science of anatomy. But it is just one of many strands of poetic
empiricism. We too easily overlook the connection between Swift's
anatomy lesson and the descriptive dissections of Pope, Mallett, Gay, and
Thomson. We too often say that the real mark of Augustanism was
abstraction and personification. These were the common possession of
French and English Neoclassicism, and they can be seen in early Pope, in
Addison's *Campaign* and *Cato*, in Thomson's *Winter* and *Liberty*, and elsewhere. But Augustanism is a broader, more difficult movement, and within
it is this counter-growth of detail – this closeness to things, which is
anything but abstract.

Secular poetry ought to interest itself in a special way with the world,
and Augustan poetry does. It stands between two great symbol-making
ages – the English Renaissance and the Romantic period. The full weight
of things in this world, neither as allegorical trumpery, nor as spiritual
analogy, is almost uniquely present in the work of Hobbes, Butler,
Rochester, Locke, Swift, Gay, and Pope. A brief review of the mundane and
quotidian subjects which dominate the texts (after 1740) which Roger
Lonsdale has recovered from the massive corpus of magazine poetry in
Britain will show to any reader the actual results of the supposedly classical
experiments of Swift, Pope, and their contemporaries.[14] These earlier
experiments were baby-steps toward the liberation from the Christian /
Classical genre complex of the Renaissance. In an early poem like *The
Splendid Shilling*, the screen of the classical and Miltonic model is still dimly
placed between the poet and a complete mundane transparency. In the
"Bootblack" section of the *Trivia*, the classical itself is mocked on behalf of
brutal realism. In a later phase, in poems of trade and agriculture the

---

[13] Swift, *Poems*, 195, 147. "The Progress of Beauty," 33–44; 113–120.
[14] See the wide variety of magazine poetry collected in *The New Oxford Book of Eighteenth Century Verse*.

classicizing elements disappear altogether, and the heroic couplet becomes a vehicle for recording the whole range of mundane human activities. Sir Charles Hanbury Williams uses the opening gesture of *The Epistle to Dr. Arbuthnot* in his "Isabella." The traces of Pope's language and rhythm remain, but the plot and imagery of domestic prose fiction have taken over.

> The monkey, lap-dog, parrot, and her Grace
> Had each retired from breakfast to their place,
> When hark, a knock! "See, Betty, see who's there."
> "'Tis Mr. Bateman, ma'am, in his new chair."
> "Dicky's new chair! the charming'st thing in town,
> Whose poles are lacquered and whose lining's brown!"
> But see, he enters with his shuffling gait:
> "Lord," says her Grace, "how could you be so late?"
> (from Charles Hanbury Williams, *Isabella: or, The Morning*, 1–8; from
> Lonsdale [see n. 12], p. 328)

This poem was published in 1740. In the twenty years which follow there are poems of every trade and sport. The street-sweepers of William White-head, the threshers of Stephen Duck, the sugar-gatherers of James Grainger, and countless others are the first true figures of modern Georgic – the Georgic of capital labor. Compared with them Thomson is a halfway house of the classical. But even Thomson (as we shall see in the next section) is a central figure in the creation of a modern spatial poetic. This great body of quotidian verse was one of the dominant strains of poetry down to the nineteenth century. The supposedly novel realism and simplicity of Wordsworth's beggars and leech-gatherers had already been outdone by the gross particularity and vulgarity of mid-eighteenth-century poetry. Wordsworth, in fact, resymbolizes and elevates the moral tone and iconic landscape of the poetry which he knew so well in his youth. The Romantic was in part a project of returning to the analogical aura of an earlier period. Wordsworth's claim in his great "Preface to the Lyrical Ballads" that the eighteenth century had only a few poems of observant natural description was an attempt no doubt to escape the burden of his own recent past. His forgetfulness has become our blindness.

Pope's mock-heroic screen in *The Rape of the Lock* and *The Dunciad* is elaborate. It may lead a good reader to imagine a complex moral allegory and a sophisticated tribute to Milton or Virgil. But such a sublime connection should never be exaggerated. It is an attempt to add prestige and seriousness to the novelistic. Augustan critics have always been embarrassed by the degradation of the lyric and epic conventions of earlier periods which constitute the real originality of Pope and Swift. They have, therefore, overvalued the instrument over the vehicle, and confused the color with the substance of Augustan poems. The true subject of Pope is the domestic and trivial sphere of Belinda – his patroness of the literal. In the same sense that Sidney and Scaliger, in claiming the highest place for Xenophon's *Cyropaedia*, understood rhyme and meter as inessential to epic poetry, so we, I believe, might be justified in thinking of the narrative verse of Butler, Pope, and Gay, for all its brilliance, as finding a place among works of modern fiction. Their meter and rhyme may be inessential decorations of good modern prose.

This gives new meaning to the old insight of Arnold that the age of Pope was a great era of prose. *The Rape of the Lock* is in the same satirical mode as the works of Fielding and Sterne – all are examples of the modern fictional plot. The connection of this poetic naturalism to prose fiction and to the whole social revolution that such a genre suggests has been argued and re-argued, but the problems presented by the broader revolution of description and figuration which created them both is still laboring toward explanation.

Augustan naturalism

In the poetry of Thomson we have the finest example of the last phase of Augustan poetry. Thomson rarely involved himself in irony, much less burlesque. He arrived on the scene when the poetry of the eye was yet to be perfected, and he produced a perennial favorite of the English reader. "There is true fame," Coleridge remarked, picking up a copy of *The Seasons* from the shelf of a highway inn, and he was right, because the innovations of subject matter and particularly the expansion of scenic poetry changed forever the horizon of English verse.

McKillop and others have shown the relation of Thomson's philosophy to fashionable optimism and the new science.[15] But is it not odd that the son of a devout minister of the Scottish Presbytery,[16] one famous for exorcisms and visions, should write poems which are fundamentally empirical and secular? No doubt the summary of key events and influences described by Thomson's biographer, Douglas Grant,[17] are accurate so far as they go, but the influence of a single schoolmaster in stripping him of unnecessary "conceits," the struggle to rise above the limitations of his dialect, reading from the essays of Steele and Addison, a supposed aversion to gloomy local Calvinism, an introduction to Newton's theory in his opening weeks in London, his constitutional idleness and latitude of

---

[15] See Alan D. McKillop, *The Background of Thomson's Seasons* (Minneapolis: University of Minnesota Press, 1961); and Herbert Drennon, "James Thomson's Contact with Newtonianism and his Interest in Natural Philosophy," *PMLA* 49 (1964), 71–80. Also, John Dixon Hunt, *The Figure in the Landscape: Poetry, Painting and Gardening during the Eighteenth Century* (Baltimore: Johns Hopkins University Press, 1976).

[16] *Dictionary of National Biography* (London: Macmillan, 1949), vol. XXI, 77.

[17] Douglas Grant, *James Thomson, Poet of The Seasons* (London: The Cresset Press, 1951).

opinion – all these are the elements of a too well-known mythology.[18]
Nonetheless, Thomson was suited by some accidents of character to thrive
in the moment of mature Augustanism, when satire had done its work in
erasing the habits of conceit, and when a descriptive art unencumbered
with paradox and with a much broader field of visual material had become
popular. In a strange way the foreignness of standard English, which he
must have felt upon arriving in London, was, I suppose, an aid in stripping
himself of cliché and educated archaism. Milton was his main source for
the literary, and Milton's eccentricities were so remote from Thomson's
that their combination was enriching without being stifling. Thomson
became in a very short time one of the great innovators of English poetry.
Winter, arriving at the press after a brief residence in England and with
limited patronage at first, precipitated a minor sensation, which grew over
the remaining twenty-two years of Thomson's life.

It is quite clear that in the period before the Civil War in England nature
had not been, in our modern, empirical sense, fully naturalized. In the
earlier period nature had been treated in two opposite ways. First as the
jewelry of God, an iconic panoply reflecting at a distance His various
virtues, a kind of specular emanation of the original creation in God's
mind, as when Raphael says to Adam in *Paradise Lost*:

> I shall delineate so,
> By likening spiritual to corporeal forms,
> As may express them best, though what if earth
> Be but the shadow of heav'n, and things therein
> Each to each other like; more than on earth is thought.
>
> (Milton, *PL* v, 572–576)[19]

The second common sense of "nature" was as an injured and decayed
wilderness – the scene of the drama of redemption. In either case the kind
of realism we have come to expect was only occasionally found in the
traditional corpus of European poetry. Even less common was the landscape of the neutral observer. The various scenic modes of the Renaissance
– pastoral, Georgic, piscatorial, astronomic, exotic – were all highly
stylized. And like their late ancient originals they maintained a kind of
moral decorum as well, showing the classes and professions, the human
landscape in conventional relations. Less common still was the de-peopled
or "de-moralized" landscape for landscape's sake with the fauna and flora
as autonomous objects of description.

If we take for the sake of our experiment the landscape of Thomson's
earliest poem, *Winter,* we may discover the peculiarity of Augustan descrip-

---

[18] For an excellent treatment of Thomson's development see Hoxie Neal Fairchild, *Religious Trends in English Poetry* (New York: Columbia University Press, 1939), vol. i, 514–517.
[19] John Milton, *Paradise Lost,* ed. Alistair Fowler (London: Longman, 1971), 292–293.

tion. In the *Second Shepherd's Play,* which takes place on Christmas Eve, there
are several passages about chapped skin, hiding in shelters from the stormy
blast, and the other rigors of the shepherd's life in winter, but there is
practically no landscape. This may seem peculiar in a play ostensibly about
the Yorkshire laborers surviving the rigors of winter, but the play mysteriously turns out to take place in Bethlehem on the original Christmas Eve,
and the Yorkshire shepherds are transformed into the first visitors of
Christ. I mention this play, though I might have mentioned Chaucer or
Langland, because with all the physical immediacy of these authors they
depend suprisingly little on effects of natural description. Never is the
moralité far from hand.

> Was never sin' Noah's flood
> Such floods seen,
> Winds and rains so rude
> And storms so keen:
> Some stammered, some stood
> In doubt as I ween.
> Now God turn all to Good.
>
> (*Second Shepherd's Play,* 183–189)

This is a typical passage, framed as it is in biblical motifs. The author of
Gawain and the Green Knight has one extended description of winter weather
on the morning of his knight's setting out finally to meet the green giant.
This passage is almost *sui generis* in late medieval English literature.

Spenser's *Shepherd's Calendar* is lacking in extended natural description of
winter even in the months between November and March. There is a total
of about ten lines of physical description in those sections of the poem,
mostly laden with clichéd epithets. In Shakespeare, winter is mentioned
frequently both in the sonnets and the plays, but with little extended
description. Like most Elizabethan winters his is utterly humanized:

> Fear no more the heat o' the sun,
>   Nor the furious winter's rages;
>
> (*Cymbeline,* IV. 2. 258–259)

> When Icicles hang by the wall
>   And Dick the Shepherd blows his nail,
> And Tom bears logs into the hall,
>   And milk comes frozen home in pail,
> When blood is nipp'd and ways be foul,
> Then nightly sings the staring owl
> "Tu-whit, tu-who": a merry note,
> While Greasy Joan doth stir the pot.
>
> (*Love's Labour's Lost,* "Epilogue")

Milton is not confronted with the problem of winter in *Paradise Lost.*

None of Dryden's or Pope's descriptive poems are winterscapes. The great
first explosion of winter description came on the heels of the first publication of *Winter* (1726). There are scores in the later eighteenth century. An
expanded field of winter imagery – swirling snows, gathering winds, ice –
becomes a staple, culminating in the remarkable "Winter-walk" in
Cowper, and carried over to the Romantics. Thomson's poem, like the
mystery play, Spenser, and Shakespeare, has shepherds, but he does not
moralize their condition. He admonishes them by means of a typical
elaboration of detail and perspective:

> Now, Shepherd, to your helpless Charge be kind,
> Baffle the raging Year, and fill the Pens
> With Food at Will; lodge them below the Storm,
> And watch them strict: for from the bellowing East,
> In this dire Season, oft the Whirlwind's Wing
> Sweeps up the Burthen of whole wintry Plains
> In one wide Waft, and o'er the hapless Flocks,
> Hid in the Hollow of two neighboring Hills,
> The billowy tempest whelms; till, upward urged,
> The valley to a shining mountain swells,
> Tipt with a wreath, high curling in the Sky.[20]   (*Winter*, 265–275)

The passage opens with a reference to Virgil's warning to the shepherds
in *Georgics*, III (349–360) about the snows of winter. It has two Miltonisms –
"watch them strict" and "billowy tempest whelms." Beyond this it greatly
deepens the visual detail of the storm, describing the wind pushing the
snow into the cleft of the valley and leaving a curl of snow at the top of a
new mountain of snow. Two mountains become three, and the sheep are
buried in the drifts. All of this is described in terms of a great wave of the
sea. The marine image is a favorite of Virgil's ("incubuere mari totumque
et sedibus imis / una Eurusque Notusque ruunt . . . et vastos volvunt ad
litora fluctus").[21]

As with the other seasons, winter has a set of visual, one might say
mechanical, parallels between the winds, the oceans, the forces under the
earth. These are only partly borrowed from Virgil. Thomson greatly
elaborates and regularizes the meteorological elements of his poem. The
scene itself is derived no doubt from Thomson's own observations of the
Scottish glens, filled as they often are by windblown sheets of snow, and
from the lost sheep of midwinter storms which were a perennial problem
for northern farmers. What is a fantasy of the North (Maeotis and *Ultima
Thule*) for Virgil is a known fact in the *Winter* of Thomson. *Winter*, written

---

[20] James Thomson, *The Seasons*, ed. J. Sambrooke (Oxford: Clarendon Press, 1981), 216. All other
quotations from *The Seasons* will be taken from this text and marked by Book and line numbers
after the quoted passage.
[21] Virgil, *Aeneid*, I, 84–86.

only months after his first visit to England, retains a larger number of specifically Scottish situations. It also maintains more of the Miltonic / Burkean sublime, while its debt to Job gives it a feeling of archaic moral power missing in the other seasons. Its language may be fruitfully compared with the stormy ocean images in "On the Death of his Mother," written at about the same time, which is also his good-bye to Scotland.

> Chilled with a sad presaging damp I stood,
> Took the last look, ne'er to behold her more,
> And mixed our murmurs with the wavy roar . . .
> Nor sunk that moment in the vast abyss!
> Devoured at once by the relentless wave.[22]

If *Summer* is a poem of the anxiety of the scientific man in a world of unfathomable space (an empirical fantasy), *Winter* is a more backward-looking poem. It is a contrast to *Summer* in just this way, an elegy for the possibility of a fully moralized landscape with a veiled nostalgia for the Calvinist totalism of Thomson's youthful religion. Without indulging in wild psychological speculation we may imagine the man (*Winter* 276–321) cut off permanently from his home and family in the swirling snows as a figure of the poet cutting the bonds with his familial scene. The shorter, original version of "Winter" also has traces of an older, punitive theology, like the one preached so dramatically by Thomson's father. This is replaced in the later *Seasons* with growing optimism and positivism. Nonetheless, the direction of Thomson's mind is always toward a greater and greater elaboration of spatial view.

Pope and Thomson had the same fundamentally empirical, even painterly turn of mind. Augustanism, while it was infatuated with personi-fication, that shriveled offspring of the Renaissance emblem, was never involved in what Professor Krieger calls "deluding generalizations."[23] Whatever may be said of its repressive ethos or "habits of rationalization," the Augustan age was capable of the most painfully particular poetry. Here are Pope and Thomson describing a spider:

> The spider's touch how exquisitely fine!
> Feels at each thread, and lives along the line:
>   (*An Essay on Man*, I, 217–218)

>   where gloomily retired,
> The villain spider lives, cunning and fierce,
> Mixture abhorred! Amid a mangled heap
> Of carcasses in eager watch he sits.
> O'erlooking all his wavering, light snares . . .

22 James Thomson, *Poetical Works* (New York: Thomas Cromwell, 1926), 403.
23 Murray Krieger, *The Classic Vision: The Retreat from Extremity in Modern Literature* (Chicago: University of Chicago Press, 1966), 144.

> The prey at last ensnared, he dreadful darts
> With rapid glide along the leaning line.   (*Summer*, 269–277)

These are very sophisticated and minute poetic observations. The last line of each passage is a nearly perfect example of these extraordinary descriptive and rhythmical imaginations. What the Romantics regained for poetry was not perception, and surely not nature, but epiphany, illumination, and analogy. The object seen, the Lockeian primary quality, the tradition of arrangement and perspective, are the common Augustan qualities. Perhaps no English poetry of the nineteenth century can equal Thomson and Pope in concentrated description. It is the Romantics, not Thomson and Pope, who "see with a theory." An intervening abstraction colors and directs the descriptive matter of most nineteenth-century poetry. Wordsworth's *Prelude* or Keats' Odes (aside, perhaps, from the "Ode to Autumn") are anything but empirical in their method. Blake regarded empiricism and naturalism with contempt.

The great Augustan poets share the sensibility of the painter, not only in specific descriptive poems like *The Temple of Fame, Claremont, The Ruins of Rome, The Seasons*, and *The Castle of Indolence*, but also in their general commitment to the "view" with its special sensual arrangement. This quality marks the most mature phase of Augustanism. Neither Cowley nor Dryden had entered this descriptive project, though they had both written with great concern about the sister arts of poetry and painting. Perhaps only Spenser among earlier poets had attempted this particular mode of charming observation. But in him there was a difference. He was not a naturalist, nor was his elegance decorative. The object of his painting was not the image itself, but the moral evocation of the image.

The general tendency of the Augustan is to break down structures of allegoresis. Plucking the visual out of its traditional iconic context and giving it the quality of immediate experience is a common gesture throughout the whole period. Pope's *Temple of Fame*, for example, differs from its Chaucerian model in being primarily a poem of observation. It is not surprising to find that the temple of eternal ice was based upon Pope's study of contemporary descriptions of "everlasting" ice and snow brought back to England by the first explorers of the Arctic.[24] The *Temple of Fame* and *The Seasons* are de-allegorized allegories in which the observing power seems to override any moral purpose. As we shall see, the exact opposite is true of Prior's *Alma*, or Johnson's "Vision of Theodore" and *Rasselas*, works which ostensibly continue but in fact attack the Augustan prejudices. Augustan "empiricism" also informs the interest Pope and Thomson (but most assuredly not Johnson) shared in gardens and landscape.

---

[24] Alexander Pope, *The Correspondence*, ed. George Sherburn (London: Oxford University Press, 1956), vol. II, 157.

The most important tendency of the Augustan imagination is its literalizing and novelty, the history of which I began to chart in the last chapter. I call it "literalizing" rather than "abstraction," because all writing is a form of generalizing. Donne and Herbert were masters of abstraction – of finding recondite speculations and constructing general propositions:

> But as all severalle soules containe
>   Mixture of things, they know not what,
> Love these mixed soules, doth mix againe,
>   And makes both one, each this and that.
>   (Donne, "The Extasie," 33–36)[25]

> Teach me, my God and King,
>   In all things, thee to see,
>   And what I do in anything,
> To do it as for Thee.   (Herbert, "The Elixir," 1–4)[26]

Donne and Herbert were masters equally of thought and image, but they did not labor over particulars. In Donne the dissolution of bodies into soul parallels the work of conceit in dissolving many particulars into their parent essence. Herbert "sees" each thing in God, the eye cannot be granted the luxury of accidental discovery. But this can not be said of Thomson. He was more expressly concerned with the particular than any other English writer before the nineteenth century. In a letter to David Mallet, Thomson claims, "I should wish to describe everything as if for the first time. My muse is not selective but greedy, and every object grows singular in my eye."[27] This is not an interest in "what oft was thought, but ne'er so well expressed," but what was never before seen or described. If we could make a catalog of things which Thomson (and a few of his ambitious contemporaries) added to the "material" of English poetry, it would be astounding. Of course he is not without a moral interest and tone We can see the commonplace scientific optimism at the end of *Summer*, and the Whig doctrine of "liberty" in *Autumn*, but what we chiefly take away from the poems is a continuous fabric of images. In fact we can go farther and say that the Whig liberty and the subsequent *laissez-faire* of Adam Smith depend on an aesthetic of personal discovery, of the private property of experience. Just as in *An Essay on Man* the human agent is pushed forward by his own particular and secret motive, the ruling passion, so in the open field of the social, the Mandevillian capitalist sees the whole world as a kind of storehouse of private delights. Each man must interpret and

---

[25] John Donne, *Poetical Works*, ed. H. J. C. Grierson (Oxford: Clarendon Press, 1912), 52.

[26] George Herbert, *Works* (Oxford: Clarendon Press, 1941), 184.

[27] James Thomson, *Unpublished Letters of Thomson to Mallett*, ed. Paul Cunningham (London: Philobiblion Society Proceedings, vol. IV, 1854), 67.

measure his own desire, and from this a greatest good will arise. This ethic
was strengthened, even prepared, by the roving empirical landscape of
Thomson. The movement from cosmos to heterocosm, from topos to
landscape, was a necessary step in removing the bondage to an essentialist
metaphysics.

Bonamy Dobrée remarks, "Thomson opens doors, which he himself
does not seem to be aware of. Apparently he thinks he is describing; he is
really lifting the shutter of intensely imaginative vision."[28] Dobrée's
example of this is a remarkable passage from the 1726 edition of *Winter*.

> the *Bear*
> Rough *Tenant* of these Shades! shaggy with Ice
> And dangling Snow, stalks thro' the Woods, forlorn.
>
> (*Winter*, 432–434)

A thing may be both "intensely imaginative" and a description. If this
were not true a good deal of our most distinguished landscape and still-life
painting would be negligible at best. It was finding new things to describe,
and placing those things in a novel and extensive scene, which was the
genius of Thomson. There was more than a little courage in this gesture.
The objects of nature – "Newton's dazzling prism broad diffused," "the
shooting lights of telescopic view," the plenitude of garden, field, and
mountain, the fauna of new continents – of which this Russian bear is an
exotic example, were new to poetry, and Thomson had the high emotion of
an explorer. His world is not the world of bookish beasts and mythical
beings like that of Lyly, Donne, Burton, or even Browne, but a world in our
modern and Lockeian sense – a world of the things that appear before us.
It is this world that has the force of surprise and novelty, which, as far back
as Addison's *Spectator* 412 (June 23, 1712),[29] had been considered among the
Augustans a quality of the highest importance in poetry. It is this world that
Thomson was describing in his letter to Mallett, a world in which the
preexisting body of creaturely emblems, symbols, and analogies are
completely transformed. Thomson's fanciful plethora crowds out the old
order of "bugbears and goblins of the mind" which were despised by
Bacon, Locke, and Adam Smith. The novelty of the Russian bear and the
Newtonian rainbow is weighted with the authority of scientific observation.

In one respect *The Seasons* may embrace the cyclical structure, the "above
and below," and the humanistic hierarchies of the late Renaissance. But the
constant interruption of the narrative with praise of the Creator, and
remembrances of the first cause, is never fully integrated with the larger
imaginative nexus. The divine encomium which ends *Summer* is a labored

---

[28] Bonamy Dobrée, *English Literature in the Early Eighteenth Century* (London: Oxford University Press, 1959) 492.

[29] Joseph Addison, *The Spectator* 412, from (London: Dent, 1945) vol. III, 279–280.

and disproportionately small tribute. The tribute of God always turns back to nature itself – to its mechanism, its vitality. One feels that God is a superplus, an excrescence in this world. While the language of creation and sustenance by God is contrived and thin, the language of the *Alma Venus*, the tutelary spirit of physical nature, is magnificent. I will give alternating examples:

> Nor to this evanescent speck of earth
> Poorly confined: the radiant tracks on high
> Are his exalted range; intent to gaze
> Creation through; and from the full complex
> Of never-ending wonders, to conceive
> Of the Sole Being right, who spoke the word,
> And Nature moved complete.   (*Summer*, 1782–1788)

> When first the soul of love is sent abroad,
> Warm through the vital air, and on the heart
> Harmonious seizes, the gay troops begin
> In gallant thought to plume the painted wing . . .
>   Every copse
> Deep-tangled, tree irregular, and bush
> Bending with dewy moisture o'er the heads
> Of the coy choristers that lodge within,
> Are prodigal of harmony. The thrush
> And wood-lark, o'er the kind contending throng
> Superior heard, run through the sweetest length
> Of notes, when listening Philomel deigns
> To let them joy . . .
> The blackbird whistles from the thorny brake,
> The mellow bullfinch answers from the grove;
> Nor are the linnets, o'er the flowering furze,
> Poured round profusely, silent. Joined to these
> Innumerous songsters, in the freshening shade
> Of new-sprung leaves, their modulations mix
> Mellifluous . . .
>   while the stock-dove breathes
> A melancholy murmur through the whole.
>   'Tis love creates their melody, and all
> This waste of music is the voice of love.   (*Spring*, 442–471)

Ruskin was correct to list *The Seasons* among the necessary preparations for "the extraordinary sort of investigations of Mr. Darwin."[30] Thomson's "finny tribes" and "connubial leagues" are the denizens of a competitive and sexual earth invented by the eighteenth century. They created those

---

[30] John Ruskin, *Fors Clavigera*, vol. II, 109 (London and New York: Merrill, 1910), 124.

"downward metaphors"[31] by which we were first brought into intimate and almost equal relation to animals.

A sea change had occurred in the contemporary descriptions of birds. The previous century had maintained almost throughout the conventional figures of theological analogy: in Thomas Randolph (1632)

> Go solitary wood, and henceforth be
> Acquainted with no other harmony
> Than the pie's chattering or the shrieking note
> Of boding owls, and fatal ravens throat.
> Thy sweetest chanter's dead, that warbled forth
> Lays that might tempests calm and still the North,
> And call down angels from their glorious sphere
> To hear her songs, and learn new anthems there.
>
> ("On the Death of a Nightingale," 1–8).[32]

Or in the case of an even later poet, Henry Vaughan (1651):

> Father of lights, what sunny seed,
> What glance of day hast thou confined
> Into this bird? To all the breed
> This busy ray thou hast assigned;
> Their magnetism works all night,
> And dreams of Paradise and light.
> Their eyes watch for the morning hue,
> Their little grain expelling night
> So shines and sings as if it knew
> The path unto the house of light,
> It seems their candle, how e'er done,
> Was tinned and lighted at the sun.[33]

Numerous parallels might be educed, where the creature still bore an intimate relation to man, and served as an emblem or *vestigium* of the divine. Through most of the seventeenth century nature was still a contrivance of grace, a lowly but useful mirror of the higher sphere. Naturalism, of course, came by degrees, but even the catalog of Milton in Book VII of *Paradise Lost* or Drayton's piscatorial catalogue in the twenty-sixth section of The *Poly-Olbion* can not with all their minute observation be compared with the naturalism of Thomson.[34] His was a new and

---

[31] I borrow this phrase from Robert Frost. It was first pointed out to me by Professor Robert Faggen.

[32] Thomas Randolph, *Poems*, ed. J. Thorn-Drury (London: Cambridge University Press, 1929), 83.

[33] Henry Vaughan, *The Complete Poems*, ed. A. Rudrum (New Haven: Yale University Press, 1985), 251.

[34] There is an important passage in Professor Spacks' *The Poetry of Vision* (Cambridge, Mass.: Harvard University Press, 1972, 123), in which she observes that: "In Thomson meaning derives from observation; in Smart meaning precedes observation. Thomson begins with a general attitude which his particular descriptions support, but the process of thought and emotion

powerful invention. It still, perhaps, has a very high place among naturalistic and descriptive poetry. Akenside was a loose and flamboyant theorist, Cowper a passionate ruminator, but Thomson's work was one of the most perfectly realized possibilities of Augustan art.

The literalizing trend of Augustan culture made popular a new and mechanical form of analogy. Here the analogy, so far from the spiritual relations described by the Scholastics, is merely one of verbal conformity or logical proportion. The emblematic material of the Renaissance and Middle Ages supported a metaphysical relation, a permanent connection between the divine and its analog. The eighteenth century reduced this connection to the relation of tenor and vehicle.

The *tabula rasa* demands no more for intellectual recognition than perceptive memory, and the "nature" produced by such an epistemology is no more than a loose field of diverse and accidentally associated objects. The baroque emblem is mysteriously potent. Bound from the first with the Logos, it bears the same relationship to imagination that the Eucharist bears to devotion. The conceit is not only, as in Johnson's phrase, the yoking of heterogeneous ideas "by violence together," but the recognition of occult resemblances between objects – primarily between the mundane and the supersensible. Where conceit is reduced to sophism or merely verbal play, as in Donne's "The Flea" and much of Cowley's and Cleveland's poetry, it is already approaching its later moribund state. This is why the development of Cowley's career is central to our study. In him and all the subsequent Augustans the conceit becomes a mechanism of simple comparison as in the Aristotelian *metaphora*.

This is also why works such as Bishop Butler's *Analogy*, with its mechanical association of animal and spiritual worlds, would ultimately appear as the weakest possible apology for Christianity, and why the good intentions of pious (but nominalist) Christians like Newton and Locke could not stem the tide of skepticism. Thomson and Pope appear squarely in the middle of this contemporary revision and, to use Wasserman's terms, *Windsor-Forest* was already a poem of association rather than correspondence.[35]

The movement of icon and allegory toward Augustan personification is seen very clearly in the decline of the Book of Hours and the emblem book (in the tradition of Quarles and Wither), and the movement toward the stylized historical–biblical pictures of the illustrated editions of Watts'

which *The Seasons* records is clearly the product of repeated stimuli. The same large movement occurs over and over: first description of real, or imagined objects; then reflection on the objects' implications and associations; finally, exhalation. The exhalation is the end product, its origins clear and explicit."

[35] Earl R. Wasserman, *The Subtler Language* (Baltimore: Johns Hopkins Press, 1959), 181–188.

Hymns for Children and Thomson's *Seasons*. The heightened realism and sentimentality of these eighteenth-century illustrations are part of the history of "naturalizing." Blake's scathing comments on Reynolds' *Lectures* and on landscape and history painting were a reaction to just such shrinkage of icon. Eighteenth-century verisimilitude eroded every element of traditional iconography.

It is not at all surprising that in painting, the older backgrounds, those touching landscapes of tree, grass, and sky, placed by Fra Angelico behind and beyond the scriptural subject, had by the time of Poussin grown forward, at last engulfing and obscuring the *figura essentiale*. If we look through the narrow arch of the casement divided by bars like a prison window in Fra Angelico's *St. Lawrence Receiving the Treasure of the Church*, we see a distant and frail, leafy greenness. This green world is wholly beyond. It is a part of the true otherness of the old natural order; infinitely below, but supporting as a symbol of vitality the central significance of the gift, the sacrament, and the martyred saint. Or more powerfully, the haunting blue tree-filled sky at the left corner of his *Annunciation*, above the wings of the angel and seen between the pillared arches of Mary's porch, appears as a dim reminder of the rood. The grass around the porch is sportive and tender, enhancing the quiet joy of the Holy Mother. At a later phase, in Titian's *Noli Me Tangere*, Christ is bending away from the beseeching Magdalen – on her side the cliffs by the road and the town, and over his head one withered tree in the grayish wilderness. She is of (or from) the world; he is, to use Dante's phrase, "a gift to death."

In so many more Renaissance paintings (like van der Weyden's *Pietà)* the division of nature and grace, the wilderness and the town, separated by the bloodied Christ, illuminate the old analogical cosmology. I remind you of this to show that nature was already an important part of the old iconology. It was background only in the sense that the whole world is the canvas of holy activity. All nature was a peaceful image of creative benevolence or a fearful emblem of the sodden path, and the place of sin. Later changes were not merely changes of technique and perspective, not a history of evolving realism, but a history, as in poetry, of consciousness and moral judgment. As Poussin moved beyond his Roman apprenticeship into his mature manner, he forsook the schemata of Raphael's biblical cartoons and turned to the architectural detail of classical ruin. At last, in his later landscapes he spread what had been the incidental and subordinated naturalism of Raphael or Domenichino across the whole width of his canvas. Such an expansion of autonomous landscape must be a self-conscious aesthetic judgment. It brings in a new world.

When we see the image of General Wolfe's dead body (in Benjamin West's great painting) imposed on the common Renaissance subject of Christ's removal from the cross, the displacement is not particularly irreverent, but neither does it borrow any life from the iconographic irony of the transformation. It is a mechanical and painterly traditionalism, but it yields no figurative depth. Wolfe is not portrayed as a saint or savior – the reference is merely structural. This is true of a good deal of eighteenth-century painting and poetry, where technique and "imitative veracity" become standards of value. Richard Jago, for example, took great pride in first getting "the true Newtonian rainbow into a poem."[36] This new stress on likeness and visual realism is mentioned everywhere in the period.

It was the study of this new naturalism in Poussin and Salvator that inspired England's three great Augustan landscape painters, Wilson, Gainsborough, and Constable. But when they turned to local subject, for the exhilarating detail of field and mountain,[37] it was not the Continental painters that inspired them most, but the great British genius of detail, James Thomson.[38]

The anxious eye: Thomson's *Summer*

It is a convention of the pastoral that summer is the season of shady repose and restful meditation. Escape from the enervating heat of midsummer and the noontide glare of the Arcadian sun is a common motif in Theocritus and Virgil. Such an escape suited the elaborate meditations of later pastoralists like Sanazzaro and Mantuan, and was repeated in English pastoral down to the time of Pope. Retreat from oppressive heat is the subject of the epigraph to the original version of James Thomson's *Summer*:

> Iam Pastor Umbras cum Grege languido,
> Rivumque fessus quaerit, & horridi
>   Dum et Sylvani: caretque
>   Ripa vagis taciturna ventis.[39]

>   (Horace, *Odes* III, xxix, 21–24)

[By now the shepherd with his listless flock, Worn out, seeks the shade and stream, and the rough home of Silvanus, while the quiet bank is forsaken by wandering breezes.]

The *locus classicus* of Roman pastoral summer is in the second "Eclogue" of

---

[36] Nicolson, *Newton Demands the Muse*, 123.
[37] See Ellis Waterhouse, *Painting in Britain 1530 to 1790* (Harmondsworth: Pelican, 1978), 236–263; and Michael Rosenthal, *Constable, The Painter and his Landscape* (New Haven: Yale University Press, 1983).
[38] About one out of five Constable landscapes are given titles from, and others are drawn from the imagery of passages in *The Seasons*. Its influence upon the whole landscape tradition is yet to be fully investigated.
[39] Horace, *Odes* III, xxix, 17–24, as misquoted in 1727 edition of *Summer*. The bracketed translations of Latin passages are my own.

Virgil, a reworking of the third Idyll of Theocritus. Corydon the lovesick
shepherd describes the ferocious summer to his cruel lover Alexis:

> mori me denique cogis.
> nunc etiam pecudes umbras et frigora captant,
> nunc viridis etiam occultant spineta lacertos,
> Thestylis et rapido fessis messoribus aestu . . .
> et mecum raucis, tua dum vestigia lustro,
> sole sub ardenti resonant arbusta cicadis.[40]

> (Virgil, *Eclogue* ii, 6–14)

> [In the end you will drive me to death.
> Now even the cows flee to the cool shade,
> Now the green lizards lurk under a bush,
> While Thestylis [prepares] for reapers worn-out with the scorching
>   summer heat . . .
> While I still trace your footsteps,
> My shrill notes beneath the blazing sun,
> Harmonize with those of the cicadas.]

It is from this scene that Pope derives his:

> But see, the Shepherds shun the noonday Heat,
> The lowing Herds to murmuring brooks retreat,
> To closer Shades the panting Flocks remove,
> Ye Gods! and is there no relief for Love?

Pope's *Summer* is a varnished imitation of Virgil's, and his characters, like
those in late-Renaissance pastoral, are mostly figures of idealized or tragic
love. The larger theme of the Horatian ode quoted by Thomson is that
fortune is cruel and we must accept the vicissitudes of life with equanimity.
Neither the amorous pastoral nor the stoical vision of summer seem to be
at the heart of Thomson's own project. It is more difficult to say what does
motivate and define Thomson's project and what relation it bears to its
great classical sources.

In *The Seasons*, Virgil is a much more central authority than Horace, in
part because the poems are ostensibly Georgic, and because after Lucretius
and the Hellenistic poets, Virgil had given the most imitated passages in
antiquity of extended landscape. Horace, who was for Pope the *métier* of the
classical, recedes into the shadow of Thomson's three great examples –
Virgil, Milton, and Lucretius. That the quotation from Horace was
omitted from all but the earliest version of *Summer* (1727) may indicate that
Thomson began to question its relevance. Indeed the first and last versions
of *Summer* are very unlike. The hundred or so lines on specifically pastoral
themes remained in the later versions, though often altered, but became a

[40] Virgil, *Opera*, ed. R.A.B. Mynors (London: Oxford University Press, 1969), 4.

smaller and smaller part of the whole performance. With the additions of
the exposition on insects (moved from a passage from *Spring* in 1730) and
microscopic vermin (266–317), of African landscape (690–896), the death
of the Stanley child (564–569), and others, the earlier idealized British
summer, ambiguous from the start, is nearly washed away. Of later
additions only the Damon narrative (1269–1370) retains some pastoral
elements, though the latest revisions (1744) of that story were not moving in
the direction of pastoral.

These observations may seem irrelevant to a reading of Thomson if we
determine that Georgic and not pastoral was the paradigm for *Summer*. But
several problems arise from the Georgic connection as well. First of all, the
amount of summer material in the Virgilian Georgic is oddly limited. In
the passage from Book II of the *Georgics* in which the seasons are mentioned
alternately (as Thomson does in the opening of each of his four seasons),
summer is the least important. It is merely waning in anticipation of the
cold breezes of winter at the end of autumn. "cum rapidus Sol / nondum
hiemem continguit equis, iam praeterit aestas [although the powerful sun
has not yet reached winter, by now the Summer is passed]."[41]

There is only one important passage on summer in the *Georgics* and that
appears in Book III at line 322. The language of the *laeta aetas* is largely a
repetition of the pastoral imagery of "Eclogue II" – the scorched grass, the
cooling stream and the shrill cicadas. Once again the goats and sheep seek
for the cooling shade, though this time under "Jove's mighty oak": "sicubi
magna Iovis antiquo robore quercus / ingentis tendat ramos," "Just where
the ancient oak with its huge trunk wreathes its great branches" was to
become a stock image in eighteenth-century British poetry from Dryden's
"pendant oaks" and from the wreathed roots and branches of the oaks in
Spenser and Shakespeare. It was by a beech that "wreathes its old, fantastic
roots so high" that the solitary wanderer of Gray's *Elegy* escaped the heat of
the day. The *sacra umbra* remains the place of ideal meditation and escape.
The single day in Virgil (like the one which circumscribes the giant
narrative of Thomson's *Summer*) begins with the morning star, moves
through the cool of the "fourth hour" to the "midday heat," and on to the
hour of the evening star. It ends with a warm moony night. Each of these
daily phases is given a single clause in Virgil. The entire day is composed in
sixteen lines, and it is more detailed than any other day of the Virgilian
calendar.

At the end of his comparison of Virgil and Thomson, the distinguished
Virgilian, L. P. Wilkinson, speaking of *The Seasons*, remarks "Though
descriptive, it has neither the eye for detail nor the ear for expressive sound
that makes the *Georgics* so vivid. Ideal rustics and wicked cities, Golden Age

---

[41] Virgil, *Opera*, 56, *Georgics*, II, 321–322.

life and *convicium saeculi.*"[42] The ear for expressive sound obviously refers to metrical virtuosity and in that respect Virgil has few peers, and certainly Thomson is not among them. But as to the "eye for detail," Thomson by any standard far exceeds his original. For while Virgil may produce descriptive clusters of unforgettable vividness, and may formulate his scenes with a verbal flourish rare in any poetry, Thomson far exceeds him in scope.

Ralph Cohen is right to call Thomson's method not so much "a poetry of sight as space,"[43] but it is in fact a poetry of sight regulated by larger spatial structures – scene, prospect, view. The range of sensoria in *The Seasons* dwarfs that of the *Georgics*, though such a fact should not necessarily be construed as a ground for preferring the later poem. Nor is Wilkinson correct that Thomson's rustics are all ideal or that he unambiguously recreates the ideal landscapes of the Golden Age. Thomson's realism is at best intermittent, but its scope is novel and impressive. The realistic elements far outweigh the idealized ones in *Summer*. I have chosen *Summer* for my exposition precisely because it was in this poem that Thomson's expanding and associative poetic, more than in any of his other works, reached its extreme.

Summer is an experiment in which those very elements of sight and space are least regulated by Georgic or Christian frames – where Augustan *judgment* found the greatest difficulty in controlling Augustan *variety*. The new objects of poetry, which had passed through their mature satirical phase in the city poems of Swift and Gay and into the maniacal city satire of *The Dunciad*, having glutted themselves upon the urban heterocosm, move on in Thomson to swallow the larger range of national and international geography. Nor did such an expansion produce an entirely neutral descriptive field, an expanded national Georgic, but included within it the whole range of satirical effects I have traced from Butler.

But in another sense a wholly original conception of neutral description is being tested in Thomson. The least important and the least representative qualities in Thomson are those of moral generalization, classical abstraction, and Christian theodicy. The existence of organic and moralizing elements points in the end to the inefficacy of teleological morality in an empirical poem. I realize that in saying this I am running counter to several of the most distinguished critics of Thomson, and it is with a good deal of trepidation that I do so. Patricia Spacks has thoroughly and incisively defended Thomson against the claim that he is a mere describer. She has shown with great dexterity the complex metaphorical layering of

[42] L. P. Wilkinson, *The Georgics of Virgil: A Critical Survey* (Cambridge: Cambridge University Press, 1968), 312.

[43] Ralph Cohen, *The Unfolding of the Seasons – A Study of James Thomson's Poem* (Baltimore: Johns Hopkins University Press, 1970), 101.

his work, and, to use her chapter title, "the dominance of meaning" over image in his project:

> In spite of his insistence that he is offering us something to "see," then, Thomson controls his descriptive passage through idea, a sense of pattern, rather than through visual detail. Not only are the actual "scenes" highly generalized, much of the presentation is not visual at all, hardly even sensuous.[44]

I have no doubt that Thomson's poetry is often abstract, that he has ideas and patterns of imagery, that his scenes are "highly generalized," and that much of his poetry is not visual or sensuous. Language by its nature limits the particularity of verbal description. Each noun serves both as a substitution for a visual idea and an abstraction from a generic notion. I would not wish to argue that there could be a truly Lockeian poetry – a mélange of simple ideas and relations; nor do I imagine that a poetry hinged to a Miltonic and sentimental Christianity on one side and Virgilian Georgic on the other could escape altogether the rigors of allusion. Allusion and imitation are always ways of shading and annexing the morality (often the metaphysical nuances) of remote ancestors without necessarily submitting to the implications of the original. Nonetheless having conceded this much, I wish to find out the grounds of Thomson's insistence that he is offering us something to "see." A descriptive poetry in the eighteenth century may be bounded by the practical limits of language but it is one that honors the eye, experience, and physical verisimilitude in a new way or to a new degree.

I have come to the question not from a desire to know whether Thomson is more true to nature than Cowper or Wordsworth, but rather why and how he wished to elude (by means of novel images and narratives of association) the iconic nexus of the preceding age – the shadow of the Baroque. I am interested in why Thomson chose to describe what we now rightly or wrongly call scenic nature. This interests me in part because for Thomson there was practically no prehistory of landscape in Europe – not even classical landscape, if we mean by it the kind of extended view we find in Thomson, Cowper, Wilson, and Constable. I wish to consider how strangely the "nature" of Spenser or the "nature" of Virgil might appear in the lens of Thomsonian description; and whether it is in fact the same "nature" at all. Perhaps an incipient positivism, a dread of the magical *locus* of Medieval nature, led the critics of the eighteenth and nineteenth centuries to honor Thomson primarily as a kind of Newton of description, but such an impulse must retain some significance for us in recalling the unusual circumstances that lead in painting and poetry to the emptying out of old forms and subject matter to make way for the literature and art of garden, field, hill, and mountain.

[44] Patricia Meyer Spacks, *The Poetry of Vision* (Cambridge Mass.: Harvard University Press, 1967), 19.

I should note that most earlier critics, particularly those in the eighteenth century, have agreed with me in pointing out that the descriptive element, the qualities of a loosely arranged empirical field, are paramount in Thomson, while more recent critics have emphasized a complex symbolical structure. The important opinion of John Aikin stresses the truth to natural history, "precise description," and scenic panorama.[45] Aikin (and many after him) also praise Thomson for his sentiment, which I take to be no more than the pathos that naturally arises from a train of images.[46] Rarely in earlier critics is Thomson given credit for *sentiment* in the far different sense (derived from the Greek διάνοια and Latin *sententiae*) of wise insights or moral observations arising from philosophical reflection. Most commonly Thomson was thought of as a great and original descriptive artist. For critics from Shenstone and Cowper down to Southey this was the great tribute to Thomson. Hugh Blair gives the common opinion in his *Lectures in Rhetoric and Belles Lettres* (1783).

Description is the great test of a poet's imagination . . . He [Thomson] studied and copied nature with care. No person of taste can peruse any one of his *Seasons* without having the ideas and feeling which belong to that season, recalled and *rendered present* to his mind.[47]

Here we have the Lockeian ideas enumerated and "rendered present." This is not classical *mimesis*, but mere imaging and remembering. Again as in Pope's scenic version of *The Iliad*, or the "fearless copy of the street," in Gay's *Trivia*, the accidental appearance replaces the ideal figure. The new kind of taste that appreciates the imaging power of Thomson is the response to a novel poetry. If not the "streaks of the tulip," at least the tulips have become important in this novel art of space. Swift found Thomson tiresome for just this reason. He told Gay that he preferred poems like *The Iliad* in which something happened. He did not have leisure to follow the poet's eye over the "whole surface of the world."[48]

[45] John Aikin, *An Essay on the Plan and Character of Thomson's Seasons*, (appended to his original edition of the poems 1778): James Thomson, *The Seasons* (London: A. Strahan, 1799) xxxiii–lxiii.

[46] This kind of associative receptivity is part of Addison's theory in *The Pleasures of the Imagination* papers. Such a power of feeling for landscape, which was Addison's chief example of an art large, varied, and beautiful, is taken up more fully by Thomson than Akenside. Johnson also praises Thomson for the spirit of visual accuracy and plenitude – his "wide expansion of general views" and "enumeration of circumstantial varieties" – and gives credit to his sentimental powers: "The poet leads us through the *appearances of things* as they are *successively varied* by the vicissitudes of the year, and imparts to us so much of his *own enthusiasm*, that our thoughts *expand with his imagery*, and *kindle with his sentiments* ("Life of Thomson" in *Lives of the English Poets*)."

[47] Hugh Blair, *Lectures in Rhetoric and Belles Lettres* (New York: Collins and Company, 1819), 404–405.

[48] Jonathan Swift, *Correspondence* ed. H. Williams (London: Oxford University Press, 1963–65), vol. II.

It was natural that *Summer* would evade the formal structures of Thomson's other seasonal poems. Thomson's *Winter,* the earliest of his important poems, though emended over many years, retains its Jobian sublimity. Winter is the natural place for a Protestant morality – one where the multiplicity of natural objects are hidden and recourse to the *deus absconditus* and all-judging Jehovah seems natural. The terror and indeterminate spaces of Thomson's *Winter* look forward to Burke's theory of the sublime. Thomson's *Autumn* is the traditional *imago essentiale* of the Georgic dominated by the tableau of harvest (Ceres, Pomona, Isis) and the surrounding Orphicism. In Thomson the mythic harvest is expanded into a national harvest of commerce. Thomson's *Spring* is a poem about the creative force of nature, the *Alma Venus* of Lucretius, or the *natur* of the late-medieval Christendom – reproductive rage that "priketh" man and beast "in hir corages." It is also a poem of idealized human love. The traditional Christian calendar of Thomson's youth was punctuated by the major feast days of Christmas, Epiphany, Easter, Whitsunday, Ascension, Trinity Sunday, All Souls', none of which occurs in summer. *Summer* was, therefore, the perfect place for a literalizing and associative schema such as Thomson's, and in it he largely escaped the formal and moral restraints of his Roman and Christian antecedents.

For these reasons *Summer* is a peculiarly local and original success of the Augustan culture; or, if it is a failure, it is the kind of failure made possible by the loosened frame of the loco-descriptive poem. Thomson used the brief summer description in Virgil to his advantage. The short African scene which ends Virgil's summer tableau (*Georgics* III, 339–349) is expanded into 439 lines.

In Thomson's experiment the Georgic elements are overwhelmed. The didactic, so important for the ancient Georgic, is almost completely lost. There are only two passages about work in the whole poem. These passages emphasize the difficulties of work under the summer sun and introduce the pattern of fantasy and escapism which colors the whole poem. The fecundity of *Spring* and the fruitfulness of *Autumn* are all but lost in *Summer.* It was written as the sister poem to *Winter,* and like that poem it mixes elements of despair and exultation. From the start summer is placed in opposition to the "genial spring" and the "jovial autumn." In the short summaries of the seasons which begin *Spring* and *Autumn,* summer is looked on with dread. For autumn harvests to mature, "from heaven's high cope the fierce Effulgence" of summer must be shaken off. Spring's "secret working hand" must do its labors before the "summer's fire." Winter is introduced as a monarch who "rules the varying year," but with providential concern for her subjects. Spring is a sweet maiden, autumn a playful Ceres with oaten pipe and sheaf.

The personified summer is from the first an ambiguous figure. He is a youth attended by "sultry Hours"[49] and his ardent look makes Spring avert her blushful eye, and leave the world to his "hot dominion." The innocence of Spring is replaced with a figure both sexually aggressive and tyrannical. Summer himself, and his vice-regent, the Sun, watch over his subject world with a "piercing" and "expectant" eye like the solar icons of seventeenth-century French monarchs. More than the other seasons he is haughty, arrogant, and sensual. As the poem moves forward he will become the tutelary spirit of the summer wanderer – the "hungry eye" of the Augustan observer in Britain and in the distant corners of empire.

The poet immediately seeks for escape from the summer. "Hence, let me haste into the mid-wood Shade, / Where scarce a Sunbeam wanders through the Gloom"(9–10). Here the author seeks inspiration in a "Hermit-Seat": "Fancy" dares to "steal one Look creative" from the "fix'd serious Eye" of the Summer monarch. He will make a similar retreat four more times in the poem. Lost in the "near effulgence" of the sun he will escape to the planetary void (104); though the Muse will not "disdain / To let the little noisy Summer-race / [insects, reptiles] Live in her Lay," the poet will seek solacing "Coolness" again as an escape from "tyrant Heat" (205). At line 469 he will "welcome" again the "Shades" to escape the "raging Noon." By then the sun has made an indistinguishable "Blaze" from "Pole to Pole": "In vain the Sight, dejected to the ground / Stoops for relief." By noon the poet anticipating Edward Young, looks "around for Night / But Night is far off." After a period of "healing meditation" in "gelid Caverns" and on the side of a "Romantic mountain" (629) the poet escapes into sleep to scenes of distant fantasy, but is thrown into the horrors of the African sun and must seek repose in an imaginary glade. By then he is trapped in a wilderness of appearances. Fantasy and reality are intertwined and Thomson, even in sleep, cannot escape the regal and pestilent sun.

From the opening the question is asked, but not until the end of the poem even partially answered, whether the poet can compete with and write within this new prospect of an immense, clear, and varied nature. "In vain the sight dejected" conjures up the fear of the spatial and imaginative immensity of a world without boundaries. But as we shall see the escape is not an easy one, for in every case it is an escape back into the world of the visual – the kingdom of the Sun. Whether fancy can find solace in the "wide prospect" of a summer day is a question that cannot be answered in the terms of the poetic which is being tested in the poem. Though summer evinces from the poet those most positive Addisonian adjectives – various, great, and beautiful – it does not offer him the easy structures of fancy of

---

[49] I will not give line references for short phrases or single words, though they are usually in the section of the poem I am discussing when they are mentioned.

the other seasons. His eye labors to attain and control that "raptur'd glance" of the sun.

After the brief introduction of summer, the poet's retreat from the Sun, and a facile encomium to the ubiquitous Whig politico and patron Bubb Doddington, God is introduced for the first time. He receives ten lines and is described in the normal Deist language of an "ALL-PERFECT HAND" who "impels" the machine of the world. He controls with magnificent precision the paths of the "Planets launched along / The illimitable Void! Thus to remain / Amid the Flux for many thousand Years" – unlike mankind whose monuments have been "swept away." Not only is man left out of the protective providence of this opening prayer, but the lower world is immediately handed over to the whims of God's angry viceroy, the sun, whose praises and wonders are described at length (81–174). The sun blesses the world with light and heat. Without him every object would be "wrapt in inessential Gloom," the same "Gloom" which the poet escapes to at line nine (and throughout the poem) and which holds the secret of the Creator at the end of the poem. "Gloom" and darkness become paradoxical. They darken and confuse the palette of the observant poet, but they offer the chief escape for him from the sun's tyranny.

The Sun is the single dominating figure of the poem. The eye of the poet is lighted by him, the jewels under the earth are formed by his secret power, the insects, reptiles, and vermin are warmed to motion in his rays, and (like the Lucretian *Alma Venus*) he is the principle of generation. We could not even see the other planets were it not for his reflected light. He is the "Parent" of seasons, and "the Vegetable world is" only his. The sun has a larger role in *Summer* than he had in any ancient poem, much larger than in Milton. He was a great source for Lucretius, but only one among the swirling bodies that make up the Epicurean cosmos. He has a similarly restricted role in the *Georgics*:

> Idcirco certis dimensum partibus orbem
> per duodena regit mundi sol aureus astra.
> quinque tenent caelum zonae: quarum una corusco
> semper sole rubens et torrida semper ab igni.
>
> (*Georgics* I, 231–234)

[Just so the golden sun rules his sphere, divided into the sure divisions of the twelve constellations. The heavens have five zones, of which one is always brightened by the hot sun, always scorched by his fire.]

The sun appears a handful of times in the *Georgics*. Once at the end of Book I as the eye which uncovers plots against the Roman government, more often in the *Georgic* III as the ruling spirit of the African landscape.

For Thomson the sun has a vast significance. It appears sixty-one times in *Summer*. But beyond its natural role in the landscape of summer, the sun takes on the role of source and muse. Thomson was fascinated by Newton's theory of light. It appears at the crowning moment of *Summer*. Yet the Newtonian sun is only one aspect of Thomson's central personification. The sun has got to serve both as the source of the visual heterocosm of the poem, and as the personified Parent and King of the Summer scene. Here lies one of the tensions of the poem. The sun which is now the source for the whole world of the summer poet is also a villainous tyrant who strikes down flowers, blasts the laborers of the field, brings the vermin tribes to infect the human race, and scorches the peoples of the tropics. Having removed God to a realm remote and abstract, the sun takes on all the problems of natural evil – he becomes the creator/destroyer of nature. But at a deeper level the sun's ambiguity symbolizes the demoralized field in which the empirical poet is forced to operate. For the traditional European poet the fall is a myth which implicates the human in the dystopia of everyday existence. Milton and Newton wrestle for control in Thomson's poem. On the one hand the glamorous certitudes of Newtonian physics should be autonomous and self-explaining, but Milton's mythology continually intrudes. Thomson alternates between a neutral, mechanistic view and a traditional dramatic one.

Nonetheless, Thomson hints at an explicit rejection of the Miltonic myth. While Milton and Thomson were both familiar with Purchas' paradisal description of the mythic Abyssinian kingdom at Mount Amara, Milton specifically rejects it as the original place of Paradise.

> Nor where *Abassin* Kings thir issue Guard,
> Mount *Amara*, though this by some suppos'd
> True Paradise, under the *Ethiop* Line
> By *Nilus* Head, enclos'd with shining Rock,
> A whole day's journey high, but wide remote
> From this *Assyrian* Garden.   (*Paradise Lost*, IV, 280–285)[50]

It was, therefore, significant that Thomson defiantly picks it for his chief *locus amoenus* in *Summer*, and specifically defends it against the horrid Jesuits who evangelized it at the turn of the eighteenth century.

> But come, my Muse, the Desert-Barrier burst,
> A wild expanse of lifeless Sand and Sky: . . .
>   and the secret Bounds
> Of jealous *Abyssinia* boldly pierce.
> Thou art no ruffian, who beneath the Mask
> Of social commerce com'st to rob their Wealth;
> No *holy Fury* Thou, blaspheming HEAVEN,
> With consecrated steel to stab their Peace,
> And thro' the land, yet red from Civil Wounds,

---

[50] John Milton, *Paradise Lost*, ed. Merrit Hughes (New York: Odyssey Press, 1967).

To spread the purple Tyranny of *Rome*.
Thou, like the harmless Bee, mayst freely range,
From mead to mead bright with exalted Flowers,
From Jasmine Grove to Grove, mayst wander gay,
Thro' Palmy Shades and Aromatic Woods . . .
There on the breezy Summit, spreading fair,
For many a league, or on stupendous Rocks,
That from the sun-redoubling Valley lift,
Cool to the middle Air their lawny Tops,
Where Palaces and Fanes and Villas rise;
And gardens smile around, and cultured Fields . . .
        a World within itself,
Disdaining all Assault: there let me draw
Ethereal Soul, there drink reviving Gales,
Profusely breathing from the spicy Groves,
And Vales of Fragrance; . . .
And o'er the vary'd landscape, restless, rove,
Fervent with Life of every fairer Kind:
A Land of Wonders! which the Sun still eyes
With Ray direct.   (*Summer*, 747–782)

This passage marks the penultimate escape of the poet from the summer scene which is the ostensible subject of the poem. Having escaped from the sun, he now retreats to the idealized African landscape. The language of the Miltonic Eden is carried over to Mount Amara. Like the bees of Virgilian Georgic the Abyssinians roam from flower to flower, having narrowly escaped the clutches of Rome. Their world is high and remote from the miseries of modern existence. They live in the aromatic shades of eighteenth-century exoticism. But more interesting than the traditional pastoral motifs are the final lines. The empirical poet must expand his spatial palette with new worlds teeming with "Life of every fairer Kind" to fulfill the requirements of the "hungry eye." His restlessness has led him in a dream to the flora and fauna of Ethiopia – to the "vary'd landscape" of a parallel world. The mythical peace and plenty of Amara do not lead him to peace and spiritual solace, but to a broader field of discrete images. Like the natives freed from the shackles of evangelism, he is free to bring the observant eye to view new "wonders."

The sun which he escaped in the preceding passage suddenly reappears in the final lines with "direct eyes." The poet must imitate this direct gaze of the Abyssinian sun. Then the reversal comes again. The utopian claims fall away and are replaced by 700 lines which catalog the swarming horrors of Africa. The sun at noon bakes with an even more ferocious power the landscape of the dark continent. The poet is trapped in a labyrinth of terrors. The snakes of Virgil and the insects of Britain are replaced by their monstrous African counterparts.

How chang'd the Scene in blazing Height of Noon,
The sun oppress'd is plung'd in thickest Gloom.
Still Horror reigns, a dreary Twilight round.   (*Summer*, 787–789)

But still more direful He,
The small close-lurking minister of Fate.
Whose high-concocted venom thro' the Vein
A rapid lightning darts, arresting swift
The vital Current Form'd to humble Man,
This Child of vengeful Nature.   (*Summer*, 906–911)

Nor stop the terrors of these regions here.
Commissioned Demons oft, Angels of Wrath,
Let loose the raging elements. Breath's hot,
From all the boundless furnace of the Sky
And the wide glittering Waste of burning Sand,
A suffocating wind the Pilgrim smites
With Instant Death.   (*Summer*, 959–965)

It seems that not only the snake is a "child of vengeful nature," but the whole panoply of poisonous herbs, lions, panthers, tigers, and even sharks collaborate to chase the rapacious wanderer off the continent. In the crowning moment of the African fantasy Thomson realizes that the spices, gems, gold, and timber of the continent are lost to those untutored in English industry. Only the horrors available to the natives, who lack "The Godlike Wisdom of the tempered breast; / Progressive Truth, the patient force of Thought; / Investigation calm, whose silent Powers / Command the World." They also lack the "Light that Leads to HEAVEN / the Government of Laws, / And all-protecting Freedom, which alone / Sustains the Name and Dignity of Man."

The "patient force of thought" appears to have temporarily eluded our author, who has come full circle from castigating the Jesuits for corrupting perfect and autonomous nature to praising British colonialism and legalism. Hinting at first that Milton was wrong to deny Abyssinian claims to a Paradise finer than the Assyrian Eden, and that the "pure aerial powers of the day / Nourished with grace" might far exceeded the reach of proud Europeans, Thomson reverses himself and condemns the African scene. Perhaps the serpents and sandstorms frightened Thomson back to British law and freedom. The sun who was the noontide tyrant in the British fields took on an even loftier ruthlessness in Africa, but remained the source of "Fervent with life of every rarer kind." We could say that Thomson was moving from fantasy to fantasy, from ideal England to empire, but we must give him credit. His African vista has no counterpart in English poetry before it. It is a studied prospect of minute detail and a congeries of numerous contemporary sources on natural history and anthropology.

Nevertheless at a certain moment the "rapacious eye," tired of its prey, must return home. The British day has not been completed. After an extended treatment of the winds, storms, and breeze-blown plagues of Africa (after the fashion of Virgil but on a larger scale) Thomson suddenly returns home. The return is one of the most peculiar leaps of the poem.

Up until line 1001 of *Summer* we have been pursuing a course of associative leaps from the horrors of the sun (the direct gaze at the heterocosmic dystopia) to holidays in pastoral meditation. But now we have a stranger turn: "Return, my vagrant Muse: / A nearer Scene of Horror calls thee home."

Just as the reader expects relief from the dangers of Africa, Thomson finds death and destruction at home. The storms of Mauritania blend with the thunder and lightning of the English Midlands. Thomson expands the Virgilian rainstorm to mammoth proportions. The sonorous, roaring, involving, swirling, crashing, blasting of the English storms ends in a narrative of strange pathos. Having introduced the "matchless pair," Amelia and Celadon, who lived a life of "Innocence, and undissembling Truth," and "passed their Life, a clear united Stream / By Care unruffled," and who walked in the "eternal Eden" of each other's smiles, Thomson with sudden reversal of emotion blasts the lovers with lightning:

> From his void Embrace
> (Mysterious Heaven!) that moment to the ground,
> A blackened Corse, was struck the beauteous Maid.
> But who can paint the Lover as he stood,
> Pierced by severe amazement, hating Life,
> Speechless, and fix'd in all the Death of Woe!
> So, faint Resemblance, on the marble-Tomb,
> The well-dissembled Mourner stooping stands,
> Forever silent and forever sad.   (*Summer*, 1214–1222)

Thomson does not tarry long over his grim tableau. No Keatsian art of the changeless lovers frozen on the funeral stone can begin to intimate the horrors of nature – the incidents of the deathly panorama which now connects the savannah to the fields of Britain. A few words later, "Nature, from the Storm, / Shines out afresh." The lover's life passes away in the casual drift of the natural. Thomson does not so much attempt to explain how bad things happen to good people, as to show how such events participate in the accidental flow of phenomena. The scene gives real edge to his later comments about "the roving eye" experienced in the "strange diversity of things." Far from a Miltonic motif of lost Eden, the Celadon and Amelia story builds on the theme of uninterpretable variety in nature herself. Unlike the "well dissembled mourner," Thomson has begun to accept the diversity of fate as a mere diversity of appearances.

One last episode must be mentioned before describing the conclusion of the poem. In the section following the encomium on swimming and the death of Amelia, Thomson moves to an extended epyllion of the Renaissance Ovidian kind. In it the lovelorn Damon, pining for his love, Musidora, sees her and her friends Sacharissa and Amoret by chance disrobe in the cooling stream near his favorite woodland haunt. In the original version of 1730, Damon views the naked girl with rapture, but she never realizes that she has been observed. In that version he is cured of his cool, stoical philosophy and his habit of solitary meditation by glancing upon her beauty. Her image "put his harsh philosophy to flight, / The joyless search of long-deluded years; / And MUSIDORA fixing in his heart, / Inform'd, and humaniz'd him into man." Typical of the anti-metaphysical aspect of Augustan empiricism, the transformation is one from speculation to spontaneous sensation. "The haughty sun" is now the instrument of natural (sexual) revelation. The eye of heaven has joined the observer's eye in its appetite.

In 1744–46 a number a revisions were added to this tale. They heighten the sensual and voyeuristic elements considerably:

> Than DAMON, thou, as from the snowy Leg,
> And slender Foot, th'inverted Silk she drew;
> As the soft Touch dissolv'd the virgin Zone;
> And through the parting Robe, th'alternate Breast,
> With Youth wild-throbbing, on thy lawless gaze
> In full Luxuriance rose. But desperate Youth,
> How durst thou risque the Soul-distracting View;
> As from her naked Limbs of glowing White,
> Harmonious swell'd by Nature's finest Hand,
> In Folds loose-floating fell the fainter Lawn   (*Summer*, 1308–1317)

The added passage has a rising tide of sexual explicitness as the narrator considers pursuing Musidora at once, but thinks better of it out of the tenderness of his heart. In the end he places a note by the bank, and when she learns it is Damon's, Musidora responds as if she is flattered by his attention and wishes to be pursued. This is a remarkable change of presentation. It has been often said that the perennial bachelor Thomson was tired of courting his own Musidora, and that this is a symbol of his impatience. In fact Thomson advances the cause of visual realism and the theme of the hungry eye into new territory. It shows the Augustan prejudice against philosophy as opposed to direct experience, but it also places love within the empirical field of the poem. It extends the passionate interest of the eye in a way which is mildly salacious. The fantasy structure has moved from exoticism to voyeurism. The poem draws both empire and sexuality into the problem of empirical curiosity.

When the solitary wanderer reaches the end of his day-long journey he walks home by night, for the first time freed from the power of the Sun, who "has lost His rage." In the later version (1744) he passes by "Twit'nam" and hopes Pope can recover from his protracted illness. He reviews the famous landscapes of Augustan verse – Hampton, Clermont, Esher. The poem of Augustan maturity, of expanded and nearly uncontrolled association, pays tribute to its models.

Thomson then retires to philosophic wisdom – listing the great statebuilders, scientists, and poets. He distinguishes the amiable muse of "classic Ages" from the "*pure intelligence*" of Newton, who explain'd the outer world as Locke "made the whole internal World his own." He pays tribute to the patrons of summer – the wizards of empiricism and astronomy. The philosophic eye extends the natural eye beyond the circle of the rapacious sun into the orbits of distant galaxies.

In the final and telling moment the narrator passes by the *ignis fatuus* of the woods, thought by common folk to be the work of fairies. Almost every important Augustan poet that preceded him had spoken of that false fire of superstition – Cowley, Butler, Dryden, Rochester, and Swift. The ghosts of the suicide and other Gothic staples appear, but Thomson, like Pope in *The Rape of the Lock*, is immune to old wives tales:

> But above
> Those superstitious Horrors that enslave
> The fond sequacious Herd, to mystic Faith
> And blind Amazement prone, th'enlighten'd Few,
> Whose Godlike Minds Philosophy exalts,
> The glorious stranger hail.   (*Summer*, 1711–1716)

Again the Augustan poet is separated from other men by a wall of disinterested observation. The horrors of superstition combine with the "blind amazement" of the enthusiast in a single image. The religion of the "sequacious Herd" equally dissolves in the light of day and shrinks beneath the nightscape of Newtonian astronomy. By philosophy Thomson exclusively means astronomy, as we discover in the great crescendo that ends the poem. At the last moment "Evidence and Truth" are "stronger than the midday sun," and science begins to replace the imperfect powers of mere perception. In the final stanza Thomson again tries to approach God. He talks for the first time of an inward eye "that at her powerful glance the phantoms rise / And disappear." He then pursues the Lockeian path from "plain Perception up / To the fair Forms of fancy's fleeting Train; / To Reason then, deducing Truth from Truth."

Having risen to this height of fancy, Thomson at the last moment sinks down again into doubt.

> Enough for us to know that this dark State,
> In wayward passions lost and vain Pursuits,

> This infancy of Being, cannot prove
> The final Issue of the Works of God.   (*Summer*, 1800–1803)

This is as hopeful as Thomson can be. A nearer and purer summary of his paradoxical epistemology is found at the end of the day.

> For ever running an enchanted Round,
> Passes the Day, deceitful, vain, and void;
> As fleets the vision o'er the formful Brain,
> This Moment hurrying wild th'impassion'd Soul,
> The next in Nothing lost.   (*Summer*, 1630–1634)

In the end the escape from the elements which crowns the central scene of the hearth at the end of *Winter* and the contemplation of the sublime immensity of the swirling winterscape prove more consoling than the microscopic and telescopic visions of *Summer*. It may seem an inversion of common sense, but of the two evils – the boundless variety of summer or the sublime obscurity of winter – the summer is the more unsettling. Summer demands an ordering of sight, a control and harmonizing of the teeming plenty which the eye can not from itself procure. The elevation of particulars and the Lockeian cult of surfaces present the imagination with a daunting task. Thomson unquestionably moved the brilliant passage on insect and vermin life from *Spring* to *Summer* in the late revisions of 1744 because he recognized them as a symbol of the stupefying variety and agitation of the poem. The swarming brood might have tainted the genial bliss of the earlier season. The "waste of music" of the birds could be imagined as the "voice of Love" in the merry contours of Spring, but the creeping and squirming mass is the proper subject of the "harried eye."

> Gradual, from These what numerous kinds descend,
> Evading even the Microscopic Eye!
> Full Nature swarms with Life;   (*Summer*, 287–289)

> Where the Pool
> Stands mantled o'er with Green, invisible
> Amid the floating Verdure, Millions stray.   (*Summer*, 303–305)

> Thick in yon Stream of Light, a Thousand ways,
> Upward, and downward, thwarting, and convolv'd,
> The quivering Nations sport; till Tempest wing'd,
> Fierce Winter sweeps them from the Face of Day.
>
>   (*Summer*, 341–344)

Add to this the expanding Thomsonian fantasies of geography, natural history, meteorology, and the sexualized body, and a project of forbidding novelty arises. In the absence of metaphysical analogy, the linked system of ontological substances, and any unifying icon and myth, the project is

impossible. It should come as no surprise that the insect passages are
followed immediately by a human parallel. The village youth "swarm over
the Mead," and rush "in one diffusive Band." They form a great Lucretian
turba.[51] As "Animals, or Atoms organized / Await the vital breath," so men
blur with insects. I mentioned in the first chapter that the human and
animal sphere began to collapse in the writings of Pope. The Arctic bear of
Thomson's *Winter* is a deliberate parallel with his tragic winter wanderer
who dies in a drift of snow. The bear is simply more at home in the
wilderness which swallows the human wanderer. The same holds for the
wanderers of Africa and the nomadic wolves of summer. The poems of
Thomson elaborate the downward metaphors of modern positivism in
their infancy. The implication for politics of conflating insects and laborers
is obvious, and a certain dispassionate Whig smugness hovers over the
poets of Enlightened description. Thomson is one of Darwin's great
precursors, but with a difference – after Linnaeus, Buffon, and Lamarck
the taxonomy of modern natural history began to mature; Thomson was
trapped in the era of improvisation.

The Blakean, Wordsworthian, and Darwinian schemata were not yet
available to rein in and illuminate the swarming Augustan landscape. The
satiric conventions of the period before Thomson, like Lockeian epistemology, offered only a bowl in which to place ideas and images. Thomson's
Winter, new as it is, is still a better escape from the limits of the empirical.
Beginning with Protestant metaphors of the ear – the howling winds and
the song sung to placate the demons of the storm – and ending in the
security of the hearth and fellowship hidden from the surrounding images
of nature, winter, in Eliot's words, "covers the earth in forgetful snow." The
morality of the Bunyanesque wanderer lost to his family and the world in
an unfathomable wilderness harmonizes with a traditional morality. It
recalls the Presbyterian fatalism of Thomson's youthful religion. None of
the numerous revisions of *Winter* could remove those marks of its origin so
inopportune for the mature program of *The Seasons*.

Of course Thomson maintained some of those moralized elements in all
the poems. He wanted to repeat the image repertoire – winds, minerals,
plants, herds, and the others – in each of the seasons. But to read the poems
as strictly moralized – as poems of traditional humanistic lore – is to strip
them of all of their special claims upon us as readers. Like the brilliant
ending to Book IV of *The Dunciad*, Thomson's concluding *Hymn* in part
negates the great and original momentum of the poem. Neither recognized
the implications of such a contradiction. Very few of their readers have
noticed.

---

[51] *Turba* means "swarm" in Latin. It is used by Lucretius to describe both a swarm of bees and
clustering atoms.

There is a tendency in many Augustan poems to try to recoup at the end what has been lost in the associative and accretive drift of the text. This was the intention of Pope at the end of *The Dunciad*. Decline of the analogical view of nature, and not taste, is the issue at the end of that poem. The dunces themselves are absolutely irrelevant to an apocalyptic decay of culture, and some of them like Dennis and Blackmore had done more than anyone else in their generation to stem the tide of change; none of them in any event would be read in the future. Burke, too, had attempted such a recouping of tradition in his treatment of the sublime. He wanted to imagine an observer unaffected and unparticipating who could preserve at a distance the illimitable emotion of the infinite, and of God. He wanted such an emotion untainted by enthusiasm and the ghosts of conventional religious experience. For this reason the sublime had to be aestheticized – placed at a suitable distance from real life. Beauty for Burke was a matter of the image, of purely visual structures. His concept of beauty was limited to casual appearance and therefore belonged to the realm of sensible experience – to Thomson's summer. But in the sublime he wished to preserve, through the sphere of emotion, the grandeur of the primitive Christian imagination.

Summer is Thomson's greatest achievement. It most perfectly embodies the ever expanding margins of the empirical project. In such a floating panoply the intellect, the choosing power, is maddened. The eye, once the window of the soul, is now at turns ardent, nervous, feasting, hungry, roving, tired, and, at last, anxious. It has become a metonymy of the uncontrollable variety of the empirical poetic. Neither the waking nor the dreaming world, the nearest nor the most exotic, the private nor the imperial can escape the endless branching and expansion of prospect. In the end the philosophic mind, the telescopic eye of Newton, must seek the peaceful shade – the retreat from chaos. But in "the unimaginable zero summer" the tyrant sun demands obedience. Like a usurping God he rules the Thomsonian day with remorseless rigor. His loyal subject, the observant poet, having cast off the shackles of analogy, must pursue him without rest.

5

The four poles of the Christian imagination in relation to Augustanism

Introduction

Like the Turk peering through the window at the madcap congregation in Hogarth's *Credulity, Superstition, and Fanaticism*, the ideal Augustan poet was at once an observer and an outsider. In Hogarth the Catholic tonsure showing through a crack in the head of the dissenting Minister beautifully epitomizes the satiric formula that conflated and combined the opposed elements of Reformation culture. The credulous folk in the congregation, like the "fond, sequacious Herd" of Thomson, represent the unsettled mob which the Augustan poets despised, and which it was the business of the established order to control. What such a crude political body represents in the practical sphere, superstitious Catholicism and enthusiastic Protestantism represent in the intellectual. By manipulating a general and unlimited satire, Butler, Swift, and their successors had traveled over the whole range of traditional ideology, affixing indelibly on each the stigma of ignorance and absurdity. The narrator of *Hudibras* had discovered the acidic spread of ignorance in nearly every human activity, Rochester had imagined "nothing" as the source and end of all our reasonings, and Gulliver (following on the metaphysical wreckage of *A Tale of a Tub*) had discovered the Yahoo as the archetypal descendent of Adam. Pope in a far subtler way had cleared a space for the quotidian by showing with gracious humor the impossibility of the angelic existences in *The Rape of the Lock*, the inappositeness of the Baroque religion, and the encumbrances of the spiritual upon the passionate and physical reality of Eloisa and the "Unfortunate Lady." Pope left the Augustan individual to assimilate herself to the idealized commercial sphere of *Windsor-Forest* and *The Moral Epistles*.

This second phase of the Augustan project was an attempt to fill up the vacuum of traditional imagination left in the wake of satire. Addison, Pope, and Gay, by opening a space for the quotidian, bathetic, and carnivalesque within a "classical" rhetoric, represented quite by accident an easy access to the dreaded sphere of popular writing – to a growing tide of the novelistic. Defoe and the other duncical novelists were involved in precisely

174

the same movement away from the Baroque that had been championed in the vulgar burlesque of Butler and Swift, but now in terms of a transparent and even optimistic realism. The uneasiness that Fielding was to feel in negotiating in a supposedly classical manner the vulgarity of his realistic subject matter simply recapitulated the ambiguity and belatedness of any claims of classicism after 1660. Locke's epistemology, the early novel, and even Newtonian physics competed to fill the gap in reality left by the bitter explosion of satire in the earlier period, and all three of those projects are combined in the empirical panorama of Thomson's *Seasons*.

Following (perhaps unconsciously) in the tradition of Lovejoy and Becker, many have imagined that the analogical plenitude of Aquinas, or the cabbalistic cosmos of Pico, could be preserved within the episteme of empiricism. Perhaps the perpetual lack of interest in metaphysical and arcane issues which eighteenth-century scholars have shared with Augustan philosophers such as Hobbes, Locke, and Hume have blinded them to the tremendous gulf between the Baroque and the Augustan mentality. The chief object of Butler, Swift, Pope, and Sterne appears to be the unsettling of the language and conventions of earlier dogma – an obvious opposition to both important forms of Reformation-era religion. All the modes of theological thought and their corresponding modes of art were challenged by Augustan writing.

I must now examine the logic of perennial Christian art, the art which confronted the satirists of the later seventeenth century, and briefly describe the response of Augustan writing to each of its kinds. If we do not pause to inspect the intellectual and spiritual scene in which or from which Augustanism grew, we may fall into the same false sense of continuity which mars a good deal of criticism of the period. If my schema in laying out the four chief forms of Baroque religious art seem far afield from the chapters that have gone before, it is because I did not wish to impose a paradigm upon the reader until I had established specific historical and poetic trends in the period which is the subject of this book. With the examples of Butler, Cowley, Pope, and Thomson already fleshed out, it will be easier to summarize the conflicts between Augustan and Baroque imagination. This chapter will also serve to connect my argument to the succeeding chapter where I describe important reactions to Augustanism both from within and from the still dominant Protestant culture. I do not wish to argue for a single unitary episteme of the eighteenth century. Those elements of older culture which the Augustans attacked have survived even till now. The Augustan is but one strand of modern western thought, but it is the strand which has formed in different ways the prejudices and habits of thought for the class of enlightened elites which encompasses both capitalists and radical intellectuals.

The fideists of Lutheran and Independent churches in Britain became the "mad enthusiasts" of Butler, the "Aeolists" of Swift, pathological and pseudo-prophetic consciences. So too "logism," the tradition of spiritual grammar in verse, was attacked under the headings of "mad acrostic" and "anagram": the morphological poems of Herbert and the emblem books of Wither and Quarles, recently so widely interpreted in seventeenth-century studies, were despised throughout the eighteenth century as the worst excesses of facile verbalism. Most importantly the wider tradition of analogy which dominated the whole period from Petrarch to Crashaw came under attack in the literalist revolution of the Augustans. None of these facts has kept several generations of eighteenth-century critics from imagining continuity – a Humanist or Renaissance Augustanism. In this they have followed the lead of the original British "Neoclassicists" themselves in imagining order could be derived out of the mere desire for order, and that there was but little price to pay for the innovations of deep and violent satire.

The three modes of traditional Christian imagination, which I have just described, proved in fact to be perennial and inexhaustible. Many of the enemies of the Scriblerians can be seen in retrospect as unfashionable throwbacks to the conventional modes of seventeenth-century thinking. So Benlowes was a flourishing metaphysical stylist and vagrant visionary, Dennis had the attitudes of a typical intellectualist Protestant of the earlier period, and Bunyan was an inspired dissenting allegorist. All of these were the express enemies of the novel Augustan program, which combining with several strains of accommodationist politics and new formulations of physical monism created an oppositional poetics. "Augustan," as I have been using it throughout, describes the tendency to satirize and sanitize the surviving elements of Civil War era culture. To think of Augustanism as Mack, Battestin, and many others have done as the chief means of preserving and continuing traditional modes of thought is paradoxical at best. The novelty of Augustan literature is precisely its lack of conformity to any of those earlier modes. Its ordering is in the most profound way a reordering of European thought. This is obvious in the case of Butler and Rochester, but no less true of Swift and Pope. This is not to say that none of these men was Christian, or that Christianity did not form a kind of counter or limit to their thought. It would be absurd to say that the Dean of an Anglican cathedral church was not a Christian, but it would be quite another matter to say that he was operating within the bounds of a traditional "Christian" aesthetic. I have simply attempted to lay out the modes of poetry which seem to me to have dominated England and Europe in the Renaissance, so that Augustan satire and literalism can be seen in a clearer light.

The four poles of Christian poetics

The problem of change in Christian poetics, or in another way, the problem of the history of Christian poetry, is rooted in the larger problem of the description of God. God himself is the chief subject of Christian art. Verbal conceptions of God, and all forms of imaging the divine, have passed through an endless dialectic. This dialectic was made more complicated by the original relationship between Judaism and Christianity.[1] The iconoclastic tendency of Hebrew art, particularly outside of Scripture, and the ancient and vexed question of the naming of God, are at once preserved and overthrown in Christian art. The Christian figure of the Father retains the ineffable quality which, in some sense, removes him from the possibilities of art; but the Son, having received the form of a creature, and having lived both within and outside the confines of time, presents an aesthetic problem of infinite difficulty. The Holy Spirit in the role of comforter, or the "one who comes afterwards," remains in an ambiguous position – being, at once, without body, and an active "historical agent." The Trinity presents to the Christian artist the limit of aesthetic activity, and the paradoxes of artistic representation.

This problem of multiplicity was further exacerbated by the adaptation of Greek and, later, Roman ideas of metaphysics and divinity. This is not to say that there was some unholy or inapposite blending of traditions, but only that Christian artistic and intellectual imagination grew up within the larger ancient intellectual culture. The question of what was truly and distinctly its own, and what was part of its special Hebrew inheritance, as opposed to what was "of Athens," was one of the earliest grounds for controversy within the church. This controversy had both doctrinal and aesthetic implications. Indeed all the famous disputes between Greek, Roman, and Protestant churches in the Reformation period had their counterparts in the debates of the early church.[2]

The logist

The first and, perhaps, the most enduring division in the Christian imagination is between its symbolic and its ontological modes. By "sym-

---

[1] The historical divisions between iconoclasm and symbolism exist within both Judaism and Christianity. The ultra-orthodox and fideist tendencies in Judaism have come into continuing opposition with the Cabbalistic and allegorizing schools. In Christian history, the Lutherans, Anabaptists, and others took up the cudgels on behalf of iconoclasm, while the late medieval and Baroque culture of Roman Christendom became increasingly symbolical, even to the point of representing the Father or Holy Ghost in Church painting and elsewhere. The case of iconoclasm in verse is still more complicated, since even the most devout Calvinists did not object to poetry which represented biblical material, including (as in Greville, Hall, Milton, and many others) descriptions of the Father, either as a person or by His conversation.

[2] Owen Chadwick, *From Bossuet to Newman* (London: Cambridge University Press, 1987), 3–22.

bolic" we mean the substitution of any image or verbal construction for God.[3] On the most primitive level the naming of God might be termed symbolic. Theology itself is an elaborate naming and describing of God, as when the Scholastics talked of the qualities, attributes, or powers of God,[4] or when the authors of the Nicene Creed speak of "One God, the Father, the Almighty, the maker of heaven and earth, of all that is seen and unseen." Here God is named, renamed, given a single *differentia*, and then seen in light of his own characteristic activity. The creeds themselves are a sophisticated verbal analysis of all that can be gleaned about God from the incipient scriptural documents, the primitive oral tradition, and apostolic catechism. Along with the beginning of John's Gospel, they mark the earliest stages of a distinctly Christian theology.[5]

Theology itself is one of the archetypal forms of Christian art. It is an art of verbal formulation in which words, though without the unique veracity of scripture, are seen in some sense to exceed their normal power of representation. This mode I term the "logist," playing upon the literal sense of merely verbal, and annexing the ambiguous force of the introductory words of John's Gospel. Those words present us with a paradoxical and penetrating attempt to describe the relation of Father and Son as a problem of, or within, language itself – "In the beginning was the Word, and the Word was with God, and the Word was God." In this mode, God is seen as the key to a universal grammar, and as the light or principle of intelligibility for all created objects. We must recall that what makes theology (with all its precious and mysterious distinctions of persons of God, divine attributes, and the rest) intelligible for Christians is God himself, as if (and this is a central argument from Basil to Anselm) language were made possible and meaningful by God. In the language of Maximus the Confessor, "The language, the grammar of the heart, and of the cosmos, and the soul (even its very substance) of the Bible is that very *Logos*

---

[3] All forms of art, Christian or otherwise, are symbolical, as is language itself, but a distinction can be made between the attempts of Christian artists to find on the one hand an unmediated knowledge and an art of that unmediated knowledge, which I shall shortly describe as mystical or fideist, and on the other an art of verbal equivalence. For the logistic thinker (Origen or Coleridge, for example), the mind can grasp, through verbal structures, the intelligible essence and character of God. This is the common psychology of Gnosticism, and other intellectualist and verbalizing forms of religious *mimesis*.

[4] The "Baconianism" and physicalism of many Restoration poets and prose writers, and even clerical writers, made them think of the "logistic" tendency of much Medieval and Renaissance theology as "merely verbal chimeras." Nominalism, in all its forms, is the express enemy of logism, which, as we shall see shortly, observes a perfect correspondence between word and divine object. In the case of Origen and the Plotinians God can be expressed verbally with an accuracy beyond other mere natural objects, because He shares with the "idea" the univocal and unqualified nature impossible in sensual knowledge.

[5] See Jaroslav Pelikan, *The Emergence of the Catholic Tradition* (Chicago: University of Chicago Press, 1971) 187–189. This is also discussed brilliantly in the second chapter of John Courtenay Murray, *The Problem of God, Yesterday and Today* (New Haven: Yale University Press, 1964).

who came down to us as Christ."[6] This mode of logism if not unique to Christianity (it is found in Stoicism and Jewish Cabbala) has perhaps seen its most complex and involuted formulation within Christian thought.

The logist imagination produced a potent form of Christian verse from the earliest times, and a good deal of early Greek Christian poetry exemplifies it.

> Σε καί γῦν εὐλόγουμεν, Χρίστε μου λόγε τηέου
> πήως ἔκ πηώτος ἀνάρχηου καὶ πνεύμα ἐξ ἀνάρχηου
> τρίτου πηώτος εἴ μίαν δόξαν ἄτηροιζομενου
>
> ὅς ἐλύσας τὸ σκότας, ὅς ὑπεστάσας τὸ πηὼς
> ἤίν ἕν πηώτι κτίσας τὰ πάντα καὶ τὰν ἄστατα ὑλᾶν . . .
>
> ἠός νοῦν ἐπηώτισα ἀντήροπου λογῷ τε καὶ σοπήι
> λαμπρώτατος τὰς ἀνὼ κάι κάτω τηεῖς ἐικόνα
> ἤίνα πηώτι βλέπα τὸ πηως καὶ γέναται πηῶς ὅλον.[7]

[Now again do we bless your name, my Christ, Word of God, light of light without beginning, all gathered into one glory. You scattered the darkness and set up the light, so that in light you build all that is . . . and you illumined the mind of man with word and wisdom, placing below an image of what is above, that in light he might see light and become the light entirely.]

Here we begin with a blessing of the name of Christ and proceed to catalog the verbal and metaphysical paradoxes implied in the concept of "Logos." There is no real imagery, but only the purest abstractions of "light of lights," and bringing of "that which was above below." "Logos" and "sophos," word and wisdom, are seen both as the nature and the gifts of Christ. The prose of Origen,[8] the poetry of Synezius, and a few intellectualist hymns in Latin of the twelfth and thirteenth centuries[9] are among the highest achievements of this mode.[10]

The logist mode is the ground of typology, for in it the words of scripture are a "living part of the person of Christ," and Christ Himself is the key to the relations between the New Testament and the Hebrew Scriptures. Origen may be said to be the first great typologist, to whom all later interpreters are in debt. The logist mind, and here we may think of Gregory of Nyssa and Clement of Alexandria as well as Origen, imagines a faith perfected by knowledge, or one might say, a faith presenting a distinct

---

[6] Kallistos Ware (ed.), *The Desert Fathers* (London: Spirtual Classics, 1976), 227.

[7] *The Penguin Book of Greek Verse*, ed. Constantine A. Trypanis (Baltimore: Penguin Books, 1971), 360–361.

[8] H. A. Wolfson, *The Philosophy of the Church Fathers* (Cambridge, Mass.: Harvard University Press, 1952), vol. 1, 33–69.

[9] F. J. E. Raby, *Christian Latin Poetry* (Oxford: Clarendon Press, 1953), 349–357, 402–414.

[10] The most astonishing example of Medieval logism is, perhaps, the "Pange Lingua" of St. Thomas Aquinas. Cf. *Annales hymnologia*, 1, 588.

object to the intellect.[11] It was, of course, Augustine who extinguished the flame of this form of Christian gnosticism in the West, though it returns in the high Middle Ages. Augustine's own complex combination of fideist and analogical modes dominated the imaginative agenda of western Christendom for a long period, and is central to the Roman and Reformed traditions.

In English the logist mode of imagination has never dominated, though some Medieval lyrics approach to it, and the *Nosce teipsum* of Sir John Davies is an interesting and ambitious attempt. Henry More's poems, undistinguished in many ways, are good examples of the logist method, as are some of the prose writings of the Cambridge Platonists. Perhaps the most remarkable achievement in English "logism" is the homiletic writing of Lancelot Andrewes. In Andrewes every word of scripture is given an almost mystical (and mystifying) weight. Each syllable of the Greek or Hebrew Testaments echoes, doubles, or enhances some other syllable, and theological demonstration falls entirely within the process of grammatical parsing. No examples arise from experience or natural analogy. The experience of reading the Bible is the whole ground of our insight into divinity, and of ethical deductions as well. All other authorities evaporate before the systematic mining and polishing of every accident of the biblical text. How far Andrewes[12] is from the method of Donne or Taylor, and from the whole subsequent tradition of exegesis, is indeed remarkable, though he was representative of a larger tradition both in England and on the Continent:

Such like seasons do we find in the *anno magno*. 1. The time of nature all in the blade; 2. of Moses, in the stalk; 3. of the prophets in the ear; 4. And when the full corn? But when at this great gathering here mentioned? When all in Heaven and all in earth gathered, that I think was the fullness of things, *plenitudo rerum*; and the fullness of seasons, *plenitudo temporum*, may be allowed for it.

This sets us over to the second part, from the seasons to the things; from the fullness of seasons to the gathering of things. And first, whereof, of what things. Of *Τὰ Πάντα*, "even all." "All;" and to shew the extent of it, subdivided into "all in Heaven," "all on earth"; and that, I trow, is "All."[13]

Here the argument is entirely verbal. The theological problems are seen as grammatical or etymological. Comparison is nominal, based upon a full-fledged faith in the most extreme amanuensis theory. In one sense, rationalism of the Spinozan or Leibnizian sort is oddly akin to this self-

---

[11] Wolfson calls this the "double faith theory." See *The Philosophy of the Church Fathers*, 112–140.

[12] The sermons of Fisher, Jewell, and others have this quality to a lesser degree, but in Andrewes logism reaches an extreme. Of course the Puritans in England and America (Johnson, Mather) use the typological method, but in them it is mixed, having been decorated with conceits and analogies of every kind.

[13] Lancelot Andrewes, *Ninety-Six Sermons* (London: Oxford University Press, 1841), 269.

confident verbalism, though it is secular and exists without the authority of revelation.[14] For the rationalist, the human mind itself, and its instrument, language, are seen as having an almost perfect economy and utility. This is, of course, expressly unorthodox, in that Christians distinguish the Divine from the angelic or the human language.[15] On the other hand, the closest approximation to logist thought in the eighteenth century is the vapidly mathematical reasoning about God by Clarke in his lectures and sermons. But logism without Logos, and without a strong consciousness of primitive theology, is an empty gesture, and falls outside the traditional axis of Christian imagination.

In that sense Locke and Clarke were not merely a new beginning in Christian logism, but the practitioners of an inherently incommensurate method. Locke's critique of historical knowledge, and his epistemological paradigm of the individual perceiver, first negate the possibility of his own later theory of evidences, and then call into doubt the example of the apostolic witness.[16] The celebrity of Locke's attitude toward figurative language had a crippling effect on several generations of Anglican homilists and poets. For this reason Hume's more sophisticated critique of miracles is merely the making explicit of conclusions implied in Locke's epistemology. In Locke, as in Hobbes, Christianity seems to be a kind of withering intellectual habit, like Greek mythology in Byzantine poetry. In Hobbes the analogy of Divine and human covenants was convenient, but in Locke the apologetic material is labored and irrelevant. There is no space left in the fully realized Lockeian imagination for the original modes of Christian thought: typology, analogy, anagogy, and fideism are all foreclosed by the logic of Locke's *Essay*.

Whatever may have been the successful applications of logist poetics, the faith in language from the late Middle Ages to the seventeenth century in England is a remarkable fact. The confidence that language could illuminate the human mind, that it was the right medium for theological intuitions, and a nearly perfect mirror of ideal nature, is found in all European literatures before the Enlightenment. It was not uncommon for the world to be seen in Dante's words "as the pages collected in a single volume," and for man to be the first page, as in the German metaphysical poet von Butschky's epigram:

The world knows no greater book than itself; but the greatest part of this book is man, before whom, in place of a fine frontispiece, God has printed his own

---

[14] This is argued in a slightly different way about Spinoza in Leo Strauss, *Spinoza's Critique of Religion* (New York: Schocken Books, 1965), 140–146.

[15] Augustine, *Civitas dei* (London: Macmillan, 1924), 327–329, VIII, iv, 2.

[16] The problems are explained in great detail in I. T. Ramsey's Preface to Locke's *The Reasonableness of Christianity* (Stanford: Stanford University Press, 1972).

likeness, and, besides, God has made him into an abstract, kernel, and jewel of the other parts of this great book of the world.[17]

This "great book" is derived ultimately from the great book of the seven seals in Revelation, the book of life and creation, which is directly consumed by the prophet.

And the voice which I heard from heaven spake unto me again, and said, Go *and* take the little book which is open in the hand of the angel which standeth upon the sea and upon the earth.
  And I went unto the angel, and said unto him, Give me the little book. And he said unto me, Take *it*, and eat it up; and it shall make thy belly bitter, but it shall be in thy mouth sweet as honey.
  And I took the book out of the angel's hand, and ate it up; and it was in my mouth sweet as honey: and as soon as I had eaten it, my belly was bitter.

(Revelation 108–10)

Our skeptical modern turn, as embodied in semantic theory from Bacon to Hobbes, and, particularly, after Locke, did not come by a gradual or inevitable process. Medieval nominalism and Luther's theory of language had no real connection to this later critique. The poetics of faith, whether Lutheran or Calvinist, was verbally self-confident. "Has not God," said Calvin, "arraigned our minds with an irrevocable grammar, and given us victorious speech."[18] The voice that spoke to Spenser or Milton was not still and small, but prophetic and lucid. Aside from the Quakers, no Christian reform cult had much denigrated the instrument of language, and while some sects favored "spiritual acrostics," others with equal vigor pursued "a figure-making God."
  Dryden made fun of several Baroque favorites including spiritual "acrosticks" and "shape poems."

> Thy Genius calls thee not to purchase fame
> In keen Iambicks, but mild Anagram:
> Leave writing Plays, and chuse for thy command
> Some peacefull Province in Acrostick Land.
> There thou maist wings display and Altars raise,
> And torture one poor word Ten thousand ways.[19]

The connection between religious writing and bad taste is explicit. The bad poet retires, like Herbert, to a peaceful retreat to torture the language and produce monstrosities of facile wit. He moves away from the iambic decorum of the Augustans to the fairyland of the Baroque.

---

[17] Quoted from Walter Benjamin, *The Origin of German Tragic Drama* (London: Verso, 1977), 140–141.

[18] John Calvin, *Commentary on John's Gospel* (London: Sheed and Ward, 1931), 116.

[19] John Dryden, "MacFlecknoe," *Works* (Berkeley and Los Angeles: University of California Press, 1972), vol. III, 59.

Those figures and those acrostics were to be the normal butt of Augustan humor – a "mere Bedlam theology of prating words," as Bishop Tillotson was to say of the mass and Baptist service alike.[20] If Pope, a fellow Catholic, could read Crashaw as "nonsense," a play of sophistries, then it is no surprise that Stillingfleet found nothing but "fopperies" in the *Revelations of Divine Love* of Julian of Norwich.[21] Leaving aside a dubious recension of Francis de Sales and the long domesticated text of Thomas à Kempis, almost nothing of the heritage of Continental meditation was left for educated Englishman in the eighteenth century, and not much more of the great Protestant devotional literature of the Baroque period had lasting appeal. All of this was part of a general eclipse of the habit of logism, typology, and illumination.[22]

The analogical

If the logistic mode is but rarely realized in British literature, the second symbolic mode, the "analogical," is extraordinarily common. The analogical mode works by a different sort of substitution. Rather than verbal formulation and equivalence, it seeks in the image of the creature an intelligible or imaginative trace of God. From the outset this must be distinguished from the arguments of design or deist rationalism. In the analogical mode the creature is seen as a sign, window, or *vestigium* of the Divine. It is known, that is, primarily as a sign. In the case of the tradition of Philo or Bonaventure, to use two extreme examples, the creature is seen as having its essence and life in this signifying relationship. For the Deist, on the other hand, while the whole field of nature is thought to be the work of God, its body and order is autonomous and finished. Nature, then, is sustained by God, not by a continual intervention, but by a finished action. This ordination, for Locke and Toland, was the supreme gift of God to His creation. In the Deist and Lockeian view the creature is not part of a language but a physical mechanism.

Newton himself had seen the problem of Divine participation, and he emphasized that gravity was not a necessary but convenient action of God, who controls all His creation by thought. None of these ambiguities bothered the older analogists. For Bonaventure or Scotus, there is no

---

[20] See Gordon Rupp, *Religion in England 1688–1791* (Oxford: Oxford University Press, 1986), 35.

[21] Ibid., 34.

[22] For a thorough treatment of the residue of typology, see Paul Korshin, *Typologies in English Literature, 1660–1770* (Princeton: Princeton University Press, 1979); also, *Typologies in English Literature*, ed. Earl Miner (Princeton: Princeton University Press, 1977), 103–134, in the article "From Shadowy Types," by Stephen Zwicker on Restoration typology. For typology and prophecy in the 1660s see Michael McKeon, *Politics and Poetry in Restoration England* (Cambridge, Mass.: Harvard University Press, 1978), chs. 1–3.

system or law of nature, but only God as the omnipresent and internal principle of order. This principle is both separate and within, as Christ is both with the Father and with the world, and as the persons of the Trinity are both infinitely remote from man and absolutely present. The idea is perfectly realized in St. Paul's phrase, "in which we live and move and have our being." Analogism of this kind captures the central tenor of Christian paradox, and, in that sense, can be seen as primitive, although its full intellectual formulation, hinted at by Augustine and Francis of Assisi, was not made clear until the time of Bonaventure, whom we shall use as our representative figure within the larger tradition.

Bonaventure is especially important to our discussion of analogy because he was the first to pull together in a rigorous way the various Neoplatonic, patristic, and Franciscan strands of "analogism." He was also one of the chief historical links in the continental and English tradition of late-medieval and Baroque meditation books. Bonaventure's *Itinerarium mentis ad Deum* is the perfect representative of the mature analogical mode of thinking.

From all this it follows that the invisible things of God are clearly seen, from the creation of the world, being understood by the things that are made; so that those who are unwilling to give heed to them and to know God in them all, to bless him and to love him, are inexcusable [Romans 1:20], while they are unwilling to be carried forth from the shadows into the wonderful light of God

[1 Corinthians 15:57].[23]

Another passage of the *Itinerarium* will more clearly distinguish the character of the analogical mind from that of the deistic.

From these two initial steps we are led to seeing God in his traces, as if we had two wings falling to our feet, we can determine that all creatures of this sensible world lead the mind of the one contemplating or attaining wisdom of the eternal God; for they are shadows, echoes, and pictures, the traces, simulacra, and reflections of that first Principle most powerful, wisest, and best; of that light and plenitude; of that art productive, exemplifying and ordering, given to us for looking upon God. They are signs divinely bestowed which, I say, are exemplars or rather exemplifications set before our as yet untrained minds, limited to sensible things, so that through the sensibles which they see they may be carried to the intelligibles which they do not see, as if by signs to the signified.

The creatures of this sensible world signify the invisible things of God, partly because God is of all creation the origin, exemplar and end, and because every effect is the sign of its cause, the exemplification of the exemplar, and the way to the end towards which it leads.[24]

This passage contains within it the Augustinian tradition of the "natural

[23] Bonaventura, *The Ascent of the Mind to God* (Indianapolis: Bobbs-Merrill Company, 1969), 37.
[24] Ibid., 19–20.

sign,"[25] the Platonic epistemology of the form of the intelligible within the sensible, the Plotinian tradition of a *via mystica* by which the soul passes through the physical towards a higher reality, and the more specifically Franciscan sense of the creature as a simulacrum and window to God. For St. Francis, the mentor of Bonaventure, this illumination of the creature was the special act of Divine love which gives us proof of our continued relation to the Creator. This "illumination" was for Francis sacramental in nature, and Bonaventure's own work is in some respects a memorial to the speculations of Francis.

All the subsequent forms of analogical Christian imagination are suggested in this passage: the Scotist notion of the "glance" (the root concept of Hopkins' "inscape"), the notion of creaturely epiphany which dominates the imagination of Christian Platonists like Coleridge, and the Renaissance mirror and microcosm. We often hear of Calvinism as the most severe departure from medieval thought, and a building block of modernity, but on the matter of natural analogy – the glance, glory, and *speculum* – Calvin comes close to the language of both Bonaventure and Aquinas:

Yet in the first place, wherever you cast your eyes, there is no spot in the universe wherein you cannot discern at least some sparks of his glory. You cannot in one glance survey this most vast and beautiful system of the universe, in its wide expanse, without being completely overwhelmed by the boundless force of its brightness. The reason why the author of The Letter to the Hebrews elegantly calls the universe the appearance of things invisible is that this skillful ordering of the universe is for us a sort of mirror in which we can contemplate God, who is otherwise invisible.[26]

It is interesting that in Bonaventure's passage, God is the form, the end, and the cause of these visible presences. In deism He is reduced to cause, and even worse to Toland's and Paley's conception of cause, so far from the richness of the Aristotelian or Medieval conception. Toland's cause does not in any sense inhere in its effect. In this way the character of God has been changed to a kind of "machinist," or worse yet, "starter of the race." It was the growth of Baconianism with its clear and absolute demarcation between the natural and the supernatural that at first imperiled the analogical world of Donne: it was the satirical Augustan program of authors like Butler, Swift, and Pope that destroyed it.

One cannot talk of the end of analogical thought without considering John Locke. Locke, at turns the great protector of property, revealer of superstitious excesses, and philosopher of surfaces was not only the mouth-

---

[25] St. Augustine, *On Christian Doctrine*, ed. D. W. Robertson (New York: Bobbs-Merrill, 1958), 34–38.

[26] John Calvin, *Institutes of the Christian Religion*, vol. 1, ch. 5, 3 (Philadelphia: Westminster Press, 1960), 53–54.

piece of the new language and the new middle-class realism, but he was a distinguished enemy of the older poetic mode. First, he pronounced against metaphor and other "equivocal figures" at enormous length;[27] secondly, and more importantly for our purpose, he wrote the final argument against the possibility of spiritual analogy. In one of his last and most distinguished essays, Locke, in answering the visionary Protestant John Norris, meticulously details his objections to Malebranche's (and Bonaventure's) claim that creatures are known in and from God. Locke's eighth objection is representative:

> If God could create a mind, and give it the sun suppose for its idea, or immediate object of knowledge, "God would then make the mind for the Sun, and not for himself." This supposes that those who see things in God at the same time see God, and thereby show that their minds are made for God, having him "for the immediate object of their knowledge." But for this I must appeal to common experience, whether every one, as often as he sees anything else, sees and perceives God in the case; or whether it be true of men, who see other things every moment, that God is not in all their thoughts? . . . This is the case of the great part of mankind; and how many can we imagine of those, who have got some notion of God, either from tradition or reason; have an idea of Him present in their minds as often as they think of anything else?[28]

This argument against the vestigial and analogical theory should be closely investigated. It offers as the chief authority in metaphysical debates the common experience of men. It equates "seeing God in or through" with seeing God *per se*. It applies Locke's principle of rational uniformity from the *Essay*, and implies that "tradition" alone (the old habit of authorities) could so mislead the human mind. It cleverly switches the field of analysis from the spiritual or virtual translucence of the creature to the problem of immediate association – "I must appeal to *experience*," says Locke, "whether everyone so often as he sees anything also sees God in the case." We are to imagine Bonaventure and Malebranche are making an *a posteriori* and visual judgment rather than a metaphysical one – that the whole idea of logical cause is a fantasy.

Locke, of course, gave this new literalism psychological weight, and should be seen not only as he was presented by Tuveson[29] and Nicolson[30] as the harbinger of man's new closeness to nature, or, as it were, the new empowering of the natural for poetry, but also as contributing to the

[27] John Locke, *Essay Concerning Human Understanding* (New York: Dover, 1959), vol. II, 41–98.

[28] John Locke, *An Examination of P. Malebranche's Opinion of Seeing All Things in God, Works*, vol. x (London: Tegg, Sharp and Son, 1823), 251–252.

[29] Ernest Lee Tuveson, *The Imagination as a Means of Grace* (Berkeley and Los Angeles: University of California Press, 1960), 131–151.

[30] Marjorie Nicolson, *Newton Demands the Muse* (Princeton: Princeton University Press, 1966), 87.

emptying out of the poetic potential of the creature. This new naturalism made possible a very small body of interesting poems, perhaps one or two enduring ones, but its encroachment upon the older imaginative material marks a nadir of the English poetic culture. Augustanism severely limited the full range of poetic effects. This was what, in different ways, both Blake and Coleridge recognized: the former in his explicit critique of natural religion, the latter in his critique of empiricism.

The God described above by Bonaventure is explicitly the principle of imagination. He speaks of that "art productive and exemplifying," which recalls us to the tradition of Sidney's *Apology*. The analogical mode of religious writing is one of infinite figuration, since its chief example is the activity of God. In Donne's words:

Thou art, a figurative and figure-making God, a metaphorical God, too; a God in whose words there is such a height of figures, such voyages, such peregrinations to fetch remote and precious metaphors, such extensions, such spreadings, such curtain of allegories, such third heavens of hyperboles, so harmonious elocutions, so retired and so reserved expressions, such commanding persuasions, and persuading commandments, such sinews even in thy milk, and such things in thy words, as all prophane authors seem as the seed of the serpent that creeps, thou art the Dove that flies.[31]

Here Donne has discovered figures of every kind to describe the figure-making character of God. "Sinews in thy milk" reminds us of the breadth and strangeness of Baroque conceit, where a figure of motherly nurture is transformed into a metaphor for potencies that "live beforehand in the person of God." Logism itself abounds in this passage. Donne brings to bear a whole grammar of associations and the Logos is the key to that grammar. But in the end he turns to two important and typical figures from the analogical repertoire, the serpent and the dove. It is important to remember that the analogical and the logistic are two ends of a single pole – the two possibilities of Christian symbolism. For this reason the metaphysical poets, especially Donne and Marvell, could use Scholastic and Platonic logism as a support for their more typical mode of analogy. The diagrams at the end of this chapter are presented to clarify these relations. Donne's techniques are far from any concept of empirical observation, and Locke's critique of the use of figures is aimed at this very "weakness" of method. Donne ransacks the natural (and scriptural) world, but he does not in our more modern sense describe the world. The objectification of nature and of the city is, collaterally, the denigration of traditional analogy. This denigration takes place outside the limits of primitive Christian art, and is

---

[31] John Donne, *Devotions upon Emergent Occasions* (Ann Arbor: University of Michigan Press, 1959), Expostulation XIX, 124.

part of the literalizing and desymbolizing tendency of Restoration and Augustan poetry and painting.

We should recognize that the Romantic era is marked by the revitalization of the analogical methods of the earlier period. It was a reaction to the strained realism and positivism of the early eighteenth century. The accidental differences – subjectivity, self-allegorizing, eccentric epiphany – can easily obscure the likeness of Romantic to Baroque poetry. What it shares is the belief in recognizable analogical relations: Smart's reworking of the Psalmic icons, the *vestigia* or traces in Wordsworth's *Prelude*, the fourfold vision of Blake, with its explicit anti-naturalism, and the Platonic "vision" in Shelley all recall and rework the aesthetic of Bonaventure's *Itinerarium*. At the same time the whole range of possibilities, the complete circle of religious modes are recapitulated in the evolution of Coleridge's thought. His earliest work moves from Unitarian (perhaps Augustan rationalism) to Lutheran fideism, and to the visionary analogism of his mature poetry and prose.

The mystical

The third mode, the "mystical," turns away from both the logistic and the analogical. It attempts by a severe discipline to find the unmediated person of God. This is, of course, a less common species of meditation, because it implies a special kind of disciplined experience. It is a mode at once suspicious of language (theology and logism) and analogy (the creature). John of the Cross and St. Teresa of Avila are Europe's most perfect examples of the mystical tradition. Their spiritual biographies are myths of abnegation, denial, and single-minded holiness. The object of their experiences was God himself, and at the summit of Mt. Carmel or in St. Teresa's chamber we leave, at some point, the possibility of art. The literature of mysticism, therefore, has two components. The first is a moral description – the drama of self-preparation and denial. The second is the confused remembrance and recording of affections during and after the experience of union. The mystical, where that word can be honestly used, is beyond the touch of *mimesis*, but the affections which surround it are a powerful subject for art.

We may say, paradoxically, that the analogical and logistic modes give us a representation of God, though the experience is at one remove, while the mystical method gives us no representation of God, though the experience is absolute. I have called the mystical and fideist modes "ontological," because they are an approach to "being" itself. The mystical mode is one of absolute presence, the fideist of absolute absence. There is a well-established rhetoric of preparation in the mystical literature, and its symbols are generally those of night, darkness, ascent, blindness, and passion. The mystic devises a lyrical drama of peculiarly severe emotionalism. Like the fideism which I am about to describe, mysticism's natural milieu is an elaborate and aphoristic moralism. The Sutras in Buddhism and some of the Vedic literature of initiation share with western mystical writing the quality of an endless and circular preparation. They also share a painful and often tedious sense of anticipation.[32] If, in the analogical mode, metaphors and analogies of the creature abound, they are the express enemy of the speculative mystic.

The fourth kind of harm is general, for the reason and the judgment of the spirit becomes very dull, as in the case of joy over temporal goods, joy in them produces its imprint more quickly and effectively and ravishes more forcibly. Thus the reason and judgment do not remain free but are clouded by that emotion of very intimate joy.

This gives rise to the fifth harm: distraction of the mind with creatures . . . Pure spirit is infallibly lost in this kind of joy, at least in the beginning. If some spirituality is felt it will be very sensible, gross, unspiritual, exterior, and unrecollected.[33]

Merton has said that Christian spiritualists are divided between the "light and the dark teachers," and the mystics are those inclined to images of night.[34] Among the aphorisms of John of the Cross is this: "In outward things light helps to prevent one from falling; but in the things of God just the opposite is true: it is better for the soul not to see if it is to become more secure."[35] We are apt to confuse mystical and visionary works of literature. There are very few works of real mysticism in the English tradition. Even Julian of Norwich has only equivocal claim to the title, since her method is primarily, like that of the spiritual Franciscans, one of seeing God in the creatures. The visionary method, on the contrary, is quite common in English literature. Vaughan and Traherne in the seventeenth century, and Smart and Blake in the eighteenth, describe elaborate patterns of creaturely illumination. Traherne's famous phrase, "a world without objects is a sensible emptiness," might have suggested to him a "spiritual emptiness" as well, but for the true mystic such an emptiness is the ideal spiritual condition. Visionary poetry, of which Traherne's is one of the last important examples in the seventeenth century, is a form of analogical art in which the poet, struck by the epiphanic force of the natural, creates a vision where each detail is suffused with spiritual significance. These two modes ought not to be confused, since they require an inverted phenomen-

---

[32] For the relations of these two kinds of art, see Ananda Coomeraswamy, *The Transformation of Nature in Art* (New York: Dover Publications, 1956).

[33] St. John of the Cross, *The Ascent of Mt. Carmel*, III, 20, in *The Collected Works* (Washington: Institute of Carmelite Studies Press, 1979), 382–383.

[34] Thomas Merton, *The Ascent to Truth* (New York: Harcourt, Brace, Jovanovich, 1985), ch. 2.

[35] St. John of the Cross, *The Collected Works*, aphorism 54, 325.

ology, but even in the seminal works of Underhill and Dean Inge, the visionary is sometimes considered a type of the mystical.[36] (Northrop Frye has brilliantly summarized the difference between these two imaginative modes in the first chapter of *Fearful Symmetry*.)[37] It could be argued that the Spanish speculative mystics share with other European Baroque artists an erotic allegory, derived in part from the Petrarchan inheritance, but this would ignore an important distinction. The erotic analogies in visionary poems like those of Marino and Crashaw are metaphors of proportion, linking God to the creature. In the mystics the erotic material merely amplifies the idea of a total devotional consummation in the human psyche.

The fideist

The last mode of religious poetry, the "fideist," is the chief subject of the next chapter, so I will be brief. Fideism, the second ontological pole, exists whenever God is perceived as an absence. This is not to say that God is perceived as not existing, but rather that His empirical (and sometimes moral) absence from the world seems to be a strong proof of His presence in another. When Ambrose Bierce called faith "Belief without evidence in what is told by one who speaks without knowledge, of things without parallel,"[38] he was not far from the central Pauline formulation – "The evidence of things unseen, and the expectation of Good to come." Bierce's joke uncovers several aspects of fideist thought. First, that faith is its own evidence, an internal recognition with no commensurate external demonstration; and secondly, that any normal sense of knowledge (or science) is put aside. Lastly, wisdom is seen as removed from the natural condition and experience of things. It is interesting to note that Origen, an inveterate logicist, took this central Pauline sentence to mean the "invisible things of God," or the "unseeable things," as if they referred to Platonic forms or angels. In fact, the "unseen things" are (as in Tertullian's argument) the very grounds for belief. Faith is that "faculty" which turns away from sensible demonstration and mundane opinion, and turns to the invisible and remote God. If we recall Christ's words to Thomas, we see that the Gospels share this notion of an unequivocal and unevidenced faith as being the highest.

The fideist shares with the mystic a vocabulary of remoteness, silent anticipation, and apocalyptic anxiety, but does not enter upon a discipline of meditation to come into God's presence. Instead, the common fideist

---

[36] Cf. Evelyn Underhill, *Mysticism* (New York: Meridian, 1955), ch. 4 and William Inge, *Mysticism in England* (London: Macmillan, 1895), 201–224.

[37] Northrop Frye, *Fearful Symmetry* (Princeton: Princeton University Press, 1959).

[38] Ambrose Bierce, *The Collected Writings* (New York: The Citadel Press, 1946), 257.

motif is an exhaustive "experiencing" of the emptiness and unworthiness of the world. In Hegel's words:

With his herds Abraham wandered hither and thither over a boundless territory without bringing parts of it any nearer to him by improving them. Had he done so he would have become attached to them and might have adopted them as parts of *his* world. The land was simply given over to his cattle for grazing. The water slept in deep wells without living movement; digging for it was laborious; it was dearly bought or struggled for, an extorted and necessary property for him. The groves which gave him shade he soon left again; in them he has theophanies, appearances of his perfect Object on High, but he did not tarry in them with a love that would have made them worthy of the Divinity and participant in Him. He was a stranger on earth, a stranger to the soil and to men alike . . . The whole world Abraham regarded as simply his opposite; if he did not take it to be a nullity, he looked on it as sustained by a God that was alien to it. Nothing in nature was supposed to have any part in God; everything was simply under God's mastery.[39]

This is a potent and thorough description of the fideist character. He is completely alienated from the natural. God is above nature, and the creature is not a trustworthy sign of the unapproachable deity. If St. Anselm's God (a type of the logistic theology) dwelt in "unapproached light," the God of Pascal, Luther, and Johnson dwells in a complete darkness. But this darkness is not only the darkness of distance or of "a God in hiding," but it is the darkening of all knowledge. The biblical type of this sort of wisdom is Solomon, as the type of analogical wisdom is David. The Davidic and Solomonic seem alternately to divide the attention of the British religious imagination. We shall see that in the eighteenth century the fideist ministers and poets alike turned from the staple seventeenth-century biblical sources in the Gospel and the Psalms to find Job, Ecclesiastes,[40] and the Pauline letters more imaginatively useful models.

Like mysticism, fideism takes for its natural elements silence, remoteness, and distance, but it adds to these the horror of night and the grave. Those two objects mark the end of two types of fideist anticipation – the one of sensation, the other of life itself. The Graveyard school of the eighteenth century (especially as it appears in Parnell's "Night Piece on Death" and Young's *Night Thoughts*) is an expression of this mode, but the "gothicization" of it in the ensuing decade greatly emptied it of power. The Gothic horror is the cartoon residuum of older Christian fideism, and is only possible in the period of the decay of biblical allegory and typology.

Fideism has been provoked in many phases of Christian culture by the appearance of gnostic or logistic intellectual threats. So Tertullian reacted

[39] G. F. W. Hegel, *On Christianity: Early Theological Writings*, trans. T. M. Knox (Chicago: University of Chicago Press, 1948), 186–187.
[40] On this see also Paul Korshin, *Typologies in England, 1650 to 1820* (Princeton: Princeton University Press, 1979), chs. 6 and 7.

to the Platonic Christianity of his time, and all Hellenized and intellectualist interpretations of scripture. He believed in the message of the Gospel
"because it is absurd,"[41] and needed no more evidence than the folly that
the world found in it. In the same way Luther is a fideist reacting not only
to temporal corruption, but to the whole tradition of Scholastic theology,
with its great weight of logism.

Never before the eighteenth century were gnosticism and "natural
divinity" so prevalent. The Deists themselves are the *ne plus ultra* of
naturalism, falling, perhaps, entirely outside the limits of the normal
Christian imagination. Nature was stolen from Christian apologists when
the tradition of *anologia entis* and creaturely illumination began to fade. The
mechanical animal of Descartes and the constructed "fantasm" of Locke
were equally denuded of iconic significance. At the moment when the old
world-view had been assailed by science and skepticism, and the old body
of spiritual figures had become inert, fideism again arose, and for one
generation dominated the Christian poetry of England. The history of that
reaction is discussed in the next chapter.

As logism and analogism are two ends of a unified symbolical pole, so
fideism and mysticism are often found together. The early work of William
Law, so instrumental in the education of Johnson and Wesley, perfectly
exemplifies fideism. The attention of that work to the manifold temptations
of everyday life, and the problems of moral perfectionism, the mix of
Solomonic moral exhaustion and abundant wisdom, the use of the
allegorical moral exemplar, and the interspersion of prayer, mark the
method of fideism. The three natural genres of fideism are the confessional
biography, the wisdom book, and allegorical spiritual-journey narrative. In
this sense it was no contradiction for Solomon to have authored (as he was
believed to have done) both Ecclesiastes, which seems to make all knowledge impossible, and Proverbs, a book of plenary wisdom. Wisdom should
not be confused with knowledge – its only object is the moral self. The
greatest expanses of fideist literature, in both western and eastern religious
writing, are walled around by wisdom. Wisdom replaces the enormous
emptiness of the natural world in fideism. It is the ground for imaginative
elaboration, and fideist culture thrives upon the unedited moral musings of
a Gautama, St. Paul, or (as we shall see) Edward Young. Of Law it is
important to notice that his later mystical tracts are merely an extension, a
kind of exaggeration, of his earlier fideistic theories. In some respects this is
true of Pascal. This is the practical effect of the kinship between the

---

[41] The anti-intellectualism and "single-faith" elements in Tertullian are thoroughly analyzed in
H. A. Wolfson, *The Philosophy of the Church Fathers* (Cambridge, Mass.: Harvard University Press,
1952) vol. II. Tertullian's reaction and ultimate schism is an obvious parallel to the militant anti-
intellectualism and fideism of Luther (or Kierkegaard). The dialectical relation of the four
modes can be seen in historical terms as well as logical ones.

mystical and the fideist. In the case of Johnson, as we shall see, a kind of pure fideism dominated his spiritual musings, and this extreme simplicity makes his case the more interesting.

The diagrams which end this section are placed there to clarify certain of these issues. It will be noticed that in historical and logical terms the four modes have several complex relations. I have already mentioned the special relations of the two symbolic and the two ontological modes, and the paradox of communicability in which they are involved. A further note should be made. Since the mystical is essentially ineffable it falls or turns to the logistic for expression. In the same way the pure formula of the liturgy or theology turns towards faith for its life. Faith, having no near object for its imitation or desire, turns at last to creaturely analogy – as in the case of the Roman Catholic Eucharist, which, empowered by faith, presents the creature as no less than the mystical person of God.

I make these points to show that my model is not static, and that it does not attempt by a kind of simplistic nomenclature to round off the jagged edges and complexities of religious poetics. The arrows added to the first diagram show the logical (and sometimes temporal) relations I have just described. The greatest products of religious imagination cannot be bound by any one of these convenient categories. All four modes coexist in the Bible, as my diagram tries to show. In ending I might remark that they are often inextricably interwoven in the finest works of Christian art, as for example the analogical and fideist in *The Faerie Queen,* and all four modes in a sublime and seamless consort in *The Divine Comedy.*

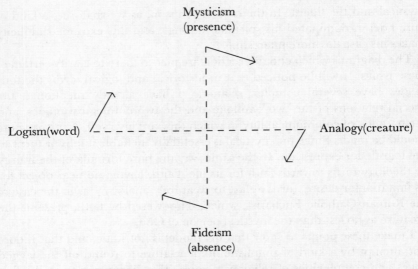

Mysticism
(presence)

Logism(word)

Analogy(creature)

Fideism
(absence)

CORRESPONDING BIBLICAL MODES

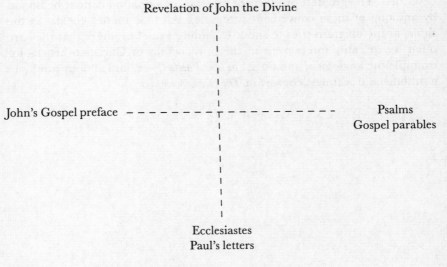

Revelation of John the Divine

John's Gospel preface

Psalms
Gospel parables

Ecclesiastes
Paul's letters

Figure 1   Four modes of Christian poetry

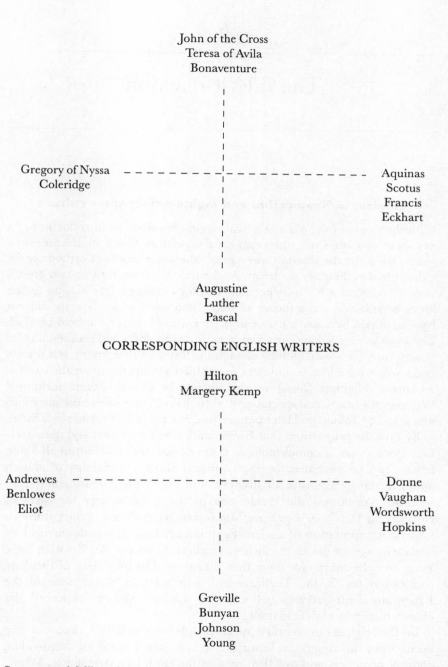

John of the Cross
Teresa of Avila
Bonaventure

Gregory of Nyssa — — — — — — — — — — — — — — Aquinas
Coleridge   Scotus
                                                 Francis
                                                 Eckhart

Augustine
Luther
Pascal

CORRESPONDING ENGLISH WRITERS

Hilton
Margery Kemp

Andrewes — — — — — — — — — — — — — — — — Donne
Benlowes   Vaughan
Eliot   Wordsworth
                                                Hopkins

Greville
Bunyan
Johnson
Young

Spenser and Milton have strong elements of all but the mystical mode; Dante
synthesizes all four.

Figure 2   Corresponding traditions

6

The fideist reaction

Fideism in Restoration and eighteenth-century culture

With the decay of the old analogical world-view and the introduction of a
new kind of naturalism, the religious imagination found itself at a crossroads. For some the solution was a gradual abandonment of orthodoxy for
either physico-theology or deism. At the time of Newton these two groups
were at odds, and his own peculiar theology claimed Christianity as the
lucky beneficiary of the theory of optics and gravitation. Gravity did not
have to obtain by a law intrinsic in matter, and so must be upheld by God.
Light was as rarefied and mystical in reality as St. John had claimed it to be
in scripture. This was apology enough for Ray and Blackmore, but it soon
had a withering effect. Could not this natural light equally prove the truth of
all known religions? Could not this divinity be known without scripture?
Was man the image and special care of this cause? These were the questions
first asked by Toland and later popularized and made formidable by Tindal.

By 1718 the proposition that Christianity was a reasoned and unmyster-
ious system was a commonplace. Bolingbroke and Warburton (if those
fellows can be imagined together) worried about the viability of church
authority in an age without mystery, and opted for a sentimental Era-
stianism. Warburton did create one of the great shaggy monsters of
casuistry in his *Divine Legation of Moses*, but its evidence, culled from an
esoteric interpretation of ancient Egyptian mythology, was doomed in an
impatient age to the dusty shelf of intellectual curios. An Erastian haze
hung over the church for more than a century. The long sleep of theology
and canon law in the Anglican fold, which began at the time of the
Bangorian controversy, lasted until the Oxford Movement forced the
church hierarchy to defend itself.

In the eighteenth century most people still believed, and we are
accustomed in Augustan histories to hear the praises of hard-riding
country preachers and practical men of the cloth like Woodforde, White,
and Sterne.[1] But good old common sense is never enough to hold together

---

[1] *Backgrounds of Eighteenth Century Literature*, ed. Kathleen Williams (Bloomington: University of
Indiana Press, 1971), cf. "The Character of Eighteenth Century Religion," A. R. Humphreys.

the claims of faith, and for a large number of seriously pious Christians this was an age of crisis. For the Christian poetic imagination this crisis was acute. The spiritual mind had nearly choked with the innumerable objects of sense. Nature had become its own best explanation. Suspended in an astronomic void of unthinkable magnitude, man seemed infinitely remote from the first cause. The creature seemed to exist in a new physical cosmos slowly receding from the biblical landscape of the Psalms, and bound by an all-explaining and autonomous mechanical law. Man, who for centuries had been his own law, the partner and image of God, was now imprisoned in this mechanical system. There was poetic logic without Logos, metaphor without illumination, and undisciplined sentiment, while the seventeenth-century staples of metaphysical conceit, microcosm, and icon had almost disappeared.

This new world of things, this thoroughgoing empiricism and concentration on worldly objects, was not suitable to traditional Christian poetry. Having first lost the analogical habit of mind, and the whole sense of intellectual hierarchy that went with it, Christian poets could not readily turn to Augustan spatial art. Although the Scriblerians (aside from Swift) had all written explicitly religious poetry, their attempts in that direction are among their least memorable. Addison's famous hymns, Gay's poetry about the night sky and the creation, and Pope's "Universal Prayer" are polished tributes to a God no longer the figural center of high-popular art. The God "that hang'st upon a tree" in Donne, or carries the letters of sinners back to the Father in the mailbag of his wound in Herbert, the tears and whirlwinds of Crashaw – these were *passé*. Christ himself recedes into the background, replaced by a remote cosmic principle, disembodied and incalculable.

> Thou Great First Cause, least Understood!
> Who all my Sense confin'd
> To know but this, – that Thou art Good,
> And that myself am blind: ("The Universal Prayer," 5–8)[2]

The sterile effect and bathetic triviality of Pope's attempt at metrical psalm writing is representative of Scriblerian piety. The opening passage of Psalm 91 appears in the Authorized Version as

He that dwelleth in the secret place of the most High shall abide under the shadow of the Almighty. I will say of the Lord, *He is* my refuge and my fortress: My God; in him will I trust. Surely He shall deliver thee from the snare of the fowler, and from the noisome pestilence. He shall cover thee with his feathers, and under his wings shalt thou trust; his truth *shall be thy* sword and buckler. Thou shalt not be afraid for the terror by night, nor for the arrow *that* flieth by day (Psalms 91: 1–5).

---

[2] Pope, *Poems*, VI, 145.

Pope renders it in the following words:

> He who beneath thy shelt'ring wing resides,
> Whom thy hand leads and whom thy glory guides
> To Heav'n familiar his bold vows shall send,
> And fearless say to God – Thou art my friend!
> 'Tis Thou shalt save him from insidious wrongs,
> And the sharp arrows of censorious tongues.
> When gath'ring tempests swell the raging main,
> When thunder roars, and lightning blasts the plain,
> Amidst the wrack of nature undismay'd,
> Safe shall he lie and hope beneath thy shade.[3]

Leaving aside the accuracy of the translation, which borrows some of its phrases from the Douay Bible, the tone is dismally pedestrian. Man as God's familiar and friend is not suggested by the original and is the worst sort of latitudinarian good feeling. The strange conceit of the bird is reduced to a cliché, "shelt'ring wing," and the "arrow that flieth by day" becomes the sting of "censorious tongues." More interesting is the inclusion of two lines of landscape borrowed from Statius and dropped into the poem to give it the proper Popeian visual frame – "Amidst the wrack of nature undismay'd, / Safe shall he lie and hope beneath the shade." This is the shade of his classical pastorals which he was working on at the time (1709). Some of the same transvaluations I described in his translations of Homer appear in the psalm, and to worse effect. Two of the later lines of his paraphrase, "I see protecting myriads round thee fly, / And all the bright *militia* of the sky" (23–24) were transposed with little alteration to *The Rape of the Lock*, showing once again the thin partition between piety and mockery. Those fictional angels of the later poem already lacked reality to Pope.

Twenty years later Pope had cast off even the pretense of religious feeling when he wrote a number of clever lampoons of contemporary religious life, including the "Epitaph [*of By-Words*]."

> Here lies a round Woman, who thought *mighty odd*
> Every Word she e'er heard in this Church about God.
> To convince her of *God* the good Dean did endeavor,
> But still in her Heart she held *Nature* more *clever*.
> Tho' he talk'd much of Virtue, her Head always run
> Upon something or other, she found better *Fun*.
> For the Dame, by her Skill in Affairs Astronomical,
> Imagin'd, to live in the Clouds was but *comical*.
>
> (Pope, *Poems*, 317, 1–8)

It is not too much of a stretch to say that by 1731 Pope, then under the sway

---

[3] Pope, *Poems*, "Psalm XCI," 1–10, in *Translations and Paraphrases*.

of Bolingbroke, might have had this same naturalistic and astronomic prejudice, and the same sense of the importance of "fun" unencumbered by the bugbears of traditional religion. Only three years before he had offered the semi-blasphemous epitaph on Newton, which Augustan critics have always treated with the utmost seriousness.

> Nature, and Nature's Laws lay hid in Night.
> God said, *Let Newton be!* and All was *Light*.

The period from 1670 to 1740 did not produce one really important Christian poem aside from hymns. The best hymns themselves, particularly those of Watts, were opposed from the start to the new interest in this world, and a full third of Watts' poems and hymns advocate turning away from the creature and the creation to think of God alone. Watts did not share the Deist sense that naturalistic poetry, and the Newtonian conception of the "intelligent maker," should be the central apology for Divinity. In his works on logic and in his secular verses he often shows the influence of Locke's ideas, but in his religious poems he rarely involves the empirical ideas of the age. The common tone and argument of Watts' *Hymns* (he wrote over 500), may be easily represented.

> Naked as from Earth we came,
> And crept to life at first,
> We to the earth return again,
> And mingle with our dust.
>
> The dear delights we here enjoy,
> And fondly call our own,
> Are but short Favors borrow'd Now,
> To be repayed Anon.[4]

This is Watts' general tone – unassuming, pious, and prosaic. His phrasing is a kind of clipped King James English. In his secular poems he can sometimes rise to a higher level of verbal complexity, especially in his Miltonic and classical metrical experiments, but most of his work seems to be catechetical in nature. It shares with later forms of eighteenth-century fideism a concentration on the grave, the Apocalypse, and most importantly, a derogation of the creature and our attraction to it. Several of his most distinguished hymns are on this very topic.

> Man has a soul of vast desires,
> He burns within with restless fires,
> Tost to and fro his passions fly
> From Vanity to Vanity.
>
> In vain on earth we hope to find

[4] Isaac Watts, "Naked as from Earth," *Horae Lyricae* (Oxford: Oxford University Press, 1977) 87.

> Some solid ground to fill the mind,
> We try new pleasures, but we feel
> The inward thirst and torment still.
>
> ("The Vanity of the Creatures")

Here the Solomonic note, which is the mark of much Protestant poetry of the period, replaces the analogical method of seventeenth-century metrical psalm and hymn writing. The themes of Watts are those typical among the Evangelicals – Pauline anticipation, self-abnegation, dramas of conversion, images of the heavenly city, lamentations on life and death, and the whole repertoire of "fideist" allegorizing – the dark way, the infinite thirst, and the war with Satan and the flesh. In some respects Watts is a holdover from the incipient forms of Calvinist religious lyric, but in another way he departs from Calvin's own naturalism.[5] His diction is so completely biblical and liturgical that, like many hymn writers, his work seems almost formulaic; yet his best songs have the air of real pious emotion, and he is still, perhaps, our most distinguished hymn writer. Let it suffice to say that in his hymns, and those of Ken and Hopkins in the generation before him, we hear the first note of fideist reaction to the new Augustan world. This dependency on Pauline and Solomonic material for so much of his verse connects him with Young, Johnson, and William Law.[6] Even Watts could not completely hold out against the general tide of thought in the period. In his later tracts he turns away from Trinitarianism and, if read closely, looks forward to the liberal Unitarians of a later period. The Hebrew divinity seemed real to him, the type of the sublime, and he preceded Prior and Lowth in claiming the Old Testament was a better model than the Roman and Greek classics for poetry. He speculated about Hebrew prosody, and wrote well on epistemological issues. But in the end he lost faith in the possibility of the Christological mystery which had been at the core of his earliest poems. The second person of the Trinity had too much of flesh and blood for most of the pious poets of the Augustan period. "Who can write of man so unlike other men and yet too like to explain the wonders of creation and the powers of eternity; it is a mystery too mysterious for our sympathy, too intimate for our faith."[7]

Twenty years after Watts' *Hymns* were published some poets, like Aaron Hill, were the victims of the floating fashions of Augustanism in religious writing. They attempted without success to incorporate the spatial poetic and the sentimentality of the 1730s. Some of Hill's early poems show a fine

---

[5] Praise of the physical creation as *speculum* and Scholastic *analogia* abound in the works of Calvin. He did not share Luther's dread of the creature. See John Calvin, *Institutes of the Christian Religion*, ed. by John T. McNeill (Philadelphia: Westminster Press, 1960), 51–53.

[6] The dependency on "Ecclesiastes" and the "Proverbs" as well as "Romans" for homiletics in the Georgian preachers is remarkable.

[7] Joseph Priestley, *Corruptions of Christianity* (London: Samuels and Reed, 1782), 227.

(if simple) flare for Calvinist pietism, but his middle poems such as *Creation* are a hodgepodge of optimistic scientism and formulaic sublimities. In the end he was swallowed up in the pseudo-Pindaric fashion of the mid-century and wrote unspeakably tedious heroic lyrics about the limits of faith and reason. A few lines may suffice:

> Doubt all faiths boldly then – undoubting God,
> Appendent to no pride, mis-rob'd like zeal,
> Hope all men blessed alike – and injure none,
> Grateful, I'll trace the fainter lights I find,
> Unenvying others blazing: – humbly, own
> My awed conviction, of man's reachless power
> To pierce omnipotence – and know it near.
> Let me, with distant reverence pondering dumb,
> Dread arrogant decision; persecute
> No fancied heresy, but clothing, calm,
> Opinions dazzled eye, bow darkly down
> And hail the unfathomed vastness![8]

Hill's mind is, to use another of his phrases, "tremblingly stuck." This sort of confused, self-lacerating bombast, which gets its weight from its quasi-Miltonic drift, is the poetry of religious crisis. It is not unlike the self-conscious maundering of the worst passages of Browning, and better, perhaps, than some other Victorian waverers. For Hill man's conviction is "awed" and his power "reachless." The poet's rhetoric shows the same mixture of falling short and leaping over that is the sign of religious emotion without an object. The tenuous balance of personal opinion against heresy is the mark of his inability to consummate the dangerous and impossible religious act. Hill's notion that the honest religious writer should "disrobe zeal" and avoid "dread arrogant decision" shows his attachment to the contemporary critique of Protestant enthusiasm and his "persecute no fancied heresy" shows a thinly veiled critique of Catholicism. The "unfathomed vastness" is a metaphor of spiritual languor, and his vaunted Augustan "calm" is the result of torpid theological compromise. Doctrine itself was a vital subject for Donne, Crashaw, Herbert, and Vaughan, but any scholastic or primitive formulation of theology (whether Protestant or Catholic) is for Augustan poets the death knell of honest religious emotion. This cult of neutral judgment, what I have called the new *via media*, has a chilling effect on both the figure-making power and the intellectual edge of the poetry.

Hill's "nature poetry" is as bad and gives a dubious and contrived report of God's workings. Like the other religious sentimentalists of the era –

---

[8] Aaron Hill, *Works* (London: Lodge, 1783) 189. From "Free Thoughts upon Faith." Quoted in Hoxie Neale Fairchild, *Religious Trends in English Poetry*, vol. 1 (New York: Columbia University Press, 1939), 452–453.

Shenstone, Jago, and Dodd – Hill's best material is derived from Thomson, but it lacks the power of Thomson's descriptions which, free from moral jargon and lifeless abstraction, pursue the natural as a substitute for customary theological cant. Being "tremblingly stuck" between the language of the Prayer Book and observant naturalism, Hill could not master the language of either. It was not until Smart (and even more effectively in Wordsworth) that these two modes – biblical sublime and physico-naturalism – were effectively combined. The Romantic author had to reimagine for himself the prophetic naturalism of the Psalmist, a naturalism which carries with it the aura of the transcendent and the archaism of analogical vision. Naturally these spiritual flitterings and downward metaphors were not enough for those who maintained more orthodox and serious religious beliefs. For them the crisis was absolute. Law and Wesley are the most obvious examples, and both found themselves outside (though never by their own choice) the Anglican church. Law was a Nonjuror, an ardent Tory, a sometime visionary, and a passionate Protestant. His remarkable handbook of Christian moral perfection, *A Serious Call to a Devout and Holy Life*, which so deeply influenced Johnson and Wesley, has the quality of moral perfectionism common to most fideist texts.

Thus it is with all the virtues and holy tempers of Christianity; they are not ours unless they be the virtues and tempers of our ordinary life. So that Christianity is so far from leaving us to live in the common ways of life, conforming to the folly of customs and gratifying passions and tempers which the spirit of the world delights in, it is so far from indulging in any of these things that all its virtues which it makes necessary to salvation are only so many ways of living above or contrary to the world in all the common actions of our life.[9]

This was strong stuff in an age of Erastian complacency. Common custom, concern for patriotic duty, rational submission, and the like were the marks of Caroline religion. Law's clarion call to piety no doubt roused the perfectionist and alienated religious emotions of Johnson and Wesley, but on the other hand, it had little effect on the thinking of Law's young charge, Edward Gibbon.[10] Law's career was entwined with the double reality of his age – enthusiasm and apostasy. He was no doubt horrified at the encroachments of Newtonian physics and latitudinarian naturalism. His references to Newton in *The Spirit of Love* are not complimentary:[11] Boehme and the mystics knew everything about forces of opposition and attraction long before Newton, and detaching those forces from the eternal divine activity is a form of blasphemy. Law perceived nature as something suddenly denuded of its old glory, standing for the first time in naked and

9   William Law, *A Serious Call to a Devout and Holy Life and The Spirit of Love* (New York: Paulist Press, 1978), 52.
10 Edward Gibbon, *An Autobiography* (London: Routledge and Kegan Paul, 1970), 12–13.
11 Law, *A Serious Call*, 375, 389.

mechanical isolation from man and God. A passage from *The Spirit of Love* perfectly captures the sense of loss and crisis.

Nature is at first only spiritual. It has in itself nothing but the spiritual properties of the desire, which is the very being and ground of nature. But when these spiritual properties are not filled and blessed, and all held in one will by the light and love of God ruling them, then something is found in nature that never should have been found, viz. the properties of nature in a visible, palpable division and contrariety to each other. And this is the one true origin of all the materiality of this earthly system.[12]

This was written at the mid-century, twenty years after *A Serious Call*, and it shows that other extreme characteristic of fideism – the rejection (in various ways) of material and apparent reality. This passage is suffused with the teaching of Boehme, but it is more than a summary of Law's visionary master. It denies any independent significance to natural things. In the post-lapsarian world a habit of materiality, with its "empty mechanic of body and force," can enter into the human intellect. This is the final stage of intellectual folly. We begin to associate nature and our own world with these "dull products of sin." This is precisely the religious conviction that motivated Bishop Berkeley to denounce the Newtonian cosmology in his *De motu*. With him (as with Law) "mechanics is apt to mislead the curious and confuse the humble." He concludes the thirty-fourth section of the *De motu* in this way:

Modern thinkers consider motion and rest in bodies as two states of existence in either of which every body, without pressure from external force, would naturally remain passive; whence one might gather that the cause of the existence of bodies is also the cause of their motion and rest, for no other cause of the successive existence of body in different parts of space should be sought, it would seem, than that cause whence is derived the successive existence of the same body in different parts of time. But to treat of the good and great God, creator and preserver of all things, and to show all things depend on supreme and true being, although it is the most excellent part of true knowledge, is, however, rather the province of metaphysics or first philosophy and theology than of natural philosophy which today is entirely confined to experiments and mechanics.[13]

Here again Newton has severed nature from its true principle, God. Physics has become a great overreacher, invading the province of theology and first philosophy. This usurpation is recalled in a good deal of fideist poetry and prose. In the pulpit Atterbury could see "the great chord of heaven and earth cut by the cold, mechanic hand."[14] It was not uncommon

[12] Law, *A Serious Call*, 366–367.
[13] George Berkeley, *De motu* in *Berkeley's Philosophical Writings* (London: Collier, Macmillan Publishers, 1965), 260.
[14] Bishop Atterbury is quoted in *Literature of the Church of England*, vol. II, ed. Rev. Richard Cattermole (London: Smithfield, 1844), 501.

for the Restoration or eighteenth-century divine to ask his congregation to turn from the sophistication of science to that one thing needful – faith. This fear is clearly marked in a passage of Berkeley:

This consistent, uniform working, which so evidently displays the goodness and wisdom of that governing Spirit whose will constitutes the laws of Nature, is so far from leading our thoughts to him, that it rather leads them a-wandering after second causes.[15]

Prior's fideism

The case of Matthew Prior is extraordinary. His reputation since the eighteenth century depends upon his witty epigrams and self-effacing love poems, which have the elegance of Waller without the mellifluousness, the toughness of Rochester without the vulgarity. The son of a pious joiner, supported from his early years by the profligate Dorset, he combines in his work the Calvinist severity of the father with the playful worldliness of the benefactor. Emphasizing the latter, A. R. Humphreys writes: "In Prior [the Augustan lyric] has a virtuoso in the easy and witty vernacular of the social world, in that truly Augustan social use of the living language."[16] This, of course, is true so far as it goes. Prior stands with Gay as the most perfect manipulator of conversational tone in this period. Had Prior never been embittered by betrayal and imprisonment, had he never tasted the full emptiness of the world, he might have remained content with these slight and masterful lyrics. But his two-year imprisonment after the debacle of the Treaty of Utrecht (of which he was an important contributor and negotiator) presented his mind with new possibilities. The "Alma", a burlesque of human knowledge, was executed in that period, and the *Solomon*, though begun earlier, was largely altered, and perhaps, completed then. These are works of great intellectual dexterity, the first envied by Pope, the latter plundered by Johnson. They show the two prongs of the fideist reaction at its earliest stage. First, the total mockery of the methods and matter of Newton and Locke; then, the retreat into the Solomonic skepticism which finds no object of solace in nature or society.

Prior is a most fascinating case because his fideism occurs within the boundaries of a developed Augustan sensibility. His Protestant other-worldliness exists almost within the antithetical mode of Augustan verse. At first glance it seems no more than a continuation of Butler's Pyrrhonic lampooning. Indeed, the opening of canto II of the "Alma", is the finest tribute in English to the method and genius of Butler.[17] Prior could

15 Berkeley, *Philosophical Writings*, 44.
16 A. R. Humphreys, "Augustan Poetry," in *The Pelican Guide to English Literature, from Dryden to Johnson*, ed. Boris Ford (Harmondsworth: Pelican, 1957), 83.
17 But shall we take the Muse abroad, / To drop her idly on the Road? / And leave our subject in

manipulate the rhythm, imagery, and language of Butler better even than
Swift, and in one sense the denunciation of all known philosophies as
delusive razzle-dazzle is merely an eighteenth-century continuation of the
master.

> Here, Richard, how could I explain,
> The various Lab'rinths of the Brain?
> Surprise My Readers, whilst I tell 'em
> Of *Cerebrum* and *Cerebellum*?
> How could I play the Commentator
> On *Dura*, and on *Pia Mater*?
> Where Hot and Cold, and Dry and Wet,
> Strive each the t'others Place to get;
> And with incessant Toil and Strife,
> Would keep Possession during Life.
> I could demonstrate every Pore,
> Where Mem'ry lays up all her Store;
> And to an Inch compute the Station,
> 'Twixt Judgment, and Imagination.
> O Friend! I could display much Learning,
> At least to Men of small Discerning.[18]   (Canto III, 152–167)

Prior's world weariness seems identical with that of Swift or Arbuthnot – a
Tory gloom brought on by political circumstances and a common-sense
rejection of new-fangled ideas and presumptuous reason. But Prior goes a
good deal further. His rejection of science in the *Alma*, unlike the anti-
experimental bias of Butler and Swift, is ultimately on behalf of Christian
(and scriptural) conceptions of the soul. This is made explicit in his prose
dialogues in which he mocks the experimental science as a replacement for
religious apology.[19] He opens his dialogue between Montaigne and Locke
by telling the British philosopher that his disregard for authority ought to
strip him of the right to quote Aristotle and Plato, and that if the older
philosophers were easier to know in their remote language their paradoxes
might be easily removed. By the end of that dialogue he denounces the
supposed certainty of perception.

If we consider even the Fabric of the Eye and the Rules of Optic, It can hardly be
thought we see the same; and yet no Words can express this Diversity. So that
there may be as much difference between your Perceptions and mine, as there is

the middle; / As BUTLER did his Bear and Fiddle? / Yet the, consummate Master, knew / When
to recede, and when to pursue: / His noble Negligences teach, / What others Folks despair to
reach. / But like pour ANDREW, I advance / False *Mimic* of any Master's Dance (*Alma*, Canto I,
1–8; 17–18).
[18] Matthew Prior, *Literary Works*, ed. H. Bunter Wright and Monroe K. Spears (Oxford:
Clarendon Press, 1971), vol. I, 504.
[19] See in Prior's *Dialogues of the Dead*, "Locke and Montaigne" and "The Vicar of Bray and
More."

between your Band and my Ruff. If so it may happen I say, that if no Mans Ideas be perfectly the same Lockes *Human Understanding* may be fit only for the Meditation of Locke himself, nay further that those very Ideas changing, Locke may be led into a new Laberinth, or Sucked into another Vortex, and may write a Second Book in order to disprove the first.[20]

He does not defer to Locke as Pope, Gay, and Thomson were to do. Empiricism in the *Alma* and *Solomon* is consistently treated as folly. He is not, as Fairchild and Spears have argued, a Pyrrhonist equally skeptical of all contemporary views.[21] He is a shifting apologist for older views. His denunciation of Newton is unequivocal:

> How oddly would Sir Isaac look,
> If you in answer to his Book,
> Say in the Front of your Discourse,
> That things have no elastic Force?
> How could your *Chymic* friends go on,
> To find the philosophic Stone;
> If you more powerful Reasons bring,
> To prove, that there is no such Thing?
> Your Chiefs in Sciences and Arts,
> Have great contempt of Alma's parts,
> But who should be presumed to tell,
> What She herself should see or feel?[22]   (Canto III, 56–67)

That there is no such thing as an independent elastic force, and that the soul (Alma), can not be judged by empirical science, which is in fact her own handmaiden, are the common ideas of Law, Berkeley, and Prior. What Prior has added is a tone at once dismissive and playful. The tone is that of *Hudibras*, but the conclusions are not those of Butler. Butler's *Notebooks* and *Hudibras* were filled with attacks on the presumption of both theology and science. The most scathing were aimed at religious argument. In Prior the reverse is true. The debates of Origen, Aristotle, and others are treated as insoluble, but the point of the first canto of the *Alma* is that old and new theories are on an equal footing – and presumption is on the side of the old. Descartes, Locke, and Newton come in for the shrillest satire.

The greatest passage in the poem recalls the method of Rochester in "Upon Nothing," where the notion of the soul as a permeating vital force analogous to Newtonian forces (an argument common in the early century) becomes the explanation and map of human folly:

---

[20] Prior, *Dialogues of the Dead, Literary Works*, vol. I, 639.
[21] See Hoxie Neale Fairchild, *Religious Trends in English Poetry*, vol. I (New York: Columbia University Press, 1939), 32–40; and Monroe K. Spears, "Matthew Prior's Religion," *PQ* 27 (1948), 159–180.
[22] Matthew Prior, *Literary Works*, ed. H. Bunker Wright and Monroe K. Spears (Oxford: Clarendon Press, 1971), vol. I, 501.

> Mark then; – Where Fancy or Desire
> Collects the Beams of Vital Fire;
> Into that Limb fair ALMA slides,
> And there, *pro tempore*, resides.
> She dwells in NICHOLINI's Tongue,
> When PYRRHUS chants the Heavenly Song.
> When PEDRO does the Lute command,
> She guides the cunning Artist's Hand.
> Thro' MACER's gullet she runs down,
> When the vile Glutton dines alone.
> And void of Modesty and Thought,
> She follows BIBO's endless Draught.[23]   (II, 251–262)

Here the soul has entered into every vice. It has become the motive force of every human activity – drunkenness, gluttony, and pandering. But the following lines adopt a tone of burlesque beyond Pope or Butler in its sexual suggestion:

> Thro' the soft Sex again she ranges;
> As Youth, Caprice, or Fashion changes.
> Fair ALMA careless and serene
> In Fanny's sprightly eyes is seen . . .
> Again Fair ALMA sits confest,
> On Florimel's experter breast;
> When she the rising Sign constrains,
> And by concealing speaks her Pains.
> In Cynthia's Neck fair ALMA glows;
> When the vain Thing her Jewell shows;
> And when the swelling Hoop sustains
> The rich Brocard, fair ALMA deigns
> Into that lower Space to enter,
> Of the large Round, Herself the Center.[24]   (II, 263–280)

This poem in tone and design is Augustan. Its content, nevertheless, repudiates a good deal of Augustan thinking. In the end the *Alma* is the model for several eighteenth-century poems that seek the primary motive of human action. Young was to meditate the "Love of Fame" as the key to moral motivation and Pope was to define the "ruling passion" as that "casting weight in each man's soul" which explains all of his actions. Prior never imagines such a unity of purpose or such a simple explanation of the chaos of emotions. His "alma" wanders the world, appearing sometimes as wealth, sometimes as lust, and sometimes as power. The soul is unknowable and its appetites shifting. The human person, fractured by desire, seeks a purpose which is unattainable in this world. While the early Young, Pope,

---

[23] Prior, *Literary Works*, vol. 1, 492.   [24] Prior *Literary Works*, vol. 1, 492.

and Mandeville sought a new economy of motivation to explain the apparent diversity of human actions, Prior remained agnostic to the end about the twists and turns of the human mind.

Prior is unsympathetic to the popular canon of the early eighteenth century. There is a nasty reduction of Lucretian atomism, and Horace, one of the tutelary spirits of the period, is rebuked in the *Alma* and parodied in *Solomon*. Pope is mildly teased in the widely misunderstood section on *Eloisa to Abelard*. Dryden is attacked here (and in a number of earlier lampoons such as *The Hind and the Panther Transvers'd*). The Augustan culture is brought under fire in the language of Augustan satire both high and low – with the polished metrical surface Prior learned from reading Waller, and with the improvisational doggerel of Butler.

In the *Solomon* the technique retains a good deal of the Augustan rhetoric and diction, but the message goes even further to denounce optimism, materialism, and latitude. Its three books divide the Solomonic vanity into three distinct species – vain knowledge, vain pleasure, and vain power. As in *Alma* and other poems of Prior, the last section seems to be the best. Perhaps it is the unwillingness to begin in *media res*, or to pace his transitional and episodic material, that elicited from Johnson the famous comment, "It wanted that without which all others are of small avail, the power of engaging attention and alluring curiosity."[25] On the other side Johnson sees this deliberation as worthy of some praise: "What he has valuable he owes to his diligence and his judgment. He was one of the first that resolutely endeavored at correctness. He never sacrifices accuracy to haste, nor indulges himself in contemptible negligence, or impatient idleness; He has no careless lines or entangled sentiments."[26] This is true of Prior both as regards style and argument. His Solomon is an unwavering pursuit of the logic of vanity. Prior's sometimes tiresome thoroughness recalls some of the key qualities of all wisdom literature. Wisdom, which I said in the last chapter is the antithesis of knowledge, takes the long, the repetitive, and the painful path. The doubling and redoubling of argument in the Book of Ecclesiastes, the Proverbs, medieval wisdom books, mystical tracts, and the Sutras enhances the sense of dearly bought and disciplined moral meditation. As we shall see Johnson himself sometimes had more than a little patience with himself.

In the "Knowledge" book of *Solomon*, Prior lashes out in all directions. The anti-gnostic and anti-logicist tendency is there abundantly:

> With outward Smiles their Flatt'ry I received;
> Own'd my Sick Mind by their Discourse reliev'd;

25 Samuel Johnson, *Lives of the English Poets*, ed. Birckbeck-Hill (Oxford: Clarendon, 1905), vol. II, 63.
26 Ibid., 65.

But bent and inward to my Self again
Perplex'd, these Matters I resolv'd; in vain.
My Search still tired, my Labor still renew'd,
At length I Ignorance, and Knowledge viewed.
Impartial; Both in equal Balance laid:
Light flew the knowing Scale; the doubtful Heavy weigh'd.

(Solomon, I, 731–738)[27]

Prior inveighs against the disputes of schools, the empty subtleties of logic and persuasion. He takes swipes at deductive (I, 705) and probabilistic reasoning (I, 445 and III, 378). Prior leaves no stone unturned in pursuing his sometimes maniacal skepticism. He labors to maintain the artifice of putting everything into Solomon's mouth. In a brilliant passage he mocks the prophetic passages of Book VI of the *Aeneid*, by having Solomon foretell the squalid and disastrous history of England:

Long shall BRITANNIA (That must be her Name)
Be first in Conquest, and preside in Fame;
Long must her favor'd Monarchy engage
The Teeth of Envy, and the Force of Age . . .
Yet All must with the general Doom comply;
And this Great Glorious Pow'r, tho' last, must dye.

(Solomon, I, 445–451)[28]

Prior parodies long stretches of Milton's Uranian prophecies (II, 730–752), Lucretius' atomism (I, 357), Ovid's creation, and even Horace. All are mentioned with ruthless anachronism by Solomon. The general anti-classical bias of the poem is brilliantly summarized in the Preface:

The Noble images and reflections, the profound reasonings upon Human actions, and excellent precepts for the government of life, which are found in the *Proverbs* and *Ecclesiastes*, and other books commonly attributed to Solomon, afford subjects for finer poems of every kind, than have, I think, as yet appeared in the Greek or Latin, or any modern language.

(Preface to *Solomon*)[29]

In a brilliant negative paraphrase of Horace's *Odes* I, 20 in which the poet feels capable of charming and placating every savage element of nature, Solomon exclaims:

Pass We the Ills, which each Man feels or dreads,
The Weight or fall'n, or hanging o'er our Heads;
The Bear, the Lyon, Terrors of the plain,
The Sheepfold scatter'd, and the Shepherd slain;
The frequent Errors of the pathless Wood,
The giddy Precipice, and the dang'rous Flood.

(Solomon, III, 119–124)[30]

---

[27] Prior, *Literary Works*, vol. I, 331.   [28] Ibid., 323.   [29] Ibid., 306.   [30] Ibid., 364.

Many readers will not miss the likeness between the diction and rhythm of this passage and Johnson's *Vanity*, and others, misled into thinking Prior was an amateur of letters, will not notice the numerous references throughout *Solomon* to Latin and Greek poetry, classical and modern philosophy, and British verse and prose. The allusive network of the poem is thicker and fuller, if less perfectly assimilated, than in any work of Pope. The learning is a serious and difficult attainment for the author (as it was in the mythic parallel for Solomon), and the sense of vanity at the end of each book is therefore more poignant.

One of the most original elements of the poem is its thoroughgoing anti-naturalism. Solomon, who the Bible says "spake of trees, from the cedar tree that is in Lebanon, even unto the hyssop that springeth out of the wall; he spake also of beasts and of fowl and of creeping things, and of fishes," (1 Kings, 4:33), is led through every arbor, garden and field to become in the end sickened by the vain plenty of the earth. It is in these sections of scenic nature that he takes the opportunity to mock the Georgic and pastoral fashions of the day. We must recall these lines were written at the time of the first great landscape and Georgic (Pope called his an historical-pastoral) poems in English. Prior was apparently not much taken by Augustan loco-descriptive and descriptive verse:

> The verdant Rising of the flow'ry Hill,
> The Vale enamell'd and the Crystal Rill,
> The Ocean rolling, and the shelly shore,
> Beautiful Objects, shall delight no more;
> When the lax'd Sinews of the weaken'd Eye
> In wat'ry Damps, or dim Suffusion lye.
> Day follows Night, the Clouds return again
> After the falling of the later Rain:
> But to the Aged-blind shall ne'er return
> Grateful Vicissitude: He still must mourn
> The Sun and Moon and every Starry Light;
> Eclipsed to Him, and lost in everlasting Night.
>
> (*Solomon*, III, 158–169)[31]

The first four lines strongly echo the language of Pope's pastorals. The "enamelled vale" and the "crystal rill" are part of the idealized abstraction of the Augustan pastoral repertoire, and their superficial brilliance awaits the destruction of the apocalyptic moment that ends the passage. Apocalyptic images and eclipses of sensation are common to all fideist poems of the period. The eclipse of sun and moon look forward to the apocalypse of both *The Night Thoughts* and *The Four Zoas*. The first couplet reminds us of the cliché language which Pope sends up in the *Essay on Criticism*.

[31] Ibid., 365–366.

If *Chrystal Streams* with *pleasing Murmurs* creep,
The Reader's threatened (not in vain) with *Sleep*.
(*Essay on Criticism*, 352–353)[32]

The "weakened Eye" and the cessation of delight in all earthly objects is the symbolic emptiness in which we meet God and come to understand ourselves. Prior, like other fideists, searches for a meditative solitude, far from the plenty of physical creation and from the miasma of political life. The two allusions to Book III of *Paradise Lost*, "dim suffusion" and "grateful vicissitude," suggest a crucial irony. Those two phrases are used in Milton's melancholy account of his blindness in the long personal soliloquy which precedes the interview in heaven. For Milton the loss of nature's grateful vicissitude is the product of his fatal blindness – his world "with dim suffusion veiled" is hidden from outward sight. The passage in Milton incorporates the common motifs of Davidic naturalism, "But not to me returns / Day, or the sweet approach of ev'n or morn, / Or sight of vernal bloom, or summer's rose / Or flocks or herds or human face divine; / But cloud instead and ever-during dark / Surrounds me."[33] In Prior's passage we also have the returning cloud, the darkening of nature, but in the context of the *Solomon* any escape from the natural, from the old round of night and day, even an apocalyptic escape, is desirable. Milton was one of the first great scenic writers, and Books IV and V of *Paradise Lost* are a chief source for the expanded field of landscape poetry in the eighteenth century. For this reason it was inevitable that Pope, Thomson, Akenside, and Warton would gather greedily from the Miltonic sensoria. But the fideists – Prior, Young, and Johnson – were not so deeply indebted to his descriptive inventions. On the other hand, Milton looms over the third book of the *Solomon*. The passage I have just quoted is at the beginning of a long catalog of the Jewish patriarchs who preceded Solomon – the greatness and the emptiness of their careers. The angel visitor who narrates the history before and after the reign of Solomon plays the role that Michael played in the last two books of *Paradise Lost*, but with a difference. Rather than promises and hope stretching down to Christ, the second Adam, Prior offers us a pattern of unbroken regret and failure. He moralizes the frailty of all human enterprise and makes Adam not the antagonist in human mythology but a tragic everyman.

> Adam, great *Type*, for whom the World was made,
> The fairest Blessing to his Arms convey'd,
> A charming Wife; and Air, and Sea, and Land,
> And all that move therein, to his Command
> Render'd obedient: say, my Pensive Muse,

[32] Pope, *Poems*, 154.
[33] John Milton, *Paradise Lost*, ed. Alistair Fowler (London: Longmans, 1971), 145.

What did these golden Promises produce?
Scarce tasting Life, He was of Joy bereav'd:
One day, I think, in PARADISE He liv'd,
Destin'd the next His Journey to pursue,
Where wounding Thorns, and cursed Thistles grew.

(*Solomon*, III, 351–360)[34]

Prior makes Adam here and throughout his long poem the type of all future human beings, even Christ, who must define themselves by sorrow and understand their birth in terms of their death.

After exhausting the possibilities of landscape and natural history in Book I, Prior moves from knowledge to pleasure in the second book. In that book he lays out the evils of every species of gratification. The poem is nearly as thorough as Bunyan or Law in rooting out the long list of dangerous temptations. If what we hear of Prior's profligate personal life was true, this asceticism must have hit close to home. We feel in the episode of Abra and the concubines some of the genuine lover's pathos of Prior's remarkable personal poetry like "Chloe Revisited" and "Jenny the Just." Sedley, Cotton, and Prior had turned the Petrarchan tradition on its head by writing poems on the ideal love of prostitutes, of which "Jenny the Just" is the most original. More than a little autobiography is injected into the portait of the soiled courtier and betrayed patriot in the powerful last line of the book:

Lost SOLOMON! pursue this Thought no more:
Of thy past Errors recollect the Store:
And silent weep, that while the Deathless Muse
Shall sing the Just; shall o'er their Head diffuse
Perfumes with lavish Hand; She shall proclaim
Thy Crimes alone; and to Thy evil Fame
Impartial, scatter Damps and Poysons on thy Name.
   Awaking therefore, as who long had dream'd,
Much of my Women and their Gods asham'd,
From this Abyss of exemplary Vice
Resolved, as Time might aid my thought, to rise;
Again I bid the mournful Goddess write
The fond Pursuit of fugitive Delight;
Bid her exalt her melancholy Wing,
And rais'd from Earth and saved from Passion, sing
Of human Hope by cross Event destroyed,
Of useless wealth, and Greatness unenjoyed,
Of Lust and Love with their fantastic Train,
Their Wishes, Smiles and Looks, deceitful all, and Vain.

(*Solomon*, II, 977–995)[35]

[34] Prior, *Literary Works*, vol. I, 370–371.   [35] Prior, *Literary Works*, vol. I, 359–360.

This is the quintessential tone of Prior's fideism. We see that central Pauline word, "Hope," and we recall the double formula, "the substance of things unseen, the expectation of good to come." The author of the Letter to the Hebrews has captured the sum of Prior's desperate Christianity. First we must remove all earthly objects, then we must open up a space for expectation. Faith cannot operate upon sensible things, but depends on a remote and unmoveable Good. Every other pursuit ends in physical and moral exhaustion. Men shall be remembered for their mistakes alone, and love and lust shall be equally disastrous. This is one of the most acute images of the Tory gloom which struck Bolingbroke, Swift, and Prior after the debacle of the Treaty of Utrecht. But unlike Swift and Bolingbroke, Prior frames his sense of melancholy in the language of Protestant moralism. He is turning away from the kind of bitter and general political satire we see in *Gulliver's Travels*, or in the letters and historical essays of Bolingbroke, and returning to a darker self-examination. He is moving from Augustan observer to participating moralist.

This may be seen if we compare three closely connected passages. In Cowley's Pindaric, "Life and Fame," he imagines human life as a younger brother to nothingness – vain and fleeting – and he pictures man standing on a

> Vain weak-built *Isthmus*, which doth proudly rise
> Up betwixt two *Eternities*;
> Yet canst nor *Wave* nor *Wind* sustain,
> But *broken* and *orewhelm'd*, the endless Oceans meet again.[36]

Taking up the same image Prior alters it subtly:

> Amid two Seas on One small Point of Land
> Weary'd, uncertain, and amaz'd We stand:
> On either Side our Thoughts incessant turn:
> Forward we dread; and looking back We mourn.
> Losing the Present in this dubious Hast;
> And lost Our selves between the Future, and the Past.
>
> (*Solomon*, III, 613–618)[37]

The passage of Cowley is in his early style of conceitful casuistry. He plays out the logic of the imagery denying the "schoolmen's" distinction between "To be or not to be," and leaves his rather abstract man standing on a perishable point of earth. Like the "imagined corners" of Donne's "round earth," Cowley's poem offers a thought experiment on living in a crumbling world. The relations of the elements of the poem are logical (even casuistical). In Prior's passage the "Point of Land" is a place from which to look backward and forward in time. The metaphors are temporal,

---

[36] Cowley, "Life and Fame," *Poems*, 201, 5–8.   [37] Prior, *Literary Works*, vol. I, 377.

and the prospects of looking forward or backward are equally dire. In moving away from a conceitful and descriptive scene (a meditative place) to a mere point in time, Prior has entered the classic fideist narrative. Like Johnson's *Vanity*, the *Solomon* takes the widest observation only to deny the significance of the image. Like the *Night Thoughts*, *Solomon* is an analysis of temporal not visual meditation. The things of the eye are swallowed up, and the nervous expectation of a desperate good are all that is left for the poet – "weary'd, uncertain, and amaz'd."

Pope borrowed from both of these poems for a famous passage in *An Essay on Man*:

> Plac'd on this isthmus of a middle state,
> A being darkly wise, and rudely great:
> With too much knowledge for the Sceptic side,
> With too much weakness for the Stoic's pride,
> He hangs between; in doubt to act, or rest,
> In doubt to deem himself a God, or Beast;
> In doubt his mind or Body to prefer,
> Born but to die, and reas'ning but to err;
> Chaos of Thought and Passion, all confus'd;
> Still by himself abus'd, or disabus'd;
> Created half to rise, and half to fall;
> Great lord of all things, yet a prey to all.
>
> (*An Essay on Man*, II, 3–14)[38]

This is great poetry. Its mastery of rhythm, antithesis, and diction is beyond the powers of the other poets, but the comparison is still interesting. In Pope's passage, which is the very *métier* of Augustanism, we have something less conceitful on the one hand, and less passionate on the other. The riddle of Pope is the riddle of a man who can no longer accept the traditional metaphysical and moral definitions of man, and who discovers himself in a world without tragedy but with an undefinable space of experience. The Solomonic man is whittled down to a point by despairing of the possibilities of life; and Cowley's merely exercises the paradoxes; but Pope's man is "confus'd," stuck, between, like the Popeian cosmos, "self-balanced." Prior's world is a sensuous emptiness, Pope's is a spatial chaos.

The third book, ostensibly about power, shows great insight into issues of kingship. (Prior had served and known intimately two monarchs, and was the only English plenipotentiary trusted by the king of France in the elaborate negotiations at Utrecht.) This is the common theme of Johnson's *Vanity* and Watts' *Hymns for Princes*, and shows a great departure from the earlier tradition of political allegory in *A Mirror for Magistrates*. But the larger purpose of Book III is to push further the fideist theorizing of the earlier

[38] Pope, *Poems*, 516.

books, to prove that we must turn to God with or without proof, that our
own imbecility and wretchedness are demonstrations of God's existence.
Here Prior comes close to the tone of Pascal's *Pensées*:

> This is the series of perpetual Woe,
> Which thou, alas, and thine are born to know.
> Illustrious wretch, repine not, nor reply;
> View not what Heaven ordains with Reason's Eye;
> Too bright the Object is; the Distance is too high.
> The Man who would resolve the work of Fate,
> May limit number and make crooked strait;
> Stop thy enquiry then, and curb Thy Sense;
> Nor let Dust argue with Omnipotence.   (*Solomon*, III, 833–841)[39]

There are many more beautiful passages in the last book, but this perfectly
describes the epistemology of fideism. The fideist is promised neither image
nor analogy, neither reason nor perception, in the endless journey to a God
who remains distant and unknowable, except as an object of promise and
hope. We can see why a fideism so extreme turns for its art to a description
of affections. The inner man is the fountain of expectation, his days given
over to what Pascal called "the long and powerful lamentation of the
heart."

   Prior's *Solomon*, for all its lack of economy, is an important document and
a powerful poem. It marks the moment where the fullness of a world of
objects, the detail of natural and social life – the great subject of the
Augustans – creates in the Protestant sensibility an anguished reaction.
Perhaps the poem will always be neglected because of the demands it
makes upon the reader: complex and multiple allusion, shifting irony, and
desolate moralism which taxes the mind. But it can still be studied fruitfully
as the moment when Augustan wit collided with the flickering fire of
Lutheranism. Any admirer of Pope will notice how many verbal hints he
borrowed from *Solomon*, which he read in manuscript even before he had
written *The Rape of the Lock*. Particularly Book II of *Solomon* is replete with the
kernel of several famous Pope lines:

> The haughty nymph in open beauty drest,
> Today encounters our unguarded breast:
> She looks with majesty and moves with state:
> Unbent her soul and in Misfortune great.
>
> (*Solomon*, II, 551–554)

> The Sun declined had shot his Western Ray;
> When tired with business of the solemn day;
>
> (*Solomon*, II, 371–372)

---

[39] Prior, *Literary Works*, vol. I, 383.

> Disturb'd and broken like a sick Man's Sleep,
> Our troubl'd Thoughts to distant Prospects leap;
> Desirous still what flies us to o'ertake:
> For Hope is but the Dream of those who wake;
> But looking back we see the dreadful Train
> Of woes anew, which were We to sustain,
> We should refuse to tread the Path again.   (*Solomon*, III, 99–105)[40]

This nearness to the Augustans, particularly to Pope and Gay, is what makes the moral revelation of the *Solomon* all the more remarkable. It is as if the tradition of ambitious observation and minute description had begun to turn upon itself. The first reaction to Augustan optimism and scientism came from within. Of course, Prior also looks forward to the morbid sentimentalism of Blair and the fideist emotionalism of Young:

> This dark opinion sure, is too confined:
> Else whence is Hope and Terror of the Mind?
> Does something still, and somewhere yet remain,
> Reward or punishment, delight or pain?
> When the sad Wife has clos'd her Husband's eyes;
> And pierced the echoing Vault with doleful Cries;
> Lies the pale corps but not entirely dead?
> The Spirit only from the Body fled.   (*Solomon*,III, 587–594)[41]

If, as Johnson claims, Prior "in private relaxation revived the tavern, and in his amorous pedantry exhibited the college," it is because he was a deeply divided and darkly aspiring talent. Nor can we go far wrong in imagining the publication of the *Solomon* in 1718 as a crucial moment in the history of fideism.

Solomon and David

Before we move on, another point about the changing character of English imagination after 1700 must be made. There was in English poetry since the time of Wyatt a cult for the Psalms of David. This continued even into the eighteenth century, partly because of the lofty place the Psalms had in the Anglican Prayer Book, partly because the Christian church had always found in the Psalms a summary of many issues of faith and doctrine.

The Psalms were also viewed from late antiquity as the paradigm for Christian poetry. David, said Jerome, is "our Pindar, Simonides, and Alcaeus, our Catullus and Serenus too."[42] But the phenomenon goes even farther than that. For Wyatt, Sidney, Vives, and Milton, David represented the heroic and kingly poet and prophet. He was a model for every mode of

[40] Prior, *Literary Works*, vol. 1, 348; 343; 364.   [41] Prior, *Literary Works*, vol. 1, 377.
[42] Augustine, *Commentary on the Psalms*, in Barbara Kiefer Lewalski, *Protestant Poetics and the Seventeenth-Century Religious Lyric* (Princeton: Princeton University Press, 1981), 39.

life, secular and religious. Augustine had argued that the Psalms were divided into three parts, corresponding to the stages of salvation:

Whichever then of these is understood, this book, in its parts of fifty Psalms each, gives an answer important and very worthy of consideration. For it seems to me not without significance, that the fiftieth is of penitence, the hundredth of mercy and judgment, and the hundred and fiftieth of the praise of God in His saints. For thus do we advance to everlasting life, first by condemning our own sins, then by living aright.[43]

There was yet another ground for admiring David, and that was his supreme naturalism. Perhaps, among all ancient poems the Psalms are the most extraordinary for connecting every object of creation to God, and for making every detail of landscape part of his praise. As Robert Alter describes it in his discussion of Psalm 121, "The archetypal sweep of the poetic landscape in this brief poem is remarkable. The speaker lifts his eyes to the mountains and, in a characteristic Biblical association of terms, moves from mountain to heaven and earth and their Maker."[44] The Psalmist is capable of the most minute observation, and of charging every natural object with divine suggestion. We may take Psalm 8 as a representative example:

> Oh Lord, our Lord,
>> how majestic is thy name in all the earth!
> Thou whose glory above the heavens is chanted
>> by the mouths of babes and infants,
> Thou who has founded a bulwark because of thy foes,
>> to still the enemy and the avenger.
>
> When I look at thy heavens, the work of thy fingers,
> The moon and the stars which thou hast established
>> [. . .]
> What is man that thou art mindful of him?
>> [. . .]
> Yet thou hast made him a little less than a God,
> And dost crown him with glory and honor.
> Thou hast given him dominion over the works of thy hands;
> Thou hast put all things under his feet,
> All sheep and oxen, and all the beasts of the field,
> The birds of the air, and the fish of the sea,
> Whatever passes along the paths of the sea.

This is a naturalistic plenitude like that of a good deal of Baroque English poetry. The analogies and emblems which we discussed in the last chapter

---

[43] St. Augustine, *Expositions of the Book of Psalms*, in *The Nicene and Post-Nicene Fathers*, ed. Philip Schaff (Grand Rapids, Mich.: Erdmans, 1983), 682.

[44] Robert Alter and Frank Kermode, *The Literary Guide to the Bible* (Cambridge, Mass.: Harvard University Press, 1987), 254.

are all in place. The analogical imagination had leaned upon this Davidic ideal for many centuries. The ascendancy of metrical psalm-writing in the sixteenth century and the constant allusion to the Psalms in the old Anglican liturgy and sermon are, therefore, quite natural.

Now, if David's world is full of spiritual analogies, praise of the works and person of God, Solomon's world is the opposite. The Solomonic wisdom is based on vanity and exhaustion, the testing in experience of the objects of creation and finding them unequal to man's spiritual thirst: "For he cometh in with vanity, and departeth in darkness, and his name shall be covered with darkness. Moreover he hath not seen the sun, nor known *any thing*" (Ecclesiastes 6:4–5). If the spirit of the sixteenth and seventeenth century was perfectly represented in its endless reworking of the Psalms, the eighteenth century and the Restoration showed its religious temper in its growing interest in the books of Solomon and Job. Not only were Prior, Young, and Johnson obsessed with the Solomonic vision, but many lesser poets throughout the period wrote paraphrases or studies of Ecclesiastes and Proverbs: S. Croxall, R. Erskine, T. Hodson, W. Tansur, J. Graeme, and J. Cunningham to name a few.[45] The important Hebrew language studies of Secker (1741) and especially Lowth (1753) gave even greater weight to these texts, and it is no exaggeration to say that they seem to outweigh even the Gospel among the subjects of homiletic exposition of the mid-century.

In one of his last sermons (1716), Dr. South, the greatest of Augustan preachers, proclaims: "If the direction of Solomon, the precept and example of our savior, and the piety and experience of those excellent men and martyrs, who first composed, and afterwards owned our liturgy with their dearest good, may be looked to as safe and sufficient guides in our public worship . . ."[46] We see who was ranked first among authorities. Likewise in the sermons of Tillotson, Solomon is often referred to as the highest authority on moral matters. On the last page of Bishop Burnet's *History of My Own Time* (1723) is the following representative passage:

I have, considering my sphere, seen a great deal of all that is most shining and tempting in this world. The pleasures of sense I did soon nauseate; intrigues of state have something in them that is more specious; and I was, for some years, deeply immersed in these, but still with hopes of reforming the world, and of making mankind wiser and better; but I have found that which is crooked cannot be made straight. I acquainted myself with knowledge and learning, and that is a great variety, and with more compass than depth; but though wisdom excelleth

[45] The poems of interest are: John Norris, *Canticles and Proverbs;* Ralph Erskine, *A Paraphrase, or Large Explicatory Poem on the Song of Solomon* (and his other books); Thomas Hodson, *The Dedication of the Temple of Solomon;* William Tansur, *Heaven on Earth;* James Graeme, *Paraphrases on some Verses of Ecclesiastes*, and many more.
[46] *Literature of the Church of England*, 463.

folly, as much as light does darkness, yet as it is a sore travail, so is it very defective, that what is wanting to complete it cannot be numbered . . . I have found that this was all vanity and vexation of spirit, though it be of the best and noblest sort, so that, upon great and long experience, I could enlarge on the Preacher's text, Vanity of vanities, all is vanity; but I must also conclude with him, Fear God, and keep his commandments, for this is the all of man, the whole both of his duty, and of his happiness.[47]

Burnet has summarized the Solomonic and fideist position. Life is a futile but necessary journey which teaches by negatives the true limits of aspiration. The emptiness of the affairs of knowledge and power lead one back to the hopes of immortality and the blessings of a God whose reasons are largely inscrutable, and who demands a severe moral discipline. This is announced to the conscience and spirit of the inner man by a habitual affection, and seeks nothing else in all the world for corroboration. The three greatest religious poems of the century (excluding Smart) – *Solomon*, *Night Thoughts*, and *Vanity of Human Wishes* – all are reworkings of the popular Solomonic themes, two of them direct imitations of Ecclesiastes, the other the most perfect expansion of the Solomonic method. In the same period the Davidic analogy, which Benlowes had made the heart of his *Theophila*, almost completely disappeared, and it would not reappear again for over a century, when it would explode on the scene in the natural phantasmagoria of Smart's *Song to David*. The reappearance of David would signal the rejuvenation of several generations of spiritual naturalism.

Young's *Night Thoughts*

It was in the 1740s that Augustan literary culture began to wane. By then *The Seasons*, which had first appeared in 1726, were complete; Pope had reached the last phase of his career; Swift, having completed his own ironic elegy, was silent; Addison, Steele, and Gay had passed away. Of course, the Augustan intellectual culture remained. Hume's *Treatise of Human Nature*, the first great edition of Bacon's works, and the work of minor poets like Shenstone, Mallet, Glover, and Somerville continued and preserved the Augustan tradition of empiricism, optimism, and naturalism.

At the same time, the fideist reaction which had begun twenty-five years earlier, was blossoming. Protestantism, both in its Anglican and Evangelical forms, began to assert itself more pointedly than it had done in the age of Blackmore and Dennis. The most common form this reassertion took was the denunciation of science, worldly pleasures, and Deist optimism. In 1739, Samuel Boyse, a young Cantabrigian, produced the first long orthodox and fideist poem of the era, *The Deity*. Although it preserved some

---

[47] Gilbert Burnet, *History of My Own Time* (London: Parker, 1821).

of the popular apologetic techniques of the day – praise of God's wonder works of heavenly design, and a tribute to British progress – its main concern was in the unapproachable and unknowable dignity of God.

> By what bright images shall be defined
> The mystic nature of the eternal mind!
> Or how shall thought the dazzling height explore,
> Where all that reason can – is to adore!
> Him would in vain material semblance feign,
> Or figur'd shrines the boundless God contain;
> Object of faith! he shuns the view of sense,
> Lost in the blaze of sightless excellence!   (*The Deity*, 107–114)[48]

Boyse, who had a large reputation as an immoral wretch, was nonetheless one of the most distinctly Christian and anti-sentimentalist characters of the period. His "idle, dishonest, petty, selfish"[49] character has, perhaps, helped to obscure his literary reputation among Christian readers of the time, but he is the most self-conscious example of the religious phenomena we have been describing. In the passage above he sees every "bright image" or "material semblance" as inadequate for God. The phrase, "Object of faith! he shuns the view of sense," perfectly captures the Pauline distrust of sensible evidence. For Boyse, as for Young and Johnson after him, God is a moral object whose essence is unknowable. The oxymoron of "blaze of sightless excellence" comes close to the language of the mystics, and there is in a certain phase of fideism a great rhetorical likeness to mystical meditation. It is obvious how far this mentality departs from the tradition of Christian evidence. The arguments of Locke in *The Reasonableness of Christianity*, legalistic and historical, and those of the Deist and Clarke, deductive and rationalist, did not sway this mature Protestant movement. Johnson himself, though he praises Butler and Clarke in Boswell's *Life*, seems basically uninterested in the larger controversy. When he begs Taylor for more evidence of the afterlife, he knows that it is not forthcoming. Religious truth for the fideist, in Atterbury's words, "never rests upon the accumulation of evidence either documentary or empiric."[50]

Through the decade of the 1740s the tide of fideist reaction grew. Whitefield's *Short Account* (1740), John Wesley's *Journal* (1741), Watts' *Improvement of the Mind* (1741), Richardson's *Familiar Letters* and *Clarissa* (1741, 48), Young's *Night Thoughts* (1742), Doddridge's *Rise and Progress of Religion in the Soul* (1745), Jonathan Edwards' *A Treatise Upon the Religious Affections* (1746), James Hervey's *Meditations* (1746), Johnson's *Vanity of Human Wishes* (1749), and Law's *Spirit of Love* (1749), are all squarely in this tradition. The works of

---

[48] Samuel Boyse, *Poems*, in Chambers, XIV, 517.
[49] Robert Southey, *Specimens of the Later English Poets* (London: Crewall, 1835), vol. II, 130.
[50] Bishop Atterbury, *Sermons and Papers* (London: Greene and Tate, 1822), 456.

Edwards and Watts propound a complex inwardness akin to the older
Lutheran meditations, while Young and Hervey contribute to the cult of
remoteness, unapproachable sublimity, apocalyptic anticipation, and the
cessation of sense. In Richardson the fideist moralism is allegorized in the
Protestant hagiography of Clarissa. The last letters of Clarissa epitomize
the world-wary and anticipating qualities of the earthly prisoner and
victim:

Since, had I escaped the snares by which I was entangled, I might have wanted
those exercises which I look upon now as so many mercies dispensed to wean me
betimes from a world that presented itself to me with prospects too alluring: and in
that case (too easily satisfied with worldly felicity) I might not have attained to the
blessedness, which now, on your reading this, I humbly presume (through the
Divine Goodness) I am rejoicing in.[51]

Clarissa too is drawn away from the objects of sense to the eternal
sphere, which would have pleased Edward Young, Richardson's correspon-
dent and fellow fideist. But it is in Young that the fideist reaction to
Augustan culture is most compelling. The *Night Thoughts* is the supreme
kenosis or emptying out of the Augustan field of natural objects, and also of
the tensions inherent in the heroic couplet, in which Young himself had
been one of the great masters. All of this emptying and loosening is done
on behalf of a kind of morbid and protracted wisdom literature, the most
peculiar in English. The worldly and circumspect stance of the *Universal
Passion* is relinquished for the loosest, most repetitive, uninterpretable
composite imaginable. The grief, the defeatism of the *Night Thoughts*, are
perfectly Solomonic – ponderous and proverbial, excavating conscience
and plunging through and past nature as if she were not there. Even the
obvious sentimentality of the triple death (Young's daughter, wife, and
friend) is simply fuel for the great moral drift of the poem. Young's poetic of
anticipation is an answer to both Augustan satire and Augustan landscape.
In moving from what I have called general satire, which is the measure of
Pope and Swift, Young recoups the possibility of traditional controversy.
The word "controversy" in all its forms appears in every part of the poem.
The poem is an argument lodged against Deism and skepticism, but it is
more importantly an argument against the canons of Augustan taste. In
this light we can understand Young's disappointment with the *Essay on
Man*, which appeared only a few years before the *Night Thoughts*.

> Dark, though not blind, like thee, Maeonides!
> Or Milton! thee; ah, could I reach your strain!
> Or his, who made Maeonides our own.
> Man too he sung: immortal man I sing;
> What, now, but immortality, can please?

[51] Samuel Richardson, *Clarissa* (Harmondsworth: Penguin, 1978), 1372.

O had he press'd his theme, pursu'd the track,
Which opens out of darkness into day!
O had he, mounted on his wing of fire,
Soar'd where I sink, and sung immortal man!
How had he bless'd mankind, and rescu'd me!   (I, 451–460)[52]

Pope had not pressed on past mere psychology and naturalism to discover the "immortal man" which is the subject of the *Night Thoughts*. He had not passed through the doorway of eternity into "day," but had been trapped in his labyrinthine musings on natural experience. The man who "never is, but always to be blest" must be prodded toward that final blessing with concentrated fervor. Though Pope's prosody and language was "a wing of fire" which had domesticated Homer, it had failed to produce work of true Christian instruction. Here as in his odd prose treatise, *The Centaur Not Fabulous*, Young attacks the Augustan belief in hidden wellsprings of personal desire. Young grew weary of Pope's and Mandeville's search for the dominant passion and the natural economy of desire, and rather than looking forward to capitalist providentialism, he goes back to the theology of enthusiasm – inward and passionate faith and prophecy. For the first time since the early poems of Norris, Christian enthusiasm is again a virtue. Enthusiasm, "that inward call from God's empyrean," is our chief cue in the endless search for salvation and spiritual transformation. Only those whose faith can ignore the tempting idols of nature can arrive at the proper degree of enthusiastic feeling. In lines that recall Pope, but in an ironic sense, Young remarks:

If earth's whole orb by some due distanc'd eye
Were seen at once her towering Alps would sink,
And levell'd Atlas leave an even sphere.
Thus earth, and all that earthly minds admire,
Is swallowed in eternity's vast round.
To that stupendous view when souls awake,
So large of late, so mountainous to man,
Time's toys subside: and equal all below.
Enthusiastic, this? Then all are weak
But rank enthusiasts. To this godlike height
Some souls have soar'd; or martyrs ne'er had bled.   (VI, 595–605)

This is not the normal tenor of Augustan religious writing. It is a poem of pointed opposition to Augustan theology and taste.

Young has no sympathy for Leibnizian theodicy. We are surrounded by the groanings and tortures of the fall and without the revelation of a general corruption we could never understand our moral imprisonment. In

---

[52] All quotations from *Night Thoughts* are from the older edition (which has some advantages over recent editions) edited by Charles Cowden Clarke: Edward Young, *Night Thoughts* (Edinburgh: William Nimmo, 1868). The passages will be marked by *Night* and lines in parentheses.

this he returns to the central narrative of fideism. Going back to the spiritual milieu of Bunyan, he speaks of the Christian wayfarer, wanderer and traveler. Man is a

> traveller, a long day past
> In painful search of what he cannot find,
> At night's approach, content with the next cot,
> There ruminates, a while, his labour lost. (IX, 2–5)

The *Night Thoughts* is a work, then, of both incomprehensible novelty and proverbial truth. It seems to look forward to Young's own critical *Conjectures* with a kind of willfulness. The poem, true to Young's theory, owes little to the ancients – there may be twenty specific allusions to them in 10,000 lines. The Ovidian and Miltonic Narcissus is invoked throughout as the type of questing man, and the contemporary astronomy made popular by Ray, Jago, and Thomson is repeated but with an opposite moral. It was quite misleading of Cassirer and others to quote from Young's "Moral Survey of the Nocturnal Heavens" (in "The Consolation" or Night x) as if it were a typical piece of Augustan naturalism. In the end Young finds even the Burkean sublimity of an apparently infinite cosmos unequal to man's spiritual hunger.

> Tell me, ye stars! ye planets! tell me, all
> Ye starr'd and planeted inhabitants! what is it?
> What are these sons of wonder? say, proud arch
> (Within whose azure palaces they dwell),
> Built with divine ambition! in disdain
> Of limit built! built in the taste of heav'n!
> Vast concave! ample dome! wast thou design'd
> A meet apartment for the Deity? –
> Not so; that thought alone thy state impairs,
> Thy lofty sinks, and shallows thy profound,
> And straitens thy diffusive; dwarfs the whole,
> And makes a universe an orrery. (IX, 778–789)

The entire universe is swallowed up in the thought of God. It is a mere place for prayer – a clue of how small the greatest expanse is relative to God Himself and to our desire for Him. How far Young departs from the Newtonian rhapsodies of Thomson is obvious. Like Johnson in *Rasselas*, Young castigates the vain naturalism of the astronomer as a symbol of helpless human ambition. In fact, *The Seasons* and the fashionable mode of extended and particular description are never far from Young's mind. Like Thomson in *Summer*, Young feels anxious about an uncontrollable expansion of prospect:

> If unextinguishable thirst in man
> To know; how rich, how full, our banquet there!

> There, not the moral world alone unfolds;
> The world material, lately seen in shades,
> And in those shades, by fragments only seen,
> And seen those fragments by the laboring eye.
> Unbroken, then, illustrious and entire.
> Its ample sphere, its universal frame,
> In full dimensions swells to the survey;
> And enters at one glance the ravish'd sight.
> From some superior point (where, who can tell?
> Suffice it, 'tis a point where gods reside) . . .
> Death, only death, the question can resolve.
>
> (vi, part i, 167–178; 199)

Young admits that the last age has seen the slow and shadowy revelation of
the material world, yet "by fragments only" and seen by "a laboring eye."
He admits also that the microscopic revelation has been followed by the
telescopic and the results are "joyous" and "stupendous." The telescopic
view intimates the wonder-working and magnitude of divinity. But such a
revelation is the simple "robe" that divinity wears, a "Mass of wonders
toss'd from his hand." Young cleverly alludes to the anxiety of naturalism
in the very language of Thomson – "a laboring eye," "ravish'd sight," and
"hungry vision." The Thomsonian landscape is not for Young an ultimate
revelation. "Death, only death" can resolve the questions which puzzle the
spirit of man. If we fail to recognize the inadequacy of the material realm,
its incapacity to quench the innate thirst for eternal happiness and knowledge, then science becomes a dangerous mode of curiosity and hubris.
Young goes so far as to reproduce (almost as parody) the structure and
substance of the Thomsonian world.

> See the summer gay,
> With her green chaplet, and ambrosial flow'rs,
> Droops into pallid autumn: winter gray,
> Horrid with frost, and turbulent with storm,
> Blows autumn and his golden fruits away:
> Then melts into the spring: soft spring with breath
> Favonian, from warm chambers of the south
> Recalls the first. All to reflourish fades;
> As in a wheel all sinks to reascend.
> Emblems of man, who passes, not expires.   (vi, part i, 680–689)

Thomson's language is here deftly and purposefully imitated. "Turbulent
with storm," "with breath / Favonian" and "chambers of the south" are
obvious Thomsonisms, and the verse paragraph opens itself out to the
more opulent and fluent rhythms of *The Seasons*. Only in the last two lines
does the voice of Young intrude with a moral twist foreign to the earlier
poem. So too the stiffer prosody of the displaced heroic couplet interrupts

the quasi-Miltonic flow of the earlier lines. The circle of fading to reflourish is oddly emblematic of the passing, not expiring of man. The seasons are a sign of the promise of immortality, but also an escape from the very circle of natural life. As in nature, so in man, "life born from death" is the promise of God's higher providence.

More exactly than any of his contemporaries Young addresses the final inadequacy of analogical thought.

> If Nature's revolution speaks aloud,
> In her gradation hear her louder still.
> Look Nature through, 'tis neat gradation all.
> By what minute degrees her scale ascends!
> Each middle nature join'd at each extreme,
> To that above it join'd, to that beneath.   (VI, part i, 712–717)

Young pursues the track of being from "dormant matter" up to man who is the hinge between the mortal and immortal creation. But he does not in the end find this linked system (which he describes more aptly and fully than Pope had done in his *Essay on Man*) the ground for confident spiritual knowledge.

> in man the series ends.
> Wide yawns the gap; connexion is no more;
> Checked Reason halts; her next step wants support;
> Striving to climb, she stumbles from her scheme;
> A scheme analogy pronounc'd so true;
> Analogy man's surest guide below.   (VI, part i, 729–734)

As sure as analogy is in the analysis of natural things, it fails to connect our aspiring souls to immortal objects. The chasm can be crossed by faith alone, and unlike Dryden's helpmate reason in the *Religio Laici*, which leads us towards but not to the goal of faith, Young's natural reason leaves us unconnected and even "at odds with holy immanence." Young was an intellectual of great (if meandering) powers, and he has laid out with systematic rigor the fideist position. Like Luther and Pascal before him, he does not trust nature as a teacher – outer design fails to produce the confident sense of God that the inner life promises. This helps us to understand Young's peculiar double sense of the word "Reason" throughout his poem. Natural reason, the child of analogy, is limited and sometimes misleading. But there is a second sense of "reason" found in every "Night" of the poem. This higher reason is the power of moral deduction beyond sensation, experience, or instinct that forces us to recognize our immortal aspirations – it is the faculty whereby we see glimmerings and anticipations of heaven, and it is the calculus of failed desire. Through this purely negative reason we draw closer to Christ's cross, the chief symbol of the hopelessness of mundane experience.

But we should never imagine that Young's objections to analogy are like those of Butler or Swift. Young is completely at home in his own theology. He is unafraid of doctrine or metaphysical reasoning, nor is he opposed to conceitful rhetoric on the grounds that such a rhetoric obscures common sense. He simply believes that faith and hope are stronger aids to man in his quest for truth than his natural faculties. Young arrived on the scene of English culture when nature had been stolen from Christian apology. It had become an autonomous and amorphous body of visual accidents. Young's fideism, like that of Wesley after him, recognized that nature has been lost to theology, and that the naturalized analogies of Bishop Butler or the Deists no longer held emotional value in a Christian context. Like Prior, Young had written a good deal of incidental prose against the Augustan optimism, new science, and especially Deism, but Young went beyond Prior to become the perfect Protestant reactionary and archaist. Prior could not have imagined Young's triumphal second sense of reason which is the very heart and structure of faith.

Although there are many passing allusions to *Paradise Lost*, Young's blank verse generally falls farther from the Miltonic tree than any other of the century. *The Seasons* has a neat and scenic Miltonism, and the *Pleasures of the Imagination* is genuinely sinuous and Latinate, but Young owes only a little to Milton – enough to mention him as a lofty and melancholy influence and move on. There is in every section of the poem a submission to mystery, to infinity, to the unknowable, which Milton could not have abided. This poetic reversal has no history, and is as purely inexplicable as any greatly popular and influential work of English. Duplicating and surpassing the nervous fideism of Prior and looking forward to its great partner poem, *The Vanity of Human Wishes*, *Night Thoughts* at turns mesmerizes, irritates and stultifies. In the eighteenth century it primarily entertained and was, perhaps, more widely read than any other poem of the period. It was the rage in Paris and Berlin well into the nineteenth century, it "broke Pushkin's heart," and brought Diderot to tears. It obviously epitomized the anxious reaching for vanishing religious emotion. It is not titillating, and has only a handful of passages that resemble the poems of the so-called "Graveyard school." The inspiration of Blair is the exotic deathliness of Webster and Tourneur. The inspiration for Young was the catechism, Ecclesiastes, and the *Book of Common Prayer*.

Looking at it from the other side of a great symbol-making divide it may seem a deadly bore. It has none of the surprise of Pope or Swift, none of the emotional outflarings of Donne, Hopkins, or Eliot. It has the pace of leisurely wisdom. The patience it has in its own slow unfolding intimates the long-suffering anticipation of the ideal fideist Christian. The narrator instructs his nephew, the worldly Lorenzo, a second self and surrogate Catholic, that patience is all. Nature teaches us nothing but its own

inadequacy. Looking forward to Kant, Young explains the disproportion
between human desire and human experience.

> What prize on earth can pay us for the storm?
> Meet objects for our passion Heav'n ordain'd.
> Objects that challenge all their fire, and leave
> No fault, but in defect: bless'd Heav'n! avert
> A bounded ardour for unbounded bliss!
> O for a bliss unbounded!   (VI, part ii, 69–74)

The *Night Thoughts* is the supreme dalliance in the field of fideist
meditation. Unlike the great "awaking" that begins the *Essay on Man* or
Book IV of *Paradise Lost*, it begins in sleep and languorous dream. Something
is hidden, buried, and put out of mind from the beginning. Neither close
reading in the Empsonian sense nor selective quotation do the *Night
Thoughts* justice. The reader must become immersed in the emotion – the
waking and dreaming rhythms. "Rayless night, finds no objects" may be
construed as the theme, and we should remember that the Latin words
meaning "the love of invisible things" hung in Young's garden. In his arbor
he placed the visual illusion of a painted bench to show unwary visitors the
dangerous distortions of sensation.

Young's mixture of witty apothegm and ponderous meditation has
irritated most readers since the nineteenth century. George Eliot wrote an
involved essay about his religious character and accidentally helped to
preserve his memory for the nineteenth century. She accuses him of the
coldness and inhumanity which he self-consciously nurtured in himself,
and said that he could not see God in a leaf or a child. In fact, Young
believed in a doctrinaire way that man could not in the final analysis see
God in anything. Nature was at best a hint or broken image of God's
grandeur, which was grandest in its remote and indecipherable aspects.
Eliot, like Leslie Stephen at a later date, simply replayed the enlightened
attitude toward Protestant zeal in the eighteenth century.

The plan of the *Night Thoughts*, in so far as one exists, is simple. The first
three and the last two books are a series of apocalyptic awakenings, the
middle books are pure catechism. Young's earliest theme was "The Last
Day" (Johnson deeply admired that early poem from which Pope and
others borrowed heavily) and the *Night Thoughts* is evenly divided by
reminders of the last fire, the universal plague, and other images of final
destruction. Like other fideists Young saw the end times as the true
beginning of the potentials of life, and death as the release to promised
satisfaction.

> it is our chain, and scourge,
> In this dark dungeon, where confin'd we lie,
> Close grated by the sordid bars of Sense;

> All prospect of eternity shut out;
> And, but for execution, ne'er set free.   (VI, part i, 404–408)

Death is the key to our release and the type of later Apocalypse. There are three repeated structural analogies which hold together the poem. First there is night as the death of the day, second the natural death as illustrated in the three central elegies of the early books, and lastly Apocalypse, which is the death of the world. Lorenzo is instructed to realize the supreme value of these three deaths. They are linked in a circling logic throughout the poem. Night expunges the distractions of the accidental and visual for the Christian meditator, death expunges the pitiful and fruitless narrative of desire in the Christian's life, and Apocalypse expunges the whole world – the last impediment between man and immortal rest. By linking these three elements in his poem Young cleverly points to empiricism, novelism, and naturalism, those three pillars of Augustan intellectual culture, as the dangerous temptations of the enlightened culture. Far from simple morbidity the poem lays out a map whereby the contemporary reader can escape the traps of contemporary curiosity. The expansive landscape of Thomson is replaced by the undifferentiated field of night. The plot of the novel is replaced by the traditional teleology of Protestant romance.

> Souls truly great dart forward on the wing
> Of just ambition, to the grand result,
> The curtain's fall.   (IV, 224–226)

The final curtain call, which obviates all the restless and curious action of human life is the cosmic Apocalypse. By my count there are no fewer than twelve lengthy descriptions of Apocalypse and judgment in the poem. Blake, who wrote *The Four Zoas* on the back of his proof sheets for his illustrations of Young's *Night Thoughts*, discovered in Young the idea of multiple and layered Apocalypse. Young's Apocalyptic rhetoric is often horrific, always grand. Perhaps more than any other English religious writer he imagines Apocalypse as the corner-stone of moral and religious logic.

> Great day! for which all other days were made;
> For which earth rose from chaos, man from earth;
> And an eternity, the date of gods,
> Descended on poor earth-created man!
> Great day of dread, decision, and despair!
> At thought of thee, each sublunary wish
> Lets go its eager grasp, and drops the world.   (IX, 217–223)

Unlike Pope's in *The Dunciad*, Young's apocalypse is moral and metaphysical rather than aesthetic.

The sleeping and waking motifs of the poem are deceptively complex. The second book begins with the guilty waking of Peter after the third crowing of the cock, and on the third night Young awakes to a pastoral solitude filled with unpleasant memories and harkenings. The middle books lay out the thorough moral training of Lorenzo, who is introduced in Night II as a kind of profligate nephew (Young had a profligate son from whom he was for a long time estranged). The place of Lorenzo is mysterious and inconsistent. He seems like a part of the narrator's divided conscience, an echo or self-examination by which Young castigates his own well-known limitations as a preacher and his servile groveling among aristocratic patrons. Young's sycophancy, which alternates throughout his work with the most other-worldy melancholy and shame, has been misunderstood by almost every critic. It is little more than the extension of his own perfectionist moralism in the teeth of Augustan practicalities. His own earlier career is for Young the very paradigm of vanity.

Let it suffice to say that no poem can approach the systematic mining of fideist possibilities which we see in Young. He wrote on these subjects most of his life, and perfected a style which mixed the proverbial and repetitive qualities of wisdom literature with the unseeing darkness of fideist epistemology. One passage beautifully summarizes the peculiar anti-naturalism and anti-empiricism of Young's mind – a mind bored and hostile in the face of the common round of social and natural experiences. Who but Young could imagine Christ's dove as a bird of infinite but unworldly variety – the endless variety of hopeful expectations that flood in upon a consciousness disgusted by the analogous variety of natural experience? The many dyes that color the mystic dove's neck are the hues of virtuous action and faith. Young replaces the multiple and associative field of Augustan imagination with a simple and iterative poetic morality. He returns to the pure teleological and apocalyptic mode of earlier English Protestants like Perkins, Baxter, and Bunyan. Young presents his reader with an exhaustive catalog of faithful and unworldly emotions, and in doing so he rebukes the novelty, variety, and largeness which Addison, Pope, Akenside, and especially Thomson, had discovered in the expanding Augustan landscape.

> A languid, leaden iteration reigns
> And ever must for those whose joys are joys
> Of sight, smell, taste; the cuckoo-seasons sing
> The same dull note to such as nothing prize,
> But what these seasons from the teeming earth,
> To doting sense indulge. But noble minds,
> Which relish fruits unripen'd by the sun,
> Make their days various; various as the dyes
> On the dove's neck, which wanton in his rays.

On minds of dove-like innocence possess'd,
On lighten'd minds, that bask in Virtue's beams,
Nothing hangs tedious, nothing old resolves
In that for which they long, for which they live.   (III, 373–385)

7

Johnson and fideism

Fideism and humanism

It was Cassirer's opinion that the chief intellectual problem of the Enlightenment was the reconciliation of Renaissance humanism and Protestant individualism.[1] Luther's world was one of severe spiritual subjectivity combined with the reinvigoration of dormant ethical militancy, and an apocalyptic drama of good and evil powers in which "the five senses and then thought itself is for naught."[2] This evacuation of knowledge and perception was an extreme position; more anti-intellectualist even than the position of Calvin, it was the great counterweight to the Catholic humanism which had begun in the thirteenth century. Luther took St. Paul for his example, and in his commentaries on Romans and Galatians he arrived near to the absolute "fideism"[3] of Tertullian.[4] He eschewed both

---

[1] Ernst Cassirer, *The Philosophy of the Enlightenment* (Princeton: Princeton University Press, 1957), ch. 1.

[2] Martin Luther, *Works* (Philadelphia: Muhlenberg Press, 1943), vol. I, 213. Johnson among all his important British contemporaries seems to me to have a fideist epistemology most like that laid out in Luther's *Bondage of the Will* and *Commentary on Romans*, and, perhaps, to have shared a deep logical and psychological sympathy with the Lutheran formulation as opposed to the liberal Anglican or Calvinist on most matters. See also, Jaroslav Pelikan, *The Christian Tradition: A History of the Development of Doctrine* (Chicago: University of Chicago Press, 1989), vol. v, 52–54 and *passim* for Lutheranism in the period since 1700.

[3] I am using "fideism" here and throughout in a specific and narrow sense. The Protestant (and occasionally orthodox) form of imagination in which the divine is understood is infinitely remote from sensation, analogy, and all discursive knowledge. The Pauline or Augustinian conception of the injured perceptive faculties, but still surviving inner voice, in which "knowledge" of God is born in expectation – an emotion of "unquestioning need" enlivened by prevenient grace – is the central tenor of primitive or modern fideism.

    Fideist art can not directly describe God, and is, therefore, an art which imitates the affections of the human agent in pursuit of the unknowable. God for the fideist is known only in relation to the human will and imagination, and not as an external or separable being. Typically the divine is seen as an ultimate end or necessary limit to human consciousness. The common motifs of fideist art are night, distance, solitude, hunger, warfare, and anticipation. The God of fideist art is a God in hiding, but known by this very absence. I have argued in chapter 6 that this sort of fideist art dominated the mid-century Christian reaction to Augustan optimism and naturalism. Its chief proponents were Berkeley, Hervey, Young, Edwards, Watts, Prior, South, Secker, Law, and Johnson.

[4] Cf. H. A. Wolfson, *The Philosophy of the Church Fathers* (Cambridge, Mass.: Harvard University

logicism and mysticism, though for the latter he has an unconscious sympathy. Faith for him was not a middle point between science and opinion, as it had been for the Thomists, nor was it a shorthand or practical exposition of a higher truth, as in the case of Bellarmine or Erasmus. Faith was the only trustworthy means of approaching the Deity, and it was in "the darkness that heals, and the light unseen"[5] that God would be found. The Christian man was blessed with an unerring moral umpire in conscience, an inner light, which neither pride of thought nor ceremonious custom could dim. It was in this formula that modern fideism was brought back into European thought – and it was this new spiritual knowledge without object or boundary that was the inheritance of men so different as Pascal, Boehme, and Johnson.

The rejection of Scholasticism and the denigration of natural reason that this Protestant epistemology entailed ran headlong into the still developing humanism of the fifteenth and sixteenth centuries. It challenged the authority of the classical *sensus communis* and the *traditio* of the historical church on behalf of the "community of the truly faithful."[6] This was the first step towards our modern form of sentimentality and subjectivity, and with it came the poetics of the embattled self, the heavenly fortress, world-weary expectation, the sublime of absence, and all the other accouterments of fideist art.

On the other hand, humanism, in both its Socratic-Christian and neo-Stoic forms, is the obvious and unwitting parent of rationalism and Deism. The God of Erasmus was the equivalent of Cicero's God. Christianity then, for about a century, was held in perilous balance with the forces of classical culture. The strain at first was felt as a violent and rending conflict within Christendom. Only later did the skeptical tensions inherent in the humanistic synthesis widen and challenge orthodoxy from within. The Baroque analogies of heaven and earth were still meaningful for Erasmus. His faith embraced the concept of universal analogy. In his *Adagia* he imagines that "every star is a jewel in the bracelet of the Lord."[7] The Humanists were from the beginning the champions of "nature." It was not Bacon, but Erasmus who first announced the liberating project. In *The Praise of Folly* he claimed that "nature the sole judge of truth, is laughing at them [the defenders of superstitious custom]

Press, 1952), vol. I, 24–43. Tertullian's position (made memorable by his phrase "I believe because it is absurd") is that faith is a form of necessary and unarguable folly – that knowledge is a hindrance to salvation, as in his *De spectaculis*.

5   Luther, *Works*, vol. 8, 382.

6   Jaroslav Pelikan, *The Christian Tradition. A History of the Development of Doctrine* (Chicago: University of Chicago Press, 1977), vol. IV, 47.

7   Erasmus, *Adagia* (Berlin: Verlag, 1983).

all the time."[8] But this nature (until the time of Hobbes) was still a window to God.

It was the eighteenth century that saw the fideist and humanistic forces, which had contributed to the social and doctrinal upheaval of the Reformation, resolve themselves into a subtler and deeper set of antitheses. The older humanism drifted toward latitude in theology, while free-thinking was, in one sense, an extreme form of the "universalism" of Erasmus, Ficino, and Pomponazzi. The kinship Augustan culture had to the peculiar genius of Montaigne, Rabelais, and More is one example of this continuity. But it is a continuity with a difference. Pope's Christianity is denuded of its analogical or visionary energy. It is the withered image of orthodoxy. In Pope's day the biblical authority had entered history, perception had replaced vision, and the classical was no longer a spiritual *preparatio*, but an independent source of wisdom and beauty.

Orthodox apologists like Bishop Butler and Sherlock took the middle ground, incorporating sometimes innocently the empiricist prejudices of the age, and attempting to defend Christianity by either ethical, historical, or scientific means. Butler's *Analogy* appealed to the age in part because its analogies are purely mechanical – arguments from animal locomotion, physics, and politics. Like Locke's *Reasonableness of Christianity*, Butler's *Analogy* came perilously close to the methods of evidence and exposition of Tindal, and finally Hume, and its use as a standard theology text at Oxford well into the nineteenth century points to something rather desperate in official Anglicanism before the time of the Oxford Movement.

Where the still existing Protestant emotion was imbued with a Lutheran intensity, it was transformed into Evangelicalism. The Evangelicals mocked the rational and scientific project of Enlightenment. Their own solution was fideistic. The tepidity of most High Church sermoners in the early eighteenth century with their anti-dogmatizing and Erastian sentiments was not enough for a "heart strangely warmed." The Wesleyan heart was indeed a good deal too strange for Bishop Gibson who authored a long public disquisition on Methodist lunacy in which he seriously attempted to describe the twice-born devotee as a victim of pathology.[9] The Anglican was likely to take reason, and in a rather narrow Lockeian sense, as the measure of true religion, while the Evangelical sort turned to a private, mysterious, and faithful devotion.

Placing Johnson upon this simple and schematic scale with Augustan humanism on one side and Protestant fideism on the other has proven impossible. For many he is the model Augustan – a man of towering good

---

[8] Erasmus, *The Praise of Folly* in *Essential Works*, ed. R. Jackson (New York: Grosset and Dunlap, 1971), 404.
[9] Quoted at length in Michael Matlock, ed. *The Eighteenth Century British Constitution* (Cambridge: Cambridge University Press, 1974), ch. 6.

sense and rock-kicking realism.[10] Richard Schwartz has attempted to place
Johnson squarely within the post-Restoration tradition of English empiricism and "scientific common sense."[11] This last phrase has a touch of the
oxymoronic, and the evidence gathered on behalf of the positivist Johnson
– his amateur interest in chemistry, his pooh-poohing of metaphysical
speculation, and his now proverbial common sense are not adequate to
explain the dark moralism of *The Rambler*, the Solomonic discontent of
Rasselas, his recently uncovered attraction for the evangelical preachers,[12]
the distinctively Pauline and fideist arguments of his own sermons, and the
spiritual aura of his *Diaries, Prayers, and Annals*.

We can, nevertheless, be amazed at the heterogeneous impressions that
Johnson makes on excellent readers. On the one side, Krutch seems almost
convinced of his agnosticism.

It may be, as has previously been suggested, that belief in the supernatural was so
nearly incompatible with the general tenor of his mind that the exception to
skepticism which he professed to make where the doctrines of Christianity are
concerned was half in vain and that he therefore did not, at the very bottom of his
mind, believe at all.[13]

"It may be," "has been suggested," "so nearly incompatible," and "half in
vain" suggest that Krutch himself was unsure of his conclusion, and it may
be that the faith or conviction of any man "at the very bottom of his mind"
is very nearly unknowable. On the other hand, for a number of nineteenth-
century writers (Carlyle among them) Johnson seemed the very type of the

---

[10] Among the numerous studies Johnson's critics have created, one should mention Paul Fussell's
The Rhetorical World of Augustan Humanism (Oxford: Clarendon Press, 1962), which greatly
exaggerates Johnson's conformity to twelve characteristic Augustan qualities. In fact, the bulk
of recent studies and newer biographies seem to undercut this view of Johnson. There is a great
chasm both in character and thought between Johnson and Swift, as there is between Johnson
and Pope. This is most obviously felt in Johnson's *Life of Swift* and *Prayers and Meditations*. Pope
and his contemporaries share with Johnson a mistrust of metaphysics and theological casuistry,
as well as a healthy skepticism of utopian politics, but Johnson has the added quality, which so
largely qualifies his grimness, of Protestant moral expectation and faith, and of its concomitant
spirit of purposeful moral struggle. He shares, as well, that private and searching form of
meditation and profound loneliness which John Sitter has recently described in his important
study. The contrast of style and purpose between Johnson and the Augustans is illustrated by
their private correspondences: Pope's, witty and public-minded, conceived for publication, and
glowing with the eclectic judgments and the famous public "embroilings" of the 1720s;
Johnson's, personal and morally grave, involved in the flux of stinging expectation and
transparent affection (as in the Hill Boothby letters of 1750 or the exchange with Mrs. Thrale in
1782). Johnson's private letters recall the style and substance of *Clarissa* more than that of
Seneca.

[11] Richard B. Schwartz, *Samuel Johnson and the New Science* (Madison: University of Wisconsin Press,
1971).

[12] See especially, Richard Brantley, *Johnson's Wesleyan Connection* (*Eighteenth Century Studies*, Fall,
1980), 45–67.

[13] Joseph Wood Krutch, *Samuel Johnson* (New York: Henry Holt and Company, 1944), 548.

God-possessed. We have the words of Stanhope (Lord Mahon) as an example:

> If then it be asked, who first in England breasted the waves and stemmed the tide of infidelity – who enlisted wit and eloquence together with argument and learning on the side of revealed religion, first turned the literary current in its favour, and mainly prepared the reaction which succeeded: that praise seems most justly to belong to Samuel Johnson. Religion was to him no mere lipservice, nor cold formality: he was mindful of it in his social hours as much as in his graver lucubrations: and he brought to it not merely erudition such as few indeed possessed, but the weight of the highest character and the respect which even his enemies could not deny him. It may be said of him, that though not in orders, he did the Church of England better service than most of those who in that listless era ate her bread.[14]

There is no doubt some truth in this exaggerated encomium, and it was confirmed by Hawkins and others who knew Johnson, but it seems less than central to a clearer understanding of Johnson. The psychological and death-haunted view of Johnson's spirituality has by now usurped that of the Anglican champion, but it is nonetheless true that serious and learned religious characters like Coleridge, Newman, Ward, Hopkins, and T. S. Eliot have always been and perhaps will always be drawn to Johnson. Stanhope's words above are also, of course, a rebuttal of Macaulay's Whiggish attack, though Stanhope himself was a distinguished Whig. What strikes us is that beyond the issues of party and denomination, Johnson rather than Bishop Butler or Warburton represented all that was best and most vital in Christian apology, and much of this depends on his particular concept of the moral and spiritual life.

It is not enough to say that one man's agnostic is another man's saint. We must attempt at last to separate the distinct strands of Johnson's religious thought by a closer inspection of his own work, and not from the stiflingly abundant and confused body of memoir, portrait, and biography. We may know that Johnson's mother was an old-style Calvinist Protestant, that he read William Law with a fervent reawakening of dormant religious emotions, that he spoke of ghosts and death in a memorable way, but Johnson's own work remains the solid ground for determining these difficult considerations.

If we make this attempt we find, I think, a fascinating dichotomy – a seeming contradiction at the heart of Johnson's thought. The clearest and least explored locus of this dichotomy is in *The Lives of the English Poets*, and it is there that I begin my analysis.

[14] Lord Stanhope, *History of England* (London: John Murray, 1859), vol. VII, 313.

The two Johnsons

In the *Lives of the English Poets* Johnson shows his deep kinship with the now obscure Renaissance Humanists Scaliger, Wowerus, Passerat, Fabricius, Poliziano, Lipsius, Pontanus, Puttenham, and others. In English we may associate Philip Sidney with this tradition, which combines the aphoristic mode, Aristotelian and Platonic aesthetics, and late-Italian critical models to produce the first great modern body of literary criticism. Johnson learned from the *grammatici* of this tradition the witty close-reading method which he uses in the *Life of Gray* and in his remarks on Addison's *Campaign*. From them he learned an elaborate interpretation of Greek *mimesis* and Latin rhetorical and poetic taxonomy. These he applied with startling success in the opening pages of the Preface to his edition of Shakespeare, where all the distinctions of medium, mode (of expression), objects of imitation, and style are laid out according to the example of Scaliger.[15]

From them, also, he gained his life-long fascination for modern Latin poetry; and he was, with Milton, the greatest English authority on Neo-Latin verse. The tenth chapter of *Rasselas*, though it appears to advance an empirical argument, is fundamentally in the Humanist manner. It is, perhaps, the last classically minded *imago poetae* in English. That passage displays the Humanist penchant for collection, akin to the Renaissance *copia*, but it has within it (as we shall observe in a moment) an uncharacteristic moralism. The critiques of the pastoral as in *Rambler* 36, 37, and 80 and the *Lives* of Milton and Phillips are one side of a debate that goes back to Castlevetro.[16] Of course, Johnson is no slavish adherent to any school,

---

[15] This has not before been pointed out even by the Chicago Aristotelians, who were so interested in the relation of Johnson to Classical and Renaissance poetics. The opening paragraphs of the "Preface to Shakespeare" deserve a more refined explication than they have yet received. They are not idiosyncratic, though they seem to turn away from the popular French Neoclassicism from which Dryden and Pope borrow. Johnson's argument is expressly divided into the categories of medium/mode/plot/lexical style/sentiment (*dianoia*) and the other qualitative divisions of Aristotle's poetics, which were regularized by the humanists of the fifteenth and sixteenth centuries. The much cruder use in Dryden of materials from Boileau (and perhaps Tasso) shows Johnson's direct knowledge of both the Greek text and the humanistic applications of it. There are also numerous examples of neo-Latin poems quoted from the text of Marino, Scaliger, Passerat, in *The Rambler* and the *Lives* which show the intimate knowledge Johnson had of that tradition. Lastly, Johnson seems to have picked up the late-Medieval or early Renaissance habit of using expressions like "the father of criticism" (referring to Aristotle), "the master of the several arts," and the like, which is eccentric at best for a critic writing in the 1770s and 1780s. The emotional sympathy he had for the younger Scaliger is obvious at the beginning of his great Latin poem, *Gnwthi Seuton*, written when he completed the *Dictionary* in 1755. "Lexicon ad finem longo luctamine tandem / Scaliger ut duxit, tenuis pertaesus opellae / Ville indignatus Studium." He seemed to think of the Humanists as brothers in the difficult and drudging labor of lexicography, criticism, and editing.

[16] Castlevetro applied his general rule of "probability" in judging the proper style and subject for pastoral, and his realistic conception of *rustica* is very close to Johnson's, who was familiar with

and his judgment is, in the most profound sense, his own; but his ideal of literature borrows a great deal from this Humanistic tradition – its sense of generic decorum, its theory of diction, the weight it places on proportion and symmetry in the use of figures, and its sometimes strenuous secularism.

It is in the light of this tradition that we are likely to interpret Johnson's critique of Christian religious poetry. It was the concern of the Humanists to master every genre and mode of ancient poetry, to regain the naturalism lost in the Middle Ages, and adapt and perfect profane art. The imitation, a form in which Johnson was one of the last great masters, was virtually invented, or reinvented (since Quintilian and others had discussed it in antiquity) by Pontanus and Poliziano. Johnson had contemplated in his youth and again in middle age a complete edition (and translation) of Poliziano's poems.[17] He also considered a history of the rise of Renaissance learning, which might have ranked among his great and singular achievements.

It was this Humanistic school of the fifteenth century that first challenged and then displaced the older religious material, the *sacra rappresentazione* of European poetry. Of course, Johnson had no such secularizing ambition, but did, in the final analysis (though for very different reasons) find scriptural drama and sacred representation beyond the reach of poetry. What made this sense of the impossibility of Christian poetry so acute in Johnson was a fideist Protestant habit of mind. The fideist divinity without analog cannot be reconciled to a Humanist idea of *mimesis*. Nature, which is the Humanistic ideal of art, is infinitely remote from Johnson's God. Johnson, more even than Edward Young and the iconoclastic divines of the mid-century, thought of God as dwelling in unapproachable darkness. More than any of his contemporaries he believed the double formula of St. Paul.[18] For Johnson faith was both insufficiently proved (in the evidentiary sense) and undeniably potent. "The expectation of good to come" was for Johnson the central premise for moral theorizing. There were for him only two forms of expectation, two distinct and psychologically connected objects of hope. The first was hope for wordly good and comfort, and that in Solomon's words was "vanity and vexation of spirit." The proximate goods and torturing desires of human experience were always and every-

his commentary on Aristotle's *Poetics*. For a summary of Castlevetro's general position, see J. E. Spingarn, *Literary Criticism in the Renaissance* (New York: Columbia University Press, 1924), 44–47. For a rather different but important treatment of Johnson's pastoral realism see Leopold Damrosch, *The Uses of Johnson's Criticism* (Charlottesville, Va.: University of Virginia, 1976), 79–92.

17 W. J. Bate, *Samuel Johnson* (New York: Harcourt, Brace, Jovanovich, 1977), 140–141 and 541–542.
18 The author of Hebrews, obviously a follower or scribe of St. Paul, is the source for "the substance of things unseen, the expectation of good to come," which very aptly describes the central Johnsonian conception of faith, as shown throughout the *Rambler*, in *Rasselas*, and at the end of *The Vanity of Human Wishes*.

where thwarted. This is the chief message of *The Rambler,* the *Idler,* and *Rasselas.* The other hope is immortal and divine. It puts an end to "dull Suspense" and "Ignorance sedate"[19] and gives dimension to every human aspiration. It is the ground for meaning and dignity in a conception of life which neither the ancients nor the Humanists could have imagined.

Johnson and the critique of analogy

Returning to *The Lives of the Poets* I must make a point which has not until now been sufficiently stressed. For Johnson poetry (and every art) is a diversion, a toy for bored contemplation, and a bauble to distract us from common miseries. Unlike for Sidney and Shelley, it does not open up spiritual and ethical vistas. Nor, as in the case of Coleridge, does it get us closer to the divine knowledge or power. Being one of the proximate goods, it should never be confused with the one true lasting good.

It is also important to know that for Johnson (unlike Blake or Coleridge) the Bible was not a work of imagination. It was not a work of imitation, nor was it the "great code" of all art. For Johnson the Bible was the special mooring for the man of faith. Its authority was vouchsafed by God himself, and unequivocal in its wisdom. Among fideists like Watts, Young, and Prior the biblical promise rose above and almost outside of normal intellectual experience. It was a work of grace and not nature. This notion is repeated in the *Lives* of Cowley, Milton, Watts, and Waller.

Sacred History has been always read with submissive reverence, and an imagination over-awed and controlled. We have been accustomed to acquiesce in the nakedness and simplicity of the authentic narrative, and repose on its veracity with such humble confidence as suppresses curiosity. We go with the historian as he goes, and stop with him when he stops. All amplification is frivolous and vain; all addition to that which is already sufficient for the purposes of religion seems not only useless, but in some degree profane.[20]

Here the accumulation of reverence, submission, humbling, acquiescence, controlling, and repose illustrate the fideist sense of human inadequacy in the face of the divine revelation. Johnson himself was a prey to these sometimes crippling emotions, and he seems to have shared with Pascal that intense realization of the terrifying smallness of human power. This is not the vocabulary of a Tory authoritarian in the style of Warburton or Bolingbroke – the uses of scripture never descend to mere manipulation of some political or ecclesiastical agent. The humbling remoteness from the

---

[19] Samuel Johnson, *The Vanity of Human Wishes* in *The Complete English Peoms*, ed. J. D. Freeman (New Haven: Yale University Press, 1971), 91.

[20] Samuel Johnson, *The Lives of the English Poets*, ed. G. Birckbeck-Hill (Oxford: Clarendon Press, 1905), vol. 1, 49–50. (All further references to *The Lives of the Poets* will be marked in text as *Life of* and page.)

biblical sublimity and the servile literalism concerning the "narrative" are qualities shared by the fideist and the mystic. Since the symbolical and the analogical faculties, which are the ground of art, have no connection to the biblical material, the Bible, like God, remains uninterpretable and alien. It is, perhaps, needless to add that the "child of faith" in the face of this overawing and unknowable text and person must finally set the world and its writing (the "frivolous" and the "profane") apart from the highest human purpose. In the face of these limitations the "curiosity" requisite to the Humanism we have been discussing approaches to frivolity or profanity. The gratuitous "amplification" – we might call it myth-making or "figuring" – which we associate with the Metaphysicals, especially when it incorporates holy images, must be suppressed. Fideist art is the art of that suppression.

Furthermore, the Classicism so often invoked by Johnson in his Humanist persona is equivocal. He insists that the pagan and the Christian worlds are of different orders. We should never confuse the pagan with the Christian situation.

The darkness and uncertainty through which the heathens were compelled to wander in the pursuit of happiness, may, indeed, be alleged as an excuse for many of their seducing invitations to immediate enjoyments, which the moderns, by whom they have been imitated, have not to plead. It is no wonder that such as had no promise of another state should eagerly turn their thoughts upon the improvement of that which was before them; but surely those who are acquainted with the hopes and fears of eternity, might think it necessary to put some restraint upon their imagination . . . [21]

"The restraint of imagination" was for Johnson a very high ideal. Fantasy and ambition could be horribly destructive, and images held in the imagination were the root of every vice. Nonetheless, he knew that men lived by hope and imagination – "from hope to hope" as he poignantly described it. The *Dictionary* is no less than a battleground for these two incompatible modes of Johnsonian thinking. If we take the word "imagination" itself we can see the tension between the Humanist, the acquisitive artist and intellectual, on the one side, and the pious fideist on the other. Johnson's first set of definitions are Humanistic. They are derived from Locke, Bacon, Glanvil, and Pope – the stable of powerful and curious Augustan thinkers to whom Johnson always credited the maturing and strengthening of English thought and poetry. They represent (with Milton) "the fancy; power of forming ideal pictures; the power of representing the things absent to oneself or others," nothing less than the power to delight and instruct. "His imaginations were often as just as they were bold and strong" (Dennis); and "where beams of warm imagination play" (Pope).

[21] Samuel Johnson, *Works*, vol. III, ed. W. J. Bate and Albrecht B. Strauss (New Haven: Yale University Press, 1969). *The Rambler* 29, 158.

This imaginative power and warmth is forgotten, even contradicted, in the second set of quotations under the heading "Conception, image in the mind." Here we find: "sometimes despair darkens all her imaginations" (Sidney); "for unfelt imaginations / They often feel a world of cares" (Shakespeare); "they by wrong imaginations / Lose a knowledge of themselves" (Shakespeare); and lastly, "Thou hast seen all their vengeance, and all their imaginations against me" (*Lamentations*). It is not difficult to see the collision of Humanist and fideist here. The curious Augustans are confronted with the world-weariness and desperate wisdom of King Lear and the author of *Lamentations*. Here imagination is a disease of discontent. It is the place of delusion. I point this out to show how precariously the artistic and moral worlds of Johnson are balanced. That balance is the very problem of *The Rambler, Rasselas,* and "The Vision of Theodore."

So the restraint of imagination, and especially the restraint of fancies that blur our religious and moral sense, were always of the utmost importance to Johnson's theory of poetry. We can see how far from the analogical poets of an earlier day Johnson really was. The fideist sees the divine and the mundane as radically and permanently separated. This conception of an infinite disproportion between the creature and creator is the particular subject of Johnson's "Review of *A Free Inquiry into the Nature and Origin of Evil.*" Nowhere else in his writing does he work out his own fideism so rigorously. Here he disavows any possibility of the medieval or Baroque *proportionalitas*, emanationism, or plenitude:

The scale of existence from infinity to nothing, cannot possibly have being. The highest being not infinite must be, as has been often observed, at an infinite distance below infinity . . . Between the lowest positive existence and nothing, wherever we suppose positive existence to cease is another chasm infinitely deep.

To these meditations humanity is unequal. But yet we may ask, not of our maker, but of each other, since on the one side creation, wherever it stops, must stop infinitely below infinity, and on the other infinitely above nothing, what necessity there is that it should proceed so far either way that being so high or so low should ever have existed? We may ask; but I believe no created wisdom can give an adequate answer.

("Review of *A Free Inquiry into the Nature and Origin of Evil*")[22]

No more explicit denial of proportion and anlaogy between the created and God could be asserted. We must not even deign to ask God such impertinent questions. Such a monolog is a part of human curiosity and, perhaps, perversity. The language of "chasm" and "deep" recalls the *Pensées*, and Luther's rhetoric of *mysterium* – the fearful isolation and separation of the natural man from God.

---

[22] Samuel Johnson, ed. by Donald Greene for *The Oxford Authors* (New York: Oxford University Press, 1984), 525–526.

He feels the claims of God's universal distributive justice are self-deceiving claims of the wealthy, and that poverty and ignorance are obviously privative and distressing in the real world. He simultaneously rejects Baroque optimism about our knowledge of God, and Augustan smugness about a world of pragmatic social balances. We may learn from such speculations as those of Pope's *Essay on Man* and Jenyns' *Inquiry* only what we learn from experience generally – our own weakness and imbecility.

There is undoubtedly a degree of knowledge which will direct a man to refer all to providence, and to acquiesce in the condition which omniscient goodness has determined to allot him; to consider this world as phantom that must soon glide from before his eyes, and the distresses and vexations that encompass him, as dust scattered in his path, as a blast that chills him for a moment, and passes off forever.

(528)

Here Johnson's world is the airy and shifting delusion of *The Vanity of Human Wishes*, something to be endured with a hopeful anticipation of the next world. And in the succeeding passage he denies, like Hegel's Abraham and the homesick wayfarer of Bunyan, that the world is to mortals a proper house or habitation, or of any intimate concern of God. Rather than being moved by its magnificence (like Addison or Thomson), he is surprised by the universe's superfluousness. Variety and novelty and magnitude, the supreme qualities of creation for the Augustans, are for Johnson morally irrelevant.

The magnificence of a house is of use or pleasure always to the master, and sometimes to the domestics. But the magnificence of the universe adds nothing to the supreme Being; and for any part of its inhabitants with which human knowledge is acquainted, an universe much less spacious or splendid would have been sufficient.

(529)

It should be noted that Johnson's attitude (and style) is in the "Review" (as elsewhere) divided between Augustan "Humanism" and Protestant homily. In a passage of Swiftian sarcasm and a style and diction borrowed directly from *Gulliver's Travels,* he says of Jenyns' notion that human suffering may be justified by divine or angelic purposes unknown to us:

I cannot resist the temptation of contemplating this analogy, which I think he might have carried further very much to the advantage of his argument. He might have shown that these *hunters whose game is man* have many sports analogous to our own. As we drown whelps and kittens, they amuse themselves now and then by sinking a ship, and stand round the fields of Blenheim or the walls of Prague, as we encircle a cock-pit.

(535)

Returning to our original problem, I think we can see *The Life of Cowley* as revealing, in an oblique way, the basic fideist quality of Johnson's thought. Johnson's critique of the conceit is no mere rhetorical exercise,

though it is practiced under the guise of a subtle exposure of metaphorical
extravagance. It recalls the tone and method of Pope's *Peri Bathous*, which
itself makes use of the lampooning technique of Erasmus. It has a mild
resemblance to Locke's theory of proportion in figures, and probably
borrows from the Humanistic conception of *decorum*. The Humanist
method is intertwined with and supports the fideist impulse.

The special nature of the biblical narrative is explicitly described in *The
Life of Cowley* during a passage on Cowley's biblical epillion, *The Davideis*.
Johnson remarks:

It is not only when the events are confessedly miraculous that fancy and fiction
lose their effect; the whole system of life, while the Theocracy was yet visible, has
an appearance so different from all other scenes of human action that the reader
of the Sacred Volume habitually considers it a peculiar mode of existence of a
distinct species of mankind.   (Life of Cowley, 91)

That is to say that the life described in the Bible, when God was still
present in the affairs of men, and when the prophetic imagination was still
active, cannot even be imagined by the now depraved human agent. We
may recall that this was also his attitude toward Milton's Eden. The
"visible Theocracy," like Eden, is of a different order from normal
experience. Our life offers nothing so grand as analogy or epiphany, no
vivid memory of glory. Our conception of God is one of absence, as
something necessarily posited. The inner man finds succor in hope, but as
in Tertullian and Pascal he has no positive knowledge of the Divine. This
goes a long way towards clarifying Johnson's infamous critique of metaphysical poetry.

[speaking of Cowley] to emulate Donne seems to have been his purpose; and from
Donne he may have learned that familiarity with religious images, and that light
allusion to sacred things, by which readers far short of sanctity are frequently
offended.   (*Life of Cowley*, 87)

This is not the reaction of a precious moralist, but of a man who refuses the
possibility of analogical parallelism between the physical and the divine.
The very notion of "religious images" strikes Johnson as absurd, and this
iconoclasm is shared by many devout and learned Christians of the age –
Wesley, Young, Secker, and Lowth. The phenomenon is not Calvinism,[23] as

[23] Some distinguished critics like Greene and Fairchild have made this error. Calvin himself was
not a strong iconoclast, especially in respect to natural analogy. In some ways he was
representative of the late-Baroque tradition of meditation, which Luther and Bucer rejected.
The Puritan divines that followed him on the Continent and in England made full use of
analogy and "theodicy." Cf. John Calvin, *Institutes of the Christian Religion* (Philadelphia:
Westminster, 1960), Book I, sections I–II, 51–55. The headings alone betray his likeness to
Bonaventure or Bellarmine – "The knowledge of God shines forth in the fashioning of the
universe and the continuing government of it" and, "The Divine Wisdom displayed for all to
see."

is often remarked, but fideism, which since the time of Athanasius, has inveighed against holy representation. If Tertullian (and Luther) could ask, "What has Athens to do with Jerusalem?" Johnson has a deeper problem: what has poetry or any art to do with truth, that is, the highest truth?

This would not have been a problem for a man who was no great lover of life or poetry, but for Johnson it was an enormous dilemma. He invested a good deal of his most serious effort in criticism and poetry, but, on account of this tenacious fideism, could never be an artist in the unequivocal and professional sense that Pope or Dryden had been. This helps to explain some of the moral paralysis Johnson felt when presented with large imaginative projects. They were for him, on one level, acts of supreme dedication and love, but on a deeper, religious level they were acts of proud conceit. It is no accident that the last *Idler* brings to his mind the idea of ultimate ends – death and divine judgment. The end of writing was not immortality but death. If we contrast his attitude toward sleep and dreams with that of the dreaming interludes of Thomson's *Summer*, or the dream visions of Pope's *Temple of Fame*, we find a complete departure from Augustan norms. The dreams of Thomson are even more fantastic exercises in variety of imagery and prospect than are possible while awake – escapes to the fanciful variegated jungles of Africa and South America. Of the place of sleep Johnson says:

All envy would be extinguished if it were universally known that there are none to be envied, and surely none can be envied much who is not pleased with themselves. There is reason to suspect that the distinctions of mankind have more show than value, when it is found that all alike agree to be weary alike of pleasures and of cares; that the powerful and the weak, the celebrated and obscure, join in one common wish, and implore from nature's hand the nectar of oblivion.

(*Idler*, 32)[24]

His anonymous writing of sermons, his *Diarie* and *Annals* were a separate (and very deeply exploratory) spiritual activity. This is why he was overcome with anxiety when asked by Mrs. Thrale and Boswell to write sermons and prayers in his later life. He no doubt anguished over the relative weight of his writing duties. He probably did not think of his spiritual meditations as a form of imagination at all, for Johnson held the spiritual life in a mysterious (and impossible) detachment from common experience.

In any event the epistemology of *The Lives of the Poets* is clear. It was an inconvenience of Milton's design that "it requires the description of what cannot be described." The surprise and delight of invention, that mixture

---

[24] Samuel Johnson, *Works*, ed. W. J. Bate and John Bullitt (New Haven: Yale University Press, 1971).

of wit and discovery, which is so difficult to define, is limited to natural things.

> A poet may describe the beauty and grandeur of Nature, the flowers of the Spring, and the harvests of Autumn, the vicissitudes of the Tide, and the iccolutions of the sky, and praise the maker for his works in lines which no reader shall lay aside.
>
> (Life of Waller, 291)

The subject of the disputation is not piety, but the motives to piety; that of the description "not of God but the works of God" (*Life of Waller*). In Johnson, unlike in Herbert or Hopkins, there is nothing which connects creator to created in a seamless web of association. Piety itself, the deepest and most private affection of the soul, is beyond art. Only the motives of piety are describable.

Another remarkable passage comes to mind: "Whatever is great, desirable, or tremendous, is comprised in the name of the Supreme Being" (*Life of Waller*). The infinity and omnipotence of God are "comprised in the name" of God. That is as much as to say that the name of God – Jesus, Father, Holy Spirit – as it is given in prayer is as close to the deity as the mind of the suppliant can wish to get. We know nothing of God's image, purpose, or power. We know him as a name, not an intelligible essence. This is not nominalism of Occam's sort, but a humble reckoning of the relation of the human soul to God. The words of scripture, the work of God, comes to us unadorned and "it can receive no grace from novelty of sentiment, and very little from novelty of expression" (*Life of Watts*). Religious effusion is to "be felt rather than expressed," and the "ideas of Christian theology are too simple for eloquence" (*Life of Waller*).

The relation of the fideist Christian to God is one of simple and heartfelt beseeching. This beseeching is done from afar and "through a glass darkly." It does not share with Baroque illumination that intelligible and epiphanic object – neither vision, nor trace. Milton should have kept "immateriality out of sight, so that his reader could drop it from his thoughts" (*Life of Milton*). This is a most peculiar suggestion. The immaterial cannot be known, and therefore, God or angels ought not be envisioned or even considered as allegorical beings. Immateriality and eternity are the great grounds and ends of hope, they are not the accomplishments of life. This is as far as the fideist argument can be taken, and not even Luther or Pascal have taken it farther.

The point I am laboring to make is this: Johnson's uneasiness with the metaphysical conceit, as with classical mythology, points to a deeply religious conviction. He was convinced that poetry was never more than a heightened and morally uplifting amusement. Those verbs he so commonly uses in the *Lives* – "amuse", "gratify," "fancy," "decorate," "illustrate," and "adorn," – are words of surface titillation. On the other hand, it is impossible to think that Johnson did not live with a deep and abiding belief in the value of Horace's rule – that the artist must instruct and delight. If for him delight is the first consideration it is partly because the highest instruction can not be given by poetry. It is also because for Johnson life must be varied and enlivened to be endured. This points to the next important consideration of his religion.

The fideist, as I remarked in chapter 5, sees life as a long and wearying journey: one fraught with dangers and follies. This was why Johnson's favorite books were those of isolated and alienated heroes like Don Quixote or Robinson Crusoe. They were the perfect types of moral existence, cut off by mad aspirations, but noble against all odds. Quixote is a parody of the Christian wayfarer and crusader, but he was for Johnson a copy of the innocent delusions and bitter extremities of normal life. His own Theodore, Rasselas, Imlac, and, perhaps, even Savage are heroes striving for the unknowable object, moving about in the circle of desire. Of course, unlike our modern masters of desperation, Johnson attends them on their way.

Wherever we go with Johnson we run into an immoveable stone. Nature is the proper object of art, but (as he says in the *Life of Thomson*) it lacks a plan. It would be easy to see Johnson as the great Augustan. But it would be dangerous. The theory of poetry announced by Imlac in chapter 10 of *Rasselas* is quintessentially Augustan. It brings Thomson or Akenside or even Pope to mind. But it must be remembered that each of the ten chapter divisions is marked by a new kind of intellectual folly – first poetry, then prosperity and peace, then power, and finally science. It would not be far wrong to imagine that Johnson, who knew the allurements of writing, held that the poet who hoped to attain all knowledge of plant, animal, and man, so that he could do nothing more than write verse, was as mad and pathetic as the hermit, the pharaoh, and the astronomer.

On the other hand, Johnson faced the problem of his own desire to write. He faced the problem of not being able to teach the one thing needful. But in all his great works there is a kind of uncanny swerve towards the unreachable, divine object. In *Rasselas*, before "The conclusion in which nothing is concluded," there is the exquisite treatise on the immortality of the soul. "But the Being, whom I fear to name, the Being who made the soul can destroy it." This is Johnson's honest sense of humility before the name of God, and his duty of exposition is done without altering the circular path of his heroes. Likewise, in the *Vanity of Human Wishes*, the disquisition on "Hope" and "Fear" comes in a great swerve from the entangled path. Rather than the *ignis fatuus* of superstitious piety, which is the chief danger to human rationality in Cowley, Butler, Rochester, and Locke, it is "The Secret Ambush of a specious Pray'r" that traps the human subject in Johnson's cosmos. Nature or history is the map of false lights and false beginnings, and the tragic exempla of Charles of

Sweden, Wolsey, and Swift run the gamut of civil, religious, and imaginative error. Unlike the Butlerian "Modern Politician," "Hypocritical Non-
conformist," and "Small Poet," their fates are not the product of a
mistaken trust in power, grace, or language, but an erroneous belief in
anything natural or temporal. They are the antithesis of the "huddled
engine" of Rochester. They are deceived by natural reason, and saved by
"Hope" and "Fear." Enthusiastic faith is for Johnson, as for the narrator of
Night Thoughts, the only true reason. The objects of hope and fear are not in
this world, but this world, and its endless warfare, teach us by negation.
This is the Solomonic note found throughout Johnson. Like Prior's endless
catalogs in *Solomon*, the promise of "Extensive view" and "Survey" in the
Vanity is nothing less than a parody of all those English and French
masterpieces of the Enlightenment. This is the chief theme of Johnson's
best sermons (*Sermons*, II, III, VI), and Solomon and Paul comprise most of
the authoritative passages and reading by which Johnson catechizes his
imaginary parishioners. The message of Solomon and Paul is the limits set
for human knowledge and the emptiness of curious speculation. Unlike
Montesquieu (writing in the same year) Johnson does not wish to explain
and exhibit "all the laws of God, creation, men and states."[25] Experience
teaches the reader at last that he is, in Yeats' words, "but a broken man."
Johnson, in all his great work, overcomes the problem of fideist art. He
finds by an act of concealment the means to point to God. The secular and
romance aspects of his work, the long journey, are merely excuses to find
the "nearer way." He always approved of allegory, because the fideist must
learn to say one thing and mean another. He must take a narrative from
the old round of imitations, but he must add the side door of faithful
instruction. The great poet, the great astronomer, are great and good men,
but that is not enough. The path must be cleared for higher aspiration.

    The fideist habit of imagination found its perfect subject in Johnson's
most mature and condensed poem, "On the Death of Dr. Robert Levet."
More than in the *Vanity* or *Rasselas* the unalloyed elements of Protestant
fideism are here displayed. In *Rasselas* the Persian convention, and in the
Vanity the Juvenalian text, serve as a screen behind which Johnson can
express his deepest conviction. The "Imitation" is one of those humanist
genres in which the values of tradition – the Roman values of moral
generalization and eloquence – can easily obscure the Christian content.
More even than allegory, imitation avoids the accusation of imaginative
transgression. But in "Levet" Johnson constructs a transparent fideism.
With muscular generality and subdued emotion he takes advantage of both
Augustan diction and the naked style of the *Greek Anthology*. "Letter'd
arrogance" and "merit unrefin'd" recall Gray's "Elegy," while the meter,

[25] Baron de Montesquieu, *The Spirit of the Laws* (New York: Hafner Press, 1949), 1.

severe in its regularity, returns to the mode of Addison and Watts. More remarkable than the technical synthesis, which marks the end of an era, is the argument. "Hope's delusive mine," "slow decline," "fainting nature," "hov'ring death prepar'd the blow," "Misery's darkest cavern known," "narrow round," and "the toil of every day" are the complete catalog of fideism. "Fainting nature" recalls Pascal's "useless earth and sky." The emotion of expectation works to a high pitch in the delusions of hope and the "hov'ring" (the long-awaited) death. In this poem "kind Nature's signal of retreat" seems bitter and unforgiving. The first thirty-two lines of the poem describe a world tiresome and brutal. They describe also the narrow, but powerful possibilities of virtue – "the single talent well employed." We cannot help but recognize Johnson's single talent, trapped as it was in the humanist/fideist paradox, here releasing itself in a sombre confession. After this exhaustive representation of life and its tortured affections we are left with only four lines. This recalls the saving moment of *The Vanity of Human Wishes*, but with even more pointed emotion:

> Then with no throbbing fiery pain,
> No cold gradations of decay,
> Death broke at once the vital chain,
> And freed his soul the nearest way.
> ("On the Death of Dr. Robert Levet," 33–36)

This is the extraordinary moment, when the soul, released at once from all its expectations, and without the "fiery pain" that fills a good deal of human experience, is freed. Nothing is said of its journey or its end. The fideist does not know the appearance of the eternal. He can not turn to analogies as in Donne's "Hymn to God, My God, in My Sickness." He can not "tune the instrument here at the door" and practice what must be done before God in heaven. Those Baroque analogies assure a likeness, a continuity between the mundane and the heavenly. Donne, whose body is a map of the world, a map which has nothing but straits to eternity, is confident of his final goal, his charge. Donne is the meeting place, the incarnation of "both Adams"[26] – the suffering Christ and the fallen laborer of Eden – and his salvation rests upon that analogy. For Johnson the futurity which gives shape to all human actions and thoughts is unknowable, ineffable. It is sufficient to see it as the necessary escape, the limit of the "narrow round" of life, and the place of the biblical promise. The "vital chain" must be broken, and it must be "at once," for there is no relation or proportion between this world and the next. "On the Death of Dr. Robert Levet" marks the end of a poetic epoch, and though fideism will be

[26] John Donne, *Poems* ed. H. J. C. Grierson (Oxford: Clarendon Press, 1922), 133. "A Hymn to God, My God, in My Sickness," line 4 of Donne's own elegy, and a high point in the analogical meditative tradition.

endlessly revived in the nineteenth century and beyond, it will never be seen in a purer form.

Donald Greene has argued that the doubleness and contradiction seen so commonly in Johnson was merely the typical eighteenth-century complexity – an illusion of paradox.[27] This seems to me to be completely false. The way Johnson assimilated the two spheres of humanist inquiry and fideist religion is indeed a paradox. Johnson had neither the simple and gloomy affections of Young, nor the vengeful humor of Prior. On the humanistic side he could live comfortably with Lockeian empiricism. The case has been made in different ways by Alkon[28] and Wimsatt[29] that his language shows the touch of Baconian jargon and new science. This is undoubtedly true, but it does not follow from a thousand entries in the *Dictionary* that Johnson was a Lockeian. Among the words mentioned by Alkon for their obviously Lockeian definitions are "idea," "knowledge," and "faculty." But this can be misleading. In each case the Lockeian definition is undercut by a following or preceding definition. For example when Locke is quoted for "faculty" he says, "In the ordinary way of speaking understanding and will are two *faculties* of the mind"; Johnson follows with an example from Swift, "Neither did our Saviour find it necessary to explain the nature of God, because it would be impossible without bestowing on us other *faculties* than we now possess."[30] Similarly he often enters a definition from Watts or Hooker after or before Locke, which either negates or ironizes the Lockeian definition. This is almost always the case. The Humanistic/fideist dichotomy is brilliantly and, I believe, systematically preserved in the *Dictionary*. In passing we should note that Johnson, who was despised for his Latinity by Hazlitt, also has a double language, for in the prayers and sermons he rarely wavers from Anglo-Saxon diction and syntax.

Johnson was not a man of his time. He was not an optimist, a skeptic, or a satirist in the normal Augustan sense. As Professor Bate has pointed out, his satire is participative and universal. His skepticism does not extend to religion, as shown by his scathing comments on the Deists and Hume. If his deathbed stories are true, and they have the ring of truth, the dichotomy I have described was preserved till the end. For in his delirium he responded with both the salute of the Roman gladiators, who carry with them the image of that Roman world of deathly contest and struggle, the long

[27] Samuel Johnson, *Twentieth Century Views* (Englewood Cliffs: Prentice-Hall Inc., 1965), 8.

[28] Paul Kent Alkon, *Samuel Johnson and Moral Discipline* (Chicago: Northwestern University Press, 1967), 65–84.

[29] W. K. Wimsatt, *Philosophic Words* (New York: Archon Books, 1968).

[30] Samuel Johnson, *A Dictionary of the English Language* (London: Johnson, Baldwin, et al., 1806), vol. I, 167.

journey of man and the simple "God bless you," which was his parting gift of hope and faith to a world that so desperately needed it.

Epilogue

Johnson solved the problem that divided the literary culture of his day by dividing himself. On one side, like Prior and Young before him he embraced in the allegorical *mythos* of *Rasselas* and *The Vanity of Human Wishes* a Solomonic fideism. In this way he rejected the mature Augustan ideology on behalf of an explicit Protestantism. Like Luther and Pascal before him he nurtured in his soul a tremendous dread of the emptiness of temporal experience – its endless suspension of moral gratification and its prospect of personal and social vanity. Although an extreme iconoclast like Johnson could not muster a belief in the analogical richness of nature which was a commonplace of the seventeenth century, he could believe in a God stripped of any natural connection to this muddled world. Like his spiritual mentor, Law, and his sometime friend John Wesley, he thought the inner yearning of the heart was the surest proof of the promise of biblical Christianity.

Literature he could not forsake. It served him as a respite and a career. But he never imagined that it could carry a message of transcendent spiritual significance. He rejected the ambitious religious analogies of the age of Donne on Augustan grounds, but not with the same motives as Butler, Rochester, Pope, or Swift. He thought of himself as a Don Quixote of the spirit, but he was in fact a Ralpho. Like that strange shadowy deputy of Hudibras he heard the voice of God in the inner workings of his conscience – "that umpire God has plac'd in us." On the other hand he was a curious man after the Augustan model. He wished to observe and understand as far as one could through the broken glass of experience, his fellow creature. Like Butler, Pope, and Swift he penetrated the veneer of character and observed the strange and often ugly workings of the human soul. But he was not like the Turk in Hogarth who observes the madness of the enthusiast (seeing the tonsure of the Catholic priest hidden from the congregation) through a window and from afar. He was never the author of a general and superior satire. He was not an observer after the manner of Thomson. His eye wearied of the empty varieties of quotidian experience. By his example he gave the greatest authority to the opinions of the generations after the Restoration, but he misunderstood the implications of Augustan common sense. Rich in paradox himself, he sheds light on the paradoxes and ambiguities of his age in an extraordinary way.

Index

à Kempis, Thomas, 5, 183
a posteriori judgment of Bonaventure and Malebranche, 186
à Wood, Anthony: *Athenae Oxonienses*, 25
Abrams, M. H, 14; *Mirror and the Lamp, The*, 133
Addison, Joseph, 3, 27, 92, 125, 126, 139, 144, 161, 163, 174, 197, 219, 229, 241, 247; *Campaign*, 142, 236; *Cato*, 142; *Spectator*, 27, 137, 151
aemulatio, 22
Aikin, John: *Essay on the Plan and Character of Thomson's Seasons, An*, 161
Akenside, Mark, 123, 133, 154, 161, 211, 229, 245; *Pleasures of the Imagination, The*, 161, 226
Alkon, Paul Kent: *Samuel Johnson and Moral Discipline*, 248
allegory/allegorical, 1, 3, 34, 64, 90, 97, 98, 110, 120, 127, 140, 141, 142, 149, 176
Allison, Alexander Ward: *Toward an Augustan Poetic*, 77, 78
Alter, Robert and Frank Kermode: *Literary Guide to the Bible, The*, 217
Anabaptist, 41
analogia entis, 1, 19, 22, 61, 130, 192
analogia, 22
analogical mode, 2, 10, 12, 27, 34, 132, 180, 181, **183–188**, 189, 192, 193, 197, 202, 218, 225, 239, Augustan opposition to, 59
Analogy, 233
Andrewes, Bishop Lancelot, 5, 6, 8, 14, 82, 92, 180; *Ninety-Six Sermons*, 180
Angelico, Fra: *St. Lawrence Receiving the Treasure of the Church*, 155
Anglicanism, 5, 13, 14, 27, 32, 37, 38, 39, 40, 41, 51, 52, 54, 80, 87, 176, 181, 196, 202, 216, 218, 219, 231, 233, 235
Annunciation, 155
Anselm, 178, 191
Aquinas, Thomas, 6, 8, 20, 52, 61, 96, 124, 126, 129, 175, 195; *Annales hymnologia*, 179; *Commentary on Thessalonians*, 50; *Latin–English Dictionary of St. Thomas Aquinas, A*, 50; Thomism, 232
Aristotle/Aristotelian, 7, 43, 44, 111, 123, 124, 154, 185, 205, 206, 236; *Poetics*, 237; Aristotle's poem *Arête*, 123
Arnold, Matthew, 6, 14, 144; *Culture and Anarchy*, 6
Assisi, Francis of, 184
Associationism (Scottish), 13
Athanasius, 243
Atterbury, Bishop Francis, 220; quoted in *Literature of the Church of England*, 203; *Sermons and Papers*, 220
Aubrey, John, 26; *Brief Lives*, 25; *Remaines of Gentilisme and Judaisme*, 105
Augustan poetics, 25, 26, 47, 52, 55, 58, 95, 141, 159, 187
Augustine, Saint, 1, 179, 184, 195; *Civitas dei*, 181; *On Christian Doctrine*, 185; *Commentary on the Psalms*, 216; *Expositions of the Book of Psalms*, 217; *Prolegomena, Confessions, Letters*, 50
Ausonius, 115, 116; *Mosella*, 115
Ayer, A. J.: *Language, Truth and Logic*, 13
Ayres, Philip, 93

Bacon, Francis, 4, 12, 26, 31, 39, 41, 42, 44, 49, 52, 62, 66, 70, 75, 78, 88, 91, 125, 151, 182, 185, 219, 232, 239, 248; *Advancement of Learning, The*, 43, 71; *Novum organum*, 28, 91
Bacon, Montague, 28, 29
Bainton, Roland: *Reformation of the Sixteenth Century, The*, 74
Bakhtin, M., 28
Baptism, 183
Baroque, 1, 3, 7, 8, 9, 10, 20, 21, 22, 23, 25, 26, 32, 33, 58, 59, 61, 63, 64, 70, 74, 75, 82, 83, 85, 93, 95, 97, 106, 120, 124, 125, 126, 128, 154, 160, 174, 175, 182, 183, 184, 187, 188, 190, 217, 232, 240, 241, 247
Baroque *proportionalitas*, 240
Barthes, Roland: 2, 21, 57; *Barthes by Barthes*, 20; *Sade/Fourier/Loyola*, 2; *Writing Degree Zero*, 58
Basil, 178
Bate, W. J., 14, 138, 248; *Burden of the Past and the English Poet, The*, 138; *Samuel Johnson*, 237
Battestin, Martin: 63, 176; *Providence of Wit*, 11

Homer, 35, 106, 112, 114, 118, 120, 121, 126, 127, 128, 131, 135, 198, 222; *Iliad*, 26, 104, 113, 120, 161

honête homme, 7

Hooker, Thomas, 3, 4, 5, 14, 52, 54, 73, 84, 96, 248; *Eikon Basilike*, 40; *Laws of Ecclesiastical Polity, The*, 51, 73

Hoole: *Art of Dehydration*, 122; *Science of Winemaking*, 122

Hopkins, 185, 200, 226, 235, 244

Horace, 3, 7, 11, 17, 23, 29, 62, 63, 92, 115, 116, 128, 131, 134, 157, 208, 209, 245; his *nil admirari*, 120; *Odes*, 156, 209; *satires*, 29; *sermones*, 127, 133

Hudibrastic (style), 11, 12, 16, 23, 26, 27, 34, 101, 122, 131

Humanism, 1, 7, 27, 39, 49, 51, 61, 62, 79, 96, 118, 119, 128, 151, 176, 232, 233, 236, 237, 238, 239, 240, 241

Humanistic conception of *decorum*, 242

Hume, David, 6, 13, 21, 23, 24, 27, 44, 45, 55, 63, 69, 70, 85, 119, 120, 175, 181, 233, 248; "Essay on Enthusiasm and Superstition," 55; *History of England, The*, 55, 86; "On Miracles," 12; *Treatise of Human Nature*, 219

Humphreys, A. R., "Character of Eighteenth Century Religion, The," 196; "Augustan Poetry," 204

Hunt, John Dixon: *The Figure in the Landscape: Poetry, Painting and Gardening during the Eighteenth Century*, 144

Hutcheson, Francis, 3

Hutton, Ronald: *Charles the Second, King of England, Scotland and Ireland*, 5

Hyde, Edward (Earl of Clarendon), 16, 30, 70, 84, 85, 89; *The History of Rebellion and Civil Warres*, 85

icon(ic), 3, 18, 59, 80, 122, 124, 140, 145, 149, 154, 160, 163, 171, 188, 192, 197

iconoclasm, 10, 56, 69, 82, 94, 104, 121, 143, 177, 237, 242, 249

Idler, 238, 243

ignis fatuus, 170

imagines mundi, 27

imago essentiale of the Georgic, 162

imago poetae, 236

imago vitae, 63

imitatio, 119

in media res, 208

Inge, William: *Mysticism in England*, 190

Isabella: or, The Morning, 143

Jack, Ian: *Augustan Satire*, 66

Jacobitism, 8

Jago, Richard, 66, 156, 202, 223

Jenyns, Soame: *Inquiry*, 241

Jerome, 216

Jewel, John, 4, 180

Johanine, 61

John of the Cross, 188, 195; *Ascent of Mt. Carmel, The*, 189

Johnson, Samuel, 5, 6, 10, 11, 15, 25, 67, 74, 76, 81, 91, 92, 109, 118, 126, 129, 134, 135, 139, 154, 161, 191, 192, 193, 195, 200, 202, 204, 208, 211, 216, 218, 220, 227, 231, 232, 233, 234, 235, **236–249**; *Annals*, 243; *Diarie*, 243; *Diaries, Prayers, and Annals*, 234; *Dictionary of the English Language, A*, 248; *Life of Swift*, 234; *Lives of the English Poets, The*, 72, 73, 79, 99, 161, 208, 235, 236, 238, 243; *Life of Cowley, The*, 241, 242; *Life of Gray*, 236; *Life of Milton*, 244; *Life of Thomson*, 161, 245; *Life of Waller*, 244; *Life of Watts*, 244; "On the Death of Dr. Robert Levet," 246, 247; *Prayers and Meditations*, 234; *Rasselas*, 149, 223, 234, 236, 237, 238, 240, 245, 246, 249; "Review of *A Free Inquiry into the Nature and Origin of Evil*," 240; *Sermons*, 246; *Twentieth Century Views*, 248; *Vanity of Human Wishes, The*, 133, 210, 214, 219, 220, 226, 237, 238, 241, 246, 247, 249; "Vision of Theodore," 149, 240; *Works*, 239, 243; Johnson and allegory, 128, 242, 246; Johnson, and Augustanism, 239, 240, 245, 248, 249; Johnson and the Bible, 238, 239, 241; Johnson on Cowley, 241–242; Johnson and descriptions of God, 237, 239, 240, 241; Johnson and fideism, 238–249; Johnson and the Humanists, 236, 237, 238, 239, 240; Johnson and Humanist poetics, 128, 236, 239, 242, 247; Johnson and Luther, 240; Johnson and poetry as entertainment, 238, 244; Johnson and poetry as instruction, 245; Johnson on Pope, 234n.10; Johnson on Prior, 208; Johnson and religious writing, 237, 242, 243

Jones, Richard Foster: "The Rhetoric of Science in England of the mid-17th Century," 122; *Studies in the Seventeenth Century*, 73

Jonson, Ben, 63, 90, 116, 134; *Alchemist, The*, 128; *Every Man in His Humour*, 39; "To Penshurst," 115; *Volpone*, 39, 128; *Works*, 116

Joyce, James, 7, 40

Judaism, 41, 79, 177, 179, 211

Julian of Norwich, 189; *Revelations of Divine Love*, 183

Juvenal, 29, 139, 246

Kant, Immanuel, 21, 55, 227; *Dreams of a Spirit-Seer*, 56

Keats, John, 72, 107, 108, 109, 122, 139, 149, 168; "Eve of St. Agnes, The," 108; *Letters*, 109

Kemp, Margery, 195

Ken, Bishop, 134, 200

CAMBRIDGE STUDIES IN EIGHTEENTH-CENTURY
ENGLISH LITERATURE AND THOUGHT

General editors
Professor HOWARD ERSKINE-HILL Litt.D., FBA, *Pembroke College, Cambridge*
Professor JOHN RICHETTI, *University of Pennsylvania*